S0-AGK-857

ACTIVISM REPLACES ISOLATIONISM:
U.S. Public Attitudes
1940–1975

by

H. SCHUYLER FOSTER
Formerly American Opinion Analyst
in U.S. State Department

FOXHALL PRESS
P.O. Box 9629
Washington, D.C. 20016

First edition.
Foxhall Press
Box 9629
Washington, D.C. 20016

Library of Congress Catalog Card Number:
83-81284

International Standard Book Number:
0-9611128-1-6

Printed in the
United States of America

To
my colleagues
in the State Department's
Public Opinion Studies Staff
1943–1965
whose intelligent and discerning analyses,
cooperatively and cheerfully produced,
have made this account possible

Elizabeth Costenbader Bellis
Fahey Black
Patricia Russell Blasche
Marion Bloom
Joan Ruine Blue
Ann Hooker Boardman
James F. Crane
Sherwin Crown
Richard E. Curl
Marjorie Treat Elting
Charlotte Moody Emerson
Shirley Gornitzky
Leonard M. Hoag
S. Shepard Jones
Mary T. Kennedy
P. Wesley Kriebel
Jody C. Lydman
Warren Magruder
Barbara Hoskins Marshall
Ethel McKethan
Waldemar A. Nielsen
Robert H. Osborn
John Patterson
Georgianna Flather Rathbun
George L. Ridgeway
Eva Sandis
Charles William Smith, Jr.
Mildred Somers
Betty Anne Royall Spiegel

ACKNOWLEDGMENTS

My greatest debt in the preparation of this study is to my colleagues in the U.S. State Department's Office of Public Opinion Studies, to whom this book is dedicated, and who collaborated in making the opinion analyses which are the foundation of the present work.

I also am indebted to Dr. Fredrik Aandahl and Dr. Edwin Costrell, then of the State Department's Office of the Historian, who most helpfully made available facilities for reviewing documents and preparing my manuscript. For ensuring continuous access to documents I am grateful to Melvin Briscoe of the Department's Bureau of Public Affairs.

In my Bibliographic Note I cite collections of public opinion polls, but I would like to acknowledge here the special helpfulness, in making such data available, of Lloyd Free (Institute for International Social Research), George Gallup, Louis Harris, Elmo Roper, and Paul Sheatsley (National Opinion Research Center).

The helpfulness of the Staff of Bookcrafters, Inc. is also gratefully acknowledged.

H.S.F.

CONTENTS

PART TWO: IMPLEMENTING BASIC POLICIES (1950–1965)

PART THREE: MODIFYING FOREIGN POLICIES (1968–1975)

ABBREVIATIONS

ABM	Anti-Ballistic Missile system
ANZUS	Australia, New Zealand, United States defense arrangements
AOR	American Opinion Report (State Department internal publication)
CEEC	Committee for European Economic Cooperation
CFM	Council of Foreign Ministers (often Britain, France, Soviet Union, USA)
DLF	Development Loan Fund
DPs	Displaced persons
ECOSOC	Economic and Social Council of United Nations
EDC	European Defense Community
EEC	European Economic Community
ERP	European Recovery Program (of U.S.)
FM	Foreign Minister or Foreign Ministers
GA or UNGA	General Assembly of United Nations
GATT	General Agreement on Tariffs and Trade
IAEA	International Atomic Energy Agency
ICBM	Intercontinental Ballistic Missile
IDA	International Development Association (lowest-interest window of World Bank)
ITO	International Trade Organization (proposed)
MLF	Multi-Lateral Force (proposed naval unit manned by NATO members)
MSP	Mutual Security Program (of U.S. foreign aid)
NATO	North Atlantic Treaty Organization
NLF	National Liberation Front (South Viet-Nam)
N.O.R.C.	National Opinion Research Center (at University of Chicago)
OAS	Organization of American States
OECD	Organization for Economic Cooperation and Development
POWs	Prisoners of War
PRC	People's Republic of China
RTA	Reciprocal Trade Agreements (U.S. program)
SEATO	Southeast Asia Treaty Organization
UNCTAD	United Nations Conference on Trade and Development
UNESCO	United Nations Educational, Scientific and Cultural Organization
UNRRA	United Nations Relief and Rehabilitation Administration

PRESIDENTS AND SECRETARIES OF STATE 1940–1975

Franklin Delano Roosevelt	(March 4, 1933) – April 12, 1945
Cordell Hull	(March 4, 1933) – November 30, 1944
Edward Reilly Stettinius, Jr.	December 1, 1944 –
Harry S. Truman	April 12, 1945 – January 20, 1953
Edward Reilly Stettinius, Jr.	– June 27, 1945
James Francis Byrnes	July 3, 1945 – January 21, 1947
George Catlett Marshall	January 21, 1947 – January 20, 1949
Dean Gooderham Acheson	January 21, 1949 – January 20, 1953
Dwight David Eisenhower	January 20, 1953 – January 20, 1961
John Foster Dulles	January 21, 1953 – April 17, 1959
Christian Archibald Herter	April 18, 1959 – January 20, 1961
John Fitzgerald Kennedy	January 20, 1961 – November 22, 1963
Dean Rusk	January 20, 1961 –
Lyndon Baines Johnson	November 22, 1963 – January 20, 1969
Dean Rusk	– January 20, 1969
Richard Milhous Nixon	January 20, 1969 – August 9, 1974
William Pierce Rogers	January 22, 1969 – September 3, 1973
Henry Alfred Kissinger	September 22, 1973 –
Gerald Rudolph Ford	August 9, 1974 – (January 20, 1977)
Henry Alfred Kissinger	– (January 20, 1977)

I

SIGNIFICANCE OF PUBLIC ATTITUDES ON FOREIGN POLICY

United States foreign policy affects every American; and every American's opinion (or lack of one) has significance for U.S. policy. The impact of foreign policy on the citizen is widely appreciated; most Americans realize that they are basically affected by the coming of war or peace, and by the foreign policies which tend toward the one or the other. But the impact of the citizen on his country's foreign policy is less visible, less dramatic, and often insufficiently appreciated. In a country with a population of over 200,000,000, the opinions of any one individual may appear to be of slight consequence.

Nevertheless, under our democratic system, the foreign policy officers of the Government are aware of the vital connection between the attitudes held by Americans and U.S. foreign policy. As Secretary of State George C. Marshall phrased it, "no policy–foreign or domestic–can succeed without public support." Sustained and intelligent support of foreign policy must come from public understanding, from the views on foreign affairs held by the individuals who constitute the public.

Impacts of Public

These individuals may affect U.S. foreign policy in multifarious ways: through voting for President and Congress; through the application of policy pressure on the Government via organized groups (business, veterans, etc.); through efforts to persuade fellow citizens to support or oppose specific policies; and through direct contact with foreign affairs or with government processes. It is evident that Americans differ widely in their interest in foreign affairs, and in the amount of activity they devote to trying to influence foreign policy. In general, among the adult population, about one half confess to interviewers for public opinion polls that they "don't follow foreign affairs regularly." Some others make foreign affairs almost a full-time concern–on special occasions, or every day.

Some presidential and congressional elections accord greater prominence to foreign policy issues than others. In 1952 some voters gave great weight to Gen. Eisenhower's promise to "go to Korea" if elected; others may have made their choice between senatorial candidates on the basis of their positions on foreign aid. Any voter can, of course, cast his vote on the basis of whatever mix of foreign and domestic issues he pleases; and in any election some voters will ascribe great importance to foreign policy views.

Election Day is "the great reckoning," but every President and Congressman is constantly aware that there is an election ahead. The President and most members of Congress take a keen interest in learning what Americans are thinking about foreign policy and many Americans are eager to let them know what they think. Each year hundreds of thousands of letters and telegrams (and telephone calls) are directed to the White House, the State Department, and offices of Congressmen to convey the foreign policy views of citizens. Through such communications, and at the hearings of Congressional committees, representatives of private organizations—large and small—place on record the positions on foreign policy which they have taken and urge their adoption as government policy. This expression of popular views is a constant process, by no means confined to election seasons.

Such direct approaches to the Government may constitute only a small part of the total public discussion devoted to major foreign policy issues, since these questions are commonly discussed in the daily and periodical press, on radio and TV, and in conferences and local meetings across the country—as well as within the family and among friends.

Some citizens may take direct action in the area of foreign policy. If they feel keenly about issues of foreign trade, for example, individuals or groups may decide not to purchase the products of "low-wage" countries, or of nations whose ideology they disapprove of. On occasion, groups in American communities have sought to organize public boycotts of goods produced in the Communist countries of Eastern Europe. Strategically placed labor unions, such as the longshoremen, have sometimes directly affected U.S. trade relations with various nations by refusing to load or unload cargoes destined for, or coming from, particular countries.

To cite quite a different field of activity, Americans abroad—and this category includes over a million persons each year—greatly affect the impressions of the United States which are developed by people in their host countries. Their conclusions as to whether Americans are trustworthy and cooperative, or greedy and war-minded, could have significant results for both the formal and informal relations of the countries involved. Similarly, the judgments reached by Americans traveling abroad affect their attitudes toward U.S. relations with the countries which they visit.

In time of war, when citizens are called upon to serve in the armed forces, they are participating in U.S. foreign policy in a most vital way; and those who feel they cannot conscientiously participate in the war necessarily have an impact on U.S. foreign policy. Citizens objecting to U.S. military policies have sometimes refrained from paying taxes to support these policies; and this technique could be employed against other policies, such as the foreign aid program or U.S. payments to the United Nations. Conversely, when a person pays taxes to the U.S. Government he may not be thinking about the fact that he is contributing to the maintenance of U.S. foreign policy; yet we could not sustain our defense and aid programs without this mass support.

Ordinarily, of course, an administration engaged in carrying out U.S. foreign policy does not have to cope with sabotage of its policies by its citizens or residents; and it can always be helped by attitudes of support. Ordinarily, too, the administration has to pay greater immediate attention to the views of the people's representatives in Congress than to the views of the people themselves. As Secretary of State Herter, who had himself served for ten years in the House of Representatives (1943 to 1953), observed in 1958: "A successful foreign policy must, . . . to be effective, command the support of the vast majority of the American people–otherwise it would not be given the tools by Congress which are essential to its fulfillment."[1] If the American voter is sufficiently unhappy about what Congress has done in the realm of foreign policy, he can replace his representatives in Congress, securing persons who will more accurately reflect the will of the American people.

Opinion Process

Of the total population, a small proportion gives constant attention to foreign policy problems and situations (aside from the full-time professional officers in the Executive and Legislative Branches of the Government). This stratum of the public includes: the growing number of foreign affairs experts in our universities and research institutions; the editorial staffs of our leading newspapers and magazines; certain press, TV and radio commentators; and the officers and staffs of private organizations–national and local–which take a stand on foreign policies.

This whole stratum of foreign affairs specialists comprises only some thousands of persons out of our total population. But these full-time specialists, through their books, articles, editorials, "columns," broadcast commentaries, organization publications and contacts, reach millions of Americans who take a regular or frequent interest in foreign affairs. This sub-public includes large numbers of businessmen, teachers, ministers, and other national and community leaders, who do take considerable interest in foreign affairs and pass on their thoughts to their numerous captive and voluntary audiences.

Millions of Americans engage in highly specific discussions of U.S.

foreign policy issues. Much of this discussion is invisible; or at least it does not come strikingly to public attention. Discussions among friends and family leave no public record, but they contribute as genuinely to the crystalization of public opinion as do the protest demonstrations, public discussion meetings, and mass rallies which are reported by the press and radio–TV. All of these visible and less visible manifestations of opinion interact and play their parts in the process by which the nation "makes up its mind" about a foreign policy. The greater the number of relevant points of view which are considered in this discussion process, the more likely it is that the national decision will be realistic and enduring.

Such discussions affect the readiness of individual citizens to play their essential roles in upholding America's commitments, whether in NATO or elsewhere. Public discussions often result in a consensus; and under our democratic tradition those who constitute the minority are aware of the extent of majority support and tend to accept the fact that the majority has spoken, and that its view should be reflected in government action (e.g., participation in defensive alliances, undertaking a large-scale aid program). Other foreign policy questions of considerable importance may excite little discussion in Congress or the press (and are tacitly accepted as not going beyond the currently perceived limits of public acceptance). Still other issues receive great attention from certain groups or publications, without ever arousing a "great debate."

The Government itself may take a leading part in developing national discussion of foreign policy issues, particularly when a major departure in policy is up for consideration. The Executive Branch ordinarily takes the lead in expounding the merits of its policy; and it can be aided or hampered by leading members of the Legislative Branch, such as the Committees on Foreign Relations and Foreign Affairs, and the formal leadership of the Senate and House of Representatives.

In the case of such major innovations as joining the UN, setting up NATO and the Marshall Plan, the Executive Branch mounted campaigns to inform the citizens of the considerations which led the Administration to propose these courses. Speeches by the President and Secretary of State were broadcast on nationwide radio, thousands of explanatory publications were distributed, and speakers from the Department of State presented the new policies at conferences and meetings in all parts of the country.

The daily and periodical press devoted millions of words to explaining the proposed policies and to reporting the views of members of the Executive and Legislative Branches and of newsworthy leaders outside the Government. Radio networks not only gave daily accounts of progress on the new measures, but staged debates between advocates and opponents which were listened to in millions of homes across the nation. The Government encouraged the formation of special national organizations of citizens to support its proposals throughout the country; and numerous pre-existing organizations brought information about the measures to their various memberships (business, labor, farm groups, veterans, patriotic, educational, church, women's, service organizations).

These extensive nationwide efforts were climaxed by legislative enactment (or treaty approval) which marked official adoption of the new policies. The information campaigns resulted also in very extensive awareness on the part of the American people of the proposed changes in foreign policy, and approval of these policies by the great majority of the people.

Some publicists tend to question the significance of a consensus which has been reached following a massive information campaign, or to suggest that any time the Government wants to "crank up" a campaign it can secure a consensus. In actual practice, it may be noted, such major information efforts are relatively infrequent. Totalitarian governments can and do mount major campaigns as a routine procedure; but democratic governments can only do so successfully when the time is ripe. A massive policy campaign requires the investment of time, effort and money on the part of hundreds of thousands of active citizens; and a democratic government will not call upon its people and their organizations, and seek to enlist the cooperation of the publishing and electronic media on matters that are not regarded as of distinctly unusual importance to the whole nation.

Many weeks of careful planning are required for such major efforts, and they need to be sustained during the months of legislative hearings and debate which normally precede legislative decision. Indeed, it may be said that a considerable degree of consensus at the public leadership level must already exist for the campaign to be mounted at all. Cooperation on the part of the news media is not automatic, nor will it be forthcoming for projects regarded as partisan rather than national in inspiration. Leaders of national organizations cannot be enlisted in the face of strong opposition within their own memberships; and public-spirited citizens in local communities will not put up the posters and summon the discussion meetings unless they are convinced that the cause is worth the effort which is involved. To a very considerable extent a policy campaign represents the spreading of a consensus from the leadership to the popular level.

The public opinion process which takes place on a grand scale during a policy campaign is essentially repeated, on a much less developed scale, whenever a new policy is adopted or an older policy modified. Government officials make known the facts which they believe call for action—or, much less frequently, people outside the government formulate their proposals and communicate them to Congressmen, the news media and organization leaders. Support and/or opposition is expressed and the public debate—great or little—is on.

Queries about Significance

Fundamental doubts about the significance of popular opinion about foreign policy are sometimes raised by writers who cite public opinion polls which demonstrate the ignorance and apathy of the American people about foreign affairs. Public opinion is also criticized because of its reputation for volatility and changeability; some complain about the docility of the public in the face of a government information campaign.

It is undeniably true that Americans are regrettably uninformed about some aspects of U.S. foreign relations; and it is inherently more difficult for the conscientious citizen to inform himself about foreign affairs than about domestic problems. Interest in foreign affairs appears to be closely related to one's education. Among Americans who have been to college, as many as 80% say that they "take much interest in world affairs;" 55% of those who have attended high school also give this response; but only 29% of those whose formal education ended in grammar school claim "much interest" in world affairs.[2] The increase in the number of Americans having secondary school and higher education, and increased public awareness of the demands of the present world, are now combining to reduce popular apathy about foreign affairs.

Moreover, on major foreign policy issues the public discussion often touches a very large proportion of the electorate, with as many as 90% of a national sample expressing a pro or con position on such issues as joining the United Nations, responding to North Korean aggression, or mounting a large-scale foreign aid program. Usually, 70% (or more) of the people have given responses to polling questions on attitudes toward the Soviet Union (or Western European countries), toward our alliances and defense commitments, toward foreign aid programs, on major national defense issues, on our relations with different regions of the world, the role of the United Nations, trade and immigration policies, and judgments on the military conflicts in which the U.S. has been engaged.

On some important—but less familiar—questions a majority of the total public have not expressed any attitudes in response to pollster's questions, e.g., what should be U.S. policy concerning the Chinese off-shore islands of Quemoy and Matsu, or attitudes toward the proposed Bricker amendment to limit the effectiveness of so-called "U.N. treaties."

It is perhaps true that Government leaders may enjoy considerable elbow-room on some foreign-policy matters which are not subject to constant or deep interest on the part of the public. But it is also true that any foreign policy issue may suddenly become of interest to the widest public; the opinion of everyone will then be important—the ill-informed along with the well-informed.

As for the volatility of public opinion, the record shows some remarkably swift responses to changes in the real situation; it also shows a noteworthy tendency for attitudes to persist despite changes in circumstances. Attitudes did change under the impact of events such as Hitler's invasion of France and the Low Countries in 1940, or the entrance of an enormous Chinese force into Korea in 1950; but in between such major events attitudes toward foreign policy display a remarkable tendency to persist.

Critics of the democratic foreign-policy process fear that the "average citizen's" attitudes on policy issues are not based on adequate information and understanding; but it is certainly a political fact that on foreign issues, as well as domestic, voters are often guided by the recommendations of those who have superior understanding and in whom they have confidence. They may "take the word" of the President, the Master of the National Grange, the head of the Central Labor Union, the Commander of the American Legion, the local editor, their minister, or a high school teacher; or they may be impressed to find that several of these leaders are lined up on the same side of an issue.

Public attitudes on foreign affairs are noted by the Executive and Legislative Branches of the U.S. Government, whether they be permissive respecting current foreign policy or whether they call for modification or reversal of policy. In the short run, the Executive Branch has to pay more immediate attention to the views of the Congress than to the attitudes of the general public, since the Congress can and does restrict U.S. policy through both legislation and appropriations. The President and the State Department are well aware that at any time the Congress may take restraining action which reflects the pressure of public attitudes.

Some members of Congress are more aware than others of the attitudes of the public on various foreign policy issues. In practice this is not usually a matter of each Senator faithfully reflecting the views of the voters of his state (and each Congressman reflecting the views of his own particular district), but of how Congress as a whole responds through its regular institutional machinery of committees and leadership. Different committees may be concerned with various aspects of foreign policy (including appropriations), and they may or may not hold extensive hearings (in Washington or elsewhere) to gather the views of American citizens and organizations; but all members of Congress, in casting their votes, tend to give considerable weight to the conclusions of the leadership and of pertinent committees as to both their substantive recommendations and their analysis of current public opinion. Each Congressman will naturally factor into his voting decision any information he has on the foreign policy attitudes of his voters and of the organizations and contributors to his election campaigns, or on the willingness of these key people to accept the judgment of their Representative on the current issue. In this fashion the policy attitudes, and the tolerances, of the bulk of the voters of the nation tend to have their effect on the Government's decision.

Alongside the views of any foreign policy experts with whom they may be in contact, both Executive and Legislative officers have to decide how much weight to give the views of the possibly ignorant and apathetic public. It is not usual, on a major foreign policy issue, for the bulk of the general public to be without any attitude; and on such questions as war and peace, or a SALT agreement, many citizens may be insistent on conveying their attitudes to Government officials.

Measuring Public Opinion

"What the public thinks" about a foreign policy problem is often regarded as relevant by Americans who are seeking to make up their own minds; and this information is often difficult to obtain. Most members of the public have no assurance that they know "what the public is thinking" about many significant foreign policy issues. The ordinary citizen—or even the foreign affairs expert—cannot gain a comprehensive picture of national public opinion without special facilities for this purpose.

In a few instances, the opinion situation seems fairly obvious. If one hears a foreign policy discussion wherever one goes, on the street corner, at work, at the market, on TV and in the newspaper, one can conclude that the "public" is interested; and if everyone is reaching the same conclusion one can also feel fairly confident about what the public attitude is—at least in that particular area. But the converse is not true. The absence of public discussion on every street corner does not necessarily mean that there is public apathy instead of public opinion. By way of illustration, the experience of one State Department officer may be noted. He was visiting his home town in the Midwest just after the North Atlantic Treaty was signed—a project to which he had been devoting much time. Concerned about how the American public was taking to this revolution in U.S. policy, he finally remarked to his father that he had been back for three days and he hadn't heard a single soul mention the North Atlantic

Treaty. "Why, the people are all for it," the father replied, "they understand that times have changed and that we need the treaty now. Go ahead and ask them about it." The officer's conversations with his neighbors soon satisfied him that his father was an accurate analyst of community opinion. He also concluded that the absence of spontaneous expressions of opinion on a particular subject need not always be interpreted as "public apathy."

In some cases where there may be plenty of public discussion, it may be difficult for the ordinary intelligent citizen to determine the preponderance of public opinion. Citizens may be in doubt even when newspapers and TV are filled with pictures and stories about thousands of people participating in protest demonstrations across the country. Members of the protesting groups, constantly talking with each other, and reading editorials and "columns" by leading publicists who share their views, can readily convince themselves that the majority of people are on their side.

On other occasions when Government policy has been attacked, as with the assaults on U.S. participation in the UN during the McCarthy era, those supporting the world organization—including some Government officials—have made misjudgments of American opinion. Periodically, there has been similar questioning about public support for the U.S. foreign aid program.

How, then, can the ordinary citizen—or anyone else—determine what public opinion really is? If a vote is taken in Congress, such action is normally accepted as representing the will of the public, and also as settling the issue, at least for the time being. But many foreign policy issues may be settled entirely by presidential action; and a Congressional vote may take place only after months of discussion and debate. How can one discover what the American people are thinking?

There are two broad methods of finding out what the people think: one is to go out and ask them; the other is to analyze what is being spontaneously said and published.

Public Opinion Polls

Some of the results of the direct method of inquiry have been available to members of the general public on a fairly regular basis since the mid-1930s, when Elmo Roper and George Gallup began publishing the findings of their surveys based upon representative samples of the adult population. In recent decades several polling organizations have asked thousands of questions about foreign policy issues, and many of these findings have been made available to the public through publication in newspapers and magazines.

Public opinion polls certainly have come closer than any previous research tools to telling us what the sum of individual Americans are thinking about their foreign policies. Such polls also have the advantage of making possible analysis of the views of sub-groups within the population: men and women; young, middle-aged and old; rich and poor; city-dwellers and rural folk; Republicans, Democrats and Independents; Catholics, Protestants and Jews. Actually, before the debate about the Viet-Nam war, the polls demonstrated that on most foreign-policy issues none of these group differences was normally associated with great differences in attitude. Moreover, there was usually little difference in views among the various American regions: East, Midwest, South, and Far West. For two decades after World War II, this homogeneity of American national opinion, in terms of the demographic categories just mentioned, was a significant characteristic.

Before polling results became available, scholars often analyzed Congressional votes in geographical terms, assuming that, for example, a bloc of Midwestern votes against a foreign policy reflected predominant sentiment in that region. This sort of analysis often fails to indicate a consistent picture. Sen. Langer of North Dakota, on one TV program, explained the fact that he voted against the United Nations Charter—one of only two negative votes in the Senate—by saying that "in his part of the country" people held different foreign policy views from those predominant elsewhere in America. Sen. Langer failed to mention that the other Senator from North Dakota voted for the Charter.

The polls strongly suggest that the real differences in foreign policy attitudes which exist among Americans are associated with other than geographical factors. One factor that is significant on some foreign policy issues is the amount of education a respondent has had. Americans who have attended college are more likely to support a positive, or "internationalist," foreign policy than are those whose formal education ended in grammar school. Those with a high school education tend to range themselves in between the other two educational groups. However, on issues where there has been specific "education" by means of a national information campaign, the differences in attitude by educational background are usually less marked.

Along with their distinctive advantages, public opinion polling results also have their limitations. Perhaps the most obvious limitation is the fact that polling questions cannot be posed in terms which are very close to those in which the problem confronts the Executive and Legislative Branches of the Government. As on many domestic problems, most citizens are simply not well enough informed to cope with the complex details, or to appreciate the pertinent background factors, which must be weighed in a decision by the Secretary of

State or a Member of Congress. Citizens able to grasp these problems may comprise only a small percentage of a national polling sample.

This limitation on the significance of the polls has not, of course, prevented Americans from having very real attitudes on whether or not the U.S. should join NATO or the UN, or send troops to Korea or Viet-Nam. And these attitudes, however carefully or lightly arrived at, have genuine political significance.

On the other hand, some polling results have led to unwarranted magnification of the ignorance of the citizens. After Pres. Truman's inaugural address, for example, a poll found that only about one quarter of the respondents had heard or read about Truman's "Point Four Program." Many of these "informed" respondents did not profess an opinion on the program, so it turned out that only about 15% of the total sample was recorded as favoring this program. But another polling organization, employing a more common sense approach, simply asked whether respondents approved a U.S. program to "help backward peoples raise their standard of living." About 65% were in favor–in contrast to the 15% found when a more limited approach was utilized.

Many Americans are unfamiliar with the official names of programs or organizations, but it doesn't follow that they are unaware of, or incapable of understanding, the essential functions of these organizations. Only about half of the people, for example, can answer the question, "What does the State Department in Washington do?"; and a similar proportion are familiar with the initials or name of NATO, the North Atlantic Treaty Organization. Yet, when asked about "the mutual defense treaty that the U.S. has with Canada and the countries of Western Europe, under which an attack against any one is regarded as an attack against all," 80% or more have called it a "good idea."

Public opinion polls can be of great value in making clear to everybody the trends of thinking among the general public on major foreign policy issues. In practice, however, the published polls do not begin to cover all foreign policy topics, and at any given time one cannot count upon the existing published polls to provide up-to-date information on more than a few of the "newsiest" foreign policy issues.

Analyzing Public Comment

Fortunately, the other major method of finding out what Americans are thinking–the analysis of spontaneously expressed opinions–makes possible a greater coverage of issues. Each day, editors and other public commentators express their views on foreign affairs questions; and from time to time major private organizations–some with membership in the millions—take public stands on these questions; and the organization positions can help illuminate the patterns of thinking within the American public.

Editorial discussions are inherently more capable of considering a foreign policy issue in depth than one or two polling questions can. Public commentators, taken as a group, are naturally more experienced and better informed than is the average respondent to a public opinion poll. Editorials frequently offer considered views on the detailed provisions of legislative or treaty proposals. Prompt editorials usually appear whenever the President makes a foreign policy statement, or when a major move is publicly taken anywhere on the international chessboard, giving clear indications of the way in which informed Americans are reacting to the news. A fairly small sample of editorial opinion can soon portray the chief themes of response which are being expressed by commentators in every part of the country.

How valuable is editorial opinion in indicating the action which the Government—Congress or the Executive—will ultimately take? On most foreign policy issues, popular opinion and editorial opinion point in the same direction, with the majority of the editorials and of the people upholding the same policy (editorial opinion is usually available more promptly than a polling result). But when these two indices are in conflict, it is usually the editorial opinion—not the popular opinion—which points to the course ultimately taken by the Government. On several occasions after World War II the Congress enacted important legislation when the polling results were adverse but editorial opinion was favorable (e.g., 1946 loan to Britain, 1947 military aid to Greece and Turkey). In more recent years editorial opinion, on such a question as Chinese representation in the UN, has been "ahead" of the popular opinion polls by months, if not years.

Evidently the Congress and the Administration have tended to act in response to the advice of Government experts and of informed opinion outside the Government, rather than on the partial information possessed by the "man-in-the-street." Editors are not only better informed themselves, but they seem to reflect the views of the whole stratum of businessmen and others having practical experience or specialized learning in foreign affairs. Any comprehensive analysis of American opinion should include the views of this segment of the public, as well as of popular opinion (and any institution or group can make an analysis of editorial opinion if it is interested enough to underwrite the project).

Nearly 18,000 daily newspapers are published in the U.S.; but some of these have no editorials, and many give little or no thought to this country's foreign relations. (Indeed, it is remarkable how few newspapers retain even a single editorial writer who devotes full time to foreign affairs.) Yet a substantial and growing number of newspapers do give thoughtful attention to foreign policy problems. Whenever a foreign policy development is reported, some editors are likely to react promptly–with gratification, alarm, or suggestions as to what U.S. policy should be. A valid sample of American editorial thinking about foreign affairs should include several papers which are outstanding in their regions, and also some newspapers with mass appeal (e.g., Scripps-Howard and Hearst chains) whose views are often closer to popular opinion than to expert opinion.

The major distinction in outlook among American editors has been that between the "internationalist" point of view, which presumes that the U.S. should pursue an active course in world affairs, and the "nationalist" approach which was dominant in America before World War II. Ever since Pearl Harbor, the great majority of American newspapers devoting much attention to foreign policy have shared the "internationalist" outlook adopted by the U.S. Government. Such newspapers have existed in every part of the country. Likewise, newspapers of "nationalist" outlook–although they are far fewer in number–have also been published in every region. In any over-all analysis of American opinion it may also be helpful to note the line-up of papers which are generally considered "liberal" and those considered "conservative."

Many varied considerations lead to support, or criticism, of U.S. foreign policies. Hence, a meaningful analysis of American opinion will involve more than a simple pro-and-con listing of newspapers on a given issue; it will describe the division of opinion in terms of the arguments and considerations advanced by the editors and commentators on each side of a question.

An analysis based upon a dozen leading newspapers has often sufficed to indicate the main features of opinion across the country. As additional editorials have become available, these have normally tended to confirm and validate the observations and conclusions initially based upon a smaller sample. (Even in a small sample one would prefer to include representation of both "internationalist" and "nationalist" outlooks.)

For readers who believe that press opinion does not reflect public opinion, some considerations may be mentioned. Skeptics sometimes point out that Franklin Roosevelt was four times elected to the presidency–each time against the opposition of the press; and some veterans of battles for public ownership, or labor disputes, feel that the press does not represent the people. There are significant differences in the situations of newspapers respecting foreign and domestic issues. On many domestic issues, a newspaper has interests which may be directly affected by labor or tax legislation, but on foreign policy issues, such as Korea or the UN, these special interests are not usually at stake, and the newspaper's own interests are simply those it holds in common with other patriotic Americans. (As for the phenomenally popular Pres. Roosevelt, it was his attitudes on domestic questions which aroused the most intense partisan and editorial ire.)

Polls are a particulary useful guide to the opinion analyst in situations where the views and actions of each citizen are of relatively equal significance, as in elections for the presidency or Congress, or in situations requiring the support of each individual, such as approval of a war, paying taxes, or observance of trade policies. For assessing the impact of public opinion on legislated or treaty-made foreign policy, public comment offers the analyst a more reliable guide than the polls do. This is true because the published comment reflects the views of that segment of the total public which takes an active interest in the issue, which is to say, exerts genuine political force upon the governmental decision (i.e., the better-informed writers, businessmen, and policy experts).

This Book

The present account of the unfolding of American opinion about U.S. foreign policy, from the time of World War II until 1975, is based primarily upon analyses which were prepared on a current basis for the information of State Department officers in Washington and their colleagues stationed abroad. It covers editorial opinion as well as polling results, and some organization views, in the belief that these various types of data are helpful in trying to reconstruct the state of American opinion respecting foreign policy issues and our relations with allies and rivals. The aim of the analysts throughout this period was to make our opinion reports as objective as possible; we felt that it was just as helpful to the Department and the Administration to call attention to criticism as to praise.

Perspective

In 1952 Prof. Frank Klingberg of Southern Illinois University published an article in *World Politics* based upon his researches in American history since 1776, which showed that there has been a tendency for periods of national "extroversion" to alternate with periods of national "introversion."[3] In the periods of "extroversion" the attention and actions of the U.S. Government have been relatively more concentrated on questions of external relations–with other countries of the world–than upon domestic problems and developments. The periods of "extroversion" have tended to last about 25 or 26 years, and those of "introversion" a shorter time, about 20 or 21 years. In terms of Prof. Klingberg's analysis, this book begins with American isolationism at the close of the "introversion" period extending from 1920 to 1941. It seems eminently understandable that an "activist" U.S. foreign policy should have developed during the following period of concentration on external affairs.

In his 1952 article Prof. Klingberg stated that if the American historical pattern of alternating periods were to continue, a shift from "extroversion" to "introversion" should be expected about 1966 or 1967. While some dramatic events in the field of race relations began to focus national attention on domestic questions in the early 1960s, it was not until the latter half of the 1960s, as we shall see, that the activism of the 1940s and 1950s began to be modified. The Nixon Doctrine, calling for a "lower U.S. profile" in the world, reflected public opinion in the new period of "introversion." The beginnings of the mid-20th century American "activism" are discussed in the next chapter.

Reference Notes

1. Department of State Bulletin, Vol. 41, p. 797.
2. 1951 poll by National Opinion Research Center.
3. Frank Klingberg, "The Historical Alternations of Moods in American Foreign Policy," *World Politics*, Vol. IV, No. 2 (Jan. 1952).

Part One

ESTABLISHING POSTWAR POLICIES (1940–1950)

II

ISOLATIONISM YIELDS (1940–1946)

It was in the very month of Pearl Harbor that Elmo Roper's interviewers for the Fortune Poll reported that a majority of Americans favored "an active part" for the United States in world affairs "after the war." This attitude on the part of Americans–so different from that of the preceding two decades–proved to be a puissant one. Ever since December 1941 about 70% of a national cross section have favored "an active part" for America, whereas 20%–or fewer–have supported the alternative of "staying out of world affairs as much as we can" (about 10% have given no opinion).

Before Pearl Harbor

American attitudes were quite different during the inter-war period. It was only five years before Pearl Harbor that Pres. Franklin D. Roosevelt gave his "America hates war" speech. Editorials across the country made it clear that the President voiced the sentiments of the nation.[1] In the same year of 1936, one of the earliest Gallup Polls reported that 60% of a national cross section believed that, "if there is another general war in Europe, the U.S. can stay out." The people's representatives in Congress endeavored to insulate America from possible war by the enactment of "neutrality legislation."

Only a minority of Americans desired a policy of participating in the existing international organization to maintain peace: in 1935, 30% felt that the U.S. "should join the League of Nations, if war in Europe is averted through the League," 57% said No (13% gave no opinion in this Fortune poll). On Oct. 5, 1937, the day before the League of Nations Assembly condemned Japan for its military actions against China, Pres. Roosevelt delivered his famous "quarantine speech;" but public comment, and the stands taken by organizations, indicated that a majority of Americans were not ready to support U.S. measures discriminating against "aggressors."

Pearl Harbor evidently brought a national realization that, no matter how hard America tried to keep out of a major war, this aim could not succeed, and that we might better "take an active part in world affairs" in the hope of thereby minimizing our involvement in war. This conclusion had not been reached when the war broke out in Europe in September 1939; it resulted from the series of traumatic events which occurred during the two years which followed. With the tragedy of Pearl Harbor we as a nation were convinced that our fate was inextricably interwoven with that of other major nations in the world.

The hatred of war which kept America out of World War I for 2 years and 8 months, and out of World War II for 2 years and 3 months, was overcome for various individuals at various stages of the war in Europe. It was after Hitler's legions invaded the Low Countries, in the spring of 1940, that a majority of Americans came to say they "expected us to go into the war in Europe," as Jerome Bruner reported in his *Mandate from the People.*[2] By the end of 1940, 60% were expecting the U.S. to enter the war; and during most of 1941 this proportion ranged from 70% to 80% or more. Contributing to this rising expectation was the belief that America's interests would be seriously affected by the outcome of the war, that a victory by Germany and Italy over Britain (and later, Russia) would be a grave danger to the U.S. From September 1940 onward, a majority of the public were in favor of "aiding Britain, even at the risk of war." In the four months preceding Pearl Harbor, the proportion supporting this policy stood at 69% or higher. In other words, the conviction of a huge American stake in the course of "world affairs" was highly developed before the Pearl Harbor attack.

A Peace Organization

With the United States actually plunged into hostilities, thoughts about planning for postwar peace were quickened–both within the Government and among the general public. Pollsters found that sentiment for "joining a League of Nations after this war is over" had increased from 37% in May 1941 to 60% in June 1942; opposition had declined from 39% to 22%.[3] By the end of 1942 Gallup reported 64% saying that our government "should take steps now before the end of the war, to set up with our allies a world organization to maintain the future peace of the world;" 24% were opposed.[4]

In 1943 national discussion of postwar planning for peace was stimulated by several Congressional bills. Rep. Fulbright (D-Ark) offered a succinct resolution: "That the Congress hereby expresses itself as favoring the creation of appropriate international machinery adequate to establish and maintain a just and lasting peace among the nations of the world, and as favoring participation by the United States therein." When Gallup Poll interviewers presented this proposal to a national cross section in July 1943, 78% said they approved, 9% disapproved, and 13% gave no opinion.

During that summer a score of Congressmen campaigned in some 30 states from coast to coast for a declaration of postwar foreign policy. "Some kind of international organization for peace" was supported everywhere by the great majority of those expressing opinions. Editorial opinion on the efforts of the touring Congressmen frequently specified a preference for the Fulbright Resolution over the B2H2 Resolution (advanced by Sens. Ball, Burton, Hatch and Hill) which specifically called for a United Nations military force to maintain the postwar peace. When Secretary of State Cordell Hull declared that the U.S. must be prepared to cooperate with other nations in the use of force to prevent future aggression, commenting editors tended to say that the Secretary had gone far enough, yet not too far. On Sept. 21 the House of Representatives adopted the Fulbright Resolution by a bipartisan vote of 360 to 29.[5]

U.S. Government leaders, long convinced of the desirability of American participation in an international organization to maintain the peace, next had to secure the approval of their chief allies, and of both major political parties at home. In October 1943 Sec. Hull met in Moscow with the foreign ministers of Britain and the USSR. They agreed on a Four-Nation Declaration (with China) in favor of creating as soon as possible a "general international organization." At home, a conference of Republican leaders at Mackinac Island had agreed to endorse U.S. participation in a postwar international organization—a move which was encouraging both to the Government and to the many editors and commentators who welcomed bipartisan agreement on postwar policy. Public opinion polls had long shown little difference among adherents of the major parties in their support of a "world organization to maintain peace" (e.g., Democrats 65%, Republicans 63% in Dec. 1942).[6]

As the presidential year of 1944 opened, public discussion showed increasing attention to the over-all problem of how best to keep the peace after the war's end. The necessity of perpetuating military cooperation among the major allies (U.S., Britain, Russia) was stressed by several prominent commentators (e.g., Walter Lippmann, Balt. Sun); but most commenting editors were opposed to anything which would be a "Big Power Alliance," preferring a general system of world organization. The sentiments of the general public were elicited by a Fortune Poll (March 1944) which found the following replies to its inquiry as to which of three alternatives "comes closest to expressing what you would like to have the U.S. do after the war":

13% said "enter into no alliance and have as little as possible to do with other countries;"
8% said "depend only on separate alliances with certain countries;"
68% said "take an active part in an international organization;"
11% gave no opinion.

Military force, however, was widely regarded as essential for maintaining the postwar peace. Such a serious group of citizens as the Commission to Study the Organization of Peace, for example, felt that the "international community as a whole" should be equipped with a "permanent force disciplined and loyal to that community and sufficiently powerful, with the support of law-abiding states, to frustrate aggression by any government or probable combination of governments." Similarly, all but one of the local groups comprising the Universities Committee on Postwar Problems "agreed that no means other than an international armed force would probably suffice to prevent or suppress aggression."

The idea of "an international police force" appealed to public opinion poll respondents during the years following Pearl Harbor. In late 1943 over three-fourths of a nationwide sample agreed that "the countries fighting the Axis should set up an international police force after the war is over to try to keep peace throughout the world." Polling analyst Jerome Bruner "granted that most Americans have no very clear idea of how an international police force works," but he stressed that the concept appealed to voters of both major parties and of all socio-economic groups.[7]

On the other hand, several journals which sought to envisage how an international police force might be set up and controlled concluded that the concept was "impractical." State Department opinion analysts pointed out that, despite the popularity of the international police force idea, polls also showed that the great majority of Americans favoring this concept wanted the U.S. at the same time to maintain a large army and navy. When asked specifically, only about one-third of the respondents felt that the U.S. army and navy should be "smaller" than the UN force.[8]

Public willingness for a world organization to exercise other significant powers, in addition to managing a police force, was indicated by various opinion polls. Majorities supported an international organization with power to: "prevent any member from starting a war against an outside country" (79%, Fortune, March 1944); "decide what military strength each member nation can have" (60%); "decide what taxes member nations must pay to support the organization" (70%); and "make laws about problems that may come up between members" (76%, NORC, Sept. 1943). As early as November 1942, several Massachusetts counties had carried on their ballots a question asking whether state legislators should be "instructed to request the President and Congress to call . . . a convention of representatives of all free peoples to frame a federal Constitution under which they may unite in a democratic World Government."[9] Seventy-five percent of those voting on this issue registered their approval. Some organizations and a few editors also advocated establishment of a powerful international organization or a world government. And, of course, some others vigorously opposed any such steps. Most journals refrained from discussing such radical proposals.

Roosevelt Statement

Soon after D-Day, and shortly before the 1944 national party conventions were to meet, Pres. Roosevelt made a brief statement (June 15) about the progress of this government's plans for serious discussions with its leading allies about setting up an international organization. Roosevelt's outline was regarded as skimpy by some commentators; but it was widely interpreted as a "minimum plan intended to produce the least possible controversy in an election year." Most of those commenting expressed pleasure upon seeing the small states accorded some representation.

An analysis of American opinion at this point, if based upon a prima facie reading of public opinion polling results, would have shown that the public wanted: 1) an international peace organization, endowed with 2) a police force, and 3) at least some powers of a world government. Each of these three goals also received vigorous backing from some quarters within the press and from some citizen organizations. Yet Pres. Roosevelt, who firmly upheld the aim of creating a peace organization, equally firmly ruled out the two goals of an international police force and an organization empowered to control its national members. (The experience of the United Nations since 1945 makes it clear that the nations of the world were not, in the 1940s, ready to carry out the goals rejected by Roosevelt.) Only a minority of the leading newspapers and organizations had espoused those goals which represented a more radical departure from the status quo. Roosevelt's opponents on these matters included the Christian Science Monitor, Chicago Sun, and Justice Owen Roberts. Ely Culbertson, head of The World Federation, Inc., bitterly complained that the President planned to revive "the old League of Nations," but with greater power for Britain, Russia, and the U.S.[10]

For the basic aim of a peace and security organization there was wide support in polling results, in the press, and among many broadly-based organizations. Shortly after Pres. Roosevelt's 1944 statement the Gallup Poll reported (July 2) an "all-time high" in popular support for American membership in a "new council or union of nations"–72% approving, 13% disapproving (15% no opinion). The Republican Party Convention had adopted a platform plank favoring "responsible participation by the U.S. in postwar cooperative organization among sovereign nations to prevent military aggression and to attain permanent peace with organized justice in a free world. Such organization should develop effective cooperative means to direct peace forces to prevent or repel military aggression." The Democratic platform favored "an organization based on the principle of the sovereign equality of all peace-loving states," and "arrangements through which the nations would maintain adequate forces to meet the needs of preventing war and which would have such forces available for joint action when necessary."

Dumbarton Oaks

On Aug. 27, 1944 representatives of Britain, the Soviet Union and the U.S. met at Dumbarton Oaks in Washington for secret conversations to seek agreement on a draft charter for the new international organization. At this time when the liberation of France and Belgium was going forward, the representatives of the three nations succeeded in harmonizing the drafts previously developed by their respective Foreign Offices on most–though not all–of the organizational problems. Agreement with the Republic of China was attained in talks with the British and Americans which followed immediately at Dumbarton Oaks. These talks ended on October 7 and the Dumbarton Oaks proposals were published October 9.

Widespread satisfaction greeted the announcement that the conferring nations had reached agreement on a large proportion of the questions involved in creating the new organization; publication of the actual agreements stimulated a flood of press and radio comment. The most general view was that a "good start" had been made at Dumbarton Oaks, that the proposals–though incomplete and tentative–furnished a firm footing for progress toward an international security system. Commentators felt that it was an improvement over the old League of Nations; they noted with approval that the Great Powers had been given large responsibilities for keeping the peace. The great majority were sympathetic to U.S. participation in this security system which involved the use of armed force when necessary to prevent the outbreak of another war. Preponderant opinion, which a few years earlier had insisted that America not become involved in war, had now come to believe–as a result of the events and discussions of the intervening years–that the best way to avoid war was to commit American armed forces to deter aggression. A minority, of course, opposed any "world organization"–notably the Chicago Tribune, Washington Times-Herald, New York News, and other "nationalist" newspapers and Senators.[11]

Among those most interested in the Dumbarton Oaks proposals were the citizen organizations in all parts of the country which for the past three years (or more) had been considering "postwar organization" to prevent World War III. State Department officers promptly provided the leaders of these organizations with the texts of the new proposals and invited leaders of interested organizations to a briefing at the Department of State on Oct. 16 at which U.S. participants in the Dumbarton Oaks conversations explained the process which had produced the drafts now under international discussion. Not only "peace" groups, but women's groups, church organizations, business and labor leaders, veterans organizations, farm groups, and many others were eager to gain a fuller understanding of the plans for future international security. Typically, they wanted their full memberships to become aware of these proposals of such great potential significance to the U.S. and to the world. Many felt that the whole American people should have an understanding of the aims and operations of the proposed security organization—particularly in view of the fact that Americans had eschewed membership in the previous world peace organization, the League of Nations.

These citizen organizations undertook to reach as many of the public as possible. Interested organization leaders got together in New York, under the chairmanship of Clark Eichelberger of the Commission to Study the Organization of Peace, to pool their wisdom and to coordinate their efforts. Among those especially concerned about a wide distribution of information were Americans United for World Organization and the League of Women Voters. They applauded the Department's decision to publish the text of the Dumbarton Oaks proposals widely (eventually 1,750,000 copies), and to send Department officers to address meetings in all parts of the country to explain the proposals and to answer questions about them.[12]

Important issues remained unsolved, even though both major political parties and the general public seemed firmly attached to the general idea of U.S. membership in a new international organization. An early October poll found 90% in favor of joining "an international organization in an effort to prevent future wars," and 82% assented to the idea that each member nation should "agree to make a part of its armed forces available when necessary to prevent any country from starting another war." Public discussion of the Dumbarton Oaks proposals focused especially on two questions: 1, the role of Congress in authorizing the use of U.S. armed forces; and 2, the rules about vetoing in the proposed Security Council.[13]

Just how U.S. military force should be brought into play, under the U.S. Constitution, was a question which was not widely discussed before the autumn of 1944. Many commentators of various outlooks were in general agreement with the view expressed by the newly-elected Commander of the American Legion, Edward N. Scheiberling, when he stated in a radio address: "We want a peace with teeth in it—a peace that can be, will be enforced." But if the threat of U.S. force were to deter a prospective aggressor, wouldn't it need to be swift and certain—as through a statement by the President's representative in the international organization, rather than through a deliberate vote by Congress which is constitutionally empowered to declare war? Discussions in and out of Congress presently made it clear that this was a knotty problem.[14]

The chief groups interested in an international organization to maintain the peace strongly argued that it need not be necessary for Congress to give its approval in each specific case of the use of U.S. armed forces (e.g., Americans United for World Organization, Commission to Study the Organization of Peace, Women's Action Committee, League of Women Voters). At a conference of organizations in November a resolution was adopted urging that "our Government, by a vote of Congress, agree that the member representing the U.S. on the Security Council will be able to pledge our nation's quota of the armed force or forces necessary for the prevention of aggression."

Several Senators also urged that Congress should not have to approve each use of U.S. forces (e.g., Austin, Ball, Burton, Connally). Most of the outstanding newspapers were also of this view (e.g., N.Y. Times and Herald Tribune, C. S. Monitor, Scripps-Howard papers). Also supporting this position were: Gov. Dewey of N.Y., John W. Davis, Wendell Willkie, Dr. James T. Shotwell, and Philip Jessup.[15]

Insistence that Congress approve every specific use of American forces came chiefly from two sources: those who tended to oppose any powerful international peace organization (e.g., Sen. Bushfield, Chi. Tribune, Hearst papers); and those who mistrusted the use of force in international relations (e.g., Christian Century, Norman Thomas of Postwar World Council). Many others were noncommittal at this time; and some, like Sen. Vandenberg, suggested that instead of a categorical answer, the issue might be resolved by setting up a sphere in which the President's authority would not require Congressional approval (e.g., in Western Hemisphere). The persistence of concern in America over this problem has been demonstrated on several occasions since 1944, as in connection with the fighting in Korea, Viet-Nam, the Dominican Republic, and the Arab-Israeli conflicts.

Among the general public, considerable hesitancy about granting the President full discretion was disclosed by a Princeton Office of Public Opinion Research poll in early September. While 31% were willing to see U.S. troops go into action following "approval of our Government representative on the international organization acting under orders of the President," a clear majority (57%) preferred "approval by Congress in addition" (12% gave no opinion). An October poll found an even division of respondents–41% for each proffered alternative. This question was phrased: "Should the U.S. wait for approval in Congress in each case when war starts before the President can send a part of our armed forces to help stop the war," or "should the President by himself have the power to send some of our armed forces if he approves of the request of the international organization?" It was clear that the nation was not ready to give whole-hearted approval to the change recommended by many earnest students of international organization.[16]

Voting in Security Council

Public discussion of the Dumbarton Oaks proposals also included important questions about the allocation of power within the new international organization. Which member nations of the new organization should decide upon the actions to be taken to keep, or regain, the peace? Would the big powers have the decisive responsibility? Could the organization coerce a recalcitrant big power? Should a nation accused of endangering the peace be permitted to "veto" measures designed to preserve the peace? What should be, in short, the rules for voting in the projected Security Council?

In public opinion polls before and after the Dumbarton Oaks conversations, a plurality (43% or 44%) consistently said they would "like to see" an organization in which all "members would have about the same amount to say in running it;" a quarter thought "the U.S. should have the most say;" and a somewhat smaller group preferred that "Britain, Russia and the U.S. together" should have the biggest "say." At the same time respondents were asked to guess how the world organization would actually be run; and half (49%) of the total voiced their expectation that the "Big Three" would "have the most to say."[17]

It was widely agreed that the new organization should be "democratic"—at least to the extent that all of the then United Nations should belong to it. Spokesmen who felt that a "genuine world government" offered the best chance of maintaining peace tended to favor an organization in which each nation would have equal power; they urged a "strong" General Assembly, rather than a predominant Security Council (e.g., Grenville Clark, Dorothy Thompson, Norman Thomas). But editorial opinion was moving toward the conclusion that the big powers must have the guiding hand.[18]

Considerable press attention was given the reported Soviet insistence on participation by members of the Security Council in decisions on disputes involving themselves. Many were strongly opposed to this idea, the Milwaukee Journal saying: "It is not our idea of justice that a person put on trial, even though presumed innocent, should sit on the jury" (similarly, Wash. Star, Los Angeles Times, Catholic Bishops, Study Conf. of the Churches on a Just and Durable Peace). Only a few were sympathetic to the reported Soviet position (e.g., Wall St. Journal, Kansas City Times); but some others felt that the question was "academic," that the new peace system would have failed anyway, if any of the great powers committed aggression (e.g.,

Sen. Ball, Ernest K. Lindley, Wash. Post, N.Y. Herald Tribune). The largest group among those commenting, focusing on the reported Russian determination to maintain a veto in the Security Council, opposed that position as patently "unfair."[19]

Another question about the new international organization centered around the role of regional organizations in the postwar security system. Some feared that international recognition of regional groups would confirm the great powers in their "spheres of influence" (e.g., Vera Micheles Dean); others, like Sumner Welles, felt that the regional organizations should receive greater recognition.[20]

There was some discouragement at the end of 1944 about the opinion situation in the U.S. and about the policies of our allies. A December opinion poll reported that only 43% of the American public recognized "the Dumbarton Oaks proposals" by that name, and nearly half of those who had heard of them had "no opinion" as to their worth as a basis for a peace organization. In Europe, several commentators maintained, Russia and Britain were pursuing "dictatorial" or "unilateral" policies in Poland, Italy and Greece, which America could not approve. Several editors agreed with Sen. Wheeler who held that, unless Russia and Britain changed their policies, it would be "pointless" to send the proposals to the Senate for ratification (e.g., Scripps-Howard papers, Salt Lake City Tribune).[21]

But the outlook changed early in 1945; and Messrs. Churchill, Stalin, and Roosevelt did get together at Yalta in February. By the time they met editorial and organization approval of the Dumbarton Oaks proposals was widespread; and public opinion polls showed as many as 90% approving U.S. participation in an "international organization to prevent future wars." Out-and-out criticism of the peace planning was largely confined to the "isolationist-nationalist" press. There did remain the unsolved questions about voting in the Security Council and how the U.S. should sanction the use of U.S. armed forces; but the over-all view was one of great hope and considerable confidence that the allies could agree on creation of an effective international organization.

Yalta Decisions

The decisions taken at the Yalta Conference had considerable impact upon American opinion about the projected international organization. The chief reaction to the Feb. 12 announcement on the Yalta meeting was one of gratification that the Big Three had reached agreed decisions respecting the prosecution of the war and important postwar actions. There was universal satisfaction with the decision to invite all of the United Nations to attend a Charter Conference in San Francisco on April 25. The three allies had given clear evidence of leadership; and they had also sought the participation of the smaller nations in the construction of the new international organization. As the Philadelphia Bulletin expressed it, the San Francisco Conference was "the best assurance that thorny issues can be finally adjusted on the lines of reasonable compromise."[22]

The agreements concerning Poland were the most controversial feature of the Yalta decisions. Most commentators tended to accept this "imperfection" as representing the best obtainable answer; but others disapproved the territorial changes benefiting the Soviet Union, and a number were skeptical about the arrangements for Poland's political future—including "free elections." Reservations about the cooperativeness of the Soviet Union in the new organization were increased with the subsequent announcement of two additional Yalta decisions: 1, the requirement of great-power unity in Security Council decisions (announced Mar. 5); and 2, the award of separate General Assembly seats to the Ukraine and White Russia in addition to the seat for the USSR (announced Mar. 29). Reports that the Russian Foreign Minister, Molotov, would not attend the San Francisco Conference were also disquieting to some.

The idea that all five permanent members must concur in a valid decision of the Secuirty Council, i.e., the great-power veto, was regretted as a "mistake" by some advocates of a powerful peace organization (e.g., C. S. Monitor, Cleve. Plain Dealer, New Orleans Times-Picayune). The idea was opposed by the "nationalist" Hearst and McCormick newspapers as a concession to Stalin. But the great majority of editors and commentators accepted this decision, as they had other Yalta decisions, as "the best obtainable." Moreover, the veto was welcomed by some Senators who had feared that otherwise the U.S. itself might be forced to take some future peace actions against its will. Ernest Lindley remarked that the general attitude in Congress "toward the Dumbarton Oaks plan as supplemented by Yalta is so favorable that many observers are keeping their fingers crossed."[23] After considerable initial disquiet over the 3-votes-for-Russia plan, and the fact that it had been kept secret for nearly two months, commentators decided that, after all, this was "not a major issue." There was general acquiescence in Sec. Stettinius' announcement that the U.S. would not ask for more than one vote in the General Assembly, and a widespread tendency to stress that the paramount aim was over-all agreement at San Francisco.

Two other topics connected with the San Francisco Conference provoked considerable advance public comment: Latin America, and trusteeship. The Inter-American Conference at Mexico City (Feb. 21–Mar. 8) had won editorial acclaim for adopting the Act of Chapultepec, providing collective security against aggression in the Hemisphere, and for dealing with other problems important to the

American republics. Most commenting editors agreed that the new regional security arrangement would buttress the proposed world organization, rather than conflict with it. The trusteeship issue occasioned greater debate, particularly over the future status of the Pacific islands which had been mandated to Japan under the League of Nations. It was generally agreed that the U.S. must have administrative control of these strategic island bases; but some Congressmen, high military officers, and "nationalist" newspapers felt that the U.S. should have full ownership of these islands. Public opinion polls made clear that, aside from military bases, additional territory was not desired by a majority of the people. A poll in January 1945 found 38% thinking that the U.S. should "own those islands outright," whereas 47% chose the alternative that the U.S. "should govern them under the proposed new international organization." College-educated Americans favored control under an international organization (59% to 31%), but those having only a grammar-school education favored outright ownership (46% to 31%).[24]

San Francisco Conference

On April 12, thirteen days before the opening of the San Francisco Conference, the nation was stunned by the news of Pres. Roosevelt's death. Within the hour after taking his oath of office, Pres. Truman stated that the Conference would proceed as scheduled. The feeling of many Americans was expressed by the Wall St. Journal which said that "the Roosevelt objectives will sweep powerfully along—for in the American mind his death will lift much of his peace planning above the bounds of controversy." Sec. Stettinius, head of the U.S. delegation to San Francisco, was known to share the ideas of Pres. Roosevelt and Sec. Hull; and there was general satisfaction that the delegation included bipartisan representation of both Houses of Congress. Among those organizations which had been actively engaged in explaining the Dumbarton Oaks proposals to the public, there was satisfaction that 42 of their number had been named as official "consultants" to the U.S. delegation. There was gratification, too, that the Kremlin had, after all, sent Foreign Minister Molotov to participate in the opening phase of the Conference. A poll on the eve of the Conference found 80% in favor of U.S. membership in the new organization, "even if we do not like some parts" of it. Only 9% said No (11% gave no opinion).

The press gave much prominence to the assembly of representatives in San Francisco, and to the Conference deliberations. Indeed, many commentators averred that the headlines may have overemphasized the differences of opinion over the admission of Argentina, the trusteeship issue, and other questions—especially the differences between Russia, on the one hand, and Britain and America, on the other. When, on May 8, there came the announcement of Russia's agreement to the Anglo-American formula on the veto power, there was almost jubilant relief on the part of American commentators. By the time Pres. Truman addressed the closing session on June 26, there was remarkably wide agreement that the conferees had produced the Charter of a worthwhile international organization. Pres. Truman called on the Senate for prompt consideration of the UN Charter, and his call was seconded by the overwhelming majority of the American press, including the Hearst newspapers.

Criticisms of the Charter, and hopes for improving it through amendment in the near future, were expressed by many commentators; but only a tiny minority of the press counseled rejection of the treaty or the adoption of Senate reservations. As the Foreign Relations Committee proceeded to hearings on the Charter, it heard testimony from a host of organization representatives—almost all of whom urged ratification. A small number of organizations representing what the Baltimore Sun termed "the lunatic fringe," opposed ratification. Among those urging approval were the Federal Council of Churches, U.S. Chamber of Commerce, the AFL and CIO leadership, American Farm Bureau Federation, American Legion, Gen. Federation of Women's Clubs, and many others.

Public comment continued to include some criticism of the provisions on trusteeship and—most of all—on the great power veto. It was contended that the veto meant that the UN could not prevent a great-power war (Scripps-Howard papers), or operate in the conciliation of disputes involving a great power (Sumner Welles), or even adopt any amendment to the Charter opposed by a great power (C. S. Monitor, Sen. Fulbright). All of these critics, however, favored ratification of the Charter. Among the general public, polls indicated opposition to the veto principle (56% opposed); but the polls also reported—shortly after the close of the San Francisco Conference—that 66% frankly "didn't know" the Charter provisions respecting the veto, and only 16% knew that Security Council action "required approval by the Big Five plus two other Council members." On the Charter as a whole, a Princeton poll reported that 54% said they had "some idea" of the Charter, and 85% wanted the U.S. to join the UN (4% expressed opposition). Nearly all commentators conceded that the Charter was "not ideal," but rather the least common denominator acceptable to 50 nations; and many warned of the tests ahead and the responsibility of the United Nations themselves to "make it work."[25]

In view of the strength mobilized in behalf of the Charter, it was "no surprise" when the Senate voted its consent on July 28, with only two dissenting votes (Langer of N.D., Shipstead of Minn.). A few commentators warned that ratification was "only a first step," mentioning that implementing legislation was yet to be adopted. But most stressed the overwhelming vote for ratification. It was three years and seven months after Pearl Harbor when the U.S. took this formal step so clearly indicative of American desire to lay aside the isolationist past, and "take an active part" in world affairs.[26]

First Year of the United Nations

When operations under the United Nations Charter started in London in October 1945, American goodwill remained strong. Editors said the Charter "must be made to work," despite the current differences among the victorious great powers. Potsdam had witnessed a measure of agreement; but mistrust had grown since the surrender of Japan, and the London meeting of foreign ministers to harmonize peace plans had ended without agreement (Oct. 2). A public opinion poll showed a drop in "satisfaction" with Big Three cooperation from 67% in September to 34% after the London meeting; three-fourths of those with opinions said that "Russia was to blame" for the lack of cooperation, because of her insistence upon trying to maintain her "sphere of influence." Walter Lippmann pointed out that Russia was not alone in trying to pursue dual, opposing policies: world cooperation and spheres of influence. Several others thought it natural that Russia should be suspicious of the U.S. "unilateral" Pacific policy (in Japan and the captured islands), retention of the bomb's secret, and American economic policy in Germany (e.g., Sumner Welles, N.Y. Herald Tribune).[27]

During the summer there had been some continuing debate over the powers to be exercised by the U.S. representative on the UN Security Council, and the character of U.S. military forces under the UN; but there was general acquiescence in Pres. Truman's announced intention of having Congress approve, by joint resolution, any U.S. undertaking on the use of American military forces under the UN. Soon after the Japanese surrender discussions of the atomic bomb showed differences of opinion about how it should be controlled, with a number advocating its control by the UN Security Council as soon as possible (e.g., Amn. Assn. for the UN, Marquis Childs, Walter Lippmann). As discussion continued, the number advocating positive measures to provide international control of the atom increased (e.g., Sens. Hatch and McMahon; N.Y. Herald Tribune, Balt. Sun; Assn. of Oak Ridge Scientists, Fed. Ccl. of Churches). Others, however, urged retention of exclusive U.S. control (Hearst newspapers). "Frankly, there are nations in the world I wouldn't trust," declared Sen. Connally (D-Tex); and the North American Newspaper Alliance reported that out of the 61 Senators and Representatives it had polled on the issue, 55 agreed with Sen. Connally. Moreover, the general public, asked to choose between having the U.S. and Britain "keep the secret" or giving it to the UN Security Council, favored retention of the secret by a sizable margin (74% to 20%).[28]

As 1945 was ending, increased public attention was given to the atomic bomb and to "strengthening" the UN Charter to meet the atomic menace (e.g., Sen. Ball, Catholic Assn. for International Peace, Scripps-Howard newspapers). Abolition of the veto was the specific remedy most commonly suggested. Sen. Taft advocated an inspection service under the UN to enforce the outlawry of the bomb, whereas Capt. Harold Stassen called for a special task force of atomic bombers under the UN, coupled with the prohibition of national bomb manufacture. An ABC (American-British-Canadian) Agreed Declaration on Atomic Energy managed to give a measure of satisfaction to most commentators: the "nationalists" interpreted it as agreement to "keep the secret;" the "internationalists" were pleased that the "secret" would soon be shared, and called upon the UN speedily to implement the ABC program. In December Congress completed action on the UN participation bill, which included authorization of the U.S. representative on the Security Council to vote the use of a U.S. military contingent by the Security Council.[29]

Another potential "test of the UN" was seen in reports of Soviet "interference" in northern Iran, where Moscow had refused to permit additional Iranian troops to enter the Soviet-occupied area. There was widespread support for the U.S. note of Nov. 24 which called for respect for Iran's sovereignty, and proposed withdrawal of all occupation troops by Jan. 1. A compromise adopted by the Security Council was applauded by commentators, especially the stipulation that the Council reserved the right to pass on the final settlement.[30]

Republican leaders, John Foster Dulles and Sen. Vandenberg, declared that America should have exerted greater leadership in the UN; some others stressed the need for caution and restraint (Sen. Connally). A public opinion poll inquiring about U.S. "reliance" upon the UN found 65% saying that Washington was relying more upon the UN "to protect itself against future attacks" than upon its own defenses. As to what U.S. policy should be, 43% said we "should be concentrating on our own defenses," while 49% favored concentrating upon "strengthening the United Nations."[31]

Throughout the first year of the United Nations, issues involving Soviet policy remained prominent. Outside the UN also, as the Foreign Ministers strove to effect a peace settlement—at least with Italy and the Eastern European nations—the struggle with Russian objectives was unremitting. To be sure, the UN dealt with other questions (trusteeship, admission of new members, Indonesia,

Greece, Siam, etc.); but those receiving greatest attention from the American public were: Soviet expansionist tendencies against neighboring countries; and Russia's position respecting the development of a UN security system, especially international control over atomic weapons.

Pres. Truman's announcement in the preceding January that the U.S. would place under individual trusteeship those Pacific islands necessary for U.S. security, was approved by many "moderate" commentators. But some "internationalists" and "liberals" asserted that this plan would weaken the United Nations; and some "nationalists" feared that the plan would not adequately provide for U.S. defense. The general public, in response to a 3-part polling question, showed a majority (53%) in favor of some sort of "international" arrangement (28% choosing the alternative that the U.S. "should not own these islands outright, but should be given full power to govern and fortify them;" and 25% holding that the U.S. "should share control of these islands with other members of the UN"). But 40% maintained that "the U.S. should own these islands outright." When the issue was taken up by the UN General Assembly in the autumn, more press comment was favorable to the "strategic" trusteeships than was opposed; but "nationalist" journals still denounced the plan for "strategic" trusteeships, and some "internationalists" (e.g., W. Lippmann, S. Welles) feared that this example of "sole" trusteeship was a cover for annexation which would undermine the trusteeship system.[32]

The American public had come a long way from its isolationist position of a few years earlier. After extensive discussion in the press and in citizen organizations, the public was giving high and sustained support to the world organization which had been proposed by the Government and advocated by the leadership of both major American parties. However, the United Nations had not fulfilled earlier hopes for an organization capable of "guaranteeing" peace. At the close of the San Francisco Conference only 40% of Americans expected that the U.S. would fight in another war "within 25 years;" but during most of 1946 as many as 60% said that they expected war within that stated period. Still, commentators were encouraged by the outcome in Iran and by achievements by the General Assembly (e.g., a disarmament resolution, establishment of the Trusteeship Council).

The willingness of the American public to participate in the United Nations, contrasted with its unwillingness to join the League of Nations after World War I, registered a sharp change in the foundation of U.S. foreign policy. Observers outside America wondered whether the change was stable; but the palpable shift in national opinion within America prompted most Americans to accept the change at face value. Moreover, the U.S. Government had taken a leading role in getting the new organization off to a sound start. It remained to be seen whether popular expectations as to the capabilities of the United Nations were realistic or exaggerated. In the most threatening case, that of Iran, the United Nations had apparently countered the threat. The experience of the first year was encouraging, if not conclusive. America was certainly demonstrating its willingness to take an "active part" in world affairs, and it was about to translate in unprecedented fashion its interest in aiding other nations.

Reference Notes

1. U.S. State Dept., Amn. Opin. Report (hereafter cited as AOR) of Apr. 12, 1943.
2. Bruner, Jerome, *Mandate from the People* (New York 1944), p. 21.
3. Bruner, op. cit., p. 236.
4. See Wm. A. Scott and Stephen B. Withey, *The United States and the United Nations* (New York 1958), p. 10.
5. AOR of Sept. 25, 1943.
6. Scott & Withey, op. cit., pp. 140 ff.
7. Bruner, op. cit. p. 45.
8. AOR of Jan. 5, 1944.
9. Bruner, op. cit., p. 38.
10. AOR for July 4 and 12, 1944.
11. AOR of Oct. 24, 1944.
12. See Dorothy Robins, *Experiment in Democracy* (New York 1971).
13. AOR for Sept. 22 and October 24, 1944.
14. AOR of Oct. 3, 1944.
15. AOR of Nov. 21, 1944.
16. AOR for Sept. 22 and Oct. 24, 1944.
17. NORC polls cited by Scott & Withey, op. cit., pp. 67 and 50.
18. AOR for Oct. 3 and 24, Nov. 20, 1944.
19. AOR for Oct. 5 and 24, Dec. 6, 1944 and Feb. 5, 1945.
20. AOR for Oct. 18 and Nov. 6, 1944.
21. AOR of Jan. 6, 1945.
22. AOR of Feb. 20, 1945.
23. AOR for Mar. 27 and Apr. 24, 1945.
24. AOR for Mar. 22 and Apr. 24, 1945.
25. AOR for June 9 and 21, July 4 and 19, 1945.
26. AOR of Aug. 2, 1945.
27. AOR of Feb. 20, 1945.
28. AOR of Aug. 2 and 21, Oct. 5, 1945.
29. AOR for Nov. 19 and Dec. 4 and 19, 1945.
30. AOR for Jan. 21, Feb. 7 and 26, May 20, June 21, Dec. 29, 1946.
31. AOR of Mar. 6, 1946.
32. AOR for Feb. 7, Mar. 20, Nov. 20, Dec. 20, 1946.

III

U.S. AID POLICIES (1941-1950)

America's aid to other countries after World War II has been impressive; so, too, was the decision to aid Britain even before U.S. entry into the war. From shortly after the fall of France and the beginning of Nazi air raids against Britain, a majority of the American public constantly felt that the United States should "help England win even at the risk of getting into war." Jerome Bruner pointed out that most of those favoring aid to Britain believed that Germany-Italy, if victorious, would "start a war against the U.S. within the next ten years," would control our foreign trade, and would limit our freedom.[1] If the popular aim was more to help ourselves than to aid others, it is nevertheless impressive that the U.S. provided to Britain and others $48.5 billion of lend-lease aid from March 1941 to V-J Day. This dispatch of money and materials to be used in fighting the "common enemy" was heartily endorsed by the American public.[2]

UNRRA

In November 1943 the U.S. took an active part in the establishment of an aid organization, UNRRA–United Nations Relief and Rehabilitation Administration–which somewhat followed the pattern of extending disaster and humanitarian relief which the U.S. had traditionally pursued on many occasions in the pre-war past. UNRRA was an "emergency organization designed to supply food, clothing and shelter to needy persons in liberated countries," plus "assistance in the resumption of urgently needed agricultural and industrial production."[3] The U.S. had taken the lead in drafting UNRRA's Charter, agreed to by 44 other nations; the U.S. paid 72% of UNRRA's operating expenses; and as much as 90% of the food and other distributed supplies were produced in America.

As early as Jan. 1943 polls had found a sizable majority (78%) of a nationwide sample of Americans backing the idea that the U.S. should help feed and rebuild other countries–even at the expense of continuing rationing and making other sacrifices after the war. Comment in the daily and periodical press, as well as statements by church, business and labor leaders, welcomed the U.S. initiative respecting UNRRA. Some commentators viewed the new organization as an "initial operation of the United Nations as a world council"–this was seventeen months before the convening of the UN Charter Conference in San Francisco.

From the outset, however, some "nationalist" sources vigorously denounced "boondoggling on a global basis" and "plans for an international WPA." The majority of editors commenting on the UNRRA conference at Atlantic City in late 1943 praised UNRRA as bringing 45 nations together in constructive cooperation, stressed that the guiding principle was not charity, but self-help, and noted that the U.S. would benefit by sharing the burden of postwar relief with others. Even so, in the House of Representatives in Jan. 1944, 57 votes were cast against the UNRRA appropriation (to 341 in favor), with opponents stressing involvement in "European power politics" and that the U.S. was being asked to pay more than its fair share.[4]

When the fighting ended in Europe in the spring of 1945, relief requirements mounted; and editors applauded when Pres. Truman called in former Pres. Hoover for consultation on what the U.S. should do to "help feed hungry Europe." The easing of U.S. rationing controls, after conclusion of the war against Japan, caused some American organizations and commentators to worry whether U.S. relief shipments would be adequate; but others were critical of the functioning of UNRRA, and began to complain about "political misuse" of supplies in various countries. Among the general public, 59% said they had "not heard of" the activities of UNRRA; but those who had heard of the organization were overwhelmingly favorable.[5]

When UNRRA reported a world food crisis in the making, Pres. Truman announced emergency food control measures and appointed Mr. Hoover to be Honorary Chairman of a Famine Emergency Committee. This Committee called upon citizens for voluntary reductions in wheat consumption and for savings in oils and fats, saying: "Americans of goodwill can do more and do it faster than any system of rationing orders."[6] Opinion polls showed the willingness of a large majority of the public to reduce wheat and meat consumption; and the voluntary program received strong support from editors. After announcement that the U.S. would not contribute to UNRRA after 1946, many commentators expressed regret that the U.S. was giving up internationalism in the food relief field; but as time went on an increasing number stressed that the U.S. had been putting up most of the money and that the international controls were not practical in curbing political abuses in the receiving countries.[7]

End of Lend-Lease

The need for U.S. aid to relieve hunger and starvation was more readily understood by Americans than were the economic repercussions of terminating lend-lease and the consequent needs of our allies for postwar financial assistance. In the few months between the end of the fighting in Europe and the unexpectedly swift end of the war with Japan, there was relatively little general discussion of postwar economic problems, although there was a favorable editorial reaction to the Bretton Woods Agreements and establishment of the World Bank. When Pres. Truman announced termination of lend-lease (Aug. 21, 1945), the initial reaction included a large measure of bewilderment that the program had ended so "suddenly." Other commentators, however, commended the President for carrying out the principle that lend-lease "should end with the end of the war." There was widespread praise for the performance of both lend-lease and reverse lend-lease; and a very favorable reception was accorded Pres. Truman's suggestion that the bulk of the lend-lease debts should be "written off." Editors felt that the U.S. had received compensation in the "coin of victory."[8]

When the Gallup Poll inquired about repayment of Britain's lend-lease debt, it found that 36% thought "England is expected to pay us back in full;" and as many as 64% said "England *should* repay in full." Another polling organization inquired about Britains's capacity to pay: 41% said "Britain can afford to pay," and 43% said "she cannot afford to pay." Official U.S. and British negotiators eventually agreed on the principle, which was also followed in the subsequent lend-lease settlements with others, of expecting payment of the agreed postwar value of civilian goods remaining after the hostilities. The British settlement became simply one item in the larger package presently agreed upon as the U.S. loan to Britain.[9]

The British Loan

When the war with Japan ended, leading U.S. and British officials appreciated that Britain would have a staggering burden to cover immediate postwar deficits and to fashion long-term plans for handling the balance of payments problem of a nation whose imports had for years exceeded her exports. Only the U.S. was in a position to provide immediate help; and the U.S. needed the cooperation of a solvent Britain in order to establish the kind of world economy and trading system it felt would be in the best interest of this country and of the world. "The loan to Britain was more than just a loan, more even than a very big loan," wrote John Campbell. "It was crucial to the success of the Bretton Woods institutions, the lend-lease settlement, world reconstruction and the liberalization of international trade." The agreed amount of the loan was $3.75 billion, to be repaid over fifty years, with interest at 2% on the credit outstanding.[10]

From the start of the Anglo-American discussions, most American press and radio commentators voiced concern over Britain's financial situation and expressed belief that extending U.S. aid would be of mutual benefit. Also from the start, vocal opposition was expressed by a minority, including some "conservative" Congressmen and anti-

British journals, which objected to "financing socialism." A Gallup Poll soon disclosed that 60% of the general public were opposed to a loan to Britain of $3 to $5 billion, with opponents frequently mentioning Britain's failure to repay its World War I loans.[11]

Additional light on popular attitudes at the time of the Anglo-American conversations was shed by a nationwide poll taken in mid-October of 1945, which inquired about loans to other war-torn countries (China and Russia) as well as Britain.[12]

"As you know, some of our allies are asking for loans from the U.S. in order to get back on their feet. If we made a loan of several billion dollars to England (Russia, China), do you think they would pay us back in full, in part, or not at all?"

	England	**Russia**	**China**
In full	10%	24%	34%
In part	35	34	34
Not at all	45	25	16
No opinion	10	17	16

"Would you approve or disapprove of making such a loan to England? (Russia? China?)"

	England	Russia	China
Approve	34%	40%	64%
Disapprove	58	50	26
No opinion	8	10	10

Educational background had a lot to do with reactions to this question: respondents who had attended college were 51% in favor of the British loan, those whose education stopped in high school were 36% in favor, and those having only a grammar-school education were 23% in favor. It is perhaps not surprising that in a population, only half of whom had more than a grammar-school education, there was not greater appreciation of complex international economic problems. Moreover, it is evident that many citizens were little touched by the press articles and radio commentaries in favor of the loan.

When Pres. Truman sent the loan proposal to Congress on Jan. 20, 1946, after its acceptance by the British Parliament, his message served to re-animate the strong majority of commentators who supported the loan; but the critics in Congress also maintained their vocality. Public discussion of the loan had been so extensive that a large proportion of the American people claimed awareness of the issue—78% said they had "heard of" it. The importance of popular understanding of the actual terms of the loan was graphically illustrated by a poll taken in early February which found a plurality in approval. This polling question stated that, in addition to the interest payments, "England has agreed to take definite steps to remove restrictions on our trade with them, and to join us in promoting world trade in general. Pres. Truman has now asked Congress to approve the plan. Do you think Congress should, or should not, approve it?" Reacting to this statement of the proposition, 46% said "Approve," 37% said "Disapprove," and 17% gave no opinion.[13]

The Truman Administration made a substantial effort to broaden public understanding of the issue. Public speeches were made by Sec. Byrnes, Under Sec. Acheson, Sec. of the Treasury Vinson; other officials familiar with the loan question journeyed to various parts of the country to present the reasons for this Administration program and to answer questions about it. State Department officials utilized their contacts with the numerous national organizations which had taken such an active part during the preceding year in acquainting their memberships and the general public with the facts about the United Nations Charter. The news media continued to give steady coverage to the developing controversy in Congress; and on the radio America's Town Meeting and other nationwide programs staged searching discussions.

When the national organizations took their positions on the loan it was evident that they were even more favorable than the nation's press: 38 supporting the loan, 4 opposing it. Business organizations were very active on the issue, and so were several of the general, religious, and labor organizations (e.g., Amn. Bankers Assn., U.S. Chamber of Commerce, Amn. Assn. for the UN, Gen. Fed. of Women's Clubs, National League of Women Voters, Fed. Council of Churches, Amn. Farm Bureau Fed., AFL, CIO). The four opposing organizations were: Veterans of Foreign Wars, American Coalition, Patriotic Order of Sons of America, and Win the Peace Conference.[14]

Supporters of the loan tended to stress the economic argument that the loan was "good business" for the U.S. Only a few used the argument which was more frequently mentioned in the later Congressional debates, that support for Britain would provide "a bastion against Communism." Among the general public, the most frequently-mentioned reason in favor of the loan was: "England needs the money." The chief opposition arguments, among both press and public, were Britain's record as a "defaulter" on her World War I debts, and belief that "it would be hard on us economically to make the loan." An opinion poll in June 1946, sponsored by the Social Science Research Council, found 38% approving the loan, and 48% against.[15]

It is interesting to note the action taken by the Congress in the face of this opinion situation of overwhelming approval by the press and national organizations, but a continuing plurality among the general public in opposition to the loan. In the Senate the loan bill passed by a vote of 46 to 34; in the House the favorable vote was 219 to 155.[16]

Did this Congressional action, in contradiction to the polling results, represent the wishes of the American public—or merely of the editors, columnists, and organization leaders? Perhaps it could be said that members of Congress voted the way that the voters would have voted, if they had given the question as much attention and concerned thought as the legislators did. Certain it is, that subsequent Congresses—holding fresh mandates from the people—proceeded to vote for more U.S. aid to more countries and for a greater range of purposes than was represented by the loan to the United Kingdom.

Greek-Turkish Aid

Scarcely seven months after the enactment of the loan to Britain, the British Government notified the U.S. that it would have to terminate the economic and military aid it had been extending to Greece and Turkey from before the end of World War II. The victorious allies of World War II had by now succeeded in agreeing to peace treaties affecting Italy and the Balkan states; but the efforts of the Soviet Union to extend its influence in other countries near its borders continued to excite deep disquiet. There were threats to Turkey, and particularly Greece, where Communists were supporting armed efforts to overthrow the government at Athens. Greece had received UNRRA aid, and the U.S. was planning considerable post-UNRRA aid for that suffering nation; but Britain had also extended economic aid and was providing advisers to train the Greek army to help put down the guerrilla action which was threatening the government. In this crisis what should the U.S. do? It was not certain that withdrawal of British aid would mean the downfall of Greece and Turkey; but neither was it certain that, on their own, these two nations would be able to withstand the pressures from the Soviet Union and keep their territories and independent governments.

The U.S. Government made a quick decision. On March 12, 1947 Pres. Truman appeared before Congress to present a message embodying what was soon to be dubbed "the Truman Doctrine." A loan of $300 million was requested for Greece (half economic aid, half military aid), and $100 million (all military) for Turkey. But the "historic" portion of this message was the President's statement of purpose. "I believe," said Truman, "that it must be the foreign policy of the United States to support free peoples who are resisting attempted subjugation by armed minorities or outside pressures." Although the Soviet Union was not named, the message was regarded as a serious challenge to Communist expansionism. Immediate and strong support of the Truman proposal came from a number of editors and Congressmen who had consistently backed Sec. Byrnes' "firm" policy toward Russia's efforts to enlarge its power. Others were not so quick to make up their minds. Popular distrust of the Soviet Union had increased rather steadily during 1946.[17]

"Do you think Russia can be trusted to cooperate with us?"

	Sep. 1945	**Oct. '45**	**Mar. '46**	**June '46**	**Oct. '46**	**Dec. '46***	**Mar. '47**
Yes	52%	40%	34%	30%	28%	35%	25%
No	33	44	45	55	58	46	63
No opin.	15	16	21	15	14	19	12

*New York meetings in November of CFM and UNGA had been interpreted by the press as reflecting improved relations with the Soviet Union.

Since the President asked for Congressional action within six weeks, there was not time for an extensive information campaign, such as had been mounted in behalf of American participation in the United Nations; but the Administration could state its case to the public through the media and national organizations, as it had done in the case of the British loan. The plight of the Greeks won wide sympathy; but could the American economy stand the strain of "trying to fight Communism with dollars" all over the world? Wouldn't the President's policy increase the danger of a conflict with Russia? Shouldn't this issue be laid before the United Nations, whose purpose was the peaceful settlement of international differences? And wouldn't American "unilateral" action, by-passing the UN, be injurious to that fledgling organization? Also, some Americans held from the outset that aiding the Greek and Turkish governments would not be helping democracy, but would be propping up reactionary and anti-democratic regimes.[18]

As editors and commentators gave their views on Pres. Truman's proposal, it was evident that by a sizable majority they supported the $400 million loans to Greece and Turkey (e.g., N.Y. Times and Herald Tribune, C. S. Monitor, Phila. Inquirer, Phila. Bulletin, Scripps-Howard, H. V. Kaltenborn, David Lawrence, Sumner Welles). Many of these supporters expressed some reluctance–regretting the "failure" of the U.S. to lay the case before the UN, or apprehensive about undertaking direct opposition to Soviet expansionism, but believing that the U.S. must take the "calculated risk" of a war. America's national interests, they felt, called for a policy of resisting Soviet expansionism as was set forth in the President's program.

Opposition to the loans came mainly from two groups: 1, the "left-wing liberals" who for some time had been critical of the Administration's policy toward the Soviet Union (e.g., Henry Wallace, Fiorello LaGuardia, Norman Thomas, PM, Chi. Sun); and 2, the "nationalists" who had consistently opposed an active U.S. part in world affairs (e.g., Chi. Tribune, N.Y. News). In addition, opposition now came from some who expressed concern about embarking on a course of "using dollars to shore up" foreign governments (e.g., John S. Knight, Chi. News, Richmond Times-Dispatch).

National organizations, which had presented such a solid front in behalf of the British loan less than a year earlier, were divided on Greek-Turkish aid, or unable to reach an agreed position. Supporting organizations included the American Association for the United Nations and Americans for Democratic Action. Ranged in opposition were the American Veterans Committee, National Farmers Union, Socialist Party, and various peace groups.

Declaring Cold War

Pres. Truman had linked the policy of U.S. aid to Greece and Turkey to a broader Cold War; and it seems clear that—despite some sharp objections—the majority of the public approved the precedent of advancing economic aid to two countries which it felt were threatened by Communist expansionism. Public opinion polls showed general support for extending aid, but they also revealed some significant differences in attitude toward various aspects of the Truman proposal. The Gallup Poll reported approval of aid to Greece by a margin of 56% to 32% (12% no opinion); the National Opinion Research Center found economic aid favored, 60% to 27%. Aiding Turkey was somewhat less favored (49% to 36%, Gallup). But military aid raised greater opposition than approval: "sending military advisers to train the Greek army" was opposed 54% to 37% (Gallup). This result suggests that there persisted some of the earlier fear that sending military aid to a country involves a risk of getting into war, which had led to the pre-war neutrality legislation. Also, only one-third of the respondents indicated that they thought that the governments of Greece and Turkey had "the backing of the majority" of their people (33% Greece, 34% Turkey). Reluctance to aid non-democratic or "repressive" governments did not always produce outright opposition to such aid programs; but it has been a continuing factor in public attitudes toward aiding foreign governments.

On the question of war risk, N.O.R.C. found a majority (52%) saying that provision of military supplies to Greece and Turkey "will make war with Russia more likely" (27% said "less likely"). The Gallup Poll, posing a substantive instead of a comparative question, found a majority (54%) saying that "lending money to aid Greece and Turkey is *not* likely to get us into war" (30% thought it "likely").

Looking further ahead, Gallup also asked: "Suppose other nations find themselves in the same fix as Greece, do you think the U.S. will have to do something about it?" By a larger margin, 68% to 20%, the answer was Yes. Seeking to elicit attitudes more specifically toward the Truman Doctrine, N.O.R.C. asked: "If Communists in foreign countries try to seize control of their governments by force, do you think it should or should not be our general policy to help those governments put down such revolts?" On this question sentiment was more closely divided: 47% said Yes, 37% said No (16% gave no opinion). Americans at this time evidently approved the purpose of the Cold War, but there was concern lest some Cold War measures result in hot war.

On the issue of by-passing the UN, some supporters of Greek-Turkish aid expressed real regret about this aspect. This was particularly true of those strong believers in the UN who disliked seeing the U.S. revert to unilateral, rather than "internationalist," action to deal with "international" problems. At the same time, some Congressional opponents of Greek-Turkish aid (but not hitherto noted for their devotion to the UN) called attention to public opinion polls indicating majority willingness to have the United Nations deal with the Greek-Turkish problems. It may be noted that one component in American popular "internationalism" was a willingness to "let George do it," a desire to dodge the responsibility and the costs of solo American action, if there were a chance that other countries (or institutions) would share the responsibility and the costs. (This became clearer later as the public showed its willingness to have the UN deal with such "hot potatoes" as Korea, Arab-Israel conflicts, and Viet-Nam.)

Still, in 1947 Americans did place great hope in the United Nations as offering a future of international peace, and they did not wish to upset this young and promising international organization. Many deemed it important to advance our support to the threatened victims of Soviet expansionism in a manner which would not diminish the capacity of the UN to usher in a peaceful world. Also, the Administration felt that the United Nations at this time was not geared up to handle such an emergency program of aid. But when Sen. Vandenberg proposed an amendment to the aid bill the Administration adopted it, making clear that the U.S. would cease aid to Greece and Turkey in any of three stated circumstances: 1, if the UN requested termination; 2, if requested by a Greek or Turkish government representing a majority of its people; or 3, if the President determined that the program's purposes had been achieved or were incapable of achievement. Vandenberg's amendment was hailed by editors as a reassuring move, and some also praised it as correcting the "mistake" of extending a "blank check" to reactionary regimes.

Polls indicated that this change was satisfactory to the general public.[19]

The whole package of economic and military aid was approved by the Senate by a vote of 67 to 23–despite the popular distaste for military aid registered by the polls and despite the opposition voiced by the "nationalists" and the Wallace "liberals." In the House the vote was 287 to 107. The Congress thus "confirmed a new departure in American foreign policy," serving notice that the U.S. would act to bolster up nations resisting Soviet pressure.[20] But there was little contemporary anticipation that this vote would lead to commitments in Asia and the Middle East.

Two months after enactment of this aid program many Americans were not too clear about its purposes. A majority (55%) continued to approve the extension of aid to Greece, but when asked about its main purpose, 35% said "relief, rehabilitation;" 24% said "stop Russia, Communism;" 7% said "strengthen democracy, combat dictatorship;" 14% cited other reasons, and 23% said they "didn't know." Eight months after passage of the act a national sample was asked about "sending military supplies to help the Greek government;" and a plurality (45%) were now favorable–marking quite a change from the attitudes expressed when Greek-Turkish aid was initially proposed. Apparently, earlier fears that sending military supplies could result in war had begun to subside in the light of experience under the program; but a substantial minority have continued ever since to be concerned about the dangers of extending military aid. By this time, too, there was discussion throughout the country of a program to aid, not only Greece, Turkey, and Britain, but all our European allies in the war.

Marshall Plan

On June 5, 1947 Secretary of State George C. Marshall, at the Harvard Commencement, made his famous offer that, if the European nations would get together to work out a joint reconstruction plan, the U.S. would see what it could do to help. "Any government willing to assist in the task of recovery," said Marshall, "will find full cooperation on the part of the U.S." The State Department was deeply concerned because Western Europe seemed to be in danger of losing the economic gains made since the end of the fighting. Under Secretary Acheson had (on May 8) delivered a public address stressing the continuing need of the war-torn countries of Europe and presenting a 5-point program for their economic recovery. The press reaction to the Acheson speech was generally sympathetic to aiding "friendly" countries; and an April opinion poll had shown 71% favorable to the principle of "continued spending of large sums to aid war-torn countries." But there were also reservations to these generous sentiments; many editors thought it would be prudent for the nation to add up the total cost of foreign financial requirements and calculate America's capacity to meet them. Also, half of the polling respondents favoring aid qualified their approval by such stipulations as "only a small amount," or "if it goes to the right countries."[21]

The aid program envisaged by Sec. Marshall differed significantly from those pursued under UNRRA and the Truman Doctrine. Its emphasis was on economic reconstruction–no military aid was contemplated; and the Marshall Plan embodied a regional and multilateral approach. The proposal was immediately recognized by commentators as a major pronouncement of U.S. foreign policy; and editorial comment showed 10-to-1 approval among a hundred surveyed newspapers. These editorials revealed a general feeling that "the era of handouts is over," and that the U.S. should extend aid only when it was assured that the aid would be used to restore economic productive capacity. An end to piecemeal aid, and the prospect of an inclusive program, were cordially hailed. Some "liberals" who had opposed aid to Greece and Turkey were sympathetic to the Marshall proposal (e.g., New Republic, Chi. Sun). Many editors favored Sen. Vandenberg's proposal of a bipartisan council to take an inventory of the nation's resources. The "nationalist" minority, as usual, rejected the whole idea of aiding foreign countries (e.g., Chi. Tribune, Wash. Times-Herald).

On June 22 Pres. Truman announced the appointment of three study committees: 1, a governmental committee headed by Interior Secretary Krug to study the effect of an aid program on America's natural resources; 2, the President's Council of Economic Advisers headed by Dr. Nourse to study the program's impact on the domestic economy; and 3, a committee of distinguished citizens, under the chairmanship of Commerce Secretary Harriman, to advise upon the limits to which aid might safely and wisely be extended. The House of Representatives also set up a Select Committee on Foreign Aid (the Herter Committee) to report on various aspects of the proposed Marshall Plan.[22]

The first public opinion poll on the Marshall Plan appeared on July 23 (Gallup Poll) and provided some noteworthy findings: only half of the general public had heard of the Plan (49%); among these "informed" citizens a majority (57%) were sympathetic to the Marshall proposal. Another Gallup question showed that informed opinion was also favorable to the idea of "giving European credits of about $5 billion a year so that they could buy the things they need in this country;" but half of the "informed" group said they were "unwilling to pay more taxes" for this purpose. The limited popular awareness of the Marshall Plan existed despite the fact that leading newspapers were giving extensive front-page attention to European and American developments respecting the Plan and also frequently editorializing upon it (in the first 18 days of July the Baltimore Sun published 13 editorials). As might be expected, educational background was significant in relation to awareness of the Marshall Plan (7 in 10 of the college-educated, 5 in 10 among those who had attended high school, and 4 in 10 among those having only a grammar-school education).

At the same time, it may be noted that actual opposition to the Plan was quite restricted—a far larger number of people were either ignorant of the Plan or refrained from giving any opinion of it. Both the educational differences and the support/opposition figures are given in the following table based upon the Gallup Poll release.

	National	**College**	**H. School**	**Gr. School**
Approve Plan	28%	47%	28%	20%
Disapprove	10	12	11	11
No opinion	11	11	11	9
Total aware	49%	70%	50%	40%
Hadn't heard of it	51	30	50	60
	100%	100%	100%	100%

It would doubtless have been difficult to enact such a far-reaching measure as the Marshall Plan with only 28% of the electorate giving it positive support.[23]

In October two polls (Gallup and N.O.R.C.) reported that the number of Americans who had "heard of" the Marshall Plan continued to be less than half of those interviewed; they also reported that only 1 in 5 respondents was aware of the major premise of the Plan—that the Europeans get together and "do something" for themselves. A comparable proportion had "heard of" the agreement in Paris in September in which the 16 countries of the CEEC adopted plans to speed up European recovery. Nevertheless, many Americans were discussing what should be the U.S. reaction to Europe's deepening needs, and additional organizations and leaders endorsed the Marshall proposal (Amn. Legion, Amn. Veterans Comm., Wm. Green of AFL, Business Action—a publication of the U.S. Chamber of Commerce). By November public discussion had increased to the point where the Gallup Poll could report that 61% said they had "heard of" the Plan. One significant development was that numerous Congressmen had visited Europe and returned to report that European needs were genuine, and that it was in America's interest to extend aid. Further news and data on the U.S. capacity to help came in the reports of the Krug and Nourse committees.

In November awareness of the Marshall proposal increased somewhat further, and enthusiasm for the Plan continued unabated in the editorial columns. The Harriman Committee report, remarkable for its unanimous agreement among leading citizens of diverse interests, received more news attention and editorial appreciation than any of the previous foreign aid studies. Many underscored its recommendation that no pressure be exerted upon aid recipients as to their form of economic organization, although the National Association of Manufacturers and some others continued to inveigh against aiding socialists (e.g., Sens. Brooks and Malone). Although much press and organization comment tended to welcome the Marshall Plan's de-emphasis of the anti-Communist aspects of the Greek-Turkish program, in Congress the most potent argument for the aid program appeared to be the threat of Communist expansion into Western Europe. Also in November, a large number of leaders in the fields of business, agriculture, labor, and education organized the Committee for the Marshall Plan under the leadership of Henry L. Stimson (e.g., O'Neal of Farm Bureau, Murray of CIO, Conant of Harvard). The Herter Committee's suggestion that the aid funds be administered by a separate agency under a bipartisan board of directors received substantial support from editors and Congressmen (e.g., Sens. Vandenberg and Taft; U.S. Chamber of Commerce).[24]

Pres. Truman sent the actual European Recovery Program (ERP) to Congress on Dec. 19, the same day that Congress completed action on a $597 million program of "interim" relief aid for France, Italy, and Austria. Strong support for the President's definite program was voiced, as usual, by most of the press and a steadily growing number of organizations; but some press observers, noting Republican efforts to reduce the relatively small amounts for interim aid, predicted "rough going" for the requested ERP amounts of $6.8 billion for the first fifteen months and $17 billion over the entire four-year period. Gov. Dewey gave his support; but several leading Republican Senators (Taft, Wherry, Millikin) advocated reduced amounts. The public opinion polls which showed support for the European Recovery Program in principle, also showed reluctance about large amounts of money (e.g., only 49% favored ERP if it meant postponement of tax reduction). The Administration stuck to its program; indeed, Sec. Marshall was accused by some press supporters of the ERP of being "stubborn" for defending the total program, based upon the needs of the European nations, throughout the course of the January hearings before the Senate Foreign Relations Committee. More often, editors and commentators staunchly maintained their support of the program, and of Sec. Marshall's "forthright" statement, as well as those made by Defense Secretaries Forrestal and Royall.

The official presentation of the program before the Committee stimulated public discussion throughout the nation–in the press, in nationwide radio debates, and in local communities where branches of national organizations (and other local groups) took an active part in this debate. The national organizations testified at the Senate hearings, demonstrating support from a wide range of representative groups–women's, veterans, religious, business, labor, and other. Outright opposition at the hearings was limited–coming from such spokesmen as Merwin K. Hart (Natl. Econ. Council), Arthur Schutzer (Amn. Labor Party), and Henry J. Taylor and Henry Hazlitt (columnists).[25]

Following its hearings the Foreign Relations Committee presented a unanimous report which "supported the Marshall Plan as the State Department had conceived and developed it. It recorded its conviction that ERP was a 'calculated risk which the U.S. cannot afford to reject'."[26] Earlier it had been agreed that the reference to $17 billion would not appear since Sen. Vandenberg and others felt that they should not attempt to commit future Congresses; and for the same reason the initial amount was scaled down to 12 rather than 15 months, but in the proportionate sum of $5.3 billion. As to the thorny question of administrative arrangements, it was agreed to create a cabinet-rank post under the President, with general expectation that a Republican would fill it.

As the time for the Senate vote approached, with press commentators and national organizations strongly in favor of the proposed ERP, State Department officials concerned with public opinion were dismayed by some opinion polls. In February a Roper poll reported 39% in favor of the Marshall Plan, and 14% opposed; but nearly half of the sample (47%) either had no opinion or simply hadn't heard of it. A Gallup Poll release on March 3 reported that the proportion who had "heard of" the Marshall Plan had increased to 79%, and that in this "aware" group approval now stood at 57%. But this meant that only 45% of the total public positively favored the program. A trio of polls taken by N.O.R.C. suggested that the greater the awareness of public debate, the less approval there was for the general idea. In the previous October 80% had said they would "approve of the U.S. sending machinery and other supplies to help the countries of Western Europe get their factories and farms running again." In December, the identical question found only 70% in favor; and in late February–early March approval was voiced by 68%. Moreover, only 23% of the national sample were recorded in favor of appropriating the "full amount" of five billion dollars which Sec. Marshall had requested.

Nevertheless on March 1 Sen. Vandenberg led off the debate in favor of the Plan on the Senate floor; and on March 13, 1948 the vote was taken, with only 17 Senators casting Nays. One factor which may have helped to crystallize attitudes in the Senate—and in the house later in March—was doubtless the news from Czechoslovakia where it was becoming clear that the Communists had succeeded in taking power. Congress completed action on the Foreign Assistance Act of 1948 in business-like fashion; and Pres. Truman signed it on April 3.[27]

At about the time of the aid bill's final passage (late March–early April), N.O.R.C. took a poll specifically on the "Marshall Plan for European recovery," and found 51% of the total sample in favor (74% among the college-educated, 55% of those with a high school education, but only 35% of those having a grammar-school education). It is interesting to note that popular support for the Marshall Plan continued to grow after Congressional enactment. In early July, N.O.R.C. found 57% saying that they were, "in general, satisfied with the Marshall Plan for European recovery," and 68% said they thought "the U.S. should continue the program for European recovery next year" (college-educated, 80%; high-school group, 74%; grammar-school group, 52%). By the end of the year (late November), the vote for continuance rose to 72% (59% among those with a grammar-school education). A remarkable change in popular opinion was thus completed from 1947 to 1948—a shift from less than 30% approval of the Marshall Plan to over 70% approval, and each of the three educational groups giving at least majority sanction. This noteworthy shift had not been produced without the persistent efforts of thousands of the Plan's supporters—in positions of national prominence and leadership, and also in local communities all across the country.[28] Although in later years much debate has been given to the amounts and detailed conditions of U.S. aid, it was this nationwide discussion which evoked the majority belief in the principle of extending (non-disaster) aid to other countries which has persisted ever since.

Point Four

A further step in the evolution of U.S. aid policy—beyond help for our recent allies—was taken in early 1949. In his well-received inaugural address, Pres. Truman advocated, as his "Point Four," technical assistance to underdeveloped countries (his first three points were also on foreign policy: support of the UN, continuation of ERP, and military support of Western Europe). Numerous commentators promptly hailed "Point Four" as an imaginative and far-seeing proposal, calculated to contribute much to world peace and prosperity. Some others demanded more information about the nature and dimensions of the proposed program, or wondered whether this might not prove to be "another" expensive scheme to "uplift the world." As the President and Secretary Acheson gave further indications of the nature of the planned program, a growing number of commentators voiced approval of the basic concept of aiding underdeveloped areas with U.S. technical skills and know-how. Commentators liked the idea of utilizing material and intellectual, rather than monetary, resources and also the emphasis on the role of private enterprise. The minority of skeptics feared vast expenditures under the new program, and the possibility that the less developed countries would discriminate against U.S. investment capital, or use our technical skills against us. A first public opinion poll (N.O.R.C.) indicated that among those who had heard of the Point Four program, 78% were favorably disposed and 15% opposed to it.[29]

Public approval of programs of economic and military aid, in both editorial and popular opinion, did not of course mean automatic support for the annual figure in the Administration's budget request. In July 1948, for example, a few months after enactment of the Marshall Plan, 68% of N.O.R.C. respondents favored its continuation, but 37% said the U.S. was "spending too much" for this purpose, while a total of 45% held that U.S. spending was "about the right amount" or "not enough."[30]

A year later comment by Congressmen on the Marshall Plan included several calls for sizable cuts in European Recovery Program appropriations; some said that economic "integration" among the European recipients was not adequate and that the U.S. should use its aid funds to "persuade" the countries to forge a closer union. In early 1950 Pres. Truman cut the Marshall Plan budget request from around four billions to $3.1 billion. This cut "satisfied" a majority of polling respondents (51%), of organization leaders, and of editors—some of whom felt that the cut was too deep. All groups, however, reflected predominant support for continuation of a large-scale Marshall Plan.[31]

Reference Notes

1. Polls from Sept. 1940 to July 1945 by Princeton Office of Public Opinion Research; Bruner, op. cit., pp. 24–25.
2. John C. Campbell and others, *U.S. in World Affairs, 1945–47* (New York, 1947), p. 344.
3. Campbell, op. cit., p. 319.
4. AOR for Oct. 11 and Dec. 4, 1943 and Feb. 5, 1944.
5. AOR for June 9, Sept. 6, Nov. 5, Dec. 19, 1945.
6. Campbell, op. cit., pp. 326–327.
7. AOR for Mar. 20, Apr. 4 and 9, May 3, June 4, July 18, Aug. 6, Sept. 19, Dec. 6 & 20, 1946.

8. AOR for Sept. 6 and 20, 1945.
9. AOR for July 4 and Aug. 21, 1945; Campbell, op. cit., p. 346ff.
10. Campbell, op. cit., p. 358.
11. AOR for Sept. 20, Oct. 5, 6 and 19, 1945.
12. AOR of Nov. 6, 1945.
13. AOR of Feb. 11, 1946.
14. AOR of May 21, 1946.
15. AOR of July 13, 1946.
16. Campbell, op. cit., pp. 363–5.
17. AOR of Mar. 28, 1947.
18. Ibid.
19. AOR for Apr. 1 and 4, 1947.
20. John C. Campbell, *U.S. in World Affairs, 1947–1948* (New York, 1948), p. 47.
21. AOR for May and June, 1947.
22. AOR for June and July, 1947.
23. AOR of July 30, 1947.
24. AOReports of December 1947.
25. AOReports of Jan. 1948.
26. Campbell, *U.S. in World Affairs, 1947–1948*, p. 504.
27. AOR for Mar. and April, 1948.
28. AOR for July and Dec. 1948.
29. AOR for Jan. and Feb. 1949.
30. NORC poll #159 (July 1948).
31. AOR of Feb. 10, 1950.

IV

IN SEARCH OF SECURITY (1945–1949)

American isolationism melted during the wartime years which culminated in U.S. entry into the United Nations; and increasing American activism on the world stage was demonstrated by U.S. programs of wartime and postwar aid to other nations. But these changes in U.S. foreign policy were not seen by the public as fully solving the problem of American national security–in the world or even in the Western Hemisphere. As John C. Campbell observed, with the end of the war and the occupation of Germany and Japan, "relations with the Soviet Union became the great problem of American foreign policy."[1]

Concern about the Soviets led to public discussion about the Cold War, control of atomic weapons, and collective security agreements respecting Europe. Security questions relating to China burgeoned at the time of the 1948 presidential election. Writing in 1947, John Foster Dulles said that the "guiding lines" of U.S. foreign policy in the two years since the war had been: "support for the United Nations and peace settlements in Europe and Asia which will eliminate the risk of future German and Japanese aggression and give the peoples a good chance to restore a condition of well-being."[2]

Soviet Aims; Germany

American attitudes toward the Soviet Union exhibited many ups and downs during the war years, beginning with the initial distress over the Nazi-Soviet pact. Later, after the Soviet Union and the U.S. were both fighting against Hitler, public opinion polls usually showed a plurality saying "Russia can be trusted to cooperate with us after the war;" and following the four-power conference in Moscow of October 1943 the plurality became a majority (54%). Americans were pleased that at that conference the Soviets, the U.S., Britain, and China undertook to refrain from making separate peace bargains and pledged their united support for a postwar organization to maintain the peace.[3]

The Yalta Conference results (Feb. 1945), as noted earlier, were acclaimed by the American press as demonstrating Soviet support for the United Nations; but some complained bitterly about "power politics" and Russian policies, and saw a "Soviet victory" in the settlement concerning Poland. Similarly the Potsdam communique of August 2 was welcomed for its specific agreement on difficult problems; but a vocal minority contended that the Russians had secured another "victory" by obtaining "primacy" in Eastern Europe (e.g., Hearst, McCormick-Patterson, and Scripps-Howard papers).[4]

Creation of the Council of Foreign Ministers at Potsdam to lead in the effort to forge a European peace settlement was also welcomed by American press commentators;[5] but these soon became distressed at the secrecy and lack of results from the wrangling sessions of the Council in London. An October 1945 opinion poll showed a sharp rise (to 50%) in "dissatisfaction with the way in which Russia, England and the U.S. are cooperating"—with most respondents holding the Soviet Union chiefly to blame. Some improvement was seen at the Moscow conference near the end of 1945.[6]

In early 1946 Winston Churchill's "Iron Curtain" speech at Fulton, Missouri accented growing doubts about whether the Kremlin was seeking domination of added territory, rather than simply "protecting herself." By the autumn of 1946 an N.O.R.C. poll found 70% of Americans concluding that "Russia was out to control as much of the world as she can," and only 18% saying "Russia has only been trying to protect herself against any future attacks." At the same time, a majority (52%) conceded that "in the disagreements between Russia and the U.S." the U.S. was "partly to blame." Also the public was evenly divided as to whether the U.S. "should try to stop any attempt by Russia to control the countries near her in Europe and Asia" (46%) or should "keep out of it" (44%). Moreover, when a follow-up question asked if we should still try to stop her "if it made war with Russia more likely," the 46% who would "try to stop Russia" dwindled to 35%. A clear majority upheld a "firm" policy in dealing with Russia in working out peace settlements, whereas only 13% said we should be "more willing to compromise."[7]

Throughout the years following V-E Day, Americans remained firm in their unwillingness to yield to Soviet pressure on, or blockade of, Berlin. Editors, and also the general public, were overwhelmingly agreed on backing the U.S. and Allied position on Berlin; and they also supported the evolving Allied views on economic and political policies respecting West Germany. Five months after V-E Day a majority (53%) felt that the occupation policy was "not hard enough," and only 2% termed it "too hard" (attitudes on the Japanese occupation at this time were similar). A December 1945 poll found 57% saying No to the question: "Will Germany every become a peace-loving nation?" Only 29% answered Yes. A large majority (77%) felt that the U.S. "should continue taking charge of young people's education (in Germany) for a long time." By February 1946 a plurality of polling respondents (41%) felt that the U.S. had made "a good start in running Germany," and an additional 31% chose the alternative response that we were "not making mistakes there," and only 14% termed it a "bad job."[8]

In May 1946 the great majority of Americans (85%) still felt that Germany would "try to start another war in 25 years if the allies didn't watch carefully." Almost as many, 80%, accordingly felt that the U.S. should join England, France and Russia to "stop any attempt to re-arm in 25 years." But our partners in the Council of Foreign Ministers failed to approve American proposals for a treaty to keep Germany disarmed, although this idea had bipartisan support in Congress and enthusiastic editorial approval.[9] By August polling respondents registered "satisfaction" with "the job" the U.S. was doing in several respects: "disarming Germany and keeping her disarmed" (69%); "punishing the war criminals" (62%); "putting Nazis out of important positions" (54%); and "reeducating the German people to prepare them for democratic government" (49% to 15%). By November sentiment about the nature of the Germans had so changed that 68% held it "possible to re-educate the German people to a peaceful way of life." By December 72% of polling respondents said they "would like to see our government help Germany get her peacetime industries going again," whereas 15% were opposed—these often citing fear of another war.[10]

Some idea of the comparative public interest in various topics in the summer of 1946 is provided by an opinion poll which inquired about five subjects. The poll found 73% taking "a good deal of interest" in "shortages of food," 64% in "our relations with Russia," 61% in "the control of inflation," 55% in "the atomic bomb," and 38% in "our trade with other countries." In the Congressional campaign of 1946, which focused largely on domestic issues, some Republicans nevertheless charged that the Democratic Administration had not been sufficiently "tough" in our relations with the Soviet Union, and that it should weed out the un-American employees in Government jobs.[11]

At the Council of Foreign Ministers meetings Secretary Byrnes had the support of most American commentators—both for his firmness against Soviet drives for advantage, and also for his conciliatory moves designed to facilitate progress in the peacemaking.[12] The actual signing of peace treaties in Feb. 1947 with Italy and the Nazi satellites prompted little enthusiasm, and some objections to the clauses calling for reparations from Italy—a country which in fact seemed to be in need of U.S. aid. By the time Pres. Truman called for aid to Greece and Turkey (in March), public concern about the future role of Germany had substantially diminished, whereas public concern about the future role of the Soviet Union had substantially increased, and the existence of the Cold War was officially acknowledged. Editors approved the Truman Doctrine, and also the U.S. turn to the economic reconstruction of Europe, including West Germany.[13] Proposals for a federalized Germany—made by France, and in America by John Foster Dulles—also stirred approving comment. The press warmly supported the keeping of U.S. troops in Germany, the new economic policy for Germany, and a federalized government–because these policies were considered "effective measures to counter Russian designs on Germany."[14] In the year and a half since V-J Day, popular trust in Russia to "cooperate with us" had gradually declined from 52% to 25% (as noted in the preceding chapter); and in March 1947 as many as 63% recorded themselves as "distrustful" of the Soviet Union.

Eight various U.S. foreign policies were voted on in a public opinion survey in April, with a plurality or more approving each of the eight policies except one: sending military supplies to Greece (34% for, 39% against). Greatest approval was for an "agreement to keep Germany disarmed for 40 years" (74%), for "continued large sums to aid war-torn countries" (71%), and for "economic aid" to Greece (67%). In July press and radio comment showed greatly increased resentment at Russia's obstructionism, and an increased determination to proceed without her in world reconstruction.[15]

United Nations; Rio Pact

For some time many Americans had felt that collective security through the United Nations was not necessarily the main answer to America's security problem. Within its first year of operation, the United Nations ceased to be the prime assurance of U.S. security for a majority of Americans, as can be seen from answers to the following N.O.R.C. question:[16]

> "Which one of these two policies do you think the U.S. should follow, in order to protect ourselves against future attacks: A, Concentrate on trying to make the United Nations so strong that no country would dare start a war; or B, Concentrate on trying to make our own defenses so strong that no country would dare attack us?"

	Make UN Strong	Strengthen Our Defenses	No Opinion
1945–Sept.	48%	45%	7%
1946–Feb.	49	43	8
1946–May	49	45	6
1946–Aug.	42	51	7
1946–Oct.	44	51	5

While Americans were debating how best to assure future U.S. security, Government officials were considering more specific plans respecting the defense of the Western Hemisphere. In May 1946 Pres. Truman sent to Congress a bill which would authorize the President to enter into agreement with other American states to send U.S.

military officers to instruct their military personnel, and to transfer to them U.S. military supplies—thus leading to standardization of military organization and equipment.[17] This proposal prompted little editorial discussion; but its critics included Sen. Taft and Henry Wallace, who argued that the measure would stimulate an arms race in Latin America, and that undemocratic regimes would use the arms against their own people. A public opinion poll in September found only 38% voicing approval of "strengthening military defenses in our part of the world by sending arms to South American countries;" but, by April 1947, after the Greek-Turkish aid proposal, a majority (53%) was registered in favor of the same polling proposition. (The questionnaire which included the earlier question had dealt largely with the unpopular regime in Argentina; the 1947 questionnaire didn't mention Argentina but included a question on arms to countries threatened by Russia.) Apparently there was less popular concern about sending arms to the Western Hemisphere than to the Eastern Hemisphere.[18]

More basic than the Administration's military supplies proposal was the plan for a permanent treaty for the collective defense of American states against aggression. A temporary war-time agreement had been reached in the Act of Chapultepec (1945) when it was also agreed to hold a conference in Rio de Janeiro in October to write a definitive treaty. But the rift between the U.S. and the Peron government of Argentina clouded the prospect for unanimous action and led to postponement of the Rio Conference. Some months later Sen. Vandenberg, in a Cleveland speech (Jan. 1947), expressed his concern that a "communistic upsurge" might occur throughout Latin America if the republics continued to drift apart. Vandenberg asked that the Rio Conference be convened; and several editors concurred. The State Department, having received word that the Peron government had taken steps to eliminate Nazi ownership and control of businesses, agreed to convening the Rio Conference that summer. In public comment it was generally agreed that the Conference should be postponed no longer.[19]

The Rio Pact (1947) stipulated that in any case of attack upon a signatory state—from outside the Hemisphere or from within—the signatories would be obliged to assist the victim of attack and to consult each other on measures to be taken. The treaty received unanimous press acclaim and was extolled as an example of international cooperation for the rest of the world, since it was designed to be an effective measure which also fitted into the United Nations framework. Commenting editors were gratified that the Conference had rejected the modifications proposed by Argentina: a requirement that agreement be unanimous in handling cases of aggression instead of the two-thirds vote which was adopted; and a proposal that the provision for swift sanctions be applied only to aggressors from outside the Hemisphere. Sen. Vandenberg piloted the Rio treaty to a 72-to-1 victory in the Senate. A public opinion poll in June showed that 72% of the public agreed that if "one of the countries of South America" were attacked, the United States should send armed forces "along with other American countries to stop the attack." (At this time only 52% agreed to similar action in case a "small European country was attacked by Russia.")[20]

The American public thus supported this new commitment to the defense of a score of allies in Latin America—in marked contrast to the U.S. isolationist policy of a century and a half which had permitted no alliances. After this significant break with the past, the U.S. went on during the next seven years to undertake mutual defense commitments with an additional score of nations in all parts of the globe (except Africa).

Atomic Weapons; Arms Reduction

At the close of the war Americans saw a potential danger to American peace and security in the continuing accumulation of arms, particularly the atomic bomb. In the period immediately after the bomb's first use commentators tended to consider it an "imperative to peace" and a challenge to the United Nations. Some suggested turning the new weapon over to the UN Security Council; but the majority of those commenting welcomed Pres. Truman's statement that the U.S. and Britain did not intend to reveal the atomic secret until means were found to control the bomb and protect the world from the danger of total destruction.[21]

The "epochal and distinguished" report of the Acheson Committee, favorable to international control, was applauded by the greater number of commentators; but its discussion revealed somewhat incompatible attitudes on the part of the general public. A majority (59%) thought that "there should eventually be some sort of international control of atomic bombs and atomic energy," rather than let "each country remain free to make its own bombs." However, only 21% thought that "the secret of making atomic bombs should be put under the control of the UN;" the majority thought the U.S. "should keep the secret to itself." Presently several national organizations undertook campaigns to educate the public on this issue, using the Acheson Committee report as a "basis for their discussions."[22]

When Mr. Baruch presented the U.S. plan to the UN Atomic Energy Commission on June 14, 1946 public comment was overwhelmingly favorable. Although some felt it risky to promise to give the bomb secret to the UN, even with the proposed safeguards, many felt it would be better for the U.S. to use its "current superiority" to secure an effective system of control than to face the dangers of an atomic arms race. There was considerable pessimism, though, about Russia's unwillingness to give up the veto in atomic matters, which most commentators felt to be essential. A number of organizations (international relations, scientific, religious, women's) voiced their approval of the Baruch plan; but polls showed that relatively few people (29%) had heard of it, and the bulk of the respondents were unwilling to sanction the eventual "turn-over" of U.S. atomic factories to an international agency. Debate within the UN, and within the U.S., continued throughout the year—with the Hearst press making a campaign "against giving away any secret of the atomic bomb;" but most commentators continued to give their support to the Baruch plan.[23]

Public discussion continued during 1947, and the general public continued to approve some accompaniments of international control and to reject others. A February poll sounded out national opinion on five conditions which might be incorporated in a scheme for international control; respondents said they would:

Accept UN inspectors to see if each country was living up to its agreements (67% to 19%);
Accept a stop on making atomic bombs (53% to 33%);
Accept placement of "all our atomic factories under the control of an international agency" (51% to 31%);

but they would reject requirements that—

We destroy all the atomic bombs on hand (49% to 39%); and that
We give the international agency "all the information it needs" about atomic energy (44% to 40%).

A repeat of this poll in October 1947 showed some increase in the proportions accepting the first three propositions; but also an increase in the proportions rejecting the last two. By October 1949, after realization that the Soviet Union also had the atomic bomb, respondents reaffirmed their acceptance of the first three propositions and they also turned in pluralities in favor of the two propositions which had earlier been rejected: 57% were now willing to destroy all atomic bombs if other countries would; and there was willingness to give the international agency "all the information it needs" (45% to 40%). A sizeable majority (68%) now approved of "the United States making an agreement that, if war breaks out, *we* won't use the atomic bomb if other countries don't;" 25% disapproved this idea.[24]

Proposals for arms reduction at the 1946 UN General Assembly evoked a burst of enthusiasm in editorials–some appreciating Foreign Minister Molotov's initiative in broaching the subject–and a hearty round of applause for the U.S. plan for arms reduction, presented by the U.S. representative (ex-Sen. Austin), for being explicit about the necessity of safeguards in the form of inspection. Editors held there must be no veto on inspection–especially where atomic energy was concerned.[25]

The first postwar public opinion poll on arms reduction found a large majority in favor of "reducing the size of our army and navy if other countries agree to do the same;" and approval rose to 83% provided "all countries agreed" to inspection by the United Nations. But only 1 out of 5 Americans (21%) expected that all countries would agree. Even if all countries did agree to arms reduction, a majority of respondents (65%) said the U.S. should "still keep a navy and air force larger than anyone else."[26] Thus, in the aftermath of the world's most destructive war, the American people were willing to reduce our armaments if other countries would do so, and particularly if there were international inspection to make sure that all arms-reducing nations kept their word. The chief focus of the world's discussion of armaments during the next years was on nuclear rather than conventional weapons. Here again Americans seemed willing to accept international controls, provided there would be effective international inspection. These themes were clearly echoed in the 1970s in the SALT talks.

Prague (1948); Cold War

In 1948 the Communist take-over in Czechoslovakia (Feb.) received wide attention in the U.S. and contributed heavily to the atmosphere of "crisis" which enveloped Washington and America in March and April of that election year. As the Cold War intensified, the proportion of Americans expecting the U.S. "to be at war in the next ten years" rose to 74% (from 28% in late 1946), and as many as 36% expected "war in the next year or two."[27]

In public comment, the strongest note was for speedy enactment of the European Recovery Program. Pres. Truman, in his March 17, 1948 address to Congress, mentioned that on that very day Britain, France, and the Benelux nations had signed the Brussels Pact, providing for a united military defense. Truman promised U.S. support for the efforts of free Europeans to protect themselves. The President's characterization of the Communist forces as threatening world peace won a large measure of editorial agreement, as did his program for revival of the U.S. military draft and the strengthening of our armed forces. A February 1948 poll had reported that Americans had changed their earlier opposition to military aid for Greece; they now supported such aid by a margin of 58% to 29%.

One week after Truman's address to Congress a poll found 49% saying they had heard of the "agreement between England, France and other countries of Western Europe to defend each other against attack;" and a majority of the total sample (56%) said "the United States should promise to back up these countries with our armed forces, if they are attacked by some other country." Almost as large a number (53%) said that they favored backing up these countries with our armed forces in case "Communists *inside* these countries tried to seize control by force." On each of these questions the college-educated respondents were appreciably more in favor of U.S. action than were those with only grammar-school education: 65% vs. 48% on backing up the Western countries; 56% vs. 48% on backing them up in case of a Communist revolt.[28]

Meanwhile the Russians were putting the squeeze on Berlin, starting their obstructionism as early as January, when they saw the concerted moves by Britain, France and the United States succeeding in efforts to rebuild the western zones of Germany. As Soviet interference with air and land communications to Berlin was intensified, American commentators gave strong support to the U.S. insistence on its rights of communication. Western withdrawal from Berlin, these writers said, would have catastrophic consequences throughout Europe (e.g., Edw. Murrow, Phila. Inquirer). An April polling question stated that the Soviets "wanted our officials and troops out of Berlin," but 85% of the respondents said "we should stay there anyhow;" only 7% held that the U.S. should "pull out" (8% gave no opinion).[29]

A month after Truman's address only 41% of a nationwide sample claimed to have heard about the Brussels agreement; but 52% of the total sample still said they would "approve of the U.S. sending military supplies to these countries of Western Europe now, in order to strengthen them against any future attack." On the other hand, when respondents were asked if "we should promise to go to war on their side, if these Western European countries are attacked by some other country," a plurality said No (48% vs. 40%).[30] Thus, in 1948 after the Communist take-over in Prague, a majority of Americans had overcome the earlier fear about sending military supplies to Europe; but they were not yet willing to "promise to go to war" in case of aggression against these countries.

Describing the steps by which America was developing its policies against aggression in the world, John C. Campbell noted that the Truman Administration—despite its pledge of support for the Brussels nations—had every "reason to believe that the Senate would shy away from a definite military commitment which could draw the

U.S. into war through the decision of some European power." The alternative to a treaty commitment, Campbell wrote, was the Vandenberg Resolution, developed by the State Department and the Senate Foreign Relations Committee, which gave its approval on May 11, 1948.[31]

This resolution, which proved to be a key development in the evolution of NATO, reaffirmed U.S. policy to seek peace and security through the United Nations and specified that the United States should associate itself with regional and other collective mutual-aid arrangements. Commentators hailed the resolution as a "revolutionary" departure in U.S. peacetime policy, showing Congressional support for the principle of "military lend-lease" to our overseas friends. A common view was that adoption of this measure would mark "the complete abandonment of the whole concept of isolationism" and indicate that the "American people are no longer divided on the question of cooperating with other nations to maintain law and international order."[32]

The climate of opinion, in Congress and out, was such that the Senate adopted the Vandenberg Resolution, by a vote of 64 to 4, one month after its approval by the Foreign Relations Committee. Disapproval in the nationwide press was noted only from the Chicago Tribune and the Hearst and Patterson papers. Some other commentators proceeded to advocate a full-fledged military alliance with Western Europe (e.g., Wm. P. Simms of Scripps-Howard; Edgar Mowrer).[33]

By mid-1948 a plurality of Americans (47%) said Germany was "not likely to become a threat to world peace in the next 20 years," while 43% still thought such a threat "likely." As the differences with the Soviet Union on German policy steadily grew, and U.S. action became more closely linked with that of Britain and France, American press comment tended consistently to approve these developments. There was one major exception: the policy of dismantling German factories in accordance with the original efforts to keep German industrial power low. As the European Recovery Program got under way it was increasingly felt that hampering economic production in West Germany was bound to enlarge the recovery program and its call on American resources.[34]

American editors strongly upheld the Western position on Berlin and thoroughly approved the decision to take the Berlin case to the UN. Also, an April poll (as noted earlier) found that 85% of the general public said we "should stay there" despite Soviet efforts to oust us. In July a Gallup Poll found 80% saying we should stay—even if it meant war with Russia. An N.O.R.C. poll reported 75% in favor of forcing the Russian blockade, "if necessary to get food and coal to the people in our part of Berlin."[35]

1948 Election; China

Polls during the summer of this election year showed the general public taking a greater interest in international questions than it had during the immediate postwar years of 1946 and 1947. "Relations with Russia" were mentioned as the top problem confronting the U.S. by 26% of the nationwide sample; and 22% named "Avoiding war." The leaders of the major parties maintained their support for a bipartisan foreign policy; and press commentators agreed. Polls showed that self-styled Republicans and Democrats held similar ideas on foreign policy (e.g., on holding our ground in Berlin); and only 3% in each party said we were "too tough on Russia."

However, one difference in position on the part of the presidential candidates should be mentioned. Gov. Dewey came out for increased U.S. aid to the Nanking government in China, which was in combat with its Communist rivals. Dewey thus took a position against the Administration, and entered a debate which had long divided editors and commentators. Public opinion polls taken following the Prague and Berlin events of early 1948 showed an increase (from February to April) in popular approval of U.S. military aid "to help the Chinese government against the Communists." Support rose from 32% to 55%; this majority sentiment was similar to that shown on military aid to European governments confronted with Communist revolt.

As news reports suggested that a Nationalist Government of China was on the verge of collapse, the debate about aid to China grew warmer. The larger number of editors held that Europe should have priority in the Cold War, and that the U.S. could not effectively stop the Communist drive in China at this time, hence they agreed with the Administration in preferring to "let the dust settle." But the debate didn't disappear with the U.S. 1948 election—or with Mao's proclamation of the People's Republic of China.[36]

North Atlantic Treaty Organization

The passage of the Vandenberg Resolution proved to afford an adequate basis for pursuing bilateral agreements for arms aid to the Western European nations. When the Brussels powers moved to open negotiations with the U.S. on a North Atlantic pact, this was regarded by most editors as "a logical and expected step." It was welcomed by a wide array of spokesmen (Winthrop Aldrich of the Chase National Bank, the Socialist New Leader, Gen. Fed. of Women's Clubs, American Legion, and others). Some commentators wondered whether military aid to Western Europe might detract from the European Economic Recovery Program; but few voiced opposition to the idea of U.S. entry into a North Atlantic Treaty Organization which would commit the nation to defend Western Europe against attack. Polls continued to show approval of military aid; but at the same time there was a fairly even division of opinion on "promising to go to war to back up these countries in case of attack." By 1949, each side in the Cold War, as George Herring later put it, "viewed the other as a threat not simply to its vital interests but to its way of life;" and before the end of the year a poll found only 19% saying we could "count on Russia to meet us halfway in working out problems together."[37]

Congressional views were carefully considered in framing the North Atlantic Treaty; and the new Democratic majority in Congress was expected to make changes in domestic policy, rather than foreign affairs. A number of Congressmen urged U.S. participation in NATO; and no Congressional voice was heard in strong opposition. In Congress and outside it was increasingly felt that a North Atlantic security pact was necessary to ensure the success of the Marshall Plan in deterring Communist aggression. Some commentators did express concern that the new pact should preserve the war powers of Congress under the Constitution; some others thought it should be set up within the framework of the United Nations.[38] These were fearful that the NATO plan could create dependence upon relatively narrow alliances, rather than the worldwide security scheme of the UN. As events had begun to illuminate the limitations upon the power of the UN to keep peace and preserve the interests of the Western nations, the majority of Americans evidently felt that it was not necessary to put all our eggs in that one basket, that we could consider other measures–although preferably "within the UN Charter"–to preserve the peace and stem the Communist advance which threatened to make the Soviet Union dominant in the world (citing the 1948 Prague take-over and 1948 Berlin blockade). Polls and editorials of 1948 showed how these attitudes developed into approval of U.S. military aid to the countries of Western Europe.

The North Atlantic Treaty was signed at Washington in April 1949; it was hailed by a host of leaders and the great majority of editors. Some church and farm leaders did feel that the treaty gave too much emphasis to military considerations; and some UN supporters still wanted a universal rather than regional pact; but outright opposition was largely confined to the anti-internationalist press (McCormick; Hearst). An opinion poll in the spring showed 79% approving the new pact, and only 11% opposed; but sentiment on sending military aid to our new allies was not that strong: 56% in favor, 36% opposed. The arguments of opposition respondents included: fear that the weapons might later be used against us; fear that sending arms might increase the chances of war; and concern lest these arms be needed for defense here. Another angle on the aid issue was reported by a Gallup Poll which found 65% of a national sample in favor of aid to NATO allies "if they agree to provide us with air bases and any other help that they may be able to give." Popular unfamiliarity with official nomenclature was again shown in a June 1949 poll reporting that 55% of its respondents "didn't know" the "main purpose" of the "North Atlantic Pact;" 15% replied that it was mutual assistance against Russia, and 9% cited mutual assistance without mention of the Soviet Union. Twelve percent opposed the Treaty, giving as their chief reasons: opposition to involvement and fear of being drawn into war.[39]

At the Senate treaty hearings many organizations expressed full support; and some minor organizations voiced disapproval. The Senate ratified the North Atlantic Treaty on July 21, by a vote of 82 to 13. Congressional action was slower on the Administration's request for $1.16 billion for military aid to NATO countries. Press comment, as noted earlier, had long been favorable to military aid to the West European countries; and popular support was shown in polls (although these did not inquire about the magnitude of the appropriation). The House passed a military aid bill, but voted to cut the authorization in half–members saying they wanted greater assurance that our aid would be effectively used through an integrated defense system. Richard P. Stebbins pointed out that Congress was still considering the aid measure in September when diplomats met in Washington to establish the North Atlantic Council; and one day later Pres. Truman announced a Soviet atomic explosion. This undoubtedly hastened final passage of the bill, including a billion dollars for military aid to Western Europe.[40]

Trends in American Opinion

Four years after establishment of the United Nations there was no national "return to isolationism." A survey at the time of the signature of the North Atlantic Treaty showed some increase over the previous year in the number of Americans saying that the U.S. "had gone too far" in its activity in world affairs–from 34% to 41%; but a majority continued to say the U.S. "had not gone too far" (59% nationwide, 71% among the college-educated). The chief complaint among the critics of U.S. foreign activity was: "too much spending," usually specifying on "foreign aid." Other critics simply said: "mixing too much in foreign affairs," or criticized the U.S. for "by-passing the UN," or for supporting reactionary regimes.[41]

This NATO-time survey also reported sustained majority approval (55%) for U.S. help in the defense of Western European countries; but there was some apparent decline in sentiment for defending a "South American nation" since 1947 (from 72% to 62%). No precise reason can be assigned for this decline; but analysis of the 1949 polling results shows considerable capacity to discriminate on the part of the respondents:

42% approved defense of both Europe and South America;
20% approved defense of South America, but not Europe;
13% approved defense of Europe, but not South America;
25% did not unqualifiedly approve defense of either area.
100%

When the 42% approving use of U.S. armed forces to defend both European and South American countries were asked if they would favor such action in behalf of "any country that belongs to the United Nations–no matter what part of the world it's in," only three-fourths of this group gave unqualified approval (31% of the total sample).

In little more than four years from the convening of the San Francisco Conference the American people sanctioned three basic shifts in their foreign policy: in place of isolationism were active membership in the United Nations, establishment of an unprecedented program of aid to numerous nations, and participation in a defense alliance with Western Europe and Canada (as well as with the other American republics). In each case the U.S. President and Executive Branch had taken the lead in presenting a policy which proved acceptable to the nation and which was formally sealed by action of the people's representatives in Congress. In each case also the proposals for change were adjudged sound by the great majority of editors and commentators, and actively supported by a number of major nationwide organizations. All of these basic policy shifts were also approved in principle by the man-in-the-street as shown by public opinion polls, although occasional reservations as to costs and detailed implementation were indicated by the polls (e.g., Marshall Plan).

Public support for membership in the United Nations, although a sharp break with past policy, reflected the long-time aversion of the American people to the carnage of war, and their conclusion (after a quarter-century of experience) that participation in international organization offered greater hope for avoiding war than did staying out of world organization. Decision to enter a defensive military alliance, for the first time since the American Revolution, came after public realization (through the experience of World War II) that the U.S. could not solve its defense needs by itself alone. The war-time search for security in Latin America eventuated in the Rio Pact which was warmly supported by the American public. The extension of U.S. military commitments to nations in Europe came after the

Soviet Union was seen as seeking for itself a place of dominance. The world-wide aid program reflected the long-time willingness of the American people to aid other nations struck by disaster—along with some appreciation that it is also in the American interest to extend such aid. These three major shifts in policy were destined to form the framework of U.S. foreign policy in subsequent decades, although time has witnessed modifications in their detailed application.

Other important foreign policies were developed during this four-year period, such as those for occupied countries, the Middle East and trade; but they did not receive as much public attention and were not the subject of as extensive information activity on the part of the Executive Branch. Yet, these policies also tended to develop in general harmony with the views which were expressed by editors and organizations representative of the American public. Proposals to control atomic weapons and reduce conventional armaments found the American public willing to strive for such goals; but in practice feasible international means could not be agreed upon. American opinion was also pleased that by the end of 1949 a West German government was in operation, although limited in powers; and there was increasing expectation that West Germany would receive eventual permission for some rearmament.[42]

Reference Notes

1. John C. Campbell and others, *U.S. in World Affairs, 1945-47* (New York, 1947), p. xii.
2. J. F. Dulles in Introduction to *U.S. in World Affairs, 1945-47*, p. ix.
3. AOR of Dec. 9, 1943.
4. AOR of Aug. 21, 1945.
5. AOR for Aug. 21, Oct. 5 and 19, 1945.
6. AOR of Jan. 8, 1946.
7. N.O.R.C. poll #145 (Oct. 2, 1946).
8. AOR for Oct. 4 and Nov. 8, 1945; Feb. 2, 1946.
9. AOR of May 3, 1946.
10. AOR for May 17, Aug. 21, Nov. 15, Dec. 11, 1946.
11. N.O.R.C. poll #243 (Aug. 21, 1946); AOR for summer of 1946, also Nov. 1, 1946.
12. AOR for Dec. 20, 1946 and Jan. 7, 1947.
13. Campbell, *U.S. in World Affairs, 1947-48* (New York, 1948), p. 18; AOR of Feb. 21, 1947.
14. AOR for Jan. 9 and 22, 1947.
15. AOR for June and July 1947.
16. See AOR for dates indicated.
17. Campbell, *U.S. in World Affairs, 1945-47*, p. 27.
18. N.O.R.C. polls of Sept. 1946 and Apr. 1947.
19. Campbell, *U.S. in World Affairs, 1945-47*, p. 232; AOR of Feb. 7, 1947.
20. Campbell, *U.S. in World Affairs, 1947-48*, pp. 112-17; AOR for Aug. 1947.
21. AOR for Aug. 11 and 21, 1945.
22. Scott & Withey, op. cit., pp. 87-89; AOR for Apr. 4 and 19, June 4, 1946.

23. AOR for June 19, July 3, 1946; Jan. 7, 1947.
24. N.O.R.C. polls of Feb. and Oct. 1947, Oct. 1949.
25. AOR for Nov. 5 and Dec. 6, 1946.
26. N.O.R.C. poll.
27. Campbell, *U.S. in World Affairs, 1947–48*, p. 492; N.O.R.C. poll #156.
28. AOR for March 1948.
29. AOR for March–May 1948.
30. Ibid.
31. Campbell, op. cit. (1947–48), p. 500.
32. AOR for June 1948.
33. Campbell, see note 31 above, also *U.S. in World Affairs, 1948–49* (New York, 1949), pp. 11–13; AOR for May and June 1948.
34. AOR for June 29, July, and Sept. 1948.
35. AOR for Aug., Sept., Nov. 1948.
36. AOR for spring and summer, 1948.
37. AOR for Oct. and Nov. 1948; George C. Herring on "Cold War" in Vol. I, *Encyclopedia of American Foreign Policy*, ed. by Alexander De Conde (New York, 1978).
38. AOR for Dec. 1948 and Jan. 1949.
39. AOR for March, April, May 1949.
40. Stebbins, R. P., *U.S. in World Affairs, 1949* (New York, 1950), p. 83; AOR for April, July, Aug. 1949.
41. AOR for April 1949.
42. AOR for Nov. 1949.

V

PUBLIC ATTITUDES AND THE STATE DEPARTMENT (1944-1950)

After following the development of public attitudes toward the major postwar policies, it is appropriate to take a closer look at the public's picture of the State Department and its place in the postwar world. Attitudes toward the Department, and its personnel, have been somewhat distinct from attitudes toward specific foreign policies which the Department was seeking to advance. Sometimes attitudes toward the Department have been hostile, sometimes favorable; and partisanship has been more evident in public attitudes toward the Department than in public judgments about specific policies.

Public Interests after War

The State Department and international relations were not foremost in the public's interest at the close of the war. Right after V-J Day the Gallup Poll asked its respondents what were the "chief postwar problems" confronting the nation. More respondents mentioned "jobs" (20%) or "avoiding a depression" (16%) than suggested "permanent peace" as a problem (15%). A little later Gallup asked what would be the most important problem "facing the country during the next year;" 42% said "jobs," and only 7% replied "making peace." In subsequent months respondents continued to stress domestic economic factors: the "high cost of living" (28%) or "inflation" (46% in Aug. 1947), or "strikes" (40% in Jan. 1947); yet during 1947 and 1948 increasing attention was accorded international problems–especially relations with the Soviet Union. By July 1948 (after the Communist take-over of Prague and obstructionism about access to Berlin), 44% mentioned foreign policy problems as most important. In 1949 there was greater public concern about foreign policy problems than domestic problems; and in May 1950 the "threat of war" was specifically named by as many as 40%.[1]

After the initial postwar stress on domestic problems (outlined above), about half of nationwide samples of the American people told polling interviewers that they took a "regular interest" in international affairs. There was a smaller degree of interest in "our country's foreign policy," and interest in "the operation of the State Department" was smaller still. Some foreign issues attracted greater public interest than others. In 1948 and 1949 as many as 30% claimed "a great deal of interest" in the Marshall Plan (and also in the United Nations); only 20% said they took "a great deal of interest" in "what is going on in Germany," or in "the way the State Department is handling its job" (although an additional 45% said they took "a mild interest" in the latter topic).[2]

Individual Attitude Patterns

The patterns into which individual Americans arranged their support or opposition to various foreign policy alternatives were investigated by the University of Michigan's Survey Research Center in 1949-50.[3] Whereas the State Department was advocating a package of inter-related U.S. policies, interested citizens insisted on making up their own packages of foreign policies. On the Department's three key recommendations about aiding Western European countries, for example, only 27% of the survey respondents approved all three of them: 1, U.S. should provide money to improve conditions in Western Europe; 2, U.S. should "go to the aid of these countries if they are threatened;" 3, U.S. should supply these Western European countries with "arms and ammunition." The first two of these policies individually received majority support (56% or more); also both propositions were approved by a group constituting 46% of the total. The arms aid proposal received less than majority approval.

These survey results showed clearly that the Administration did not have, out in the country, a solid majority group of citizens who supported all of current foreign policy—even with reference to a single important area (Western Europe). Whereas the Administration viewed the three policies just discussed as an inter-related and logical whole, this entire pattern of thought was accepted at this time by only one-fourth of the American public. Thus the Department received considerable public backing for each of the three specific policies separately, but such piecemeal support could not exert the same force as would have a body of citizens adhering to an integrated policy by a reasoned pattern of thought.

Knowledge of State Department

From 1944 to 1948, in connection with its recently-adopted plans to give the public an increased amount of information about U.S. foreign policy, the Department commissioned four public opinion polls to assess the public's knowledge of, and attitudes toward, the Department and the Foreign Service of the U.S., as well as toward particular foreign policies.[4] These polls demonstrated that public knowledge and experience were definitely limited: 9% of the nationwide sample said that they had at some time seen or talked with a Foreign Service Officer; and less than 40% could correctly describe the "main job" of the State Department. (Such public ignorance has prompted some people to question the wisdom of democratic control of foreign policy; but the real test has to be the wisdom of the policies adopted under popular government–rather than the quiz scores of citizens on tests involving official nomenclature.) The poll showed that knowledge of the State Department's role was significantly related to the respondent's educational background. In the 1944 poll, for example, 72% of the respondents who had attended college correctly described the "main job" of the Department; but only 43% of those who had been at high school did so; and only 16% of those whose education stopped in grammar school. (According to the 1950 census, a sizable majority of all Americans (67.5%) had no more than a high school education.)

The 1944 poll included popular evaluations of the Foreign Service and of the State Department. The "American diplomat" was more often viewed favorably ("intelligent," "tactful") than unfavorably ("politician," "grafter"). A majority (53% in 1947) also felt that our Foreign Service was "doing a better job" than that of most countries. In evaluating the State Department, however, respondents in these immediate postwar years expressed more "dislikes" than "likes." On the positive side, Americans praised the abilities of Department personnel, and also "liked" their role in "furthering peace." On the other hand, they voiced criticisms of the personnel and complained about U.S. foreign policy: "not tough enough," "not clear enough," or "too secret." In several 1948 polls a majority of respondents (from 53% to 63%) said that the "government officials in charge of foreign policy were not telling the people all they should about foreign policy." This majority belief in the inadequacy of government-supplied information bespeaks some mistrust of the Truman Administration; but it did not prevent the majority approval of specific foreign policies which has been described above.

In a late 1945 poll N.O.R.C. asked respondents to compare the job being done by the State Department with the performance of two other federal Departments. The figures below indicate a greater public willingness to rate the State Department as mediocre or poor than either of the other two Departments.

	War Dept.	**State Dept.**	**Interior Dept.**
Good job	55%	30%	27%
Just fair	27	34	18
Poor job	5	10	5
Total making ratings	87%	74%	50%

Two criticisms of the Department which were frequently expressed in editorial opinion were not upheld by the polls, viz, the charges that under Pres. Truman "military men" and "businessmen" had too much influence in the Department. At this time Gen. Marshall was Secretary of State (1948) and important ambassadorial posts were also occupied by generals and admirals; and Department officials who were prominent in American business had been active in urging the British loan and organizing the Marshall Plan. The 1948 poll asked: "In general, do you feel that businessmen (military men) have too much to say, or not enough to say, in deciding our policy with other countries?"

	Too Much To Say	Not Enough	About Right	No Opinion
Businessmen	34%	32%	15%	19%
Military Men	17	40	25	18

While about a third of the public did feel that businessmen had "too much to say," almost as many declared that they didn't have "enough to say." As for the "military men," only a sixth of the general public felt that they had too much influence, whereas as many as 40% said they had too little "say."[5]

Despite some public tendencies to depreciate the Department, there was always a core of citizens who were appreciative of the Department and its efforts to "further peace." A number of editors and commentators were in this group. Another sympathetic group within the public was made up of the partisans of the Administration (i.e., the Democrats) who appreciated the President's past accomplishments and who were confident of his good intentions in seeking solutions to current problems amid great difficulties. These groups often amounted to a plurality favorable to the Secretary of State and his major policies during the immediate postwar period, as we have seen; and a majority of the editorials on foreign policy were also usually favorable.

Security Risks

Sen. Joseph McCarthy (R-Wis) attained wide public fame in 1950 when he released a letter to Pres. Truman (Feb. 11) charging that 57 Communists were still working in the State Department. Actually, at that time, "public opinion" about the number of Communists in Government jobs was little different from what it was at the time of Mr. Truman's presidential victory in 1948. This conclusion is based upon findings of the Texas Poll, whose results on national questions were usually similar to those of nationwide polls. In November 1948 and May 1950, the Texas Poll[6] asked this question (and reported educational breakdowns):

"Among people who have jobs in the federal government in Washington, do you think there are many communists, some, or no communists at all?"

	Nov. 1948	May 1950
Many communists	17%	15%
Some communists	64	64
None at all	2	3
Don't know	17	18
	100	100
Total saying "some" & "many"		
College-educated	94%	88%
High School	84	81
Grammar School	63	67

It was soon after V-J Day that charges appeared in the press and radio to the effect that some Government employees were not loyal to the U.S. Even before the war was over, the media had reported that the editors of *Amerasia* and a State Department officer had been arrested for conspiring to make illegal use of classified documents. The Department officer was exonerated and reinstated; but the possibility of the State Department harboring security risks had been publicized. In 1947 several members of the House of Representatives (elected in 1946) publicly discussed their doubts about State Department personnel; the U.S. Chamber of Commerce issued a report demanding action by Congress to remove Communists from all government posts. In the Marzani case, a former State Department employee was convicted of concealing his membership in the Communist Party; and this conviction was ultimately upheld by the Supreme Court.

In June 1947, the State Department announced the dismissal of ten employees as security risks, setting off a considerable debate in the press. The Department was applauded by a few (e.g., Springfield (Mass) Union, Jamestown (N.Y.) Post-Journal); but a larger number of commentators criticized the Department and Sec. Marshall for their failure to hold hearings, or otherwise ensure that the ousted employees had been fairly treated (e.g., Wash. Post, the Alsops, Marquis Childs, I. F. Stone). Some writers suggested that the Department had responded to pressure from the newly-elected Republican Congress.[7]

When the Department embarked upon a new "security program" in October of 1947 the majority of commentators continued to be critical; the New York Times said it was still possible that an American citizen "can be tried without a bill of particulars rendered, without being given an opportunity to confront his accusers." Newspapers upholding the Department's new program included the

Chicago News, Kansas City Times, and Newsweek; whereas the critics included the Christian Science Monitor, New York Herald Tribune, Philadelphia Inquirer, and Elmer Davis. Criticism subsided appreciably after the Department announced that the ousted ten officials would be permitted to "resign without prejudice."[8]

But the presidential year of 1948 saw the return of the "loyalty" issue. Gov. Dewey pledged a clean-up of the Communists in Washington following his election as a Republican president. Very few Americans as this time contended that the State Department was pursuing a pro-Communist policy (in face of its Greek-Turk aid program, its strong stand on Berlin, etc.), but during the summer the House Un-American Activities Committee held extended hearings on the charges that former Department official Alger Hiss had, years earlier, conveyed classified documents to the Communists.[9] In December Hiss was indicted for perjury for his statements before the Committee.

McCarthy Charges

So Sen. McCarthy was merely picking up an old issue when he charged in 1950 that 57 Communists were still working for the State Department. Assistant Secretary Peurifoy promptly sent McCarthy a telegram saying that he knew of no Communists on the State Department payroll and asking him to name the 57. Thereafter the Senator frequently reiterated his charges of disloyalty in the Department, and just as frequently Department spokesmen reiterated their denials and asked the Senator for his evidence.

McCarthy was also promptly asked by the Tydings subcommittee in the Senate to lay his charges before that subcommittee. The Chicago Tribune's news report cited the Senator's "orderly presentation of facts" before the subcommittee, as did radio commentators Fulton Lewis, Jr. and Three-Star Extra. But most editors across the country maintained that the Senator had failed to substantiate his charges of Communist infiltration of the State Department (e.g., Milwaukee Journal, New Orleans Times-Picayune, St. Louis Post-Dispatch).[10]

Dean Acheson had become Secretary of State a year earlier (in Jan. 1949), to the accompaniment of considerable favorable press comment. An opinion poll in April 1950 found 59% of its respondents saying that Acheson was doing a "good" (23%) or "fair" job—and only 12% saying a "poor" job (29% gave no opinion). This favorable judgment may be compared to the 58%-to-13% vote of approval given to Secretary Marshall in a 1948 poll.[11]

Yet in 1950 the charges that there were "Communists holding jobs in the State Department" were very widely listened to; 79% of a national sample said in an April poll that they had heard of such charges. Moreover, a sizable majority (63%) said they did feel that "some of the people who work in the State Department are not loyal to the United States;" only 23% said they felt that "all the people" at the Department were loyal. When the respondents were asked a further question as to "how much harm these (disloyal) people are doing to the country's interests," 28% said "a great deal of harm," 31% said "some harm," and 2% said "none." Another question found a majority (56%) agreeing that "the State Department itself is doing all it can to keep disloyal people out;" but 27% denied that.[12]

The same April 1950 poll also showed an abrupt drop in approval on the trend question about "the way our relations with other countries are being handled by government officials in charge of our foreign policy." This finding prompted Department officials to wonder to what extent the widely-published charges by McCarthy might have contributed to the reversal in the trend of public approval which was indicated by the polling results given in the table below.[13]

Approval/Disapproval of Handling of Foreign Policy

	Approve	**Disapprove**	**No Opinion**
March 1948	40%	31%	29%
July 1948	47	34	19
Nov. 1948	57	18	25
March 1949	51	30	19
April 1950	33	47	20

Respondents were also asked in this April poll about their over-all impression of State Department officials: a majority (56%) replied that they had a generally "favorable" impression, 22% reported an "unfavorable" impression, and 22% gave no opinion. Among the "unfavorable" respondents, one-third said they based their judgment on the "disloyalty" of Department personnel (i.e., 7.7% of the total sample). Nearly as many respondents ascribed their "unfavorable" impression to the "incompetence" or "inefficiency" of Department officials; and one-fourth of those "unfavorably" impressed dismissed Department officials as "politicians."

With respect to Sen. McCarthy's continuing charges, roughly 6 out of 10 commentators expressed faith in the loyalty and integrity of State Department employees, including the Baltimore Sun, Christian Science Monitor, Dayton News, Denver Post, San Francisco Chronicle, Walter Lippmann, Stewart Alsop, Drew Pearson, and Mrs. Eleanor Roosevelt. At the same time, in all sections of the country some newspapers and commentators expressed doubts and suspicions about the Department (e.g., Dallas News, Indianapolis Star, Los

Angeles Times, Phila. Inquirer, and three newspaper chains: Hearst, Knight, Scripps-Howard). Some of these critics of the Department based their views upon disillusionment over the trend of events in China and the conviction of Alger Hiss (in Jan. 1950), rather than on any evidence adduced by McCarthy. Only about 1 out of 10 actually supported the Senator's charges.[14]

But substantially all of those commenting agreed that a thorough and impartial investigation was needed to dispel the current misgivings about the Department. Many felt that investigations by the Tydings subcommittee would be inadequate because it seemed to be split along partisan lines—also the Executive Branch was withholding access to the loyalty files. Several commentators suggested a special investigating commission which should include persons of such eminence as Herbert Hoover, Justice Roberts, Bernard Baruch, and Maj. Gen. Donovan.

Many State Department officials, outraged by what they perceived as "damage" done by McCarthy's "unsubstantiated" charges, were stunned by a Gallup Poll (May 21, 1950) indicating that among the general public the McCarthy charges were seen as doing "more good than harm," as shown in the following table.

	National	Republicans	Democrats
More good	39%	50%	35%
More harm	29	22	33
No opinion	16	15	14
Hadn't heard of charges	16	13	18
	100%	100%	100%

Republicans, it is clear, were much more likely to stress the "good," but a plurality of Democrats also returned that judgment.

This matter was further pursued by an N.O.R.C. poll which asked respondents "in what way" they thought the McCarthy charges were "good for the country." The reasons included: exposing Communists before they could do damage, alerting the public to the danger, getting things into the open, stimulating greater care in hiring employees, and warning Communists away from such employment. Reasons given as to why the charges were "bad" for the country included: making other countries doubt us, creating distrust among our own people, erosion of confidence in government and leaders, hurting of some innocent people, and tipping off Russians to U.S. alertness.[15]

Actually, the "loyalty risk" issue didn't loom very large among the reasons given for "disapproving" the handling of our foreign relations by the 37% who did disapprove in an N.O.R.C. poll. The "disapprovers" were more likely to mention "sending too much abroad," leniency with Russia, or the "lack of any real policy;" only 2% of the sample cited the presence of Communists in the State Department as grounds for their disapproval. It may also be noted that those respondents who thought disloyal workers were doing "a great deal of harm" were just about as supportive of U.S. foreign policies as were other respondents.[16]

The reassuring word that the trend of popular approval for the "handling" of foreign relations had been resumed was conveyed by a poll taken just before the outbreak of war in Korea: 48% expressing approval, only 37% disapproval. This June poll also found on a basic trend question a clear majority (54%) holding that the U.S. had *not* "gone too far" in "concerning itself with other parts of the world"– 36% did say "gone too far."

It was also in June that Sen. McCarthy attacked Gen. Marshall for being too pro-Communist; commentators acted with overwhelming hostility to this charge; many editorials excoriated the Senator. A decline in popular approval of McCarthy was registered the following month (July); nevertheless an August poll showed greater public concern about disloyalty in government than did any of the polls on this subject taken before the Korean war. At this time also many headlines about "reds in Government" heralded the current hearings by the McCarran subcommittee.[17]

Role of Partisanship

Anxiety lest U.S. foreign policy lose its bipartisan base had been growing in the spring of 1950, and some Republicans charged that the Administration was making foreign policy without consulting minority spokesmen. Contemporary commentators, however, felt that this anxiety was substantially relieved by certain political developments: Sen. Vandenberg's letter to Paul Hoffman, head of the European Recovery Program, calling for "unpartisan" consideration of U.S. world responsibilities; appointment of former Republican Senator John Sherman Cooper to serve as consultant to Sec. Acheson on NATO matters; and appointment of former Republican Senator John Foster Dulles to serve as adviser to the Secretary on broad problems. Some critics maintained that Cooper and Dulles were not adequate representatives of a wide range of Republican thought; but commentators generally felt that these appointments appreciably brightened the prospects for bipartisan cooperation. On this matter the general public was divided, as found by an N.O.R.C. poll of July 1950 when 34% of the sample held that "not enough attention" was being given to "the views of Republican party leaders" by the "officials in charge of our foreign policy," whereas an equal number of respondents felt that the attention being given was either "enough" (29%) or "too much" (5%).[18]

When a concrete policy proposal (e.g., join NATO, send aid) was the subject of a poll or an editorial, the response was usually nonpartisan in character, showing bipartisan approval. But if the question inquired about the way in which the leaders of the Administration were "handling" their responsibilities, a high degree of partisan response could enter in—especially when respondents could recognize the subject as one engaging their loyalties in a current partisan controversy (e.g., U.S. policy toward China). But these partisan differences never became automatic or thoroughgoing, with all Republicans "disapproving" of the Administration's handling of all foreign affairs, or all Democrats "approving."

It was traditional for partisan division to occur on such questions as whether the Administration had "done all it should have" in trying to prevent Communists from taking over China, or from entering the U.S. Government service. Postwar concern about Communists in the Government was shared by Republicans and Democrats; and a majority of polled Americans felt it was a "good thing" for the country to have this problem thoroughly investigated. Americans felt that the President and Secretary of State should be vigilant to prevent the infiltration of the State Department by disloyal workers. And partisan division of popular opinion was rare on policies which had been adopted by bipartisan Congressional vote, such as supplying military assistance to Western Europe, or policies which had been carried out by bipartisan personnel such as the Japanese peace treaty.

Public support for basic foreign policies was not necessarily integrated with support for the national leaders who had proposed these policies. Polls and editorial opinion alike upheld U.S. membership in NATO and the UN and participation in the Marshall Plan; but these attitudes did not entail support for Pres. Truman and Sec. Acheson in their Far East policies or their handling of the "security risks." Conversely, unhappiness with some Truman-Acheson policies did not mean any diminution in support of the national, bipartisan programs which were basic to postwar U.S. policy.

Reference Notes

1. See *The Gallup Poll* (New York, 1972), Vols. I and II.
2. See N.O.R.C. polls of Feb. 1948 and June 1949.
3. Survey Research Center, University of Michigan, *America's Role in World Affairs: Patterns of Citizen Opinion*, Ann Arbor, 1952.
4. U.S. State Dept., Amn. Opin. Reports of Oct. 5, 1944, Jan. 16, 1946, Feb. 2, 1947, Apr. 23, 1948.
5. N.O.R.C. poll #155 (2/25/48).
6. U.S. State Dept., Amn. Opin. Report of Oct. 17, 1951.

7. U.S. State Dept., Amn. Opin. Report for July 1947.
8. U.S. State Dept., Amn. Opin. Report of Oct. 31, 1947.
9. U.S. State Dept., Amn. Opin. Report for Sept. 1948.
10. U.S. State Dept., Amn. Opin. Report of Mar. 14, 1950.
11. N.O.R.C. polls #279 (4/12/50) and #157 (4/22/48).
12. U.S. State Dept., Amn. Opin. Report for April 1950.
13. N.O.R.C. polls taken in months indicated.
14. U.S. State Dept., Amn. Opin. Report of May 22, 1950.
15. N.O.R.C. poll of June 14, 1950.
16. U.S. State Dept., Amn. Opin. Report of June 8, 1950.
17. U.S. State Dept., Amn. Opin. Reports of June and August 1950.
18. U.S. State Dept., Amn. Opin. Report for April 1950.

VI

ASSESSING INTERNATIONAL SOLUTIONS (1946–1950)

As the United States was developing its policies to meet the postwar crises in free world security and in the world economy, it was also discovering how far the United Nations organization could go to help solve both immediate and long-range problems, such as the issues of Palestine and Human Rights. Also occupation problems were met and dealt with in Japan and in Germany; questions of immigration and trade were viewed as domestic as well as international problems.

Disappointment with the UN

After a year of experience with the UN a number of Americans concluded that the organization was not strong enough to prevent war; and some leaders and groups continued to advocate a basic shift to world government. Most writers, however, felt that while world government might be a reasonable ultimate objective, any major alteration of the UN Charter in the near future was impossible in view of basic differences among the Big Three.

The great power veto in the UN Security Council was seen by many as a major obstacle to peace. The Soviet Union had exercised its veto on several occasions, notably on proposals to control the use of atomic energy and on the admission of new members into the UN. Popular dislike of the veto was shown by a poll taken in October 1946: 85% favored admitting new UN members by majority vote; 57% felt that a member nation should not have the right to veto the entry into its country of a UN committee attempting pacific settlement of an international dispute; and 51% even said they opposed the U.S. having the right to prevent the UN from dispatching American troops to help stop a war. Of course, correct information about the veto under the UN Charter was not very widespread—only 38% realized that the U.S. did have the right to prevent the UN from calling out American troops, for example.[1]

A number suggested that the veto power be abolished or limited in order to strengthen the peace-keeping machinery (e.g., Phila. Inquirer, Chi. Sun, Milwaukee Journal). Others, however, defended the veto, pointing out that the U.S. from the beginning wanted it included in the Charter, and that some day the U.S. might want to use it itself (e.g., Wash. Star, San Diego Union). When Mr. Baruch made the limited proposal of abolishing the veto in atomic matters, he was strongly supported in most press and radio comment.[2]

The first poll about "the progress the UN has made so far" was taken in May 1946; and "satisfaction" and "dissatisfaction" were found to be equal (37% each). After a brief period of Russian co-operation in the UN (in 1946), Gromyko's rejection of the Baruch atomic proposals and the unleashing of a virulent anti-American campaign in worldwide Soviet broadcasts dimmed earlier hopes. During most of 1947 and 1948 popular "dissatisfaction" with the UN was greater than "satisfaction."[3]

The alternative concept of world government held considerable popular appeal. A Roper Poll found in 1946 that 63% favored "having the U.S. go along with" the following proposition, that "every country in the world elect representatives to a world congress and let all problems between countries be decided by this congress, with a strict provision that all countries have to abide by the decisions whether they like them or not" (20% were opposed). In the same month (Aug.) the Gallup Poll reported a majority (54%) supporting the following proposition, that "the UN organization be strengthened to make it a world government, with power to control the armed forces of all nations, including the U.S." That Americans had not thought through the implications of having an "international police force" strong enough to prevent war can be illustrated by the N.O.R.C. finding that 75% favored U.S. participation in an "international police force," but only 15% were willing to see U.S. forces smaller than those of the international force.[4]

Another measure of popular disappointment with the United Nations was provided by a pair of polls, taken in 1945 and October 1947, using the following question:[5]

> "In general, what chance do you think the UN Organization has, to prevent wars between big nations–good, fair, or no chance at all?"

	1945	1947
Good chance	36%	22%
Fair chance	43	48
No chance at all	11	23
No opinion	10	7
	100%	100%

Many asked: "Can the United Nations succeed with Russia in it?" By the spring of 1948, after the Czech coup and the 23rd Soviet veto in the Security Council, a poll found an almost even division of opinion: 46% calling it "hopeless to try to work along with Russia in the United Nations," and 45% saying "there is still a chance we can make the UN work with Russia in it." When Americans were asked whether the UN difficulty was attributable to its organization or the conduct of its members, a majority (61%) said that "the present UN weakness is due chiefly to the way the countries in it have acted," and only 16% said it was "due chiefly to the way the organization is set up."[6]

How much did Americans blame U.S. policy and actions for the UN difficulties? The April 1948 poll found that a majority (62%) thought that the U.S. "had done all it should to make the UN more successful," but 24% felt the U.S. "should have done more." These minority respondents were then asked what more the U.S. should have done; most said the U.S. should have "given more active leadership, been more decisive," or been "more consistent on Palestine," or "tougher with Russia." Only a few held that the U.S. should have "a more conciliatory policy," or that it "should not by-pass the UN."[7]

World Government?

Many prescriptions to improve the prospects for peace were in the air during this postwar period; and the Fortune Survey sought to measure the comparative popular appeal of some of them by offering these three propositions:

> "1. America should give up the idea of an international organization and instead form separate alliances with friendly nations;
> "2. America should continue to count mainly on the United Nations organization and do all it can to make it work;
> "3. America should start now to organize a world government in which we would become a member state."

Only 10% (in Jan. 1947) were ready to turn their backs on international organization. A clear majority (55%) pinned their hopes on the United Nations; but the minority favorable to world government increased from 16% to 20% from January to December 1947.[8]

Despite its minority status with the general public, the idea of "world government" had won an impressive place in American leadership opinion, including members of both Houses of Congress. The largest organization favoring world government, the United World Federalists, in 1948 had 400 chapters from coast to coast and a paid membership of 35,000. Pres. Cord Meyer, Jr. stressed his belief that the development of atomic weapons made some kind of world government inevitable within the next few years. The Committee to Frame A World Constitution, headed by Robert M. Hutchins, urged a detailed world government. Ely Culbertson advocated basic "reforms" of the UN, lectured widely, and gained greater political support than the rival world government groups. Clarence Streit favored a federation of democratic nations "modeled broadly on our own constitution." All of these leaders, in the words of John C. Campbell, stressed the "absurdity of trying to organize a peaceful world without more fundamental restrictions on national sovereignty."[9]

The momentum achieved by various Congressional proposals to amend the United Nations Charter was so great that Sec. Marshall felt impelled to testify at the hearings of the Foreign Affairs Committee on May 5, 1948. He told the Committee that the unsatisfactory state of world affairs could not be corrected by abolishing the UN veto on issues involving aggression, or by any other forms of reorganization. He added that we needed to keep the door open for negotiations with the Soviet Union. Marshall's stand drew an overwhelmingly favorable response in editorial comment (e.g., Balt. Sun, Los Angeles Times, Wash. Post). Walter Lippmann added: "Let us not, like an over-anxious gardener, pull up the seedlings to see whether we cannot make them grow faster." The editorials also supported the Vandenberg Resolution, which called for U.S. "association" with regional alliances under the UN Charter, rather than amendment of the Charter.[10]

In 1949 trend polling questions showed that, for the first time, popular opinion had changed from predominant "dissatisfaction with the progress of the UN" to "satisfaction." (The "dissatisfied" dropped to 36% and the "satisfied" increased to 47%.) Now, on the eve of the signing of the NATO treaty, the world outlook was brighter than it had been in the preceding year which witnessed the Prague coup and the Berlin blockade. When respondents were asked why they were "satisfied" with UN progress, they didn't cite specific UN actions, but simply said the UN was doing well in view of the difficulties confronting it. The negative role of the Soviet Union was cited most often by those who were "dissatisfied." By July 1949 the "satisfied" rose to 53%, and they now included a plurality of the college-educated (48%). This "satisfaction" coincided with a decline in the proportion expecting war "in the next ten years," from 62% in November to 48%.[11]

Despite the increased appreciation of the United Nations, a "world federation" resolution was introduced in the House of Representatives in June, sponsored by 71 Democrats and 28 Republicans. This asked that it be a "fundamental objective" of the U.S. to seek the development of the UN into a limited world government. A public opinion poll about this time reported 53% saying it was "not a good idea" to make the UN a world government "with power to control the armed forces of all nations, including the U.S." An N.O.R.C. poll found only 22% saying the U.S. "should call a conference right now to set up a world government;" whereas 29% said we "should wait till later before we go ahead." Cross-tabulations showed that attitudes toward world government were not related to current dissatisfaction with the UN; the "satisfied" and the "dissatisfied" displayed similar attitudes toward the prompt establishment of world government. When respondents were asked about the main differences between the UN and world government, 49% of the replies were either "don't know," or very vague, or irrelevant.[12]

Pres. Truman's address at the laying of the cornerstone in New York (1949) prompted many editorial tributes to the UN; and most of the advocates of international federation appearing before the Foreign Affairs Committee–whether espousing Atlantic Union or world government–were careful to state that they did not wish to "disrupt the UN," but to "strengthen it" into a world law-enforcing organization. Support for this movement came from church and service groups (e.g., Natl. Council of Churches, Kiwanis, Junior Chamber of Commerce). Leaders of the Atlantic Union Committee, which desired to develop NATO into a political union, included: former Justice Owen Roberts, Will Clayton, and Robert Patterson. The number of state legislatures adopting resolutions in favor of world government continued to rise, reaching 21 by May of 1949. On the other hand, the Hearst press reported that a committee to oppose world government had been formed by representatives of the American Legion, V.F.W., D.A.R., and other patriotic organizations.[13]

Further Congressional hearings on resolutions advocating world or Atlantic federation were scheduled for early 1950, and the Department made another analysis of current opinion. Few commentators were supporting the resolutions, but prompt establishment of a world federation was advocated by prominent individuals and organization officials. Among the general public only 14% supported world government and thought it possible of attainment by 1974. While a United States of Europe was favored by press and public, there was little desire to combine the U.S. with Western Europe in a single federation. As to strengthening the United Nations, a majority (58%) favored giving it power to "call out American troops, along with those of other countries, to help stop an aggressor;" but only 22% said that the troops should move promptly "without approval by our own Congress."[14]

Hearings witnesses both commended and criticized the State Department for its opposition to moves in the direction of world or Atlantic federation. The Georgia legislature had retracted the endorsement it gave to world government in 1946; but a considerable segment of the press was critical of the State Department's "negative" position and deplored the Department's unwillingness even "to explore the possibilities of international federation" (e.g., Sen. Kefauver, Dallas News, Wash. Post). The disappointed Minneapolis

Tribune suggested that the Department had "cynically . . . climbed into bed with the Chicago Tribune." The Scripps-Howard papers supported the Douglas-Thomas proposal which called for an international agreement permitting effective international action against an aggressor by a two-thirds vote which included three of the Big Five. But many newspapers remained skeptical of the practicality of the Congressional proposals; these papers approved the official U.S. position which accorded highest priority to strengthening the United Nations under its existing form (e.g., C. S. Monitor, San Francisco Chronicle, Wash. Star).[15]

In the spring of 1950 Herbert Hoover gave impetus to a movement of opinion quite counter to world government, when he appealed for a "phalanx of free nations" to combat Communism and suggested that the United Nations be reorganized without the Communist nations. Hoover's plea for a "moral crusade" won some editorial approval, but most editors strongly opposed the idea of ousting the Communists from the UN as irrevocably splitting the world into two camps. Some papers did support Hoover's proposal (e.g., Knight papers, Chi. Tribune); and polls showed the general public moving toward support of a UN without the Soviet Union.[16]

But the prompt action of the UN in the Korean crisis produced a renaissance in the prestige of the UN, and also tended to concentrate attention on current UN actions rather than on the ultimate shape of the international organization. Moreover, the gains registered by the organizations backing world government stimulated opposition; and in 1950 a referendum in Oklahoma marked a decisive defeat for the world government proposal. As pointed out by Francis S. Bourne in 1955,[17] most of the state legislatures eventually rescinded their resolutions favoring world government; and the Congress, instead of acting in the direction urged by the 115 members supporting world government, forbade appropriations to any organization advocating "one world government."

The state legislatures, of course, had neither experience in, or responsibility for, U.S. foreign policy. And their shifting resolutions do not appear to have reflected a major shift in opinion on the part of the general public; rather these legislative actions seem to have reflected the various activities of private organizations–their publicity and political pressures–and probably also some changes in the "climate of opinion." In the late 1940s that climate was favorable to building international institutions designed to maintain the peace; in 1950 the charges advanced by Sen. McCarthy and the circumstances of the war in Korea combined to raise questions about Americans who stressed international institutions, or an international police force, or such symbols as the UN flag.

Human Rights

In early 1947 commentators devoted considerable discussion to an international bill of rights which was then under consideration by the Economic and Social Council of the United Nations. While recognizing that it would be impossible for the United Nations to enforce such rights, most of those commenting believed that a bill of rights would produce long-run educational benefits. A few, however, felt that the undertaking was "so loaded with dynamite" that it should not be attempted. Polling its members as to which rights were considered "most important," the American Association for the UN found that 97% cited freedom of expression–including freedom of assembly and religion; and 74% named the "right to participate in the Government." Other rights were ranked lower: right to economic security, 68%; right to education, 61%; and right to a fair trial, 56%.[18]

At the Geneva meeting of the ECOSOC Human Rights Commission the U.S. advanced a draft which drew approval from a number of "internationalist" newspapers, although the New York Times and others noted that the U.S. was not fully living up to all of its principles–particularly in its treatment of Negroes. When the Soviet delegate proposed an investigation of the treatment of blacks in America, the Chicago Times and the Washington Times-Herald agreed–on condition that the same commission investigate the plight of slave-labor in the Soviet Union. The International Declaration of Human Rights was adopted by the UN General Assembly in Paris a year later; and this action was applauded by most observers as a "truly noble" experiment in human progress, but there was no supporting move in Congress at this stage of the American civil rights debate. The Chicago Tribune termed this "hypocritical document" a reflection of the "futility of everything the United Nations undertakes."[19]

Immigration (1943-1948)

American sentiment about immigration policy has tended to vary considerably, depending upon the segment of "the public" which is involved. Editors have often appreciated the reasons which underlie Executive requests for increased immigration, and thus have given their support; polls of the general public have usually shown some reluctance about an increase. Among organized groups, church and ethnic organizations have often strongly supported enlarged immigration, whereas some other groups have tended to be much less favorable.

During World War II, in the autumn of 1943, some polls were taken about a postwar relaxation of the complete ban on Chinese immigration. A Gallup Poll in September found more opposition to relaxation than approval, with greatest opposition coming from farmers and unskilled workers who appeared to be motivated by economic fear as well as racial concern. In October another poll asked a series of questions and found: 23% opposed to any immigration of Chinese, 6% in favor of unlimited Chinese immigration, and 59% in favor of admitting "a limited number" (12% gave no opinion). In a follow-up question it was stated that "the Chinese people feel badly about (the) discrimination" which allowed unlimited immigration of South Americans and specific quotas from European countries; and it was added that the President "had approved a proposal before Congress to change the law so that about 100 Chinese a year could come in." This proposition then received the support of 65% of the sample, with Republican and Democratic respondents giving equal support. All educational groups favored the proposed change, but in different degree: those with grammar-school education, 56%; high school, 64%; and college, 83%.[20]

Pres. Truman's announcement on Dec. 22, 1945 of plans to facilitate the entrance into the U.S. of displaced persons from Europe occasioned a moderate amount of public comment; the directive was generally viewed as "humane and necessary." Some wanted to liberalize U.S. quotas (e.g., New Republic, Max Lerner); opposition to the admission of refugees in the press was limited to "nationalist" sources (e.g., Westbrook Pegler, Patterson papers). Numerous organizations supported the admission of DPs (e.g., Catholics for Human Rights, American Friends Service Comm., the AFL *Trade Union Courier*). However, a Gallup Poll reported only 37% of a national sample in favor of admitting "more" or "the same number" of persons from Europe as were allowed to enter before the war; 51% of the respondents desired "fewer" immigrants.[21]

An August 1946 poll asked whether the U.S. should let some of the "800,000 homeless people in Europe" come here now. Only 23% said Yes; 71% said No. Nudged by a follow-up question asked of opponents, an additional 27% agreed that "we should let some of them come here now if other countries agreed to take some of them, too;" but 44% remained adamantly opposed.[22]

In the election year of 1948 approval of legislation to admit DPs was increasingly expressed in the press and by labor and other organizations. Greatest support was given to Rep. Stratton's bill which called for the admission of 400,000 DPs over a 4-year period. Popular opinion, however, continued to be largely unfavorable, although hostility did tend to lessen with greater information about the problem. Reasons cited by opponents included the housing shortage, fear of depressed wage scales, and the possibility that the DPs might become a community burden. These factors were also stressed by some organizations (VFW, DAR).[23]

Greater popular support than was found in earlier polls was registered in an April 1948 survey that offered some explanatory information to the respondent.

> "In Europe there are many displaced persons who are afraid to return to their old homes because the Russians now control those countries. Congress is now considering a plan to let some of them come into the U.S. Do you approve or disapprove of letting 200,000 of these people come during the next two years to live in this country?"

	Sept. 1946	**July 1947**	**April 1948**
Approve	23%	28%	40%
Disapprove	71	65	53
No opinion	6	7	7
	100%	100%	100%

The bill which Congress passed in June provided for the admission of 200,000 DPs over a 2-year period; but it was widely criticized by editors and organizations as discriminating against Jews and Catholics and being generally inadequate. Still, these sources—and Pres. Truman—did consider the law "better than nothing."[24]

Palestine (1945-1950)

Since World War II Palestine has loomed large in American discussion of foreign policy. In October 1945 the Fortnightly Survey of American Opinion (State Department internal publication) noted that "the drive of U.S. Jewish people to have Palestine opened to unrestricted Jewish immigration" had gained the support of Gov. Dewey, Mayor LaGuardia, and members of Congress. Commentators of various political outlooks added their approval. Profound sympathy for the Jewish people in Europe had been expressed by American sources during the spring as news came of the liberation of the concentration camps in Germany by American troops. Later the State Department received many thousands of letters and telegrams urging pressure on the British government in behalf of the Zionist cause.

Some commentators said in late 1945 that the U.S. should accept responsibility for seeing that the British permitted unrestricted immigration into Palestine, even if armed force should prove necessary to prevent Arab uprisings against increased Jewish immigration (e.g., Edgar Mowrer, PM, Cecil Brown). A number asked that the problem be turned over to the United Nations (e.g., Sumner Welles, C. S. Monitor).[25] When Pres. Truman said he did not favor a Jewish Commonwealth in Palestine, little comment was stirred—although some "liberals" voiced regret, and some "moderates" praised his "courage." Some of the newspapers expressing sympathy for the homeless Jews added that Arabs had rights in the region, too, and that the U.S. had wide "strategic interests" in the Middle East (e.g., Des Moines Register, Wash. Star, Balt. Sun).

Appointment of the Anglo-American Committee of Inquiry on the Palestine problem was received unenthusiastically–with faint hope (e.g., N.Y. Herald Tribune), or as "an evasion of responsibility" (e.g., Phila. Record). But considerable comment was accorded the Committee's report in the spring of 1946, which recommended that 100,000 Jews be admitted to Palestine as soon as possible, and that Palestine come under United Nations trusteeship. In spite of fierce protests by both Arabs and Zionists, most commentators viewed the Committee report as "fair"–a "conscientious, humanitarian" document. A few influential commentators (e.g., N.Y. Times) felt that the U.S. should now assume responsibility with Britain for keeping order in the area; but some "nationalist" sources (e.g., Patterson press) and Congressmen contended that the U.S. should not contribute money or troops to keep order in "Britain's mandate." A growing number of commentators recommended that the whole problem be turned over to the UN for settlement.

British Foreign Secretary Bevin's opposition to admitting 100,000 Jews into Palestine, and his alleged "slight" against New York City aroused a storm of criticism from Zionist sympathizers in Congress and out. Raymond Swing commented that it was true that the U.S. was not showing "hospitality" to refugee Jews and was shying away from sharing military responsibility in Palestine. The Gallup Poll reported that 78% thought it was "a good idea" to allow 100,000 Jews to immigrate into Palestine; but a large majority (74%) were against sending American troops there to "help England keep order." However, 72% favored letting the UN deal with the problem.[26]

An N.O.R.C. poll reported that only 28% of the national sample took either a "great" or "considerable" interest in "our policy toward Palestine" (72% took "little" or "no" interest). In this poll eight foreign policy subjects were inquired about, and Palestine excited the smallest degree of interest–less even than the Paris Foreign Ministers meeting or Franco Spain. The Gallup Poll release remarked (June 19) that, "although the problem of the Jews' entry into Palestine has received front-page treatment throughout the country for many weeks, only half the people in the survey said they have been following discussions relating to it." Like Gallup, N.O.R.C. found only a minority (28%) saying that the U.S. should "help Britain keep order" in Palestine–with the majority (61%) tending either to give general "isolationist" objections or to say, "It's England's problem."

American commentators expressed regret in Britain's delay on any decision about admitting 100,000 Jews into Palestine, and dismay over the terrorist bombings in Jerusalem. Public correspondence to the White House deplored the delayed decision on refugees; but some commentators expressed greater sympathy for the British position. Pres. Truman announced (Aug. 16) that the U.S. had "no solution" to offer on Palestine; but he did suggest that the U.S. could admit more refugees, including some Jews. The President's failure to offer a Palestine plan aroused some criticism; but a sizable group commended his immigration suggestion as being helpful to all displaced persons.[27]

A presidential statement of Oct. 4, 1946 urged immediate entrance of Jewish refugees into Palestine, recommended that other countries lower their immigration bars to displaced persons, and envisaged a long-range settlement of the Palestine problem along "partition" lines. This statement elicited warm praise from "liberal" and Zionist sources; but a larger number of commentators—including influential "moderate" and "conservative" spokesmen—were critical of such an "empty gesture" aimed at "getting votes in the off-year election." When Britain decided to turn the issue over to the United Nations, this decision received general approval among American editors. Some added that in the UN the U.S. might be compelled to assume its "share" of responsibility for a settlement, claiming that the U.S. had been "long on advice" and "short on action."[28]

When the UNGA convened in the autumn of 1947 many commentators were sanguine about settlement of the Palestine problem, and they generally agreed with Zionist spokesmen in upholding the "partition" plan favored by a majority of the UN Special Committee on Palestine (e.g., N.Y. Herald Tribune, Chi. Sun, Walter Lippmann). A number of observers, holding that the crux of any solution would be the UN's ability to enforce it, said that the U.S. must assume its full share of the enforcement burden. When the UNGA backed the partition plan, and the affirmative votes included both the U.S. and the Soviet Union, editors hailed the decision as a "historic achievement." But few wanted to see U.S. troops used to enforce the partition plan against recalcitrant Arabs or Jews. News of continuing strife in Palestine renewed worries about the peace prospects; and some Congressmen and editors wondered whether the U.S. should have pushed partition, thus alienating the Arab world and giving the Soviet Union an opportunity to enter the "strategic" Middle East.[29]

Early in 1948 discussion in the UN Security Council, on how the General Assembly's resolution calling for partition could be implemented, made clear the continuing opposition of the Arab states and the unwillingness of other UN members to provide the military force which evidently would be required to push partition into actuality. Pres. Truman, Sec. Marshall, and Amb. Austin made statements which were strongly attacked as backing away from partition, or even as "betrayal" (e.g., Max Lerner, N.Y. Post, Eleanor Roosevelt, Philip Murrary, N.Y. Herald Tribune, 40 organizations participating in an AAUN-sponsored Emergency Conference to save the United Nations by supporting the Palestine Resolution). Calling for a "positive" U.S. policy, these critics urged that the U.S. lift its embargo on arms to the Middle East so that the Jewish forces might acquire arms, and that the U.S. play a leading role at the UN in the establishment of an international force.[30]

An opinion poll (taken Feb. 27–Mar. 2) found that the intense interest in Palestine problems shown in the media and by organizations was not shared by a majority of the general public. The poll found that 28% had not heard of the partition plan, and an additional 15% had no opinion on it; 38% did approve of "dividing Palestine into these two countries," and 19% did not. However, people did have opinions on the U.S. embargo—82% wanted it continued against both Arabs and Jews, and also on whether American soldiers should participate "if the United Nations does decide to send an international police force to keep order in Palestine." This was approved by a vote of 50% to 43%, with 64% of the college-educated respondents approving (33% among those with only a grammar-school education). But if the UN couldn't agree to send an international force, 83% said the U.S. should not send American troops to Palestine by itself.

When Amb. Austin announced (Mar. 19) that the U.S. favored a UN trusteeship for Palestine, rather than immediate partition, heavy public discussion ensued. A minority approved this policy shift in view of the tense situation in Europe and the Mideast; but the great majority of commentators were critical. Some shared Zionist distress at abandonment of the partition plan; but far more widespread was the concern of both "liberal" and "conservative" spokesmen over the spectacle of the U.S. as "weak and vacillating," and the adverse effect on the prestige of the UN (e.g., C. S. Monitor, Chi. Tribune, Detroit Free Press, the Alsops, Sumner Welles). Some complained that the "reversal" demonstrated the influence in the U.S. of the military, and showed that oil and strategy were given precedence over "justice."[31]

Deep gloom pervaded April comment in view of the approaching British withdrawal and the mounting warfare between Arabs and Jews. Pres. Truman's declaration, that U.S. troops would participate if the UN undertook to police Palestine with an international force, was received with reserve because most commentators held that the President should send troops only with the concurrence of Congress; and such approval seemed doubtful. But the President's "swift and dramatic" recognition of the state of Israel, promptly upon the expiration of the British mandate, received immediate approval from observers of almost all points-of-view. Some did deplore the "whirling dervish" course of U.S. policy; and most said the U.S. should take the lead at the UN to halt the "spreading" warfare in the Middle East. Several Eastern newspapers urged UN action to protect Israel and stop Arab "aggression," whereas papers in the South and Midwest tended to doubt that the UN would be able to take any effective action. As expectations dimmed that the UN would actually create an international force for Palestine, a poll indicated that 62% would approve such UN action; and support for U.S. participation in such a force increased from 43% to 51%.[32]

Sustained popular approval of the U.S. arms embargo (73%) was shown by a June poll, which also reported that 54% sympathized with neither group in Palestine (34% favored the Jews, 12% the Arabs). Indeed, this poll showed only 24% taking a "great deal" of interest in news about Palestine, whereas 45% took that much interest in U.S.-Russian news. When asked for an over-all judgment on the U.S. handling of the Palestine problem, 35% said they were "satisfied," 26% were "dissatisfied" (many mentioning its "inconsistency"), and the largest number (39%) gave no opinion.

Hope for peace in Palestine rose and fell; but news of the assassination of Count Bernadotte in September 1948 was an especially rude shock. Blame for the act was often ascribed to the Stern Gang; but commentators differed as to whether the Government of Israel had any responsibility. Bernadotte's recommendations to the UN, published after his death, caused controversy. These were endorsed by Britain and Sec. Marshall and a clear majority of the American press; but they were sharply opposed by pro-Zionist commentators who charged that depriving Israel of the Negeb and Jerusalem would hinder the growth of the fledgling nation, and that the U.S. had once again "reversed its Palestine policy."[33]

Israel's victories in the Negeb against Egyptian forces prompted some to minimize the usefulness of the Bernadotte proposals, and to suggest that a final settlement would probably have to be made by the Jews and Arabs themselves. Israel's resort to force was generally deplored; but an increasing number of observers expressed sympathy with Israel's claims to the desert region. A public opinion poll showed that few respondents had heard of the Bernadotte proposals, and fewer than 1 in 10 had a definite opinion about them; the majority continued to sympathize with neither the Jews nor the Arabs.

At this point observers saw "another Palestine policy reversal" in Pres. Truman's Oct. 24 statement reaffirming the Democratic platform's support for the original UN partition plan–this move being taken as a repudiation of Sec. Marshall's support for the Bernadotte plan at the UNGA meeting in Paris. In these weeks preceding the presidential election of 1948, the pro-Zionist minority maintained strong pressure for "complete" U.S. support of Israel, including de jure recognition and a loan from the Export-Import Bank. Some editors expressed sympathy for the plight of the Arab refugees; but the chief tendency in editorial opinion was in favor of "direct" Arab-Jewish negotiations as the most "realistic" means of reaching a settlement. The renewal of fighting before the end of the year, despite establishment by the UNGA of a 3-nation conciliation commission, was dismaying to observers hoping that the Palestine problem would go away. In the new year (1949) the successful talks in Rhodes, under the auspices of Ralph Bunche, inspired fresh hope for an Israeli-Egyptian detente. In limited comment, observers now endorsed U.S. de jure recognition of Israel and an Export-Import bank loan to Israel of $100 million.[34]

The worsening plight of Arab refugees was the subject of press discussion in the summer of 1949, with some observers urging either UN or U.S. development of the Mideast to improve the refugees' situation. Reports that the U.S. had taken a "firm" stand vis-a-vis Israel on the refugee issue prompted some approval—and some sharp attacks from pro-Zionist sources. Dr. Bunche's success in developing a Syrian-Israeli armistice was warmly hailed by some. Some also welcomed the UN economic survey of the Near East as the "greatest hope" for solution of the refugee problem; but the New York Post "couldn't cheer the project" until the U.S. stopped trying to wring "fantastic concessions" from Israel.[35]

In the autumn a proposal for UN "curatorship" for the religious shrines in Jerusalem, with the New City going to Israel and the Old City to Jordan, was endorsed by the New York Times, the Herald Tribune, and the Louisville Courier-Journal. But Catholic and Protestant organizations protested this plan, insisting upon a "truly international regime;" and pro-Zionists upheld Israel's claims to all of Jerusalem. The December 1949 General Assembly vote in favor of internationalization, despite opposition from both Israel and Jordan, was widely regarded as unenforceable and hence unfortunate—although it was endorsed by American religious leaders. Meanwhile the UN Clapp Report proposing work-relief for the Arab refugees received some sympathy in light discussion.[36]

American opinion ultimately supported some U.S. admission of postwar refugees, but this decision had little impact on the problems of Jewish refugees. Pres. Truman's recognition of Israel, amid the Arab-Jewish fighting in Palestine, won approval in America; but it was not followed by calmness in the United Nations or the Middle East.

Trade (1945-1950)

During World War II there was occasional public discussion of post-war economic goals; and as the fighting in Europe drew to a close the American House of Representatives voted extension of the Reciprocal Trade Agreements program. Public comment was favorable to this action, some commentators heralding the vote as a "first victory" for the Truman Administration. Strong support came from the Scripps-Howard papers, and from such Republican papers as the New York Herald Tribune. Opposition was voiced by the Hearst papers, the New York Sun, and a few other dailies reflecting the interests of specific industries (e.g., wool, textiles, pottery).

As a group American editors had become pretty active believers in the reciprocal reduction of tariff barriers to international trade. They favored the clause in the extension bill which authorized a further cut up to 50% of U.S. tariff rates (as of Jan. 1, 1945, rather than on the higher Hawley-Smoot figures of 1930); and this feature was adopted with the concurrence of influential Republicans in both Houses. This action confirmed a long-term trend away from the economic isolationism of the Hawley-Smoot period, although some nationalist newspapers studiously refrained from comment on the issue (e.g., Chi. Tribune, Wash. Times-Herald). Less than 30 newspapers, out of 150 examined, registered out-right opposition to the legislation. Organizations approving extension of the RTA included the American Farm Bureau Federation, Congress of Industrial Organizations, U.S. Chamber of Commerce, and Federal Council of Churches.[37]

Polls showed that many Americans were not well informed about trade issues, with only 63% giving correct definitions of a "tariff" in a 1944 poll. About half of the total sample (47%) agreed to the reciprocal proposition that the U.S. should "reduce its tariffs on goods other countries want to sell here, provided they reduce their tariffs and other restrictions on our goods." Only 10% expressed disagreement with this proposition. A Gallup Poll of 1945 reported that about 1 in 10 respondents was familiar with the Trade Agreements program; and most in this group (75%) felt the program should be continued.

The Republicans won a majority of seats in 1946 in both Houses of Congress; but there seems to have been little change in editorial opinion, or in organization stands, on trade policy. The Administration, which was pushing two international programs at the Geneva Conference on Trade and Employment, was hampered by protectionist endeavors at home. Wool interests succeeded in obtaining legislation, including the possible imposition of a special import fee on wool, which caused the conferees in Geneva to doubt the outcome of their labors for an International Trade Organization (ITO) as well as for the General Agreement on Tariffs and Trade (GATT), if the U.S. were to feel free to take unilateral measures undermining the success of their joint efforts. The wool support law produced loud complaints in the U.S. press and radio. Pres. Truman vetoed the law, and allowed the wool issue to be solved by methods not involving import restriction.[38]

The Geneva Conference was then able to move again—after a 2-month halt pending resolution of the U.S. wool problem. Indeed, the pessimists were surprised to see the Geneva Conference registering agreement on a substantial and encouraging reduction of international tariffs. An agreement was signed by 23 countries embodying thousands of tariff reductions which went into effect at the beginning of 1948.[39] This meant a reduction on about 3500 separate items in the U.S. tariff, or over half of all imports dutiable under the Hawley-Smoot tariff; and many other duties were bound at the 1947 level. This achievement was hailed as a "landmark in the history of international economic relations." As usual, unfavorable comment came from the New York Sun. Time magazine felt the agreement added up to "more barter and bilateralism and probably to a reduced flow of goods from country to country." A Gallup Poll summarized the Geneva agreement and its principle of reciprocal tariff reductions; it found 63% of the national sample approving this agreement, 12% opposing it, and 25% giving no opinion.[40]

On March 1, 1948 Pres. Truman asked Congress to renew without change the 1945 Trade Agreement Act, which was to expire on June 12. His request was strongly backed by press sources ranging from The Nation to the Wall St. Journal, some holding that failure to renew the Act would be "a step back on the road to isolationism." Many sources favored also U.S. approval of the Charter of the International Trade Organization (signed at Havana on March 24 at the close of a session following the Geneva preparatory meeting which had also achieved the tariff reductions). But several commentators, including the Wall Street Journal, doubted that the ITO would be effective; U.S. News & World Report asserted that in the ITO Charter "the exceptions outweigh the rules."[41]

The Republicans, now in charge of the Congressional committees dealing with trade renewal, demanded strong restrictions on the President's authority to enter into trade agreements. With the general public receptive to the principles of reciprocal tariff reductions, and editors strongly in favor, the Congress did renew the legislation—but with tightened restrictions upon the tariff authority of the President. Promptly after the 1948 elections returned a Democratic Congress, several editors called for speedy action to restore the Reciprocal Trade Agreements Act without the "crippling" amendments by the

80th Congress; they also urged formal approval of the ITO. Business groups, however, registered opposition to the ITO Charter (e.g., National Foreign Trade Council, U.S. Chamber of Commerce). In September 1949 Congress did renew the RTA, but only after Senate Republicans sought to re-enact the "peril point" provisions regarded by the Executive as unduly "hampering" trade policy.[42]

Occupation of Japan (1945-1950)

Considerable attention to U.S. relations with Japan was accorded by the American public, beginning promptly with V-J Day. The naming of Gen. MacArthur to head the occupation government of Japan, the "most complex problem" in U.S. history, was widely praised. The terms of the Japanese surrender received overwhelming support throughout the country, even though the man-in-the-street had earlier expressed firm insistence upon "unconditional surrender" and strong antipathy to Emperor Hirohito. Some commentators did stress the difficulties of using the Emperor, or said that his retention intensified the problem of bringing about a democratic Japan (e.g., N.Y. Times), while Sen. Bankhead (D-Ala) and others claimed he should stand trial as a "war criminal."

In September 1945 considerable criticism was directed at Gen. MacArthur for his policy of accepting and utilizing existing Japanese institutions, which critics feared would leave untouched both "the same old gang about the Emperor" and the socio-economic structure of Japan (e.g., C. S. Monitor, Wm. Shirer). However, publication of the policy directives for the occupation elicited comments of general satisfaction on the part of commentators—with some seeing a close correspondence between Administrative policy and American public opinion (e.g., Thomas Stokes, N.Y. Herald Tribune). Meanwhile, a public opinion poll found that 68% felt that the "allied program for the treatment of Japan" was "not hard enough;" 21% said it was "about right," and 1% said it was "too hard." Gen. MacArthur's moves decreeing civil liberties and taking control of Japanese banks were applauded by the media, as was the State Department's declaration that state shintoism would be terminated.[43]

Some prominent commentators expressed uneasiness about the "unilateral, nationalistic" U.S. policy for control of Japan—not sharing control with our allies (e.g., Chi. Sun, W. Lippmann, Sumner Welles). When this issue was put to the general public, opinion was found to be closely divided, but with noteworthy differences according to educational background, on the broad questions of "letting England, France and Russia take an active part in helping to settle problems in the Pacific." The poll results were:

	National	College	H. School	G. School
Let others share	46%	62%	46%	38%
Leave up to U.S.	49	36	50	54
No opinion	5	2	4	8
	100%	100%	100%	100%

But when Sec. Byrnes announced that Russia was insisting upon a control council for Japan on the Berlin model, editors supported the Secretary's position that the ineffectiveness of unanimity rule in Germany precluded its application to Japan.[44]

A majority of Americans (64%) believed that we would have to police Japan for many years, according to a Gallup Poll (Nov. 3), because "we cannot trust the Japs, and they have to be entirely re-educated." Favorable press comment was inspired by Gen. MacArthur's directive aimed at breaking up the Zaibatsu, his order abolishing the feudal system, and his list of Japanese who should stand trial as war criminals, including members of the royal family and Japanese officials prominent in every field.

A poll taken in February 1946 reported that a substantial majority (69%) felt that the U.S. had made "a good start on the job of turning Japan into a peaceful nation," and an additional 12% said. "we haven't made any serious mistakes." Only 4% said: "We're doing a bad job." (These findings were appreciably more favorable than the current results on the occupation of Germany.) In the autumn many commentators hailed the Diet's adoption of the new U.S.-approved Constitution, although some skeptics felt that the document was "too advanced" for the average Japanese citizen. By now, a majority of the American public deemed it "possible to re-educate the Japanese to a peaceful way of life."[45]

An end-of-the-year N.O.R.C. poll (1946) disclosed that a majority (61%) of Americans favored U.S. help to Japan to get her peacetime industry going again (72% favored such aid to Germany). The poll also found 72% saying that Japan should be given "the same opportunity as other nations" to sell goods to the U.S. These public attitudes were in harmony with the statement of Under Secretary Acheson, in his pre-Marshall Plan speech at Cleveland, Miss. on May 8, 1947, that "we must push ahead with the reconstruction of those two great workshops of Europe and Asia–Germany and Japan–upon which the ultimate recovery of the two continents so largely depends."[46]

When Gen. MacArthur advocated prompt negotiation of a peace treaty and an early end to the occupation, these proposals received a primarily favorable press–although some editors had reservations.

A peace treaty was termed "a logical move" to end the financial drain on the U.S. caused by unsettled reparations and trade problems; and the Administration's proposal of an 11-nation "veto-less" peace conference was widely supported. Public interest in an early peace conference was pointed up by sustained comment from business journals, editors and radio commentators, while leaders and the general public continued to applaud Gen. MacArthur's administration of Japan (86% in a Minnesota Poll).[47]

The 1948 visits to Japan of George Kennan, and of the Draper mission of industrial and governmental experts, sparked reports that the U.S. was contemplating an end to reparations, and assistance in building a peaceful Japanese economy. Initial comment was favorable, often stressing the desire to see Japan self-supporting instead of a burden to the American taxpayer. A July poll found continuing majority approval (59%) of "our government helping to build up Japanese industry" (35% disapproved). In the same survey a majority (55%) declared they felt Japan was "*not* likely to become a threat to world peace during the next twenty years;" but as many as 81% favored "continuing to keep occupation troops in Japan;" only 13% chose the alternative of "bringing them home now."[48]

In early 1949 commentators debated Japan's importance to the U.S. as a Pacific "base," with the majority holding that the U.S. should remain in Japan "for some time." A poll showed that the majority in favor of keeping troops there had declined from 81% to 68%; but only 17% favored "bringing them home now." Some commentators held that U.S. troops should be retained in Japan solely for military purposes, and that the occupation be shifted to a civilian administration which could help the Japanese run things on a "business basis." High American appreciation of the MacArthur occupation was again reported by the Gallup Poll: 26% voiced "enthusiastic approval," 55% gave "general approval," 5% disapproval (14% no opinion). At the same time Gallup reported that a majority (57%) felt that the U.S. "should *not do more* to help Japan get back on her feet," whereas 31% did favor greater U.S. expenditures for that purpose. In May commentators welcomed announcement of the end of reparations from Japan; but some did urge sympathetic consideration of the effect of this move upon the Philippines and other victims of Japanese aggression.[49]

Conclusions

Earlier chapters have outlined the public's approval of basic postwar policies respecting participation in the United Nations, adoption of aid programs, and setting up NATO. At the same time Americans were assessing the practicability and adequacy of such international institutions as the United Nations. Americans were disappointed with the UN as peace-keeper and as guardian of human rights; but only a minority (20%) embraced the alternative of world government. The American public had to be coaxed to accept much increase in immigration; but it was sympathetic to European Jews finding a haven in Israel—provided this would not involve U.S. military action without our fellow UN members.

The chief attribute of the public's position on trade policy was the steady increase in acceptance of liberal trade, even with Japan—but not yet with Communist countries. Gen. MacArthur's efforts to free and democratize Japanese institutions also received public support.

Thus the public which re-elected the Truman Administration in 1948 continued to give support to its foreign policies in most fields: trade policy and occupation policies for Japan and Germany, as well as support of the UN, foreign aid, and collective security respecting Europe and Latin America. The public was reluctant about immigration, and divided over policy toward China. For the most part, the leadership of the Government was accepted by the public.

Reference Notes

1. N.O.R.C. survey #145.
2. AOR for June 26 and July 26, 1946.
3. AOR of Dec. 27, 1948.
4. AOR for Aug. 19, 1946 and Dec. 27, 1948.
5. AOR of Nov. 18, 1947.
6. AOR of Apr. 19, 1948.
7. AOR of Dec. 27, 1948.
8. Ibid.
9. AOR for Mar. 19 and July 6, 1948; Campbell, *U.S. in World Affairs, 1947–48*, p. 410.
10. *Dept. of State Bulletin* for May 17, 1948; AOR for May 1948.
11. AOR for May and July 1949.
12. AOR for June and July 1949.
13. AOR for May 25, July 18, and Oct. 1949.
14. AOR of Dec. 29, 1949.
15. AOR for Feb. and Mar. 17, 1950.
16. AOR for May 10 and Aug. 22, 1949.
17. Bourne, Francis S., "The Public Opinion Poll as Opinion Evidence in the World Government Movement 1946–54," M.A. Thesis at Columbia University.
18. AOR for Feb. 21 and June 19, 1947.
19. AOR for Dec. 16, 1947; July 19 and Dec. 1948.
20. AOR for Oct. 12 and Nov. 3, 1943.
21. AOR for Jan. 8 and 21, 1946.
22. N.O.R.C. survey #243.
23. AOR for March and Mar. 29, 1948.
24. AOR for June 1948; N.Y. Times of June 26, 1948.
25. AOR for Oct. 19, Nov. 5 and 19, Dec. 4, 1945.

26. AOR for May 20, June 19, and July 3, 1946.
27. AOR for Aug. 6 and 20, Sept. 4, Oct. 18, 1946.
28. AOR of Mar. 7, 1947.
29. AOR for Sept., Oct., Nov., Dec. 1947.
30. AOR for Feb. and Mar. 10 & 16, 1948.
31. AOR of Apr. 2, 1948.
32. AOR for May and June 1948.
33. AOR for Sept. and Oct. 1948.
34. AOR for Dec. 1948 and Jan. 1949.
35. AOR for June, July, Aug. 1949.
36. AOR for Nov. and Dec. 1949 and Jan. 1950.
37. AOR for June 9 and July 30, 1945.
38. AOR of Jan. 16, 1947.
39. Campbell, *U.S. in World Affairs, 1945–47*, pp. 247–9.
40. AOR for Nov. 14 and Dec. 5, 1947.
41. AOR for March 1948.
42. AOR for Apr. and Nov. 1948 and Sept. 1949.
43. AOR for Oct. 5 and 19, 1945.
44. AOR for Nov. 5 and 19, 1945.
45. AOR for Mar. 6 and Oct. 18, 1946.
46. AOR of Jan. 22, 1947; *Dept. of State Bulletin*, May 18, 1947, p. 994.
47. AOR for Mar., June, July, Sept., Nov. 1947.
48. AOR for Apr., May and July 1948.
49. AOR for Mar., Apr., May 1949.

Part Two

IMPLEMENTING BASIC POLICIES (1950–1965)

VII

KOREAN WAR AND ITS IMPACT ON POLICY (1950-1952)

Pres. Truman was at his home in Independence, Missouri, on the Saturday night when North Korea invaded South Korea (June 24, 1950–U.S. time). He was surprised and shocked at the news; so were the American people. The President moved swiftly to meet the crisis. His moves–summoning an emergency session of the United Nations Security Council; proposing the resolution calling for a cease-fire in Korea which the Council adopted; pledging U.S. arms aid to South Korea–were promptly and warmly approved by the American public.

Attitudes on War

Virtually all of the press and radio comment viewed the surprise invasion as Soviet-inspired, and calling for united action by the non-Communist nations of the world. Commentators offered few specific suggestions for action; but they backed U.S. leadership in developing a program to halt and reverse the invasion. Korea was not widely regarded as of great strategic importance, but editors felt that the U.S. had a vital moral and psychological stake in the conflict.

"Pres. Truman's prompt and forthright decision to try to restore peace in Korea with American planes, ships and arms," said the Philadelphia Inquirer in a representative comment, "deserves the unstinting backing of every American, as well as people everywhere who believe in international law and decency." Similarly the New York Herald Tribune said: "The President has acted with a magnificent courage and terse decision" (similarly, Wash. Post, Edw. Murrow, Elmer Davis).[1]

Prof. Robert W. Tucker, writing after the growth of dissent in America re Viet-Nam, has sought to explain why there was so little American dissent to the Korean action.[2] "The attack upon South Korea followed closely upon the coup in Czechoslovakia, the blockade of Berlin, the first Soviet explosion of an atomic device, and the Chinese Communist accession to power. These events were widely interpreted as a mounting Communist offensive which was increasingly taking a military form and which, if left unopposed, might well eventuate in an armed attack against Western Europe."

Many commentators in 1950 took particular satisfaction in the fact that the U.S. had chosen to act through the United Nations, making its moral position clear before the world, and backing up the UN cease-fire resolution with force. Within a few days the Gallup

Poll reported that 81% of a nationwide sample approved the U.S. decision to send military aid to Korea (13% disapproved); and 57% said that this new move would lead to peace rather than "another world war" (29%).[3]

The President's actions were opposed by only a tiny fraction of American opinion, which included the far left, the McCormick press, and a few Congressmen. These critics contended that Pres. Truman had "exceeded his authority" in dispatching American forces without consulting Congress (e.g., Chi. Tribune, Sen. Taft). When Sen. Taft went further and called for Sec. Acheson's resignation, little support or sympathy was expressed in public comment outside the Hearst papers.

Pres. Truman's separate order, interposing the U.S. Seventh Fleet between the Chinese mainland and Formosa, received relatively little discussion, but most of those discussing it accepted this new policy as an integral part of America's defense program in Asia—although some did criticize the U.S. for reversing its "hands-off" policy on Formosa, or noted that the new policy was lacking UN sanction. At the same time public comment stiffened its opposition to extending recognition to the People's Republic of China; and a number added that Japan should have a "vital" role in a coordinated Pacific defense policy.

Awareness that the military situation in the Far East presented major difficulties was expressed by most commentators; and some observers also mentioned the weakness of the Korean government of Syngman Rhee. In the following weeks came a grim acceptance that the Korean struggle would be long and hard, and consequent acceptance of Pres. Truman's U.S. mobilization program; and there was increased approval for arms aid to Western Europe and to other threatened countries. Accordingly, when Prime Minister Nehru offered mediation in the UN on "Soviet terms" (including a UN seat for Peking), rejection of this offer by the United States was widely and strongly supported, most observers stressing their opposition to "any deals" before the aggression was repelled.[4]

A July 1950 poll by N.O.R.C. found 75% of a national sample approving "the decision to send American troops to stop the Communist invasion of South Korea" (21% disapproved). Spokesmen for large and influential organizations—including labor, religious, and veterans groups—also strongly supported the U.S.-UN stand. This determination was expressed at a time when the N.O.R.C. poll (July) found a majority (54%) saying they expected "another world war within the next year or two"—the highest expectation of war since the close of World War II. When a Gallup Poll (July 8–15) probed popular understanding of the war in Korea, a clear majority (58%) either stressed "Communist aggression" or the U.S. effort "to stop

Red expansion;" but as many as one-fourth of the nationwide sample couldn't explain "what the war in Korea is all about." On related policy issues, the N.O.R.C. poll reported a majority believing that it would be "more important" for the U.S. to stop an invasion in Europe than to stop one in Asia—if we "had to make a choice." Still, as many as 7 out of every 10 respondents said that they would approve U.S. participation in a Pacific mutual defense pact with non-Communist countries "like India, Australia, and the Philippines."[5]

As to the goals of U.S.-UN fighting in Korea, some American spokesmen as early as July 1950 suggested that the UN army should not stop at the 38th parallel, but should occupy part or all of North Korea in order to permit a unified Korean government and end the threat of a future invasion (e.g., Sen. Taft, Gen. Eisenhower, several media commentators). Such suggestions were encouraged by the UN military gains of August and the arrival of British ground troops as part of the UN forces. The Chicago Tribune was distinctly in the minority in warning that on the northern border of Korea "we shall be face to face with the hordes of Russia and red China with a new line more explosively dangerous than the 38th parallel ever was."

Following Gen. MacArthur's "brilliant success" in mid-September in landing troops at Inchon and re-taking Seoul, the question of the future of North Korea became more pressing. Most of those discussing this question favored the destruction of the North Korean army in order to permit laying the basis for an independent and united Korean government, to be chosen by Koreans South and North in elections supervised by the United Nations. A September poll (N.O.R.C.) found a popular majority (54%) saying the UN army should cross the 38th parallel and try to occupy North Korea; only 29% said the UN army should stop at the border on the Parallel. Those in the majority felt that we should prevent recurrence of the invasion, "finish the job," and guard against an incursion by the Soviet Union. The minority felt that "our job" would be finished at the border, that further penetration could invite war with Russia and/or China, and that there had already been enough loss of life.[6]

In this September poll the large majority of 81% said the U.S. was "right" in sending its troops to stop the Communist invasion of South Korea; only 13% said the U.S. was "wrong." As many as 66% said that in the event of other Communist attacks the U.S. should "help defend" the attacked countries. Over-all approval of the way in which "government officials" were handling our foreign relations was expressed by 50% of the sample; only 35% disapproved. In a mid-October poll over-all approval rose slightly—to 54%.[7]

Sec. Acheson's proposal to strengthen the United Nations, by enabling the General Assembly to take prompt and effective action against future aggression in case the Security Council were paralyzed by a veto, won overwhelming approval from the nation's press. Indeed, some editors (as in earlier years) wished to go further than the "national contingent" idea and create a "separate" international police force (Denver Post, Scripps-Howard papers). Outright opposition to the Acheson proposal was largely confined to the Hearst and McCormick newspapers. A Gallup Poll found 83% in favor of a U.S. contribution to a "UN world army–ready at all times to be sent anywhere in the world where trouble breaks out." But the majority was reduced to 55%–instead of 83%–when the question asked whether or not the UN should be given the power to call out U.S. troops.[8]

Public support for the NATO pledge remained strong despite (or because of) the war in Korea. A March 1950 poll had found 81% saying they thought our "agreement with Canada and the countries of western Europe to defend each other against any attack" was a "good idea." A month after outbreak of the Korean war this figure rose to 87%; it dropped to 78% following the massive incursion of Chinese Communists into Korea, and rose again to 84% in August 1951. Support for "sending military supplies to the countries of western Europe now" ranged from 69% to 73% after the start of the Korean fighting.[9]

After Chinese Intervention

November 1950 opened with grim editorial concern over reports that Chinese "volunteers" were participating in the Korean war on the side of the North. Although the full-scale Communist Chinese attack in Korea didn't come until the end of November, the increasing role of the Chinese had an enormous impact upon American opinion which was promptly reflected in the November poll on the trend question about the "handling of our relations with other countries." In October there was an approving majority (54% to 29%); in November this figure turned around to a disapproving plurality (43% to 38%). In between these two polls came the Congressional elections of 1950 with much controversy over foreign policy; the Republicans gained seats in both houses of Congress and claimed that the voters had thereby "repudiated" U.S. foreign policy. Some commentators agreed that the election demonstrated popular distrust of the Administration's conduct of foreign policy; some saw the election influenced by Sen. McCarthy's attack against the State Department, and the polls did show an increase among those saying that disloyal employees were doing "a great deal of harm"–from 19% in April to 28% in November. In fact, however, the Republican gains did not produce an actual majority in either House.

Nevertheless, Republicans in the new Congress demanded a thorough "house-cleaning" of the State Department–from the Secretary on down. But editors were almost unanimous in disapproving this "irresponsible" move, and in applauding Gov. Dewey and other Republican leaders for supporting a "united front" on foreign policy at this critical time. An early December Gallup Poll reported a plurality (30%) favoring Sec. Acheson's "replacement," while 21% wished his retention; as many as 49% refrained from any judgment on the Secretary.[10]

Now, for the first time since World War II, signs appeared suggesting some wavering in the broad public support of a strong U.S. policy of world leadership. Herbert Hoover, in mid-December–after the Chinese forces had reversed the military situation in Korea, delivered his radio address counseling a reduction in U.S. commitments, and suggesting withdrawal from the defense of Western Europe to the defense of the Western Hemisphere. In response to Hoover's speech, and a similar one by former ambassador Joseph Kennedy, there ensued a "great debate" among press and radio commentators and Congressmen. In the voluminous discussion the idea of withdrawal from Europe was decisively rejected (e.g., N.Y. Herald Tribune, Edw. Murrow, Knight press). Some, however, did see the Hoover speech as a valuable warning against the "laggardly approach" of our NATO allies to creation of an effective defense system, or accepted Hoover's point that it was useless to try to defend other nations unless they were determined to defend themselves (e.g., Hearst and McCormick papers). The outcome of the nation-wide debate made clear that, despite the war in Korea, Americans had confirmed their commitment to Western Europe.

A year-end poll reported a majority (56%) disapproving the "idea of sending large numbers of American troops to help build up the defense of Western Europe," and 36% in favor. However, when these "disapprovers" were asked if they "would approve of sending more troops to Europe if the countries of Western Europe increased the size of their armed forces," an additional 34% said Yes, making a total of 70% giving conditional or full approval. Three months later (March 1951), after the Chinese military advance had been stemmed, a polling majority (54%) "approved the idea of sending American troops to help build up the defense of Western Europe."[11] Sustained approval for sending U.S. arms aid to Western Europe (71%) was reported by a Jan. 1951 poll. Also 66% said that in the event of war with Russia, "we would really need the support of our allies to defeat her."[12]

Meanwhile, disapproval continued to be predominant in the public's opinion of the way government officials were "handling our relations with other countries." As the following table shows, from the entrance of the Chinese into the Korean war this majority disapproval persisted over the next two years, until the very end of the Truman administration.

Public Attitudes on the "Handling of our Relations with Other Countries by Government Officials"

	Approving	Disapproving	No Opinion
June 1950	48%	37%	15%
July 1950	48	36	16
Sept. 1950	50	35	15
Oct. 1950	54	29	17
Nov. 1950	38	43	19
Dec. 1950	36	47	17
Feb. 1951	36	50	14
Mar. 1951	37	47	16
Apr. 1951	28	58	14
May 1951	34	51	15
Aug. 1951	32	53	15
Oct. 1951	37	49	15
Nov. 1951	30	58	12
Jan. 1952	32	56	12
Feb. 1952	38	47	15
Mar. 1952	32	57	11
Apr. 1952	36	53	11
June 1952	43	45	12
July 1952	32	57	11
Aug. 1952	30	61	9
Oct. 1952	34	51	15

The preceding figures do not necessarily reflect attitudes toward the State Department as such, because respondents often have other "officials" in mind. In November 1950, for example, respondents were asked: "Which officials do you especially disapprove of?" About one-third of the "disapprovers" named Sec. Acheson, and a similar proportion named Pres. Truman; but nearly a third simply said they "didn't know" which officials they "especially disapproved of."

Respondents have tended to base their approval or disapproval of the handling of U.S. foreign affairs either on policy grounds, or on the manner in which the officials have conducted our foreign affairs, or a combination of these two factors. Certainly a "disapprove" response didn't necessarily mean disapproval of basic policies, such as membership in the UN or NATO; but it could have meant a feeling that our foreign policies were "going too far" (isolationist replies based on the Korean war) or weren't "going far enough" ("too easy on Russia"). Complaints about the "manner of conducting our foreign affairs," in October 1950, included disapproval of official dissension and confusion—complaints that various officials in Washington presented clashing accounts of our foreign policy, or that they "reversed themselves," or were "inconsistent." A substantial group of "disapprovers" also declared that the officials were "not qualified," or were "inefficient." In this Oct. 1950 poll the chief reasons given for disapproval were: Dissension/confusion, 22%; Too easy with Russia, 19%; Inefficient, not qualified, 18%; and Isolationist reasons, 14%. It may be added that in this poll only 8% of the "disapprovers" specifically charged that the officials were "pro-Communist."

Breakdowns of a December 1950 poll show that, after the massive Chinese intervention, the greatest disapproval of U.S. officials came from the college-educated, Republicans and Independents.

	Approving	**Disapproving**	**No Opinion**
National	36%	47%	17%
Democrats	44	39	17
Republicans	25	59	16
Independents	28	59	13
College	30	62	8
High School	36	50	14
Grammar School	37	39	24

The "great debate" sparked by Herbert Hoover was accompanied by a deepening split in opinion on the prosecution of the Korean war itself, some continued to advocate a "firmer," more belligerent policy on the part of the U.S. and the UN to combat the aggressors; but the greater number—including "moderate" spokesmen—intensified their approval of a "diplomatic approach," seeking a negotiated settlement which would save U.S. fighting strength for "more crucial areas." These commentators held that the U.S. must not become embroiled in a war of attrition with China, in view of the possibility of a Communist thrust in Western Europe; they strongly rejected appeasement, but sought an "honorable settlement," some suggesting that a neutralized zone on both sides of the Manchurian border would be a "fair compromise." But such proposals were anathema to the advocates of a "firmer" policy.[13]

Americans were substantially agreed in feeling that the Chinese Communists had joined in "aggression" in Korea, and they were dismayed at the delay (until late January) of the UN General Assembly in condemning Peking as an "aggressor." At the same time, the deep objections of many of our allies in the United Nations to risking involvement with Red China aroused some misgivings about the risks of the U.S. course concerning China. UN military gains during January brought some revival of optimism after the deep pessimism earlier in the month; but vigorous debate continued on the merits of of U.S. withdrawal from the Korean peninsula, or of "staying and fighting."

Public opinion polls, and letters to editors and to Congressmen, gave evidence of some demand for withdrawal. The Gallup Poll reported that 66% of a national cross section said: "Now that Communist China has entered the fighting in Korea with forces far outnumbering the United Nations troops there," we should "pull our troops out of Korea as fast as possible." In this poll only 25% said we should "keep our troops there to fight these larger forces" (9% gave no opinion). However, a Minnesota Poll of this period offered its respondents three options, and found 29% favoring permanent withdrawal, 23% favoring withdrawal until the U.S. was stronger, and 34% opting to stay in Korea as long as possible. The January Gallup Poll also reported a plurality (49%) holding that, "in view of developments since we entered the fighting in Korea, the U.S. made a mistake in deciding to defend South Korea;" 38% said it was "not a mistake" (as compared to 65% taking this position in an August 1950 Gallup Poll). The National Opinion Research Center, also in early January, asked a different question about the Korean war; it found 55% saying the U.S. "was right in sending American troops to stop the Communist invasion of South Korea." This was a substantial reduction from the 81% who had taken that position in September.

On non-Korean foreign policy issues, 65% of a national cross section said in the January N.O.R.C. poll that they still favored "an active part in world affairs" for the United States, likewise supporting arms aid to Western Europe and to Asia; and 78% continued to favor our mutual defense agreement with Canada and Western Europe. But, as noted earlier, there was a substantial–if temporary–reduction in approval of the principle of "sending large numbers of American troops to help build up the defense of Western Europe"–from 57% in September to 36% in January of 1951.[14]

During February the temper of public discussion of world affairs became more optimistic than it had been for several months. The improved UN military situation in Korea apparently quieted, to a considerable extent, the previous concern over the security of U.S. forces there; and the general trend of foreign affairs led many to believe that the free world was gaining strength, and that another world war was less likely to occur. In this atmosphere an N.O.R.C. poll found that, in contrast to sentiment of the previous month, 67% now wanted to "stay on as long as possible" in Korea. A Denver Post poll also found a majority favorable to "staying" in Korea–including 39% who favored "using all our power to win, including the atom bomb and air raids on Manchuria."[15]

March press discussions revealed a growing desire for settlement of the conflict, with some commentators–perhaps spurred by Gen.

MacArthur's statements from the field—pressing for decisions on re-crossing the 38th parallel and bombing Manchuria. Some others, however, echoed Gen. Ridgway's remark that termination of the war on the 38th parallel would be a "tremendous victory" for the United Nations. According to a Gallup Poll of mid-February, 73% believed the UN should "stop fighting" when it reached the 38th parallel "if the Chinese agree to stop fighting at that point." A later Gallup Poll found a plurality (43%) in favor of dividing Korea at the 38th parallel, whereas 36% were opposed (21% giving no opinion). Commentators generally agreed with Gen. MacArthur that no military decision was possible until UN or other decisions were made about goals in Korea. The St. Louis Post-Dispatch observed: "The UN could use this period of stalemate for a new effort to reach a settlement with China." Similarly, Erwin Canham said on ABC radio: "We can only hope that under our constant pressure the Chinese will some day decide to reach agreement" (also Stewart Alsop, Dayton News).[16]

Amid continuing debate in America Gen. MacArthur issued his March 24 statement offering to discuss armistice terms with the enemy field commander, and adding—contrary to Administration thinking—an implicit threat to carry the war to China if the Communists persisted in fighting. A number of commentators praised the General for taking the initiative toward peace (e.g., N.Y. Herald Tribune, Wash. Post, David Lawrence); some others favored the General's initiative but doubted whether he had furthered the cause of peace by asking the Chinese Communists to acknowledge "their own overwhelming defeat" (e.g., N.Y. Times, Walter Lippmann, Elmer Davis). In the continuing discussion of the role of the 38th parallel, most commentators were now opposed to full-scale advance beyond it—a reversal of the position they had taken before the Chinese intervention. Respecting the proposal to use Chiang's troops against Red China, the largest number expressed opposition, fearing that this would embroil the U.S. in all-out war against Peking and also weaken the Western alliance.

MacArthur Dismissal

Pres. Truman's dismissal of Gen. MacArthur on April 10 triggered a vast, emotional debate, with much stress upon personalities, politics, charges and countercharges, as well as upon the issue of whether application of the General's policy recommendations would bring on war with the Soviet Union. Gen. MacArthur's tumultuous return to Washington, and the Congressional hearings on Far East policy, kept the debate stirring for several months. Polls soon made it clear that the President's action was not popular with the general public: 62%

expressed disapproval of the dismissal in a "spot" Gallup Poll; 58% in an N.O.R.C. poll sent to the field on April 18. This view was expressed by 50% of college-educated respondents and by 59% of the other educational groups. Analysis by political affiliation showed Democrats opposed to the dismissal, 53% to 36%; Independents opposed 51% to 30%; and Republicans opposed 72% to 17%.

But, contrary to the trend among the general public, opinion expressed by the press, radio and organizations tended to uphold the President's removal of Gen. MacArthur, to emphasize that civilian leadership must prevail over military, and that the General's issuance of policy statements left the President no alternative but to relieve him of his command. This split between the general public and the articulate commentators extended beyond the issue of dismissal to the General's recommendations for future Korean policy. It has been noted earlier that the commentators tended to oppose U.S. assistance in placing Chiang's troops on the mainland, whereas the N.O.R.C. poll of mid-April found 58% of the general public expressing approval of "giving the Chinese Nationalist government under Chiang Kai-shek all the help it needs to attack the Communists on the mainland of China," 25% disapproving, and 17% giving no opinion. Similarly, commentators tended to oppose the U.S. bombing of Manchurian bases, whereas the April poll showed 56% saying that U.S. airplanes "should cross the Korean border and bomb Communist supply bases inside China" (26% were opposed).[17]

It is interesting to note that the commentators and the man-in-the-street were in accord on basic aims; what they differed on was their estimates of the consequences of particular military steps. When respondents were asked if the U.S. "should take strong steps against China, even at the risk of all-out war with the Chinese," only 27% said Yes; 65% favored the alternative of "trying as hard as we can to stay out of a big war with China." Moreover, 71% felt that "if we did get into a big war with Communist China," Russia "would go to war against us, too." Evidently, the majority of Americans felt that Gen. MacArthur's recommended military policies could secure victory without the bigger war which was feared by the Administration, by fellow members of the United Nations, and the majority of American commentators.

Indeed, one of the major differences between Gen. MacArthur and the general public, on the one hand, and the Administration and the commentators, on the other hand, was that the former gave slight consideration to the reactions of other United Nations members, including our NATO allies. Two further attitudes registered by the general public in the April poll should also be noted: 1, 68% said "we should continue to keep our troops in Korea," rather than "pull them out now" (favored by 21%); and 2, there was continuing approval of having sent "American troops to stop the Communist invasion of South Korea"—63% in April against 60% in March.

In comments on the General's address to Congress there was a noteworthy tendency on the part of the majority of commentators to question MacArthur's assumptions: viz. that his course could win the Korean war, that it would not "necessarily" bring the Soviet Union into the fray, and that it would not have any harmful effect on the Western alliance (e.g., Wash. Post, N.Y. Times, N.Y. Herald Tribune, Walter Lippmann). Among those giving sustained support to MacArthur and his plans were Sen. Taft, the Chicago Tribune, Wash. Times-Herald, N.Y. News, the Scripps-Howard papers, and American Legion Commander Erle Cocke, Jr. Pres. Truman's announcement at this time of the successful negotiations leading to the Anzus defense pact with New Zealand and Australia was hailed by all as a welcome development.

As the Congressional hearings went on through May and June there was much reiteration of views by the supporters of Gen. MacArthur and by the supporters of the Administration's limited war policy. Sentiment against Red China hardened, and the United Nations embargo against war materials to that country was warmly and generally welcomed. In May the repulse of the second big Communist offensive occasioned increased speculation about the possibility of a cease-fire; and in June most commentators viewed the idea of a truce at the old border with approval, and tended to feel that the Administration's limited war policy had been proved sounder than any program advanced by its critics.[18] The critics, however, remained unconvinced.

At the end of June a Gallup Poll reported a majority approving "a truce at the 38th Parallel in Korea, with peace terms to be worked out later" (37% disapproved). Sec. Acheson's presentation at the hearings drew wide applause; and a number commended the Committee report which warned foreign nations of America's basic determination and unity. In fact, the policy battle was over; Gen. MacArthur's speech-making tour of Texas—in which he also attacked the Administration's domestic policies—played to half-empty houses.

In July the armistice talks at Kaesong pursued an on-again off-again course—with commentators expressing cautious optimism about their eventual outcome. In a Gallup Poll 74% approved U.S. participation in the talks. Among commentators, the preponderant view was that the Korean war was a "victory" for the principle of collective security, and a valuable spur to the free world's rearmament. The minority contended that the armistice represented a "defeat" for the whole UN. According to the Gallup Poll, the popular view was less clear-cut: 33% supported the view that a UN victory at the 38th Parallel would mean that the Communists "came out best;"

30% said such an outcome would mean that the UN "came out best;" 22% said neither side would be ahead (15% gave no opinion). Most Americans, in the summer of 1951, appeared happy to hope that armistice talks would end the fighting.[19]

After the first Kaesong truce talks the problem of the Korean war continued to trouble the American public till the very end of the Truman Administration–and after. The fighting was less intense much of the time, but there was always the possibility that it might escalate, and for two solid years from mid-1951 there was the fact that there was "no peace."

Attitudes on the Fighting

When the Gallup Poll asked the American people if the Korean war were a mistake, the larger number of respondents continued to say Yes–as they had ever since the Chinese attack in force.[20]

"In view of the developments since we entered the fighting, do you think the U.S. made a mistake in deciding to defend South Korea, or not?"

	Yes, mistake	No, not a mistake	No opinion
1950–Aug.	20%	65%	15%
1951–Jan.	49	38	13
1951–Feb.	50	39	11
(College)	(43)	(50)	(7)
(H. School)	(50)	(41)	(9)
(G. School)	(52)	(35)	(13)
1951–Oct.			
"Useless War"	56	33	11
(Repubs)	(65)	(26)	(9)
(Dems)	(49)	(37)	(14)
1952–Feb.	51	35	14
1952–Oct.	43	37	20

People who thought the war a "mistake" tended also to believe that a truce line near the old border between North and South Korea would be a victory for the enemy (49% to 24%), whereas those who did not see the war as a mistake tended to feel that such a truce would be a victory for "our side" (39% to 29%), according to the Gallup Poll of Feb. 1952.

At the same time that American polling respondents were telling the Gallup Poll interviewers that it was a mistake for the U.S. to "defend South Korea," a majority of them were telling the interviewers of N.O.R.C. that the U.S. was "right" in "sending American troops to stop the Communist invasion of South Korea."

	Right to send troops	Wrong	No Opinion
1950–Sept.	81%	13%	6%
1951–Jan.	55	36	9
1951–Feb.	57	32	11
1951–Mar.	60	30	10
1951–Apr.	63	27	10
1951–May	60	30	10
1951–Aug.	60	30	10
1951–Nov.	54	37	9
1952–Jan.	56	34	10
1952–Mar.	50	40	10
1952–July	55	38	7
1953–Sept.	64	28	10

How can the difference in responses to the Gallup and N.O.R.C. questions be explained? Apparently, when Gallup asked about the Korean fighting, respondents thought about the carnage; and the greater number of them called that a mistake. When N.O.R.C. recalled the circumstances which had led to the war in Korea ("Communist invasion"), a majority continued to say that the decision to send troops was correct–whether or not they felt that the action had turned out to be worthwhile. Presumably most Americans who told the N.O.R.C. that the U.S. decision was "wrong" (fairly consistently about one-third of the total) said to Gallup interviewers that the war was a mistake. Also presumably, most of those respondents who thought the the war was "not a mistake" (also one-third of the total) told N.O.R.C. interviewers that the U.S. was "right" in sending troops to stop the invasion. In between these relatively solid opinion groups (aside from the 10% or so who usually stated no opinion) were many Americans who tended to think the Korean fighting was a "mistake"–unless they were reminded of its purpose. On the "rightness" of the decision to send U.S. troops, it is interesting to note that the highest figure (since 1950) was registered in September 1953, two months after signature of the armistice.

Beginning in August 1952, N.O.R.C. asked another question: "As things stand now, do you feel that the U.S. effort in Korea has been worthwhile (worth fighting)?"

	Korea Worth Fighting	**Not Worth It**	**No Opinion**
1952–Aug.	39%	54%	7%
1952–Oct.	32	56	12
1952–Nov.	34	58	8
1953–Jan.	39	52	9
1953–Apr.	36	55	9
1953–July	32	58	10
1953–Nov.	38	50	12

These figures are manifestly similar to the Gallup findings about the Korean fighting as a "mistake;" and they suggest that the question which many Gallup respondents actually had in mind was whether the war had been "worth fighting." (It is interesting that twenty years later, in the spring of 1973, Dr. Free reported polling figures very similar to those registered in November 1953: "good thing the U.S. took part in Korean War," 37%; "better if we had managed to stay out," 49%.)[21]

Breakdown of the talks at Kaesong at the end of August 1951 found American commentators firmly backing the UN Command's position, and exasperated with the conduct and tactics of the Communists. Polls reported that 70% thought "our government has done all it should" to reach agreement at the peace talks, and that a majority (54%) still favored having U.S. planes "bomb Communist supply bases inside China." November's agreement at Panmunjom on a cease-fire line was cautiously welcomed; and some commentators were encouraged to hope that a truce might be obtained that winter. Only a minority (19%) wanted the truce talks "broken off."[22]

During the election year of 1952 there was some continuing discussion of Korean matters. In March the Russians charged that the UN forces had employed germ warfare in Korea; American editorial reaction ranged from indignant disbelief to outraged alarm. The U.S. handling of the charges received warm support; but it was widely expected that the germ warfare propaganda charges would be accepted by peoples in Asia in addition to those behind the Iron Curtain. In America, 64% said they had heard these charges; 5% said they thought "there might be some truth in them," while 55% said they were "completely false."[23]

Editors continued to uphold the UN positions at the truce talks; they applauded the stand of the UN General Assembly against forced repatriation of prisoners taken during the Korean fighting. When UN inquiries of Chinese and Korean prisoners found as many as 40% not wishing to return to the Communist side, editors felt that this finding might reduce the chances of Communist acceptance of the UN's "compromise solution" of the impasse on prisoners. In April an

American public opinion polling question stated that many of the prisoners held by the UN side were "afraid they (would) be put in prison or even killed if we send them back," whereupon 50% of the respondents said we "should refuse to send them back," but 37% said that "in order to speed up the truce talks we should send them back anyway." A follow-up question informed respondents that "the Communists now say they won't give back the men they have captured from us unless we send back all of theirs;" and 41% then changed their minds and said that in that case "we should agree to return them all in order to get our own men back." Fourteen percent continued to say, "we should still refuse to return them."[24]

In the spring of 1952 popular opinion as to future U.S. policy for Korea was sharply divided, according to a poll offering three alternatives: 28% said the U.S. should pull its troops out of Korea; 31% wanted the UN forces to stand on the existing battle line; and 34% said "we should go on the attack against the Chinese Communists." Editors summing up the situation foresaw a prolonged stalemate; but they also saw these gains from America's Korean actions: prevention of the conquest of South Korea and the checking of further aggression in Asia; the rearming of the West; strengthening of the United Nations and collective security arrangements. On the debit side they placed the tremendous cost of holding South Korea, and Communist China's consolidation of its position. Among the general public, only 19% favored "making more concessions" to secure an armistice.[25]

After the nomination of Gen. Eisenhower and Gov. Stevenson to be the presidential candidates, numerous observers saw these contenders as so close to each other on world affairs that the issue of foreign policy would be removed from the 1952 campaign (e.g., David Lawrence, Anne O'Hare McCormick). But Gen. Eisenhower won wide editorial acclaim for his October pledge to "go to Korea," if elected, in order to re-examine all possible courses of action toward a settlement of the war. When asked in a Gallup Poll, 67% of the people said that Eisenhower "could handle the Korean situation better" than Stevenson; this was a much higher figure than the mere plurality who said they would "like to see the Republicans win" (48% to 46%).[26]

State Department; Japan (1950–52)

A poll a year after outbreak of the Korean war (N.O.R.C. July 1951) reported a noteworthy increase in the proportion of respondents who could give a correct answer as to the "main job of the State Department"–43% as compared with 33% in 1948. It seems quite likely that the publicization of the Department by Sen. McCarthy, and the ensuing discussions enabled an increasing number of citizens to recognize the formal name of the Department of the Federal Government which handled relations with other countries. This N.O.R.C. poll also asked an interesting group of questions when it called upon respondents to give their ratings of various officers concerned with foreign affairs.

"When it comes to handling our foreign affairs, would you rate Pres. Truman (Sec. Dean Acheson; other officials in the State Department) as very good, good, only fair, or poor?"

	Very Good or Good	**Only Fair or Poor**	**No Opinion**	**Total**
Pres. Truman	38%	56%	6%	100%
Sec. Acheson	36	39	25	100
Other officials	37	24	39	100

Over one-third of the respondents gave good ratings to all three categories of these officials associated with the Truman Administration; but a majority didn't hesitate to give the President low marks. Also, respondents were less willing to render a negative verdict against the Secretary and other Department officials than they were to blame the President. When asked to explain their low ratings for Pres. Truman, respondents cited mainly personal grounds ("incompetent," "impulsive"); but some mentioned his Far Eastern policy and his dismissal of Gen. MacArthur. Sec. Acheson was criticized for: his Far East policy; and being "too friendly" toward Communism and the Soviet Union (also toward "England"). Criticism of Department "officials" was more in terms of criticism of any Government jobholder: "They are political yes-men," "lack competence," or "argue too much among themselves."

The extent of continuing public interest in the problem of "Communists in our Government" was attested by the fact that at the end of 1951 no less than 53% of a nationwide sample said that they took "a great deal of interest" in that topic—more than in "the peace talks" in Korea, 48%; or "our Government's foreign policy," 38%.[27]

After the outbreak of war in Korea a number of commentators stressed the need for a vigorous, coordinated Pacific policy which would assign a vital role to Japan in containing the Communist advance in Asia. They also favored a "separate" peace with Japan; some were worried about a possible "red grab for Japan." At a time of growing press support for permitting a Japanese army (Sept. 1950), a poll asked respondents whether the Japanese "should or should not be allowed to set up an army of their own." This was favored by a narrow plurality, 47% to 43% (whereas in the case of Germany 56%

favored a German army "to help strengthen the defense of western Europe").[28]

By the end of 1950, and with a change in question-wording, an ample majority (61% to 25%) were found to favor letting the Japanese "set up an army of their own to help strengthen the defenses against Communism." A Gallup Poll had earlier found 72% in favor of the U.S. "taking steps now to build up an army of Japanese soldiers to be ready to fight the Communists if Japan is attacked." Commentators speculated that if the UN forces were compelled to evacuate Korea it would not be long before Japan became the main target of Soviet aggression; they saw a need for speedy restoration of Japan's sovereignty and for her re-armament.[29]

The U.S. note to the Soviet Union refusing "to any one nation" the veto power in negotiating the Japanese peace treaty was enthusiastically endorsed; and the word that the U.S. was sending John Foster Dulles to Tokyo to speed work on the treaty produced another round of applause. The tentative U.S. outline for a liberal treaty, and Mr. Dulles' invitation to Japan to join in a mutual defense agreement after signature of a peace treaty, were warmly approved by most of those commenting. A few, however, urged the U.S. to keep in mind the "understandable anxieties" over Japanese rearmament held by some of the non-Communist nations of the Pacific area.[30]

In June 1951 editors welcomed Mr. Dulles' success in bringing about British agreement on the Japanese treaty; but they were inclined to think that a peace treaty could not be put into effect while fighting continued in Korea. A month later they were enthusiastic about the U.S. decision to go ahead with a treaty conference in San Francisco on Sept. 4; and in the meanwhile they hailed the U.S. defense treaty with the Philippines as well as the ANZUS pact with Australia and New Zealand.

Here we may take time out from the Japanese negotiations to emphasize that, at a time when a majority of Americans had been saying for months that it was a "mistake" to enter the Korean war, they nevertheless supported the undertaking of additional defense commitments to: Australia, New Zealand, the Philippines, even the ex-enemy, Japan. Also, support for our NATO commitments, and the defense of Berlin, continued to be expressed by a majority of editors across the country and in polls of the general public. This public attitude was certainly a far cry from the pre-war days of isolationism.

The actual signing of the Japanese treaty stimulated a surge of confidence in the free world's ability to meet and defeat Soviet Russia on the diplomatic battlefield; and there was individual acclaim for Amb. Dulles, Sec. Acheson, and Gen. MacArthur for their roles in bringing the treaty to fruition. Twenty percent of a national sample said they had seen the San Francisco treaty conference on television, and a total of 71% said they had heard or read something about the treaty; 52% called the treaty "good," and only 3% found it "bad." This poll also reported that 67% now supported a Japanese army; and as many as 82% said they would "give Japan the same opportunity to sell her goods in this country that we give to other nations" (12% would not). In a poll at the end of the year (1951) 67% said they thought "we can count on Japan to cooperate with us" (as compared with 78% for England, 62% for France, and 55% for Western Germany).[31]

In October 1951 a Gallup Poll release was headed: Acheson Gains In Popularity Following Jap Treaty Confab. Dr. Gallup called attention to a "sharp change" since the previous winter in popular attitudes about Dean Acheson's acceptability as Secretary of State. In December 1950 respondents had favored the replacement of Mr. Acheson by a margin of 30% to 21%; now the margin was favorable to his staying, 29% to 25%; but among Republicans a plurality still favored his departure (49% to 19%). An N.O.R.C. poll of the same period (#313) also showed popular sentiment in favor of Acheson's retention of office: 47% to 31%. But a somewhat larger number of respondents were willing to answer a question on the Secretary's over-all handling of his office, and they returned a negative plurality: 48% to 35%.

In the early months of the presidential year of 1952 a Gallup Poll reported that a majority of independent voters regarded as a "strong argument" for the Republicans the allegation that "the Democratic Party has let too many Communists get into important positions in Washington." At about the same time N.O.R.C. reported popular sentiment still favorable to Sec. Acheson's retention in office—by a margin of 38% to 32% (which was less support than was registered just after the Japanese peace treaty). In May the trend question on approval/disapproval of the handling of foreign affairs by "government officials" registered the highest approval (43%) since October 1950 (before the massive Chinese entry into Korea).[32]

By March 1952 commentators, distressed by the "talkathon" at Panmunjom, hailed as the one bright spot in the Far East the Senate's ratification of the peace treaty with Japan and the related security pacts. They held that this "act of statesmanship" marked the extension of bipartisan foreign policy to the Far East, and also materially advanced U.S. defense plans covering a vast, vital Pacific area. Editors joined in greeting Japan as an "ally" and member of the "family of free nations;" but they were also aware of Japan's political and economic problems under her restored sovereignty. The need for Japan to export in order to survive was widely recognized by editors; and many seconded Gen. Ridgway's call for "close" Japanese-American cooperation.[33]

The results of Japan's "first free and unsupervised" election in October were most satisfactory to press and radio commentators; and the "ballot-box defeat" of the Communists was hailed as "Communism's worst Asian setback" since the end of World War II. But editors also noted that difficult economic problems lay ahead; and in a poll 77% now said that Japan should have "the same opportunity to sell her goods in this country that we give to other nations."[34]

But in the summer of this presidential year of 1952, when hopes for a Korean peace were at their lowest point, the greatest popular disapproval ever on foreign policy was recorded (61%). The same poll also reported a high figure for the number of respondents saying that "some of the people who work in the State Department are probably not loyal" (71%). The vote on Mr. Acheson's job as Secretary of State was negative: 50% "only fair" or "poor" vs. 32% "good" or "very good." These opinion trends continued through Election Day to the end of the year. In mid-November a majority (55%) still said they "disapproved Pres. Truman's ideas about foreign affairs."

The problems concerning Americans on the United Nations staff of questionable loyalty to the U.S. were publicized by a grand jury report in New York issued after the election, as well as through earlier hearings by House and Senate committees. The grand jury returned no indictments, but editors found its report "highly disturbing" and were inclined to blame the State Department for not preventing the employment by the UN of alleged American subversives. At this time also the Department's suspension from employment of John Carter Vincent provoked divided comment in the press, with some welcoming the Civil Service Loyalty Board's recommendation that Vincent be dismissed, and others expressing concern over the idea that Vincent be "punished without a trial" in order to guard "national security."[35]

Impact of War on Other Policies

The initial impact of the Korean War upon pre-existing policies was to heighten popular apprehension about the Soviet Union, and to increase appreciation of the United Nations in view of its quick moves to stem the North Korean aggression. The war also strengthened public support of the idea of collective security; Americans gave stronger support to NATO and to the provision of economic and military aid to our friends in Europe as well as in Asia.

But the entry into the war of huge numbers of Chinese soldiers greatly modified these original reactions. People exchanged their overwhelming approval of the war for the belief that the war was a "mistake"—unless they were reminded that the battle was undertaken to halt Communist invasion. (And a sizable minority were unshaken by reminders of the Communist threat.) The paucity of help in the war from UN members led to some reduction in appreciation of the United Nations; but there was continued support for NATO, and the foundations were laid in popular approval for ANZUS and SEATO. The public welcomed Japan as an ally and a trading partner. Majority belief in economic and military aid also continued.

Public acceptance of a large-scale U.S. program of economic aid had been established with approval of the Marshall Plan in 1948, and extended in 1949 with the Point Four program of technical assistance. The immediate impact of the Korean War on the majority of Americans—unlike that on former Pres. Hoover—was to increase their approval of measures to defend Western Europe. The largest increases noted were on two polling questions: support for a West German army increased from 40% in June 1950 to 54% in July; and support for U.S. arms aid to Western Europe increased from 62% to 73% in that same time interval. Also, support for "continuation of the Marshall Plan" rose from 56% to 64%; in fact, such approval was maintained throughout the planned life of the program, into 1952; and public support for a substantial U.S. program of economic aid to friendly countries continued for many years.

Meanwhile, editors hailed signature of the Schuman Plan (in April) as the first long step toward European federation, and many were hopeful that this economic union would be followed by steps in the military sphere, including a German contribution to Western defense. At the same time, the McMahon-Ribicoff resolution, which called upon Congress to reaffirm American friendship for the Russian people, was approved by editors and the general public (73% "good idea"). Reports on NATO progress from Gen. Eisenhower, and statements of similar import by Congressmen returning from Europe, gave considerable encouragement to American commentators; and they welcomed plans for a unified European army which would eventually include forces from West Germany.[36]

During the time of the heaviest Chinese military attacks in Korea, support for economic aid to Europe dropped a bit, but such support remained above the majority level (59% in Jan. 1951, 58% in Feb.; it came back to 61% in 1952). In June 1951 U.S. economic aid to "friendly countries" was upheld by 77% of N.O.R.C. respondents, and by 75% in October. When respondents were asked to give the "main reason that some countries have gone Communist since the last war," they stressed the significance of the economic situation. The largest single category said: "bad economic conditions, poverty, hunger" (mentioned by 32% of the total), and an additional 20%

said, "The Communists promised better conditions, better times." In the June 1951 survey, 27% said that, "in case of a war against Russia, we could defeat Russia by ourselves if we had to," but as many as 66% said "we really need the support of our allies in order to defeat her."[37]

As to economic aid for friendly governments "in Asia, to help them develop their countries," 63% of N.O.R.C. respondents gave their support in a poll soon after outbreak of the war (July 1950). In 1951 this figure increased to 71%. Support for Point Four aid was also predominant in press and organization comment. In late 1950 (Nov.) 62% subscribed to the proposition, "It is a good policy for the U.S. to try to help backward countries in the world to raise their standard of living;" in Feb. 1952 this figure had risen to 69%, and by Aug. 1952 it stood at 73% (with 20% agreeing that "some of these funds" should be given through the United Nations, and 16% saying "all" of the U.S. funds should be via the UN).[38]

Military aid to Western Europe was considered worthwhile throughout the months of the Korean War. Sending military supplies, "to strenghen them against any future attack," was backed by a majority vote varying between 64% and 75%. Sending of military supplies to "help those governments in Asia that are threatened by Communism" was also supported during the Korean War, majority approval ranging from 65% in July 1950 to 54% in July 1952.

But when the question was on the amount of aid to be appropriated, the figures were quite different, as has been noted in earlier discussion of foreign aid. N.O.R.C. asked respondents in Oct. 1950 whether, if we had to spend more on military supplies to Western Europe, we should "keep up the amount we are now spending on the Marshall Plan." About a third (32%) said "keep up the amount;" 41% said "cut it down some;" and 14% said "stop it altogether." After ten more months of fighting in Korea (in Apr. 1951), a larger number said they would keep the Marshall Plan amount the same (44%); and a somewhat smaller number (35%) said they would "cut it." Although 6 out of 10 respondents favored aid to "backward" countries, when a Minnesota Poll suggested spending $900 million for this purpose in "Asia, Africa, and Latin America," only 17% gave approval and 64% disapproved.[39]

At the end of 1951 N.O.R.C. asked its respondents how they felt "about the amount of money the U.S. is now spending to help the Western European countries build up their defenses against Communism." A sizable plurality (45%) said "we are spending too much;" 39% said the amount was "about right;" and 6% said it was "not enough" (10% gave no opinion). In March 1952 respondents were told that Pres. Truman was asking an increase in the amount of "aid to other countries" from 7½ billions to 8 billions; 60% promptly said this was "too much," 28% called it "about right," and 2% thought it "not enough" (10% gave no opinion). One month later the "too much" group had declined to 52%, and the "about right" group risen to 32%; but these figures make clear that attitudes toward large total expenditures were quite different from the Feb. 1952 figure of 87% who called it helpful to send economic aid to our allies.

In the summer of 1952, as expenditures for the U.S. military build-up became more and more evident, complaints about the cost of "foreign aid" came from a substantial minority of editors and Congressmen. A number asked: Can the U.S. afford continued aid on such a grand scale? Why doesn't Europe do more on its own? At the end of 1952 Sens. Sparkman and Wiley warned Europeans that their rearmament "slowdown" could invite cuts in American aid to Europe. It has been pointed out earlier that respondents' complaints about spending on foreign aid contributed to their over-all "disapproval" of the handling of foreign policy.[40]

After the 1952 election a Committee headed by Commerce Secretary Sawyer won widespread press approval for its recommendations that economic aid to Europe be reduced and terminated at the earliest practicable date, and that the overseas staffs be reduced and consolidated. Some thought that the report had come "a bit late;" and it was widely hoped that the report would give impetus to the movement for "trade, not aid."[41]

In the field of trade policy, early 1950 moves by the Administration to encourage increased imports to the U.S. from Europe, and the Torquay negotiations for further tariff cuts, drew criticism from some elements of industry and the press (Hearst, McCormick, and Knight papers). The particular object of the attacks on a liberal imports policy was the so-called "slave-labor" imports from the Iron Curtain countries. The most outspoken critics, including some labor union leaders, were from the textile, hat, rubber footwear, and oil industries. However, the general press tended to welcome higher American imports in order to avoid the necessity of continued grants of aid to foreign countries.[42]

When the Korean War started many spoke out against U.S. or allied exports to the Soviet sphere of strategically useful materials. Still, a number felt that Sen. Wherry's (R-Neb) proposal to cut off ERP aid to nations exporting such materials was "too drastic." Also, most commenting editors upheld Pres. Truman's rebuke of longshoremen refusing to handle crabmeat and other imports from Iron-Curtain countries. Popular sentiment against trading with the Soviet Union increased from 60% in 1948 to 74%—with respondents saying it would be "better to stop all trade with Russia" rather than permit the "sale of such things as machinery, in return for such things as minerals we need from them."[43]

At the 1951 hearings on renewal of the RTA, numerous national organizations voiced strong support for renewal (U.S. Chamber of Commerce, Amn. Farm Bureau Fed., CIO), whereas criticism came from the watch, fur, glass, and other industries. Press commentators expressed sharp disappointment when the House passed a renewal bill which included the peril-point, escape-clause, and other weakening amendments. A February poll showed 28% in favor of unilateral tariff cuts, and an additional 39% in favor of reductions on a reciprocal basis (total 67%).[44]

After the 1952 election a poll found 34% saying it would be a "good thing" if we "reduced our tariff on goods that we buy from other countries," and an additional 33% said that the U.S. should reduce its tariffs "providing other countries reduce their tariffs on goods we want to sell them"–total approving reductions, 67%. At the same time, only 22% felt that tariff reductions would help them personally–most of these cited lower prices as a benefit. But 60% felt that some people in the U.S. would be hurt by tariff reductions–50% naming manufacturers and producers, 46% citing workers, 21% businessmen, and 17% farmers. Government aid to those businessmen hurt by lower tariffs was favored by 59%; and 66% favored aid to workers and farmers harmed by lower tariffs. At the end of 1952 a poll showed 71% approving the idea that "the U.S. should reduce its tariffs on goods that other countries want to sell here, providing they reduce their tariffs on goods we want to sell them."[45]

During the seven years following World War II the Democratic Administrations had the satisfaction of seeing Cordell Hull's reciprocal trade principles upheld in the United States and, indeed, incorporated in the international General Agreement on Trade and Tariffs (GATT) adopted by a score of trading nations. These principles won increasing acceptance among American editors and major organizations; but in Congress the protectionists apparently had increasing success in watering down these principles and in raising obstacles to East-West trade. Also, the Administration failed in its postwar objective of establishing an International Trade Organization–to which it had devoted much time and energy–because it had failed to convince the business community and the Congress of its worth.

The 1948 immigration law was extended to the end of 1951; and early in 1952 Congress enacted the McCarran-Walter bills which revised and codified our immigration laws (Immigration and Naturalization Act of 1952). The new law ended the exclusion of Orientals, but it retained the "national origins" basis of our immigration code; and the majority of press commentators called upon Pres. Truman to veto it because of its "racist, restrictionist, and reactionary" features (e.g., N.Y. Times). This attitude was also expressed by influential sections of the labor movement and the churches. In addition, a number of commentators agreed with the Bulletin of Atomic Scientists that the State Department's "excessively rigid and indiscriminate application of the McCarran Act" was hampering the progress of science.[46]

But this latest immigration legislation was upheld by a vocal and sizable minority. "This nation has had its fill," said the Nashville Banner, "of Harry Bridges (plural), Hans and Gerhart Eislers, of Raissa Browders, etc." (similarly, Scripps-Howard papers, McCormick press; DAR, American Legion). Opinion polls also showed popular reluctance to increase immigration, although persons who had escaped from Communist countries were more acceptable than other Europeans. A Gallup Poll of December 1951 examined attitudes toward admitting escapees and, by including in the favorable total those who gave "qualified approval" to their admission, reported a small margin in favor. The significant differences in attitude according to educational background are made clear by these breakdowns.

	National	**College**	**H. School**	**G. School**
Admit escapees (inc. "qualified")	43%	61%	45%	37%
Not admit	40	22	37	48
No opinion	17	17	18	15
	100%	100%	100%	100%

An April 1952 poll, inquiring about admitting "an extra 300,000 Europeans to enter the U.S. and become citizens," encountered opposition from 57%—compared with approval from 36%.[47]

Pres. Truman appointed a commission on immigration which held hearings throughout the country and heard many pleas from organization spokesmen for amendment of the immigration law. Because candidates Eisenhower and Stevenson both favored modification of the existing Act, the matter did not become an election campaign issue. A post-election poll found increased opposition (63%) to admitting "an extra 300,000 Europeans"—but a slight majority (51%) in favor of admitting "people who have escaped from the Communist countries of Eastern Europe." Respondents who disapproved said they were concerned lest the escapees turn out to be Communist spies, or that the U.S. wouldn't have jobs or room for the immigrants.[48]

United Nations (1950–52)

The war's impact on popular sentiment about the UN is of interest. In February 1951, after some criticism of the UN, an N.O.R.C. poll found that 78% wished the U.S. to "continue to belong to the UN" (90% among the college-educated), and only 12% took the position that "we should pull out now." A poll in May found the minority in favor of Atlantic Union (21%) at the same level as had earlier been recorded in favor of a "conference to set up a world government right now." Another minority (also 21%) expressed willingness to give the United Nations power to call out American troops without the specific approval of the U.S. Congress.[49]

In late 1951 Americans backed the U.S. arms limitation proposal in the UN General Assembly, as showing the positive efforts of the Big Three free-world nations to counter the "phony" peace offensive by the Soviets. Although only 43% said they had heard of the U.S. proposal, 70% said "we should agree to limit the size of our armed forces if other countries agree to do the same," and 80% favored letting UN inspectors "go into any country, including the U.S., to see if it was actually keeping down the size of its armed forces."[50]

As a part of the "anti-internationalist" upsurge in 1951, strong critics of the Covenant on Human Rights argued that it would supersede the U.S. Constitution's guarantee of individual liberties (e.g., Sen. Bricker; Hearst press). Because the Human Rights Declaration was one matter on which the Truman Administration did not win legislative support, and one which was not pursued by the succeeding administration, it may be well to glance ahead a couple of years and note the position of Sec. Dulles. He told a Congressional Committee: "We do not . . . look upon a treaty as the means which we would now select as the proper and most effective way to spread throughout the world the goals of human liberty."[51]

In 1952 the vociferousness of UN critics gave rise to considerable fear among friends of the United Nations that American popular support of the UN had been seriously eroded. Concerned citizens in local communities told State Department officials of an upsurge of local attacks upon the UN and UNESCO. In fact, some officers of such eminent organizations as the American Bar Association and the American Legion did engage in sharp attacks; and a number of smaller organizations seemed to be having a greater impact than hitherto with their traditional attacks (e.g., U.S. paying an "unfair" share of UN expenses; UN treaties superseding U.S. constitutional guarantees).[52]

Analysis of editorial opinion at this time did disclose that the few newspapers which were unfriendly to the UN had been more active in recent months; but there had been no appreciable increase in their numbers. Similarly, the national organizations which had actively backed the UN from its inception had maintained, or even increased, their support and educational efforts–although the perception in many quarters was one of rising national hostility to the United Nations. Finally, a June 1952 public opinion poll showed an increase (since Feb. 1951) in the proportion of Americans wanting the U.S. to "continue to belong to the United Nations"–from 78% to 85%– and a decrease in the number wanting to "pull out now," from 12% to 6%. Moreover, this poll disclosed that there had been a modest increase, over the previous year, in the number "satisfied" with UN progress (from 43% to 47%); and only 21% of the national sample said they "had heard or read any criticism against the United Nations during the last few months." (However, a few months later as many as 41% said they had heard criticisms, nearly half of these mentioning the charges that the UN had employed disloyal Americans.)[53]

Altogether this 1952 atmosphere concerning the UN makes an interesting case to put alongside the 1948 activity in behalf of world government. In that earlier case many concerned citizens had the impression that the public was moving pell-mell into an insufficiently considered commitment to world government; but analysis of editorial opinion and of popular opinion disclosed that the sentiment for radical change was confined to a minority (perhaps 20%) of the total public. In 1952 concerned citizens had the impression that the U.S. was moving toward withdrawal from the United Nations; but public opinion analysis made clear that the minority in favor of that course was even smaller (about 6%) than that favorable to world government. Indeed, the general public–sometimes accused of "mercurial" or "sheep-like" behavior–appears to have remained rather steady in its attitude toward international institutions during this time of striking events in the world.

Reference Notes

1. AOR for June 27 and 28, 1950.
2. Tucker in R. E. Osgood and others, *America and the World* (Baltimore, 1970), pp. 43–4.
3. AOR for June and July 3, 1950.
4. AOR for July 1950.
5. AOR for July, Aug. and Sept. 8, 1950.
6. AOR for Sept. 1950.
7. N.O.R.C. polls ##288 and 291.
8. AOR for Sept. 27 and Oct. 31, 1950.
9. AOR of Oct. 24, 1951.
10. AOR for Nov. and Dec. 1950.
11. N.O.R.C. polls ##295 and 300.
12. AOR for Jan. 1951 and Feb. 1952.
13. AOR for Dec. 1950.
14. AOR for Jan. 1951.
15. AOR for Feb. 1951.
16. AOR for Mar. 14, 28 and Apr. 11, 1951.
17. AOR for May 1951.
18. AOR for May and June 1951.

19. AOR for July 1951.
20. *The Gallup Poll*, Vol. II (New York, 1972).
21. Address by Lloyd A. Free before American Association for Public Opinion Research, 1973.
22. AOR for Aug., Sept., Nov., Dec. 1951.
23. AOR for March 1952.
24. AOR for Apr. 1952; N.O.R.C. poll #323.
25. AOR for May and June 1952.
26. AOR for July, Aug., Oct. 1952; Gallup Poll, Sept. 7.
27. N.O.R.C. poll #315.
28. AOR for June 1950; N.O.R.C. poll #288.
29. AOR for Sept. and Dec. 1950.
30. AOR for Dec. 1950 and Jan. 1951.
31. AOR for Sept. and Oct. 1951, Jan. 1952.
32. N.O.R.C. polls ##317 and 325.
33. AOR for April and May 1952.
34. AOR for Oct. and Nov. 1952.
35. N.O.R.C. polls ##329 and 333; AOR for Dec. 1952.
36. AOR for April and July 1951.
37. N.O.R.C. poll #303.
38. AOR for Sept. 20, 1950 and Mar. 6, 1951.
39. Minnesota Poll of Jan. 22, 1951.
40. AOR for July 9 and Dec. 1952.
41. AOR for Dec. 1952.
42. AOR for April and May 1950.
43. AOR for Sept. and Oct. 1950.
44. AOR for Jan. and Feb. 1951.
45. N.O.R.C. polls ##333 and 334.
46. AOR for Oct. and Nov. 17, 1952.
47. Ibid.
48. AOR of Dec. 9, 1952.
49. AOR for Oct. 24 and Nov. 20, 1951.
50. AOR for Nov. 1951; N.O.R.C. poll #314.
51. AOR of Dec. 5, 1951; *State Department Bulletin*, Vol. 28, p. 592; see also Richard P. Stebbins, *U.S. in World Affairs, 1953* (New York, 1954), p. 55.
52. AOR of Jan. 15, 1952.
53. AOR of June 20 and 25, 1952; N.O.R.C. poll #334.

VIII

ENTER EISENHOWER AND DULLES

Even before Pres. Eisenhower was inaugurated it was evident that the public viewed him and his foreign affairs advisers in a profoundly different way than it had viewed their predecessors. A poll taken a fortnight after the 1952 election showed only 30% approving "Pres. Truman's ideas about foreign affairs" (55% disapproved); whereas twice as many (59%) said they approved "Eisenhower's ideas about foreign affairs" as "far as they could tell now." The "appointment of John Foster Dulles to be the next Secretary of State" was also approved by a clear majority (58%). This state of public opinion existed even though press and radio commentators saw little difference between Truman's foreign policy and Gen. Eisenhower's proposals; and the Eisenhower-Stevenson campaign had not been notable for debate on foreign policy.[1]

The shift in attitude toward the Government leaders was evident in opinion about Korea and other Asian areas; it facilitated the later public support for SEATO. Faith in the new Administration increased public approval of the State Department; yet some doubts remained. The Eisenhower Administration took an active interest in Latin America, including Guatemala; and it also invoked the United Nations on significant occasions. Relations with Europe and the Middle East—also very important—form the subject of the following chapter.

Over-all Shift in Attitudes

The contrast in public attitudes toward the outgoing foreign affairs officials and the Eisenhower officials could hardly have been greater. And the new public confidence in government officials persisted for a number of years—with a dip in appreciation after the 1954 Geneva conference on Far Eastern questions, and a new high mark set after the Geneva summit of 1955. There was still a partisan component in polling respondents' judgments on some topics. In the February 1953 poll, for example, those who had voted for Eisenhower gave 83% approval to the officials handling foreign affairs, whereas 63% of Stevenson voters shared that verdict; but this did mean approval of the new administration by a substantial majority of the Democrats as well as the Republicans.

The figures on Sec. Dulles, similarly, stand in marked contrast to those on his predecessor (the "positive" figures include ratings of "good" and "very good;" "negative" includes "only fair" and "poor").

Public Attitudes on Handling of Foreign Affairs by Government Officials

	Approving	Disapproving	No Opinion
Oct. 1952	34%	51%	15%
Feb. 1953	71	14	15
Apr. 1953	72	13	15
July 1953	64	20	16
Sep. 1953	62	21	17
Nov. 1953	57	26	17
Jan. 1954	66	20	14
Apr. 1954	64	21	15
July 1954	56	31	13
Sep. 1954	63	23	14
Oct. 1954	62	26	12
Mar. 1955	65	22	13
May 1955	66	21	13
Aug. 1955	73	21	10
Oct. 1955	74	13	13
Nov. 1955	70	19	11

Public Attitudes toward Secretary of State

	Approving (or positive)	Disapproving (or negative)	No Opinion
Aug. 1952	32%	50%	18%
Apr. 1953	60	4	36
July 1953	57	10	33
Aug. 1953	45	17	38
Sep. 1953	51	8	41
Nov. 1953	49	11	40
Mar. 1954	56	14	30
Apr. 1954	61	7	32
May 1954	57	10	33
July 1954	66	10	24
Sep. 1954	64	8	28
Oct. 1954	66	12	22
Jan. 1955	61	8	31
Mar. 1955	69	10	21
May 1955	66	10	24
June 1955	61	12	27
Aug. 1955	69	6	25
Oct. 1955	68	7	25
Nov. 1955	71	9	20

Pres. Eisenhower's inaugural address and its "strongly international" tone drew a warm and enthusiastic response in newspapers across the nation. "There was strength, but no sword-rattling," said the Cleveland Plain Dealer in a representative commentary. To many Democratic spokesmen the inaugural address was a comforting reaffirmation of the basic principles of past U.S. policy. The trend polling question now found 73% of the general public supporting "an active part for the U.S. in world affairs," one of the highest points registered in the series which began in 1942.[2]

Sec. Dulles' first official address was likewise very favorably received, with some editors saying it heralded a "stiffer attitude" toward our European allies and a new, confident approach to world problems. A few commentators, however, wondered whether the new Administration was over-estimating the power of propaganda and "liberation" to overcome the Communist empire (e.g., Walter Lippmann).

The new Administration's efforts to encourage European unity, and its maintenance of the basic foreign aid program, were approved in public comment. Sen. Lodge's appointment as Ambassador to the United Nations, and his moves to clear up the "subversives" question there were also widely approved, although in Florida (also Dallas and Los Angeles) there were citizen campaigns to withhold all funds from the UN until the "subversives" were fired from the Secretariat.

In a February poll 84% of a nationwide sample said we should continue to belong to the United Nations, while only 10% said we should "pull out now." The same poll showed an increase to 79% in the proportion believing the State Department was "doing all it can to keep disloyal people out"—compared to 56% in the previous October. Indeed, this February poll showed that 10% said they had "more confidence in the State Department than in other government departments in Washington," 76% said they had "about the same" degree of confidence, and only 2% voiced "less confidence in the State Department" than in other Washington departments.[3]

Korea; Indochina; China

Gen. Eisenhower was very widely appreciated as the victorious general in Europe, and as head of the NATO forces; and after his inauguration the press gave top attention to his pledge to visit Korea and try to produce peace there. In late 1952, half of the people (51%) said they felt that the President-elect "can do something" toward getting peace in Korea, while 38% said they thought the war would "go on about the same." Aside from general expressions of confidence, respondents were most inclined to say that Eisenhower would mount a fresh attack destined to succeed (25%), or that he would gain more soldiers from Korea (11%) or from other countries (10%) who could bring the fighting to victory. By the month after Eisenhower's inauguration 78% declared themselves "satisfied" with the way in which the President was "handling the Korean situation." Presented with three alternative courses concerning Korea, 23% of polling respondents advocated "pulling out," but 29% called for "holding the present line," and the largest group (38%) wanted the U.S. to "go ahead and attack the Chinese Communists."[4]

The attack course was urged by Time magazine and the Indianapolis Star, and also by American Legion Commander Lewis Gough. But Lt. Gen. Eichelberger (Ret) was prominent among those opposing new military action (also N.Y. Herald Tribune). Meanwhile, some discussion was accorded the fighting in Indochina, between the French and Ho Chi Minh forces, with Joseph Alsop urging increased aid to the French and Sec. Dulles expressing confidence that Pres. Eisenhower would find ways to end the war there as well as in Korea. The President's "first step" in the Far East was his order to the Seventh Fleet to cease trying to prevent Chinese Nationalist forces from landing on the mainland. This change won editorial approval in discussions considering many possible shifts in Far East policy which could achieve the gradual "disengagement" of Western forces in the area. The Formosa policy was supported in a Gallup "spot-check" by a margin of 65% to 14%; and it was applauded in the press, radio, and Congress.[5]

In March commentators began to think that a Korean truce could be in sight, as Peking indicated possible willingness to compromise the prisoner-of-war issue. Satisfaction with the way the Eisenhower Administration was handling the Korean problem was again registered by a majority of the public and the press. Some partisan difference continued in evaluations of the Korean War: half of the Stevenson voters still felt the war was "worth fighting;" whereas 61% of the Eisenhower voters said it was "not worth" it. On other issues, however, the poll found remarkably little difference in the views of these two political groups.[6]

Increased U.S. aid for the Indochina war was backed by a majority of Americans; they argued that relaxation of the "economic pressure" on France would pay dividends in Western Europe; but the opposing minority feared that increased U.S. aid could make Indochina "another Korea." In April, as many as 67% said either that we should "send more aid to Indochina to help the French and Indochinese armies in their fight against the Communists" (23%), or keep that amount "the same" (44%). In the next month 55% held that "our own air force should take part in the fighting if it looks like the Communists might take over all of Indochina;" but only 33% declared themselves in favor of "sending American troops also."[7]

Signing of the Korean armistice in July was hailed with "relief and thankfulness" that the fighting had ended, and the majority regarded it as a "significant achievement." But observers recognized that the truce was "only the first step" to peace, even in Korea. A major accomplishment was seen in the successful stand against forced repatriation of war prisoners; the Christian Science Monitor and others also saw a "mighty gain" in the fact that UN "battle-readiness" had been demonstrated (e.g., Balt. Sun, St. Louis Post-Dispatch). This conclusion, however, was disputed by the Hearst and McCormick papers; they accepted the "stalemate truce" but could find "little to cheer about." A Minnesota Poll reported its respondents deeply split as to "which side had won the bigger victory in Korea;" 26% said "our side," 26% said "the enemy side," 21% said "neither side," and 25% gave no opinion.[8]

Nevertheless, majorities approved (in an N.O.R.C. poll) U.S. plans to sign a defense treaty with South Korea (51%) and to help in the reconstruction of the war-torn republic (64%). Throughout August the 30-day period for prisoner exchange was watched with anxious concern by press observers; and polling respondents expressed skepticism, by a more than 2-to-1 margin, that the fighting in Korea "was really over." Commentators also were skeptical about the prospects that a UN-sponsored conference would be able to agree on the political status of South Korea. They were divided as to whether an international conference should be an across-the-table meeting of participants seeking to settle the Korean problem, or a round-table session to include such non-belligerents as India and the Soviet Union which would try to settle the whole complex of Far East issues. A considerable number criticized U.S. opposition to the inclusion of India (e.g., Wash. Post, Walter Lippmann), but the UNGA decision not to include India was hailed by others as a "U.S. victory" (N.Y. News; Hearst papers). Meanwhile, the firm U.S. stand against UN consideration of seating Peking was welcomed by commentators; and they approved Sec. Dulles' warning to Red China against aggression in Korea or Indochina, also the "solidarity" displayed at the Washington meeting of ANZUS.

The passage in October of a 3-month period without the convening of the Korean conference produced no particular concern in public comment. The rules established by the Neutral Nations Repatriation Commission for interviewing POWs who didn't wish to be repatriated aroused some initial concern; but it soon became apparent that so few were converted by the Communist "explainers" that this episode was regarded as the Communists' "worst propaganda defeat since the Berlin riots of last June." Commentators applauded the U.S. decision to expose at the UN the Russian-directed efforts to extract germ-warfare confessions from Americans captured in Korea, and also to submit the Army's "shocking" report on Communist atrocities against UN prisoners which editors felt should provide a convincing reason for denying the seating of Peking in the UN. Meanwhile, Japan's decision in favor of a U.S.-assisted modest rearmament program was in harmony with the wishes of press and public.[9]

Pres. Eisenhower's announcement, at the end of 1953, that two U.S. divisions were to be withdrawn from Korea was approved by the great majority of commentators. In January an N.O.R.C. poll asked respondents to name "some of the good things" the Eisenhower Administration had accomplished in foreign affairs during its first year; the largest number mentioning any one topic (48%) said: "They stopped the fighting in Korea." When interviewers asked about foreign policy actions which they did not approve of, over 70% were unable to mention any. Also, half of the respondents reviewing the "world situation" said it was "getting better."[10]

Whereas the situation in Korea had undoubtedly improved, in Indochina there were Vietminh gains prompting some Americans to suggest that U.S. military moves would be necessary if Indochina were to be saved (e.g., Alsop brothers, Sens. Douglas and Sparkman). By April 1954, 52% of polling respondents thought it "likely that American troops will be sent to fight in Indochina within the next year;" and 64% either said we should "do more" to help in Indochina (25%) or should continue on the existing scale (39%). The majority who said our air force "should take part in the fighting if it looks like the Communists might take over all of Indochina" rose to 61%, and the proportion favorable to sending "American troops" in that event rose to 40% (49% said we should not). The McCormick press, however, wanted the U.S. to get out of Indochina altogether; and Wallace's Farmer & Iowa Homestead expressed a preference for a French negotiated settlement over the dispatch of U.S. troops.[11]

Opposition to recognizing the Peking government, opposition to seating Peking in the UN, support for an export embargo—all these positions were maintained by the great majority of press and public. Indeed, the most vocal school of critics protested any indication that the U.S. might "re-examine" any aspect of the current policy hostile toward Communist China; but a number of editors did feel that such a "reexamination" would be prudent—even though few advocated any move toward recognition in the near future.[12]

Geneva Conference; SEATO

Agreement at last on the holding of a conference on Korea was reached at a Big Four meeting in Berlin. The great majority of press comment was favorable; but in Congress there was sharp criticism by some lest a meeting including Communist China become a first step toward U.S. recognition of Peking. Few were optimistic about the prospects of actually reaching agreement on Korea; some saw a better outlook for the added conference topic of Indochina. At this point a poll showed 64% of the general public wanting the U.S. to defend any other country attacked by the Communist Chinese; but only 11% would have the U.S. act "alone;" 50% said we should act only with the United Nations.[13]

Shortly before the Geneva Conference convened (April 26), Vice President Nixon suggested that to prevent a Communist victory in Indochina it might be wise to send American military units there, including some ground troops. In the ensuing discussion, press and Congressional opinion strongly upheld the U.S. decision *not* to send air aid in response to a French plea. "We must be alert to the danger," said the Washington Star, "of rushing to the rescue of people who have little or no heart for fighting their own battle" (similarly, Scripps-Howard papers, Wall St. Journal). Hopes for agreement at Geneva were not high to begin with, and became little better as the conference wore on; commentators saw little indication that the solid Chinese-Russian bloc intended to be "reasonable" on either Korea or Indochina. Pres. Rhee's agreement to nationwide Korean elections under UN supervision was seen as a "clear refutation" of Communist charges of stubborn obstructionism.[14]

Press discussions of the Indochina problem included much favorable comment on Sec. Dulles' proposal for united action to stem the Communist drive in Southeast Asia, and also some irritation at the hesitation of Britain and others to join in such a project. Among the general public, 60% favored "signing an agreement for the defense of Southeast Asia along with such countries as the Philippines, Siam and Australia." Opposition to U.S. military action "alone" was shown by another question reporting 69% in favor of collective military action to "keep the Communists from taking over all of Indochina," but only 21% favoring U.S. military action "if other countries are not willing to join us." Editors were also reassured by Sec. Dulles' speech indicating that the U.S. would not take unilateral action in Indochina, or any military action there without prior approval by Congress, and that the United Nations should give moral sanction to our action.

British-French delay in agreeing to collective action in Southeast Asia prompted the Senate Majority and Minority leaders, Knowland and Johnson, to call for a reappraisal of our foreign policy. They were particularly disturbed by signs that our allies were preparing to bring Communist China into the UN, and they maintained that the U.S. should withdraw from the UN if Peking's representatives were seated. Editors agreed with them in opposing the seating of Peking at that time; but the larger number rejected the idea of a U.S. walkout—thus taking a position in line with polling results among the general public.[15]

The Indochina armistice which marked the close of the Geneva conference was labeled by many—in Congress and out—a "communist victory;" but the majority of commentators were disposed to accept the truce as the lesser of the evils which faced the West in Indochina. Many welcomed Pres. Eisenhower's observation to the effect that it was not our place to be critical of the truce unless we had an alternative to offer; and a number agreed with Rep. Richards who said that something might yet be saved from the "wreck" if a united allied front were established in Southeast Asia. There was relatively little detailed discussion of the truce terms, and U.S. "disassociation" from the armistice agreement was generally upheld; but some regretted even the Geneva presence of Under Secretary Bedell Smith, as others regretted our failure to assert "more leadership" during the Indochina negotiations. At the conclusion of the conference commentators noted two important "lessons" for the free world: 1, We must see to the removal of the last vestiges of colonialism in Southeast Asia; and 2, we must proceed without delay to establish a NATO-like Southeast Asia defense pact.[16]

The post-conference announcement that four of the six U.S. divisions remaining in Korea were to be withdrawn was welcomed by most of those commenting; they added that the withdrawal did not mean "abandonment" of South Korea. After threats from Peking to liberate Formosa, Pres. Eisenhower's "calm but firm" declaration of U.S. intent to protect Formosa against aggression was upheld by editors throughout the country.[17]

News that a conference to consider a Southeast Asia Treaty Organization (SEATO) was scheduled for Manila in September was welcomed by the great majority of commentators; but a minority contended that, instead of pursuing its "passion for grand coalitions," America should be seeking "hard-and-fast arrangements for precise ends" with such anti-Communist nations as Nationalist China, Korea, Philippines, Pakistan and Thailand (e.g., Luce and Scripps-Howard publications).

Signing of the SEATO agreement was highly gratifying to a large segment of the press; these editors welcomed the Manila emphasis on self-determination and economic cooperation, and also the U.S. declaration that it would act immediately only in case of a Communist armed attack in the treaty area. At this time two-thirds of the general public felt that helping Asian countries raise their standard of living would make them "much less likely to go Communist." Indeed, these people thought it "more important" to send these countries "economic aid" than "military supplies." Altogether, the

Manila achievements were deemed a "promising start" on Southeast Asian defense.[18]

How far the U.S. should go in defending the Nationalist Chinese was a question given fresh emphasis in the autumn of 1954 by Peking's shelling of the off-shore islands of Quemoy and counter-measures by Taipei. American editorial views ranged from that of the Dallas News, which felt that capture of Quemoy by the Communists would cause the U.S. great loss of face, to that of the Chicago Sun-Times, which held that Quemoy was not important enough strategically for the U.S. to risk involvement in a mainland war with Communist China. The prevailing trend of opinion seemed to stress the risks of involvement at a point where the U.S. would be "at a distinct disadvantage so close to the Chinese mainland." When the UNGA voted to postpone action on the seating of Peking, this "American victory" was hailed by press and public alike. Indeed, a majority of the public (59%) felt that "we should continue to oppose Communist China in every way we can;" but 26% said we should "try to improve our relations with that country;" and some editors suggested that it was time for the U.S. to state the conditions under which Peking would be acceptable to us in the UN.

The outburst over Quemoy cooled down, and at the end of October those expecting "another Communist attack anywhere in the world" diminished to 21% (compared with 43% in September). But in November Peking's sentencing to prison on espionage charges of 13 U.S. aviators downed during the Korean war was unanimously denounced as "outrageous" by American commentators–some calling for the use of U.S. force to rescue the captives. But a number of other commentators welcomed reports that Pres. Eisenhower had (in September) vetoed a Joint Chiefs of Staff recommendation that the U.S. bomb the Chinese mainland in order to prevent a Red capture of the Quemoys (e.g., C. S. Monitor, Watertown Times).[19]

As 1954 drew to a close, commentators took satisfaction in the absence of any large-scale fighting in the Far East; but they agreed that Asia was still "troubled," and that Red China remained a "threat." Only 5% in an N.O.R.C. poll favored recognition of Peking. But evidently the general public gave only limited attention to "saving" Southeast Asia; only 1 out of 3 Americans claimed to have heard of "the recently signed Southeast Asia Defense Treaty." Still, the principle of U.S. participation in such a defense treaty was approved by 76%–a higher proportion then ever previously recorded.[20]

With this SEATO treaty the U.S. expanded to their furthest extent its defense commitments to other nations–now embracing Latin America, Western Europe, and much of Asia. This expansion, which laid a basis for the subsequent involvement in Indochina, was supported both in editorial comment and in popular opinion polls at a time when a majority of Americans said that the Korean war had been a "mistake." Despite that war's costs and frustrations, a majority of the public evidently felt that it would be worthwhile for this nation to extend its pledges of defense against Communist aggression. It is true that the American public much preferred to have other countries join us in the military measures we might undertake against an aggressor, but the public gave its approval to the SEATO treaty despite its disappointment over the failure of other United Nations forces to play a major military role in Korea.

Presentation to the Senate in early 1955 of the defense treaty with Nationalist China and of the Manila Pact occasioned fresh support for these documents in editorial opinion, and popular approval was sustained. Several editors welcomed the "understandings" incorporated in the Foreign Relations Committee's report which were interpreted to mean: no commitment to defend Quemoy, and no affirmation that Chiang had sovereignty over Formosa. When Sec. Dulles, in a speech before the Foreign Policy Association, stated that the U.S. would defend Quemoy and Matsu if they were attacked as a part of an attack upon Formosa, the greater number of commentators said he had engaged in "as much candor as the circumstances seem to permit." Some, however, warned that the "flexible" American policy was a "hazardous game" which could bring war by "miscalculation" (e.g., N.Y. Mirror, Hanson Baldwin, Indianapolis Star). Others continued to argue for and against a public declaration that the U.S. would defend the islands "at whatever cost."[21]

Release by Peking of four U.S. airmen at the end of May prompted both "rejoicing" and "wariness." The joy was alloyed by the thought that some Americans were still in Chinese prisons, and editors cautioned against "undue optimism" regarding any "real change" in Peking policy. Meanwhile, commentators took satisfaction from the continuing "de facto cease-fire" around Formosa. However, the calls from Mr. Justice Douglas and others for the seating of Peking in the UN were matched by expressions of strong opposition by Sens. Thurmond and Knowland; and the Gallup Poll showed 67% still opposed to Communist China—although this degree of opposition was less than the 79% in August of 1954.[22]

The Administration's decision to hold talks with Communist China at the ambassadorial level (which got under way at Geneva on Aug. 1 between Ambassadors Johnson and Wang) were supported by both press and public. Peking's announcement that the U.S. flyers would be released encouraged some commentators to hope for an atmosphere so improved that the talks could go beyond the immediate problem of obtaining the release of 41 U.S. civilians still held in Red China. But a number maintained that Peking's "good faith still takes a great deal of proving."

Announcement then of Peking's decision to release all the American civilian captives set off general rejocing and many tributes to Amb. Johnson for his "skillful" handling of a "vexatious assignment." Still, most of those commenting felt that the Chinese deserved no reward for "belatedly righting a grave wrong;" but they did approve our "discussing other practical matters" with the Chinese. A few favored an early conference between Sec. Dulles and Chou En-lai (e.g., Wash. Star, St. Louis Post-Dispatch).[23]

The UNGA vote postponing for another year any action on seating Peking elicited hearty and unanimous approval in public comment; but the Washington Post called attention to the growing opposition in the UN on this issue and suggested that the U.S. make a "thorough exploration" of the questions involved in seating Peking. Gallup reported that 71% of his interviewees were opposed to a seat for Peking, although the pro-Peking minority had risen to 17% (8% in 1954, 10% in June 1955). At the same time an N.O.R.C. poll reported that 55% favored U.S. trade with Communist China "if this trade does not include war materials" (39% were opposed to limited trade).

Respecting Indochina, commentators welcomed Pres. Diem's victory over Bao Dai and said it vindicated America's decision to aid his government. Some warned, however, that Diem "must convert his country into a real democracy if he wants it to resist the pseudo-democracy of the Reds" (Boston Herald). The need for continuing U.S. economic and military aid was stressed by the Kansas City Star.[24]

State Department (1953–55)

The advent of a Republican Administration seemed to do nothing to diminish Sen. Joseph McCarthy's concern about the loyalty of U.S. civil servants. A poll taken in Feb. 1953 did show a large increase in the proportion of people saying the "State Department is now doing all it can to keep disloyal people out of the Department"—a rise from 51% in Sept. 1952 to 79%. In July this figure became 80%.[25]

But the continuing assertions by Sen. McCarthy's Government Operations subcommittee sparked press reports of "negligent filing methods" in the Department and some angry editorials. A Washington Times-Herald editorial asserted: "The evidence which Sen. McCarthy is bringing forth indicates that the Reds and the perverts ruled the roost, and that honest people who protested did so at the danger of destruction of their careers." The Wall St. Journal wanted to see "this investigation go right ahead." Some, however, felt that the Department's new administration would remedy the situation (e.g., N.Y. Herald Tribune).[26] A May N.O.R.C. poll reported that a majority of the general public (55%) deemed it more important to "find out all the Communists in America, even if some innocent people are accused," than to protect "people who might be innocent, even if some Communists are not found out."

Sec. Dulles' decision, clearing John Carter Vincent of charges concerning his loyalty, yet accepting his retirement from the Foreign Service, was received favorably by most press and radio commentators. Some earlier editorials on the Vincent case had asserted that "it has been a deliberate policy" of the Department "to cover up past mistakes and to protect those who made them" (e.g., Cleve. Plain Dealer, Gannett papers). The Phoenix Republic was one of the papers saying the Department's "continuing defense" of Vincent illustrated its "weakness in dealing with world-wide communism." After Vincent's retirement, critics of the Secretary's decision warned that it could curb "objective diplomatic reporting." Marquis Childs concluded that Dulles "handled the Vincent case in as humane a manner as possible, but with a little more candor Dulles might have said that Vincent's usefulness was ended not by his own acts but by the attacks directed against him by Sen. McCarthy and others."[27]

When Sen. Mundt (R-SD) called for removal of "remnants of the old Acheson team" from policy-making posts in the State Department, several editors warned that such Congressional pressures could have a "crippling" effect on the Foreign Service. Sec. Dulles' "vigorous tribute" to the Foreign Service in a public address was welcomed by editors as a boost to Department morale (e.g., Chi. Sun-Times, Wash. Post). Later several sources denounced Sen. Mundt's statement that he arranged to have $8 million for the Oaho Dam in South Dakota included in the budget by subtracting a like amount from funds for State Department personnel (e.g., Marquis Childs, Raleigh News & Observer).[28]

The pattern of popular opinion about Sen. McCarthy and his activities was well brought out in a Gallup Poll (released June 23, 1953), which permitted respondents to indicate their sentiments by offering five degrees of approval and five degrees of disapproval. The following table also gives, for comparative purposes, the popular judgments of Sec. Dulles and Pres. Eisenhower. Dr. Gallup pointed out that "the number of voters expressing extreme disapproval of the Wisconsin senator outnumber, by a margin of about 3-to-2, those expressing great enthusiasm." In the cases of Messrs. Eisenhower and Dulles the table showed heavy emphasis on extreme approval. One-third of the public gave "no opinion" on either McCarthy or Dulles; but the total approval-disapproval score was much more favorable to Sec. Dulles (62% to 6%) than to the Senator (35% to 30%). Strong-

Popular Approval/Disapproval of 3 Public Figures

Value	McCarthy	Dulles	Eisenhower
+ 5	6%	15%	57%
+ 4	4	11	11
+ 3	9	16	13
+ 2	6	10	3
+ 1	10	10	5
– 1	7	2	3
– 2	4	1	*
– 3	3	1	*
– 4	2	1	*
– 5	14	1	1
No opinion	35	32	5
	100%	100%	100%

*–less than 1%.

est disapproval of McCarthy was registered by college-educated respondents, "whose dislike of the Senator exceeded their enthusiasm by more than 4-to-1," Dr. Gallup added.

Alongside this evident popular appreciation of the Secretary of State it is interesting to note the way opinion divided among newspapers and other commentators. According to a Public Studies Division report (Aug. 5, 1953), a sizable majority of newspapers, 52 out of 81, were either noncommittal (non-critical) or upheld the Administration and its foreign policy. Eight additional papers supported U.S. foreign policy, but were critical of the Department's conduct of it (e.g., Wash. Post, St. Louis Post-Dispatch). The 21 papers which were critical both of U.S. policy and the Department included newspapers from three prominent chains (McCormick, Scripps-Howard, Hearst).

Out of 44 syndicated columnists, 29 were more or less sympathetic to the Administration and its foreign policy; 12 tended to be critical of both (e.g., David Lawrence, Fulton Lewis, Jr. of MBS); and 3 were critical of the Department but not of policy (e.g., Marquis Childs, Thomas Stokes). Out of 39 radio programs, 28 were neutral or sympathetic, 6 criticized both policy and Department, while 5 focused their criticism on the Department (e.g., Elmer Davis, Edward Murrow).

The Department's announcement in the autumn that, as a result of its security measures, 306 American employees and 178 foreign employees had been dismissed drew praise in some quarters (e.g., Memphis Commercial Appeal, Houston Post). However, other longtime critics of Department personnel contended that hold-over employees had "foisted their own plans and schemes onto their busy superiors" (Sen. Martin (R-Iowa; Human Events).

In 1954 charges were still being seen in the press to the effect that the State Department was harboring many "discredited" holdovers from the Acheson-Truman days. At this point, however, five prominent retired diplomats (Messrs. Armour, Bliss, Grew, Phillips, and Shaw) published a letter calling attention to the "sinister results" of recent "flimsy" attacks on Foreign Service personnel. A majority of those commenting in the press and on the radio concluded that strengthening the morale of Departmental and Foreign Service personnel had become a major problem; they accordingly welcomed announcement of a new commission to survey personnel conditions.[29]

The Wriston Committee's report in June was warmly received, as inspiring "new hope" among the personnel. Specific editorial approval was accorded the scholarship plan facilitating advanced training, the idea of integrating the Department and Foreign Service personnel, and the Committee's feeling that U.S. representatives abroad should be allowed to report the facts as they saw them, without being attacked because their recommendations did not reflect the point of view of partisans at home. Still, said the New York Times, "no reorganization or expansion plan can boost morale overnight within the beaten and battered State Department."[30]

Dismissal of John Paton Davies from the Foreign Service (Nov. 5, 1954) was the occasion of heavy and sharply divided press comment, with the weight of sentiment critical of the dismissal. Those approving or accepting the dismissal included the Scripps-Howard and Hearst chains, the New York Herald Tribune, and David Lawrence. Many of these commentators had for some time been concerned that "security risks" were still active in the government, or stressed that Davies had been given a "fair" hearing. Criticism of the dismissal was voiced by several large-city dailies and nationally syndicated columnists (e.g., Des Moines Register, the Alsops). C. L. Sulzberger said: "The thought of 'trying' American diplomats for past opinions or wrong guesses is abhorrent" (in N.Y. Times). Fearing that the Davies decision would "seriously damage the effectiveness" of the Foreign Service, several editors renewed their call for a high-level commission to study the "whole question of loyalty and security in government."[31]

A study of polling results in early 1955 demonstrated that there were few differences on foreign policy which could be associated with the respondent's attitude toward Sen. McCarthy. In other words, the line dividing people on the McCarthy issue did not appear to be parallel to any line dividing Americans on foreign policy—as far as could be ascertained on the basis of examining attitudes on a score of foreign policy issues. Those who thought "favorably" of

McCarthy were somewhat more approving (75%) of the general handling of foreign affairs than were those who thought "unfavorably" of him (65%). The pro-McCarthy respondents seemed slightly more favorable to the idea of "defending Formosa alone if necessary" (59%) than were those in the anti-McCarthy group (57%). The "antis" were somewhat more favorable than the "pros" toward "help to Latin America for education and health" (87% vs. 83%). In short, Sen. McCarthy was not receiving the support of a group of Americans who were "against" U.S. policy or otherwise shared a foreign-policy outlook.[32]

A May 1955 poll included several questions on "the Foreign Service of the U.S." These questions indicated that the number of people correctly informed about the Foreign Service (20%) had not increased since a comparable poll in 1946; but popular estimates of the job being done by "our ambassadors and consuls" had improved: rising from 40% "good job" and 13% "fair job" in 1946 to 51% "good job" and 20% "fair job." Respondents candidly said they took less interest in the Foreign Service than in several other foreign policy subjects as indicated below.

	Great Deal of Interest	**No Interest**
H-bomb tests	47%	11%
Formosa situation	32	23
Central and South America	23	35
United Nations organization	21	20
Work of Foreign Service	11	38

As an aid to placing in perspective popular knowledge about the Foreign Service, here are some other polling findings of about the same time:

53% said they had heard of the North Atlantic Treaty Organization
36% could tell what was meant by "the electoral college"
20% identified the Foreign Service correctly
10% knew that Quemoy and Matsu were near mainland and under Nationalist control
6% could state the purpose of the proposed Bricker Amendment.

United Nations (1953-56)

Pres. Eisenhower's appointment of Henry Cabot Lodge to be U.S. Ambassador to the UN was welcomed by press and public; and it was received as evidence that the Eisenhower Administration considered the UN important. Elmo Roper pointed out that Lodge was well and favorably known to the public, with nearly 6 out of 10 persons aware of him, and these 5-to-1 in considering the appointment a good one. Lodge moved swiftly to clear up the question of the loyalty of Americans employed by the UN; but his successful efforts did not inspire as much editorial discussion as had the presence on the UN staff of questionable Americans. Awareness of this situation had contributed greatly to the increase in criticism of the UN which was reported in January 1953 by N.O.R.C., when 41% said they had heard criticism (compared with 21% in June 1952). By February 71% in an N.O.R.C. poll said they felt that the U.S. was "now doing all it should" to take care of this problem. When respondents were asked if they thought that the UN was "in any way dangerous to U.S. interests," only 15% said Yes; 73% said No (12% gave no opinion).[33]

The Bricker amendment proposal was reintroduced into the Senate in 1953, with the sponsors including some Senators not previously regarded as hostile to the UN. Backers also included the McCormick press, the D.A.R., and some American Bar Association leaders. They felt an amendment to the U.S. Constitution was necessary to protect the rights of American citizens against UN-sponsored treaties. Opponents of the amendment felt it was not needed, and that an amendment might tie the hands of the Government and hamper its capacity to act expeditiously (e.g., N.Y. Herald Tribune, Wash. Post). Sec. Dulles opposed the amendment in an April 6 statement before the Senate Committee; and other Administration statements also tended to stimulate increased opposition to the amendment in the press. The bulk of press comment now either opposed the amendment or advocated further study. Opposition to the amendment came also from religious leaders, labor leaders, and Negro spokesmen who saw a danger in restricting the Executive's control of foreign policy at this "critical stage" of world affairs. Some commentators deplored the Administration's jettisoning of the Human Rights and related conventions. Amendment supporters remained undaunted (e.g., N.Y. News; women's patriotic organizations).[34]

As the attacks against the United Nations continued, a number of its supporters expressed concern. Such a strong proponent as Norman Cousins wrote in United Nations World that "most Americans are losing confidence in the UN as an adequate and effective force in maintaining peace in the world." Actually, over against the bitter attacks by a busy little minority, and the lukewarm attitude of many Americans toward the UN, there was the continuance of impressive support for the world organization–not least from the national organizations whose activities have already been referred to.

A Senate declaration against seating Peking in the UN reflected majority opinion in the press and radio; but efforts to cut off all U.S. contributions to the UN if Peking were seated did not receive majority support in the Senate or outside. A Gallup Poll found 60% disapproving a UN seat for Communist China; but only 19% said the U.S. should withdraw from the world organization if Peking were seated.[35]

Sec. Dulles' address to the UNGA (Sept. 17, 1953) was well received as making clear this country's willingness to explore the road to peace if the Russians would give some evidence of sincerity. While sharp criticism of the UN continued from some quarters, many editors called it "the world's best hope for peace." An October poll reported that a majority of Americans (58%) believed that the UN was "not powerful enough" to fulfill its goals. An opinion report of the same month noted that "the noise and intensity of the attacks (on the UN) have sometimes caused citizens to have unfounded doubts about the extent and depth of popular support for the UN. "The actual strength and persistence of public support, and the logic of events, have more than sufficed to contain the dissatisfactions and hostilities stirred up by the attacks."[36]

Following the UN decision to take action against the aggression in Korea, American pluralities continued to declare themselves "satisfied" with the UN, even though Americans also wished that the other UN members would take greater part in the burden of the fighting; and "satisfaction" continued to be predominant after the Korean armistice (49% to 36%).

A Roper Poll inquiring into basic attitudes reported (Dec. 1953) that only 9% of a national sample wanted the U.S. to adopt an isolationist policy and pull out of its international arrangements, whereas a majority (52%) were in favor of a stronger international organization. A Texas Poll, however, reported that sentiment for actual world government had diminished since 1950, from 33% to 23%.

A number of newspapers which had long been severely critical of the UN were now outspoken in their demand for the Bricker amendment; the Wheeling Intelligencer called it "the most important step proposed since the Bill of Rights to safeguard the American citizen." But a larger number of papers were opposed to Sen. Bricker's formulation, calling it unnecessary and likely to paralyze conduct of foreign relations by the Executive Branch. Many of these papers were against any amendment, hammering away in almost daily editorials (e.g., Boston Herald, N.Y. Times, Wash. Post). Some others would have accepted a compromise amendment (e.g., Scripps-Howard); but no wording proved to be acceptable to two-thirds of the Senate. Of the general public only a small proportion were informed about the amendment; the Gallup Poll found 13% with some knowledge of it. Four percent favored it; 7% opposed it, 2% gave no opinion.[37]

Throughout 1954 polls and editorials maintained their strongly negative attitude on seating Peking in the UN; but a number of papers agreed with the Des Moines Register when it said that the U.S. should make clear that it is not irrevocably committed to its stand on China, and make clear what Chinese actions are necessary to change the U.S. position (e.g., Milwaukee Journal, Wash. Post).[38]

The 10th anniversary of the United Nations and the commemorative session at San Francisco prompted considerable comment evaluating the 10-year record. The judgment most often repeated was that the UN had failed to live up to expectations, but it had been worthwhile. If the UN "has been less than it might have been," said the Fort Worth Star-Telegram in a representative commentary, "it has been more than many thought it ever could be." Editors applauded Pres. Eisenhower's address as expressing the desire and will of the American people for peace, and their support of the UN.[39] A nationwide poll at this time (1955) found that sentiment for continued U.S. membership in the UN stood at the highest level (88%) registered over the preceding five years; and sentiment for "pulling out" (5%) was at its lowest. College-educated respondents were 97% in favor of continued UN membership; those with high-school training 91% favorable; and the grammar-school group favored it 80% to 8%. Moreover, "satisfaction" was at its highest figure ever–74% were "satisfied with the progress that the United Nations organization has made so far."

The admission of 16 new members to the UN was welcomed by many as an approach toward universality of UN membership, which would "strengthen its right to speak as a world organization" (Phila. Bulletin). While welcoming the "package deal" on the admission of new members, some others criticized the U.S. for not accepting the deal which would have admitted Japan along with Outer Mongolia, whose candidacy was opposed by the U.S. A poll in April 1956 registered continuation of the high proportions which in 1955 had favored continued U.S. membership and "satisfication" with UN progress.[40]

Latin America (1953–56)

Pres. Eisenhower's Pan-American Day address in 1953 was widely acclaimed by American editors, some of whom referred to the "neglect" of Latin America by the previous administration. Also, editorial praise was virtually unanimous for the President's announcement that his brother, Dr. Milton Eisenhower, would lead a "fact-finding" team to report on economic and social conditions in Latin America in an effort to strengthen inter-American cooperation. The strongest recommendations resulting from the "fact-finding" tour were in the economic field—the suggestions for continued U.S. aid and increased trade and private investment, plus liberal U.S. policies on tariffs, technical assistance, and development loans. Many editors deemed it essential that the Administration implement the report's recommendations. Editors also welcomed the report's "timely alert" to Latin American Communist activities, although some regretted that it did not include similar references to "fascism and militarism" in the hemisphere (e.g., C. S. Monitor, N.Y. Times). Bitterest criticism of the report came from the Washington Times-Herald which called it another appeal for the "give-away" of U.S. funds "in all directions."[41]

When the U.S. delegates took off for the Tenth Inter-American Conference (1954) in Caracas, predictions were that the Latin countries would fail in their hopes for helpful economic aid, and that the U.S. would fail in its effort to obtain a strong resolution against the penetration of Communism into the hemisphere. Guatemala's expulsion of two American newsmen on the eve of the Caracas meeting, and the Arbenz government's charges that the U.S. was part of a conspiracy to invade Guatemala, contributed to demands for a strong U.S. stand at Caracas against "the growing menace of communism in the Americas" (e.g., Sen. Smathers, D-Fla; Rep. Jackson, R-Cal).

The inability of the U.S. Administration to reach clear decisions on its own economic stands, which prevented agreement at Caracas, was regretted by commentators; but they accepted the Caracas decision to hold a special conference of finance ministers later. Sec. Dulles' "sterling diplomatic performance" in securing a resolution opposed to Communist infiltration of the hemisphere won wide editorial appreciation. Most observers approved the U.S. delegation's "diplomatic" avoidance of any clash with Guatemala, and regarded the conference resolution as "isolating" the Arbenz regime and converting the Monroe Doctrine into an "effective modern instrument" against the menace of "international Communism." The resolution was a "striking victory for freedom and self-government in this part of the world," said the Washington Post.[42]

Disclosure in May of a shipment of arms to Guatemala from Communist sources in Eastern Europe was thought by editors across the country to deserve the gravity with which it was viewed in Washington. The dominant reaction was that such an arms shipment affected all the Americas, and required joint hemispheric consideration; editors welcomed Sec. Dulles' revelation that the American republics had been asked to study the situation. Many commentators felt that the arms shipment proved that Guatemala was "the beachhead" for

Communist designs in the Western Hemisphere, some adding their emphasis on the danger to the Panama Canal of a "Communist-armed-and-dominated Guatemala." Doubts that any significant action would result from invoking the Caracas resolution were expressed by some who recalled past Latin American reluctance to "publicly scold" a fellow republic (e.g., Des Moines Register, Richmond Times-Dispatch).[43]

Overthrow of the Arbenz regime in May was welcomed by U.S. commentators who expressed hope that a cease-fire in the civil war would lead to a stable Guatemala government in the "good neighbor" tradition. Many added with satisfaction that the successive displacements of the Arbenz and Diaz regimes constituted "a complete rout of the Communists." In a representative comment, the Philadelphia Bulletin said that "any direct action (by the U.S.) is likely to be interpreted in other parts of the world as an exercise of imperialistic ambitions." A few editors held that any U.S. action would be justifiable which would safeguard "the long-range welfare of the U.S." (Hearst papers). Some others declared that it was "beyond doubt that the counter-revolutionary regime could not have had airplanes without our connivance, if not assistance" (N.Y. Mirror; similarly Prov. Journal, Eric Sevareid). According to Sevareid, no American government could "sit idly by and watch a piece of real estate that close to the Panama Canal become a Communist base of operations." A number praised Amb. Peurifoy for his "key role . . . in bringing about the resignation of Arbenz."[44]

The aim of the Soviet Union to keep a hand in the affairs of the Americas was thought to be highlighted by its UN veto of a motion to refer the Guatemala case to the OAS rather than to the UN Security Council (e.g., N.Y. Times, Chi. Sun-Times). Amb. Lodge's admonition to the Soviets to stay out of the hemisphere was applauded (e.g., Phila. Bulletin, Houston Chronicle). Similarly, wide support was given in the press to Sen. Lyndon Johnson's resolution declaring U.S. determination to prevent interference by Soviet Communists in hemisphere affairs and to insure OAS action to that end. Several, however, thought that among the "lessons" of Guatemala for the U.S. was to recognize a greater need to undertake Point Four and economic aid in Latin America.

A majority (55%) approved of "the way our government has dealt with the trouble in Guatemala" in an early July opinion poll, but the unusually high proportion of 40% gave no opinion (5% disapproved). Among the college-educated, 72% approved and 6% disapproved. When respondents were asked whether "there's any real danger that any of the countries in South America will go Communist in the next few years," 43% thought there was, and 33% thought not (24% gave no opinion). Asked to suppose that "some country in

South or Central America does set up a Communist government," 65% said that in that case they would "favor trying to get them out, even if we have to use armed force;" 26% were opposed. A further question to the 65% found that 31% said "we should use armed force only if other American republics join us," but 30% felt "we should go ahead on our own" (4% gave no opinion on this follow-up question).[45]

When the Armas government of Guatemala issued its "democratic and progressive" program, its recognition by the U.S. was approved by virtually all commenting editors. Several noted that the U.S. had "had a firm and friendly hand in the establishment of the new government," and maintained that the U.S. therefore had a "special obligation" to use this step of recognition to spread more friendly relations throughout Latin America. A few, however, were dismayed that the Armas government had "suspended" the land reform legislation (e.g., St. Louis Post-Dispatch).

Convening of the Rio Conference on Inter-American Economic Affairs in November 1954 occasioned considerable press approval of Treasury Secretary Humphrey's promise of expanded Export-Import Bank loans to the Latin American countries, and further reduction of trade barriers, as well as participation in a new International Finance Corporation to provide investment funds. Pres. Eisenhower's concept of the "good partner" as successor to the "good neighbor" won editorial approval (e.g., San Francisco Chronicle). According to the Atlanta Constitution, the Rio program was, "for effectiveness and public relations purposes, the best thing to come out of Washington" since the Point Four program.[46]

U.S. efforts to "improve education and health" in Latin America were favored by an overwhelming majority (82%) of Americans, according to a poll at the end of 1954. Willingness to help Latin American countries build up their industries was also noteworthy (66%); but when offered a choice most respondents wanted to have our government "encourage American businessmen to take care of this," rather than lend money to the Latin American countries for this purpose. The more education a respondent had, the more willing he was for the U.S. to help, and to spend money in helping, the Latin American countries.[47]

At the beginning of 1955 editors welcomed the ending of the brief hostilities between Nicaragua and Costa Rica. From the time of Costa Rica's first complaint of Nicaraguan "aggression," editors urged that the U.S. act only through the OAS. Some organizations (CIO, ADA) did call for direct U.S. military aid to Costa Rica to prevent a coup before the OAS would be in a position to restore peace; but most observers advised that the U.S. "adhere to the conventional cooperative procedures that we helped establish." Afterward, most editors were pleased that the "State Department eschewed" unilateral action; they praised the role of both the U.S. and the OAS. Strong editorial support was given to the sale of U.S. planes to Costa Rica under OAS sanction–the "first military application" of the Rio pact.[48]

With 41% saying in a December poll that the U.S. was "not giving enough attention to the problems of South and Central America," commentators welcomed announcement of Vice President Nixon's goodwill tour in early 1955 of Mexico, Central America, and the Caribbean area. Editors praised Nixon for doing the U.S. "a heap of good" in the area, and said that he should give Washington a "better understanding of Central American problems." Marquis Childs called Nixon a "remarkably effective ambassador of goodwill;" but some felt it would take "far more than goodwill tours to convince these people we are really interested in their welfare" (Kansas City Times).[49]

Early in 1956 Soviet offers to the Latin American nations of technical assistance and manufactured products in exchange for surplus agricultural products were discussed by the American press with mixed emotions. Some dismissed the Kremlin's propositions as not promising enough to be taken seriously in this hemisphere (e.g., Time, Balt. Sun); but others, in alarm, cited Guatemala as a case of what could happen with closer ties to the Communists (e.g., San Diego Union, Detroit News). Some concluded that it was time for the United States itself to offer a sustained program of assistance (e.g., N.Y. Herald Tribune).[50]

During Pres. Eisenhower's first administration the public gave more attention to relations with Latin America than it had done since its approval of the Rio Pact. The idea of extending U.S. economic aid to nations in the area won approval which was expressed from time to time during the four-year period. Of keener public interest, however, was the possibility of Communist expansion into the New World, which was seen in the importation of Communist arms by the leftist government of Guatemala. In 1954 the American public was seemingly unanimous in hailing the demise of that government, and only a few editors discussed the actual U.S. role in the change of governments there. Certainly there was no hint that twenty years later–after Viet-Nam and Watergate–a majority of American editors would voice disapproval of the idea that the U.S. should engage in efforts to overthrow governments in foreign countries.[51]

Conclusion

The initial welcome for the Eisenhower-Dulles administration of foreign affairs was heightened by its termination of the Korean War, its establishment of SEATO, its recourse to the United Nations, and its encouragement of the ousting of left-wing control in Guatemala. The change from Democratic to Republican administration had meant no diminution in America's activist role in the world; the shift from pre-war isolationism effectuated under Roosevelt and Truman was maintained. Indeed, America's active role in the defense of free world countries was expanded in both Asia and Latin America.

Public approval of foreign policy was as notable at the end of Eisenhower's first term as it was at its beginning, partly because of developments in relations with Europe and the Middle East which are examined in the following chapter.

Reference Notes

1. N.O.R.C. poll #333.
2. N.O.R.C. poll #337; AOR for Jan. 1953.
3. N.O.R.C. poll #337; AOR for Feb. 1953.
4. N.O.R.C. polls ##334 and 337; AOR for Jan. 1953.
5. AOR for Jan. and Feb. 1953.
6. AOR for Mar. 1953.
7. N.O.R.C. polls ##339 and 340; AOR for Apr. and May 1953.
8. AOR for July 1953.
9. AOR for Oct. 1953.
10. AOR for Dec. 1952 and Feb. 1954.
11. AOR for Jan. 1954; N.O.R.C. poll #335.
12. AOR of Feb. 12, 1954.
13. AOR for Feb. 1954.
14. AOR for April and May 1954.
15. AOR for June 1954; N.O.R.C. poll #353.
16. AOR for July and July 21 and 28, 1954.
17. AOR for Aug. 1954.
18. AOR for Sept. 1954.
19. AOR for Oct. and Nov. 1954.
20. AOR for Dec. 1954.
21. AOR for Jan., Feb., Mar. 1955.
22. AOR for June 1 and July 1, 1955.
23. AOR for Sept. 2 and Oct. 5, 1955.
24. AOR for Nov. 1, 1955.
25. AOR for Mar. 12 and Aug. 2, 1953.
26. AOR of Feb. 12, 1953.
27. AOR for Jan. 5 and 23, March, and Mar. 11, 1953.
28. AOR for May 6 and July 27, 1953.
29. AOR for Feb. 1954.
30. AOR for June 1954.
31. AOR for Nov. 1954.
32. AOR of Jan. 13, 1955.
33. AOR for Jan. and Feb. 1953.
34. AOR for April and May 29, 1953.
35. AOR for June and June 17, 1953.
36. AOR for Oct. and Oct. 15, 1953.
37. AOR for Jan. and Feb. 1954.

38. AOR of Oct. 21, 1954.
39. AOR for July 31 and Aug. 26, 1955.
40. AOR of Jan. and June 1956.
41. AOR for Apr. and Nov. 1953.
42. AOR for Feb., Mar., and Apr. 16, 1954.
43. AOR for May 1954.
44. AOR for June 1954.
45. AOR of July 21, 1954.
46. AOR for Nov. and Dec. 22, 1954.
47. AOR of Feb. 15, 1955.
48. AOR for Jan. 1955.
49. AOR for Feb. 1955.
50. AOR for Feb. 1956.
51. AOR for Oct. 1974.

IX

EUROPE; MIDDLE EAST (1950–1956)

Eleven days before Pres. Eisenhower was inaugurated the Gallup Poll reported that 69% of the public were in favor of an Eisenhower-Stalin meeting. For years a majority of Americans had favored a Truman-Stalin meeting (57% in 1952), even though only one quarter thought that the two leaders could "reach a satisfactory agreement;" even fewer thought "we could count on Russia to live up to that agreement" (11% in 1952).[1]

The death of Stalin was announced in Moscow a few weeks after the Eisenhower inaugural; and Georgi Malenkov, head of the triumvirate which succeeded Stalin, issued some statements conciliatory toward the West. Nearly half of the American public (47%) thought that Stalin's passing would make it "easier" for us to get along with the USSR. Pres. Eisenhower's responsive—yet "firm"—reply to Malenkov was highly gratifying to most commentators; they agreed that "the next move" was up to the Soviets. The mood of the time—with the Korean war not settled—was one of great caution about the duration of this "new era of seeming cooperation." An increased proportion of the general public saw a "chance" that Russia "will change her policy and make real peace during the next five years"—from 17% in 1951 and 26% in 1952 to 42% in April 1953. In that month support for an Eisenhower-Malenkov meeting reached 75%, and as many as 51% expressed confidence that a meeting would produce a "mutually satisfactory agreement." But Americans continued to believe that it was "more important to stop Communist aggression" (64% compared to 67% in 1952) than to "stay out of war" (27%).[2]

When Eisenhower was inaugurated East Asian questions were most pressing; but relations with the Soviet Union—and the rest of Europe—had to be considered at the same time. Questions of aid and trade persisted; and events in the Middle East built up to the war in Palestine in 1956. All these developments were contemporaneous with those described in the preceding chapter covering Latin America, the UN, and the State Department, as well as East Asia and the Pacific.

Arms; Atoms

In the flood of speculation about future U.S.-Soviet relations commentators generally agreed that before any top-level meeting with the Russians there should be the maximum solidarity among the leading NATO governments. When Prime Minister Churchill suggested that the Big Three heads of Western governments meet in Bermuda, American commentators welcomed the idea—whether or not it would lead to a summit meeting including the Russians. In early 1953 a number of editors and Congressmen were suggesting that in many respects our European partners had failed to do their share in the common defense. There was also some feeling that our allies were too eager for a summit meeting with the Soviets, and editors endorsed the U.S. position that before consenting to a summit conference there should be evidence of good intent on the part of the Russian leaders. They were disappointed by Soviet refusal to participate in renewed talks on an Austrian treaty.[3]

With the Bermuda meeting postponed on account of Churchill's illness, and with revolts in Eastern Europe dimming the chances for an early summit with Kremlin leaders, a division of opinion became apparent between Americans who backed the Administration's policy of "watchful waiting," while steadily building up the free world's strength (e.g., Kansas City Times), and the critics who advocated greater U.S. efforts to "fan the fires of anti-Communist revolt" (e.g., Sen. Potter, R-Mich). A July poll showed diminished popular optimism about securing an agreement with the Soviet Union, with 61% seeing "no chance that Russia will change her mind and make real peace." But the idea of a summit meeting to include the Soviets was at a new high, with no fewer than 86% favoring such a conference.[4]

Announcement by the U.S. that the Soviets were producing hydrogen bombs moved editors to urge a review of American military planning and civil defense arrangements, with many feeling also that it was time to renew efforts to secure international control of nuclear weapons. Until adequate controls were established, it was widely agreed, there must be no slackening of U.S. nuclear programs. Some added that it was time to release information on the potentialities of nuclear weapons to the American people, and to share more information with our NATO partners.

Considerable press attention in October 1953 was devoted to the idea of a nonaggression pact between the West and the Soviet Union, which had been suggested by Prime Minister Churchill, Adlai Stevenson, and others. Some favored such an offer by the West as tending to expose the Soviet "peace bluff"; but doubters stressed the "formidable obstacles" to freezing the existing borders in Eastern Europe. Sen. Knowland declared that he would oppose any pact which would leave "enslaved" peoples in Eastern Europe. Most commentators expressed deep skepticism about any treaty, citing the "Soviets' long record of bad faith."[5]

Discussion of another aspect of our relations with our allies was prompted by Sen. Joseph McCarthy's attack on the "immoral trading" of these allies with the Communist "enemy." Most editors and Congressmen warmly welcomed Sec. Dulles' reply to McCarthy, reaffirming U.S. policy on the proper treatment of other sovereign nations, and the President's firm endorsement of it. As the Worcester Telegram put it, "A truculent U.S. approach might present Russia with its greatest prize–a quarreling and fragmented free world."

The much-postponed Bermuda conference finally took place Dec. 4–7, with Messrs. Churchill, Eisenhower and Laniel participating. "Seldom, if ever," wrote Richard P. Stebbins, "has a meeting among the heads of great governments been so long planned, so anxiously awaited, surrounded with such secrecy, and produced so little visible results as the Bermuda meeting." Nevertheless, editors gave the Bermuda communique a generally favorable reception, welcoming the reassertion of Western "solidarity" on several issues, and the scheduling of a Foreign Ministers meeting with the Soviets in Berlin. The Washington Star stressed the West's "need to confront Mr. Molotov with a genuine display of continuing unity on all major issues."[6]

In Bermuda Pres. Eisenhower informed his colleagues of a U.S. proposal for a major international conference on the peaceful uses of atomic energy that he would present to the UN General Assembly on Dec. 8. Eisenhower's UN speech was welcomed by editors as bringing a fresh outlook and offering a practical approach. It was also considered a massive blow in the Cold War, and that if the Soviet Union finally rejected the proposal the U.S. and other free world countries should go ahead with the peaceful atomic energy conference. Adverse criticism was confined to few (e.g., Wash. Times-Herald, N.Y. News, Daily Worker).

The four-power FM meeting in Berlin, held in January–February 1954, reached agreement on scheduling a Far Eastern conference and, with respect to European issues, demonstrated both Moscow's intransigence and the West's solidarity. Although the final decision on the European Defense Community was still up to our European partners, Sec. Dulles' diplomatic skill in countering Molotov and presenting the Western case won high praise from a variety of commentators. Among the general public, after the Berlin conference a plurality (48%) still expressed dissatisfaction with the way "our allies are cooperating with us in the struggle against world communism;" this feeling was particularly strong (59%) among respondents who expressed a preference for the Republican party. Still, Americans recognized (72%) that the U.S. needed allies and must try to work with them, "even if they don't always do what we want them to."[7]

Two military aspects of U.S. foreign policy were heavily discussed at this time: "massive retaliation," and the H-bomb. As part of the "new look" in U.S. policy, the "massive retaliation" defense policy won general praise as a "positive" policy–despite warnings by ex-Sec.

Acheson and ex-Amb. Kennan against over-reliance on the deterrent power of super-weapons. The March 1 test of a hydrogen bomb at Eniwetok appeared to strike deeper into the public consciousness than any other recent nuclear development. Editors called for extraordinary efforts toward establishing international control of nuclear weapons and agreements to prevent their use; yet many said it would be foolhardy for us to stop our research, and deemed it necessary to keep our weapons in readiness to deter nuclear attack by the other side. Nevertheless, polls showed half of the American people in favor of turning over some of our atomic material–assuming similar contributions from other countries–to a UN agency for the development of peaceful uses (42% were opposed). Similarly, a plurality of the people–as of the press–favored Pres. Eisenhower's request to Congress to permit greater cooperation with our NATO allies in the field of atomic weapons.[8]

Continuing efforts to reach agreement with the Soviet Union for control of nuclear weapons were favored by 79% in an April Gallup Poll; but only 1 out of 10 favored going so far as to soften our demands for strict inspection. At the same time, some editors of "internationalist" outlook were fearful that the European Defense Community would fail and the Western alliance disintegrate; whereas editors of "nationalist" outlook were dissatisfied with the attitudes of our European partners and urged a reappraisal of our commitments.

Some Senators and Generals wanted the U.S. to sever relations with the Soviet Union and reorganize the United Nations without the Communists (e.g., Sen. McCarran, Gen. Mark Clark); but Pres. Eisenhower's firm rejection of such a course won overwhelming editorial approval. A poll found 67% favoring continued exchange of ambassadors with Russia (23% would break relations), and 56% saying it was "better to have Russia remain a member of the UN" (whereas in July 1950, 63% had said the UN would be "better off without Russia"). Following the truce in Korea, Americans were now hoping for closer contact with Moscow, rather than any rupture. A majority of the general public (64%) continued to believe that it was "more important to stop Communist aggression" than to "stay out of war;" but respondents agreed that "if our allies stayed out" of war, we should "stay out, too."[9]

French rejection of the EDC treaty in August dealt a "great blow" to the free world, and U.S. commentators made no attempt to minimize it. With the Baltimore Sun they declared that "a search must now be made for a second-best plan." The Chicago Tribune, however, frankly advocated a return to "isolationism," instead of "alliances." The Oct. 3 decision at the London Foreign Ministers meeting, agreeing on German sovereignty and rearmament under NATO, made American editors jubilant. Popular support was evidenced by a poll showing 56% in favor of "getting German troops into the defense organization of Western Europe," and only 34% saying "we should keep Germany disarmed." (It will be recalled that following the war Americans supported a treaty to keep Germany disarmed.) Maintenance of U.S. troops in Germany was also upheld by a majority (54%). A specific polling question about "two treaties under which West Germany would become independent and would be allowed to rearm" found 59% in favor (68% among the college-educated). As many as 70% of the general public now said: "We can count on West Germany to cooperate with us."[10]

U.S. proposals at the UN General Assembly on international cooperation in developing atomic energy for peaceful purposes were generally approved in press comment. Some called the program "a modest beginning" (Scripps-Howard papers), but most editors felt it placed the U.S. in a favorable light before the world. Mr. Vishinsky's disarmament and atomic control proposals at the GA kindled some hope that the Soviets had become more cooperative in this field, but editors soon concluded that there was no substantial change in Moscow's position. Still, said the Philadelphia Inquirer, "it is well to keep on trying for agreement and to continue testing the Soviet stand." In October, Amb. Lodge's announcement to the UN of the decision to allocate 220 pounds of fissionable material to the international program was viewed by commentators as providing dramatic impetus to the atoms-for-peace program.[11]

1955 opened with substantial approval of the way "Pres. Eisenhowever is now handling our problems with Russia and world communism" (5 to 1 in approval). Americans continued to think that war with Russia was coming "sooner or later." At the same time, there was some editorial appreciation of the offer by the Soviets to share scientific knowledge gained in the operation of an atomic-driven power plant. Some American journals wished to end H-bomb tests; but a January poll disclosed that 84% of the general public favored continuing these U.S. tests. Appointment of Harold Stassen in March to develop disarmament policy was hailed as having "a priceless effect on opinion at home and abroad." But a fresh Soviet disarmament proposal was viewed with great skepticism.[12]

Sen. George's (D-Ga) suggestion of a high-level meeting with the new Soviet leaders, Bulganin and Khrushchev, commanded much public attention, and most commentators voiced cautious approval—even though few were optimistic as to the results. Soviet-Austrian agreement on an Austrian treaty (announced April 15) aroused mixed feelings: gratification that the Austrians were finally achieving independence and freedom from occupation; but also misgivings about the future of Austria's "neutrality" and doubts about the effect of the treaty upon German attitudes toward rearmament.

Scheduling of a Big Four summit meeting for the summer of 1955 was welcomed by press and public (78% approving); and a majority (53%) thought agreements would be reached at the top; but only 13% said Russia would "live up to" such agreements. Opposition to the summit was largely confined to voices as extreme as that of Sen. McCarthy or the Boston Post, who believed that any kind of negotiation with the Soviet Union was "hopeless"–if not "appeasement." Most commentators declared that the summit would be "worth trying" in view of the Western solidarity signalized by West Germany's entrance into NATO and such conciliatory Soviet moves as signature of the Austrian treaty. As the time for the Geneva session came closer, there was growing approval of the Administration's approach; and confidence in the solidarity of the Big Three was strengthened by the Foreign Ministers' talks in New York and at the UN anniversary meeting in San Francisco.[13]

The summit meeting at Geneva was promptly adjudged a success by the press and the public; creation of a "friendly" atmosphere among the Big Four was held a worthwhile advance. A popular majority (64%) approved the "way Pres. Eisenhower dealt with the Russians," and 52% thought that "some good" had come from the meeting; 17% saw "a great deal of good." In the heavy nationwide editorial discussion greatest emphasis was placed on Pres. Eisenhower's "brilliant" success in taking the initiative at the summit and making America's peaceful intentions clear to the world. Many editors considered the "true significance" of Geneva to be the mutual recognition that nuclear war was unthinkable. Several pointed out that the Soviets hadn't budged a single inch in the Geneva talks; yet it was felt that the lessening of tensions at Geneva made it much less likely that current East-West conflicts would lead to war. The minority of critical commentators contended that Moscow was only seeking to induce the free world to relax its defenses; but the majority approving Geneva were agreed that the U.S. and its allies must continue to maintain a high level of military strength and alertness.[14]

Pres. Eisenhower's "open skies" proposal for U.S.-Soviet aerial inspection–and exchange of defense blueprints–was viewed as "dramatic" and "challenging." The most common point of agreement was that it was a great propaganda stroke; it was welcomed by the great majority of press and Congressional commentators. While James Reston termed the proposal "unrealistic," the Philadelphia Bulletin declared: If "the Russians sincerely want peace, a way to begin it has been pointed out by Pres. Eisenhower." The reaction of the general public was to disapprove (56%) the proposal to "let Russian planes take photographs of our military bases in the United

States, if the Russians let American planes take similar photographs in Russia;" only 39% approved. Polls in subsequent months showed continuing majority opposition, with pluralities believing that "this kind of inspection would make a surprise attack on the U.S. more likely" (43%), and that "we could not find out from these photographs whether Russia was making preparations for a surprise attack" on us (70%).[15]

During the summit session editors paid little attention to the Soviet proposals for an international agreement to ban the use of atomic and hydrogen bombs. A June public opinion poll reported that the public was opposed to a plain prohibition (54% to 40%), but favorably disposed toward an international agreement incorporating controls for enforcement–a total of 81% favoring prohibition "if there were some kind of international control to see that all countries live up to the agreement."

Pres. Eisenhower's idea of increased contacts between U.S. and Soviet citizens was strongly endorsed by both the press and the public, with the editors citing with approval the recent exchange of visits by Russian and American farm experts. To these observers the chief value of the farm visit lay in the opportunity for the Russians to meet Americans and realize that they were peace-loving people. The approval that the general public had long bestowed upon the U.S. international exchange of persons program was now extended to exchanges with the Soviet Union–not only in the case of farmers (79%), but of musicians and athletes as well (72%). On these exchange questions, educational background was associated with wide differences in attitude; exchanges of scientists were favored by the college-educated (66% to 30%), but scientist exchanges were opposed by those having only a grammar-school education (52% to 35%).[16]

For some time, American commentators had tended to support our allies' pleas for an increase in non-strategic trade between Western Europe and Eastern Europe. A poll taken a few weeks before the Geneva summit showed that a majority (51%) had come to accept this view held by the press, thus registering a marked change since 1953 when only 26% approved and 67% disapproved. (Incidentally, 49% had come to approve allied trade with Communist China in non-strategic materials; 45% still disapproved.)

At the summit it was agreed to hold a 4-power Foreign Ministers meeting in the autumn; and a majority of the public (60%) felt that the four countries would be able to reach some agreement. A majority (56%) also said they would be "willing to have the U.S. give in on some things that Russia wants," rather than "insist on our point of view on everything." Some commentators feared that public acceptance of "the spirit of Geneva" could go too far; and they welcomed the President's speech to the American Bar Association indicating that Eisenhower was "fully aware of the dangers" of summitry.[17]

The lessening of international tensions was thought to have been furthered by the atoms-for-peace conference which also met in Geneva (Aug. 8–20), in accordance with Eisenhower's 1953 proposal and the UN General Assembly resolution. According to some American editors, the coming together of over 70 countries to cooperate in exploring the potentialities of the peaceful atom was in itself a development which would have an important influence toward peace. The press generally welcomed the role of the conference in eliminating much of the secrecy surrounding atomic development, the New York Times saying: "This competition to spread knowledge is the most hopeful sign of our times." According to the Milwaukee Journal, the conference "contributed immeasurably toward lessening fear of the atom and replacing it with hope that man can be the master of this gigantic force."

Pres. Eisenhower's illness (in September) moved many editors to point up the importance of his "personal eloquence and sincerity" at the summit in convincing the Communists, as well as some of our skeptical allies, that America was genuinely dedicated to peace. With diplomatic conferences coming up, some felt that the "lack of the President's personal participation" could make a "profound difference" (e.g., Eric Sevareid); but most shared Sec. Dulles' belief that the direction of U.S. foreign policy had been firmly charted on the basis of a bipartisan American consensus. Meanwhile, Party Chief Khrushchev's remarks about the ultimate victory of communism over capitalism were seen by some as a "pail of cold water in the face of those still basking in the Geneva spirit."[18]

Still, an October poll reflected significant changes attributable to the Geneva summit. The proportion expecting an "all-out war with Russia during the next two years" dropped to 9%, as against 28% in January 1955; and the proportion saying "we can avoid a big war with Russia entirely" grew to 43% from 25% in January. (In subsequent months these figures fluctuated somewhat, but they were much the same a year later in the autumn of 1956.) At the same time, most Americans did not feel that the danger of "Russia making a surprise attack on this country during the next ten years" had disappeared; 15% saw "great danger" of this eventuality, and 63% saw "some danger;" only 18% saw "no danger at all."[19]

Europe After The Summit

Sustained American support for the U.S. policy of collective security was shown by an October poll in which 80% registered their approval of the NATO mutual defense treaty. Moreover, only 16% of the general public expressed willingness to replace NATO by a general security pact—with "the U.S. and Russia and all of the other countries of both Eastern and Western Europe promising to defend each other against any attack." If, however, a European pact were to supplement NATO it would have the support of a majority (59%). This latter concept also had strong press approval. It should be added that in October 1955 Americans showed less irritation with their European allies than they did during 1952 and 1953—years of Korean fighting. A plurality now registered "satisfaction" with the way our allies were "cooperating with us in building up armed forces for the defense of Europe." It may be added that popular sentiment for maintaining or increasing the current level of U.S. armaments was greater at the end of 1955 than at the beginning of 1953 (85% vs. 63%).[20]

Americans were not too surprised at the failure of the post-Geneva efforts to reach specific agreements on the German and disarmament problems. They continued to favor mutual reduction of armaments, provided there was adequate international inspection of the process. Under existing circumstances Americans were strongly in favor of continued U.S. tests of the hydrogen bomb (83%); yet two-thirds thought it would be a good idea if all countries, including Russia and the U.S., would sign an agreement "to stop any further H-bomb tests." A similar proportion favored a U.S. undertaking that "we won't use the atomic or hydrogen bomb if other countries don't."

Americans also continued to favor the unification of Germany, and the integration of West German armed forces with those of NATO. A steady debate went on over the prospects of attaining these two goals, with critics of U.S. policy contending that Moscow might achieve a Germany united by Soviet action and tied to the Communist bloc by massive trade concessions (e.g., Chester Bowles). To counteract the "astute Communist propaganda," C. L. Sulzberger said it would be necessary for the West to show Bonn that she has a "real political and economic future" in the NATO coalition.[21]

As the presidential election year of 1956 opened there was little tendency to blame the U.S. or the West for the failure of rapprochement to bring us closer to the Soviet Union. Approval of the conduct of foreign relations by Washington officials remained at a high level, and specific approval for Sec. Dulles reached a new high of 71% approval. In January Pres. Eisenhower's "calm and skillful" rejection of Premier Bulganin's proposal for a treaty of friendship was cordially applauded by many editors and Congressmen. Adlai Stevenson was among the many who upheld the President's contention that the treaty of friendship already embodied in the UN Charter "will be furthered by deeds, not mere documents."[22]

Changes in the Kremlin, the criticisms of Stalin, dissolution of the

Cominform, and the Bulganin-Khrushchev "invasion of Britain" in the spring of 1956 were interpreted by Americans as constituting a change of tactics which should prompt a reappraisal of U.S. policy. The Scripps-Howard papers said that Adlai Stevenson's "grim appraisal" of the state of the world "made more sense" than the Administration's "nonsense about the Soviets failing." But there was agreement with Pres. Eisenhower that "we must first of all maintain our military power," and also his argument that armaments alone cannot solve our problems. There was general satisfaction that Bulganin and Khrushchev in Britain found the Anglo-American alliance "impenetrable." The public tended to retain its skepticism about the Kremlin's "new look," and in July a poll found as many as 63% saying "there is no chance that Russia will change her past policy and make real peace with us during the next few years"—a figure larger than any registered since the death of Stalin. Now, in 1956, 26% did see a "chance" that Russia might change.[23]

During the summer campaign for the presidency there was wide agreement in the press and among the general public that the Republicans' most effective argument was: "They got us out of Korea and have kept the country at peace." Later, considerable discussion developed over Adlai Stevenson's proposal that the U.S. take the lead in discontinuing hydrogen bomb tests. Editorial comment was preponderantly critical of Stevenson's position, and favorable to Eisenhower's position that the Russians cannot be trusted, and that security would be endangered by a cessation of testing. The Stevenson supporters, including most of the scientists debating the issue, maintained that U.S. research up to the point of explosion could be continued, and that Soviet violation of a test ban could be detected and heralded to the world. On the Stevenson proposal the general public was rather evenly divided, with 41% approving the N.O.R.C. proposition that "the U.S. take the lead in offering to stop hydrogen bomb tests, assuming that Russia and England do the same;" but 47% expressed disapproval.[24]

By election day American voters were giving attention to two new crisis developments: the revolt against the Hungarian regime; and the conflict in the Middle East. During November American sympathy for the Hungarian rebels was clear, and commentators insistently called for stronger UN action against the Soviet Union and the Kadar regime, or for greater U.S. assistance to the refugees. The press made clear the strong feelings aroused by the Hungarian tragedy; yet there was general agreement that employment of armed forces would run a risk of starting World War III and of speeding the "destruction of the very people we are trying to help" (e.g., Jos. Harsch). An opinion poll in the middle of the month reported 63% thinking "our government did all it should to help Hungary win freedom from Russia," and 22% feeling that the U.S. "should have done more." The Administration's offer of foodstuffs and relief supplies was unanimously approved, and the offer to admit an increased number of refugees was likewise applauded.[25]

A minority cast some blame on the U.S. because of earlier broadcasts conveying "implied promises of liberation," but the majority tended to concur with Walter Lippmann's conclusion that the "tragedy of Hungary was that it tried to by-pass Titoism." Some voices favored severing diplomatic relations with the Soviet Union (e.g., Rep. Hays, D-Ohio); but a majority (68%) held "it is better to have Russia remain as a member of the UN," than to be outside. At the end of the year 83% said "our government has been doing all it should to help Hungary," whereas 11% thought it "had not"–most of these saying we should have sent more relief or admitted more refugees, rather than mentioning sending arms or troops.

Middle East (1950–1956)

To understand American public attitudes about the Middle East conflict which broke out on the eve of the American presidential election of 1956 it is helpful to resume the account which we have traced as far as the outbreak of the Korean War. In late 1950, when Britain refused Egypt's demand for withdrawal of its troops from the Suez Canal Zone, commentators tended to side with Britain, saying that the free world needed continued British protection of the Zone (e.g., Kansas City Star). A year later, when Egypt abrogated the treaty with Britain, American editors voiced alarm lest the "dangerous" currents of nationalism and fanaticism in the Moslem world create a power vacuum into which Communism might move. Egypt's refusal to join in a Middle East defense pact was regretted, as was the failure of the Mossadegh government in Iran to work out a reasonable solution of its oil dispute with Britain. Most of those commenting expressed sympathy with the aspirations of Middle Eastern peoples in their struggles against "colonialism." A number advocated programs of economic and technological aid to help develop the area; and several stressed the need for "concrete action" to solve the problem of the Palestinian refugees. But where nationalism threatened the security of the region, as it did in the case of the Suez Canal, most observers were firm in the view that defense of the free world must take priority, and they were accordingly sympathetic to proposals for a Middle East Command.[26]

Prime Minister Churchill's suggestion on his 1952 visit to Washington, that the U.S. send "token" forces to Suez elicited a mixed response which was largely unfavorable. There was some support for the proposal from commentators who tended to accept some U.S.

"responsibility" in this area without defining the nature of the "responsibility." According to a February poll, two-thirds of the public were aware of "recent troubles between the British and the Egyptians," but only 22% thought that the U.S. should "try to help" England and Egypt "settle these problems." On the specific issue of the British troops in the Canal Zone, 39% said they sympathized mostly with Britain's refusal to get out, 21% mostly with the Egyptians, and 40% sympathized with "neither" side.[27]

Events in Palestine itself prompted little public discussion during the election year of 1952. However, one autumn poll is of interest. Respondents were asked how important they thought it was for the U.S. to "cooperate closely" with various countries. Over half (55%) called it "very important to cooperate closely" with West Germany, 45% with France, 42% with Iran, and 34% with Israel (among the college-educated 50%). The chief reasons given in the Israeli case may be grouped under the heading, "Israel deserves our help" (viz. new country, working hard; threatened by Communism; Jews were persecuted). Some respondents cited ways in which "Israel could help us" (viz. potential allies, strategic aid; trade, oil, resources).

U.S. relations with Iran in 1953 had no immediate effect on Palestine issues, but they became important in themselves a quarter-century later after the deposition of the shah. In 1953 American commentators generally were fearful that the "leftist" premier, Mossadegh, would somehow draw Iran into the Soviet orbit; so they were relieved by his departure from office. Public discussion of his going and the return of the shah did not include any mention of U.S. involvement in these political events, but former Ambassador Henry Grady did criticize U.S. efforts to "elbow out" the premier with economic pressure. Discussion was generally favorable as to whether the U.S. should extend economic aid to the government of the restored shah. The N.Y. Herald Tribune hoped that the money would "undo the work of Mossadegh," and said that was "about the limit to which a Western power can safely go in attempting to influence the course of events in Iran."[28]

In the first year of the Eisenhower Administration the Arab-Israeli border strip commanded the attention of the UN Security Council, which attention was widely welcomed by American editors. They saw a fresh opportunity for the Security Council to transform "the uneasy armistice into a durable peace" (e.g., Phila. Inquirer, Prov. Journal). Most editors not only denounced Israel's raid into Jordan, but supported the stern U.S. note of protest (e.g., San Francisco Chronicle, Denver Post). Announcement by the U.S. that it was suspending grants-in-aid to Israel (Oct. 20), because of her failure to carry out the orders of the UN truce team respecting the Jordan River hydro-electric dam operations, was also endorsed by editors (e.g., C. S. Monitor, Louisville Courier-Journal, Wash. Star).[29]

But by far the loudest public response was the protest of leading rabbis and Zionist organizations, plus some political figures including New York Senators Lehman and Ives, and also Ralph McGill (Atlanta Constitution) and the CIO Executive Committee. The Dayton News said "the U.S. State Dept. is in the position of pre-judging a case which the Security Council of the UN is about to try;" and Max Lerner accused Sec. Dulles of "appeasing" the Arabs "to keep Arab oil from Russia," and saw the U.S. embarked on an anti-Israel policy "such as the Near East desks at the Sate Department–all of them trained in Arab sympathies–have long demanded." Peter Lisagor, in the Chicago News, said "it is an open secret that Sec. Dulles is intent upon convincing the Arabs that American policy is not unduly pro-Israel under the new administration." Israel's termination of work on the Jordan River project, and the Oct. 28 renewal of U.S. economic aid, won applause from a number of commentators (e.g., Erwin Canham, Wash. Star, Dayton News). With the resumption of U.S. aid coming a few days before the Nov. 3 election, some charged that the U.S. action was taken for the sake of domestic political gains (e.g., St. Louis Post-Dispatch, Jas. Reston, N.Y. Post). But several others saw the U.S. action as constituting "a sensible approach to the adjustment of an extremely difficult problem" (e.g., Chi. News, Scripps-Howard papers, Detroit Free Press).

When the UN Security Council a month later (Nov. 24) condemned Israel for the Kibya raid, the prevailing reaction was that while some sort of censure was called for, the resolution should not have ignored the Arab attacks on Israel prior to the Kibya event (e.g., Wash. Post, Kansas City Times). Some saw a flaw in the resolution's failure to press the Arab delegations to accept some proposal for Arab-Israeli negotiation as suggested by Amb. Eban (e.g., C. S. Monitor, N.Y. Times and Herald Tribune). The earlier U.S. note of protest was disapproved by Hearst's New York Journal-American and the New York Post. Some editors stressed that the plight of the Arab refugees in Palestine was an important hindrance to Near East peace (e.g., Wash. Post, Anne O'Hare McCormick).

In the following months editors continued to deplore the recurring acts of violence across the Palestine frontier, and they often demanded that the United Nations attempt to produce a final settlement. The U.S. policy of "impartiality" between the two sides tended to produce greater editorial criticism than approbation. The Washington Post, for example, said that U.S. "impartiality seems to involve a constant rapping of the knuckles of Israel, which plays into the hands of Arab intransigents." Zionist spokesmen were persistently critical of the U.S. policy.[30]

The Anglo-Egyptian agreement providing for Britain's withdrawal from the Suez Canal Zone (July 27, 1954) occasioned much editorial discussion most of it welcoming the prospects of improved relations in the area, and hopeful about developing a Middle Eastern defense system. Some, however, feared that the agreement could weaken Israel's position vis-a-vis Egypt.[31]

Next year Sec. Dulles proposed (Aug. 26, 1955) several steps to settle Arab-Israeli conflicts and offered U.S. assistance to the states of the area, provided they would agree on boundary problems. Editors applauded the U.S. position, but most were restrained in their predictions on the outcome.[32]

News of a Soviet program of arms and economic aid to various Arab states moved some American editors to complain of the "failure" of U.S. Middle East policy; and hundreds of letters–largely from American Jewish organizations–called on the State Department to offer U.S. arms aid to Israel, or a U.S.-Israel security pact. Others felt that U.S. arms to Israel would only result in more Soviet weapons to Arabs (e.g., Scripps-Howard and Knight papers). When asked about the "recent fighting between Israel and Egypt," 59% of the respondents said they had "heard of" it. They distributed the "blame" in this dispute as follows: 6% to Israel, 12% to Egypt, 14% to both or neither, 27% not stating an opinion, and 41% unaware of the fighting. In the same poll a plurality said they supported Sec. Dulles' proposal that the U.S. join other countries to prevent any attempt "to change by force boundaries agreed upon by Israel and her neighbors" (those who said the U.S. should not undertake such a guarantee numbered 36%).[33]

Considerable sentiment was expressed in favor of "stepped-up" U.S. economic aid to the states of the area as a counter-balance to Soviet military and economic infiltration (e.g., Des Moines Register, Boston Herald, Phila. Bulletin). Some supported aid for the high Aswan Dam; opposition came from some other quarters, including Congressmen from cotton states (e.g., Rep. Whitten, D-Miss.).[34]

The Dec. 11 attack on Syrian outposts, in which over 50 Syrians were killed, was dismaying to American editors. The Louisville Courier-Journal observed that the border attacks "have gone on so long that to blame one side more than the other is difficult;" but the majority of commenting editors criticized Israel for the attack, including some warm friends of the Zionist state (e.g., Sen. Lehman, Hearst's N.Y. Journal-American, N.Y. Post). The UN Security Council's censure of Israel was approved by a majority of editors, the New York Herald Tribune saying that the world "cannot condone violence which could so easily set off a war." However, some called this third censure of Israel "unfair," contending that the Arab states had yet to be censured (e.g., Detroit News, Phila. Inquirer, David Lawrence).[35]

An intense demand for the U.S. to supply arms to Israel came less from editors and commentators than from prominent individuals (including former Pres. Truman, Mrs. Roosevelt, Walter Reuther) and a number of Congressmen. When the U.S. announced that it was shipping 18 tanks to Saudi Arabia, there was a sizable outcry, especially from those favoring arms for Israel. An embargo was clamped on any arms to the Middle East for 43 hours–enough for the Administration to explain that the tank shipment was in accordance with a 1953 mutual defense agreement with Saudi Arabia, and to win a somewhat grudging O.K. from a majority of commenting editors. Many, however, criticized the "bungling" of the whole episode which was seen by them as indicative of the "lack of a firm policy." Opinion polls continued to show public belief that it was important for the U.S. to "cooperate closely" with Israel (72%) and also with the Arab countries (67%).[36]

Announcement that Pres. Eisenhower and Prime Minister Eden in their Washington talks had discussed the need of preventing war in Palestine was welcome to many editors; but others were "sorely disappointed" with the "generalizations" in the joint statement and concluded that the U.S. and Britain "have no idea of what to do" (e.g., Kansas City Star, Chi. News, Portland Oregonian). Some hoped that a workable course of action would arise from the tripartite talks, including the French; but the Soviet Union's warning against a Big Three declaration to use any troops in the area drew heavy condemnation of this "brazen criticism." Editors urged that the Kremlin not be allowed "to bluff the Western powers out of any joint action" intended to stabilize the Middle East.

The April news that Secretary-General Hammarskjold had succeeded in securing an Israeli-Egyptian cease-fire agreement elicited enthusiastic editorial acclaim; which was extended after the Secretary-General's achievement in getting similar agreements from Syria, Jordan and Lebanon. Some, however, felt that Hammarskjold had merely "re-established the state of things which existed when the Arab-Jewish war stopped in 1949" (San Diego Union, Hearst papers). When presently the Democratic platform pledged to ship arms to Israel, some U.S. editors criticized this commitment as "unnecessary and dangerous."[37]

Pres. Nasser's "bomb-shell" decree in July nationalizing the Suez Canal was promptly denounced as a "despicable act of banditry" in heavy press and radio comment; but the great majority of commentators felt that the issue of ownership was separable from that of assured use of the strategic waterway. U.S. participation in efforts to assure continued navigation of the Canal was widely endorsed, as was Pres. Eisenhower's emphasis on a "peaceful" settlement of the Canal problem.[38]

Prior to Nasser's abrupt Canal move, editorial discussion about withdrawal of U.S. funds to help construct the high dam at Aswan had concluded with virtually all commentators approving the withdrawal. Editors resented Nasser's efforts to "play off" the U.S. and Britain against the Soviets, and they approved the action of the Senate Appropriations Committee in opposing the use of Mutual Security funds for the Aswan Dam. Some editors had suggested that Russia might step into the "vacuum" and build the dam, but no one had mentioned the possibility that Egypt might retaliate by nationalizing Suez. Aided by hindsight, some editors now criticized the "precipitate" manner of U.S. withdrawal from the dam project.

American editorial opinion regarded nationalization of the Canal as a threat to the economic "life-line" of Britain and France, rather than a threat to this country's interest as a user of the Canal; and the editors were also alarmed over the military preparations of Britain and France which presented the possibility of a war whose limits could not be predicted. Troubled by Nasser's "blunt" action, the editors supported free navigation of the vital waterway. A few urged the U.S. to range itself alongside Britain and France; but most frankly stated that our support of the allies should not go so far as to endorse a "forcible" solution. Some asserted there was "nothing that we need do about" the crisis (e.g., Chi. Tribune, Houston Chronicle). Speaking of the U.S. role, the Wall St. Journal said in a representative comment: "It is no small tribute to Mr. Dulles' statesmanship that he has directed the justified wrath of Britain and France into a search for peaceful solutions."[39]

The action of 18 nations, out of the 22 attending the Aug. 16 conference of Canal users in London, to attempt to establish international control of the Suez Canal received virtually unanimous backing in American editorial opinion. Soviet attempts to draw a "parallel" between the Suez and Panama Canals were called "far-fetched" by most commenting editors; but some did say that before the episode was over the U.S. would be called upon to justify its "exclusive jurisdiction" over the Panama Canal. During September editors continued to laud Sec. Dulles' success in restraining any resort to arms in the Canal crisis; a number also commended Adlai Stevenson's exclusion of Suez from "partisan politics."[40]

Popular opinion, also, approved the U.S. positions on Suez: 7 out of 10 said we should "keep on working" for the idea that "other countries besides Egypt should have some share in the operation of the Suez Canal," and only about 1 out of 7 said that we should "go along with Egypt's plan to operate the Canal itself." On whether Britain and France were "justified" in "threatening the use of force," opinion was rather closely divided; but only 1 out of 6 felt that the United States should "help" these allied nations in case they decided to use "armed force." The taking of the Suez issue to the UN Security Council by Britain and France was approved by most editors; and a poll found overwhelming approval–88% to 5%–for having the Suez question "come up before the United Nations organization."[41]

Americans were stunned when Israeli, French and British troops entered Egypt in late October. Criticism of Israel was severe–in line with the reaction against Israeli reprisals against Jordan earlier in the month. Pro-Zionist spokesmen, however, agreed with Hearst's New York Mirror that the Israeli move was a "brilliant political stroke" to "avoid being choked to death while the Great Powers appease Nasser." American editors were "incredulous" when Britain and France vetoed the U.S. move at the UN Security Council to order Israel's withdrawal from Egyptian territory; and criticism was even more bitter than when our two European allies had sent their own troops into Egypt in a "reckless step which jeopardized" world peace. There was great relief when Britain and France agreed to a cease-fire in Egypt and to the presence there of a UN emergency force.[42]

Popular feeling was well marked out by a mid-November poll which carefully probed national sentiment with follow-up questions.

"Do you think England and France were justified, or not justified, in using armed force against Egypt?"

England and France justified	25%
Not justified	55
No opinion	20
	100%

If respondent said "Justified":
"Do you think the U.S. should have done more to help or encourage England and France in this action?"

U.S. should have helped more	7%
No, U.S. should not have	17
No opinion	1
	25%

If respondent said "Not Justified":
"Do you think the U.S. should have taken a stronger stand than it did against this action by England and France?"

U.S. should have taken stronger stand	18%
No, shouldn't have done so	34
No opinion	3
	55%

On the general handling of foreign affairs, approval was greater in November, 74%, than it had been in late October (65% approval).

At the same time, press and public wished the U.S. to return as soon as possible to a friendly basis with our European allies. In the poll, 80% agreed that "we should keep on working with our allies, even if they often fail to do what we want." Commentators wished to restore the effectiveness of our NATO alliance against the continuing Communist menace. The President's order putting into effect an emergency oil program for Europe was warmly welcomed.

Editors, who were already disturbed by Soviet measures to put down the revolt in Hungary, were indignant at Soviet threats of sending "volunteers" into Egypt. They applauded Pres. Eisenhower's pledge to resist such intervention through the instrumentality of the United Nations, although some editors felt that the President's warning should have been "stronger."

Immigration; Trade; Aid (1953-56)

In early 1953 Pres. Eisenhower proposed the admission, over a 2-year period, of 240,000 Europeans–above the regular quotas. Approval of this proposal came from the great majority of commenting editors and broadcasters, as well as 32 national organizations interested in aiding refugees from Communist-controlled countries. Opposition to an influx of refugees was registered by some Congressmen, editors, and organizations–including the American Legion and the General Federation of Women's Clubs (by a margin of 4 votes). College-educated Americans continued to be in favor of admitting additional refugees; but in a May poll a national plurality narrowly disapproved of the plan (48% to 47%), even though the polling question mentioned the President's support and also stated that "there are many people in Europe who have left their own homes because their countries were taken over by the Communists." Following passage of an emergency refugee program in August, some continued to deplore the small numbers actually admitted.[43]

Two years later (1955) an N.O.R.C. poll reported that 52% approved the idea of "letting a limited number of refugees (from Communism) enter the U.S.–over and above the normal numbers we would let in anyway;" 43% disapproved. This poll also found that 39% of the sample thought that "too many" immigrants were being admitted, 37% said the number was "about right," and 13% felt that "not enough" were being admitted. When respondents who had said we had "too many immigrants now" were asked which "particular groups or nationalities" they had in mind, nearly half replied: "None in particular, just too many." At the end of 1956 an N.O.R.C. poll found 48% saying the U.S. had admitted "about the right number" of refugees from Hungary, 11% said "not enough," while 34% said "too many." Nearly 190,000 had been admitted under the Emergency

Act by the end of the year. In Eisenhower's second term editors welcomed a White House Conference on U.S. participation in World Refugee Year, and many applauded the President's 1960 proposal for increased immigration. But the critics also continued their previous arguments, and no change resulted.[44]

At the time of Pres. Eisenhower's first inauguration there was a burst of protectionist activity to counter the steady increase in support of a liberalized U.S. trade policy. Hence, trade was regarded as a "delicate issue" confronting the new administration, which decided to recommend to Congress a 1-year renewal of the reciprocal trade agreement policy, accompanied by a 1-year study of over-all foreign economic policy.[45]

A "dramatic change in thinking on tariff" was reported in June 1953 by the Gallup Poll, which found much greater sentiment for "lowering" the tariff (39%) than for "raising" it (13%). Gallup also reported, in consonance with some earlier polls, that the "traditional difference between the Republican and Democratic parties has practically melted away so far as the rank-and-file of voters themselves are concerned." But in Congress Republicans on the Ways and Means Committee were able to include several restraints on trade, along with the one-year extension of the Reciprocal Trade Agreements Act.[46]

Next year Pres. Eisenhower settled for another 1-year renewal—to the distress of many of his allies in the press and in business. According to Jos. C. Harsch, "the White House accepted the conclusion of the Congressional leaders that it would be impossible to handle the trade program this year (1954)" (in C. S. Monitor). At this point the Administration's recourse to escape clause procedures to raise tariffs on Swiss watches produced a storm of criticism, not only from foreign countries feeling a need to sell exports in America, but from editors and business spokesmen in the United States.[47]

After the 1954 Congressional elections it had been assumed that the chances of RTA approval were enhanced by the Democratic victory, and early in 1955 Pres. Eisenhower sent his new economic program to Congress, including a 3-year extension of the RTA legislation, although "subject to the present peril point and escape clause provisions." Pres. Eisenhower "takes the international long view on foreign trade," said the Watertown (N.Y.) Times, "a view that his party should take, but a view that his party has failed to take in many years." The majority of press and business commentators agreed that the U.S. must import if it wished to export, and that a high level of trade served the national interest. But several papers of "nationalist" outlook continued to oppose a liberal trade program (e.g., Wheeling Intelligencer, Columbus Dispatch). The Hearst papers said Congress should wait for a Tariff Commission report before acting; and the Salt Lake City Tribune advocated that Tariff Commission recommendations for tariff increases be sent to Congress, instead of the President, and that they become effective unless vetoed by either House of Congress.[48]

An opinion poll of May confirmed that a substantial majority of Americans continued to uphold the policy of reciprocal tariff reduction, although the opposition had increased slightly during the time of protectionist campaigning. The poll also confirmed that political party preference made little difference in the trade policy attitudes of rank-and-file respondents. As in earlier polls, respondents favored government assistance to those adversely affected by tariff reductions. Congress passed the extension bill on June 21.[49]

Although Pres. Eisenhower took office at a time when there was considerable unhappiness about the degree of European cooperation, a basic program of military and economic aid was upheld by the press and in public opinion polls—along with the usual hopes for reducing the size of the appropriations. Military aid was backed by 70%, and economic aid by 65%. Some said they wished to see greater European progress toward a unified defense before extending additional aid to Europe.[50]

The Eisenhower budget for the Mutual Security Program included policy changes—reduced amount, and "greater emphasis" on military aid and on the needs of the Far East—which were welcomed in editorial comment. Some editors and Congressmen complained they were seeing "more of the same" Truman-Acheson aid program. Respondents in an N.O.R.C. poll were told that the aid program was being cut from eight billions to six billions; a majority (52%) called the new amount "about right." Public discussion continued amid Congressional efforts to reduce the amount and presidential appeals against such "slashes." Editors lined up on each side—then seemed to accept Congress' "compromise" decision.[51]

Several influential Senators of both parties recommended in 1954 that future aid should depend on the increased cooperation of recipient countries with U.S. policies in Europe (EDC) and Southeast Asia (Knowland and Wiley, R.; Mansfield and McCarran, D.). When N.O.R.C. respondents were told that the President was requesting three and a half billions instead of five billions, 56% said this figure was "about right." Editorial supporters of the Administration maintained that the U.S. could not afford to step down from world leadership by telling allies to "shift for themselves."[52]

After the 1954 elections, in which the Democrats won control of both Houses of Congress, Pres. Eisenhower appointed a new Council on Economic Foreign Policy, headed by that "old government cost-cutter," Joseph Dodge. The Wall St. Journal and Hearst papers argued that further U.S. "hand-outs" were neither necessary nor desirable; but many editors maintained that economic aid to "key countries" was the best defense against Communist expansion—including in Asia. A January 1955 poll found 78% saying we should continue to send economic aid to "countries that have agreed to stand with us against Communist aggression;" and a plurality (47% to 41%) favored continued aid to "some countries like India, which have *not* joined us as allies against the Communists." As many as 79%, in an April poll, favored our government spending money "on technical assistance to backward countries of the world, under which American experts help them to solve their farming and health problems."[53]

In December 1955 much comment considered how the U.S. should meet the post-Geneva Soviet "challenge" in offering economic and technical aid to Asian and African countries. Most press commentators continued to be sympathetic to a large-scale U.S. aid program, especially for Asia; but the critics in the press and Congress were also outspoken. Some in Congress favored substantial military assistance and reduction of economic aid, whereas the general public increasingly felt that economic aid was "more important" than military aid "to keep Communism from spreading in Asia"—(74% in November 1955, against 65% a year before).[54] A Gallup Poll (released Feb. 3, 1956) reported that a majority (57%) favored continued expenditure of "about four billion dollars" a year "to help prevent countries from going Communistic." Gallup found little difference in attitude by party preference, but considerable difference by age: respondents aged 21-to-29 were 65% in favor; those 30-to-49 were 58% favorable; those over 50 only 49% favorable.

Sec. Dulles' "eloquent plea" at Philadelphia for long-term economic commitments in Asia elicited strong support from the great majority of commenting editors. Hearst's New York Journal-American saw "no reason" why America should be "panicked by Soviet economic warfare," and "every reason" why the Administration should be "granted the powerful weapon of limited long-range foreign aid." According to an early 1956 poll, popular support for aid to neutral "countries like India" increased to 53%; but, rather than approve long-term aid, a majority (65%) said we should "refuse to commit ourselves beyond one year at a time." As the discussion continued, polls showed new highs in support of technical assistance to "backward countries" (85%), and of economic aid to our anti-Communist allies (87%); but sentiment for aiding neutral countries "like India" dropped back to 43%; and 50% registered opposition.[55] Foreign aid did not appear as a partisan issue in the 1956 campaign, and it dropped out of sight during the big crises over the Hungarian revolt and the Middle East war.[56]

Thus, during Pres. Eisenhower's first term there was appreciable lowering of the tension with the Soviet Union, although this rose again during the 1956 Palestinian war, which also cooled our relations with France, Britain, and Israel. As the Korean war moved into history, it was accompanied by diminution in the amounts of military aid and economic aid favored by the American public. Support for a liberal trade policy, however, tended to persist–despite some Congressional victories by the protectionists.

Under Eisenhower, as under Roosevelt and Truman, the American public supported an active role in world affairs for the U.S. This was notable respecting Europe and the Middle East, as well as in Asia and Latin America. While there was some reduction in foreign aid, there was sustained concern and activity in the defense of free world countries and in efforts toward a peaceful world.

Reference Notes

1. Gallup Poll of Jan. 9; N.O.R.C. poll #323.
2. AOR for Mar. and Apr. 1953; May N.O.R.C. poll.
3. AOR for Jan. and May 1953.
4. AOR for July and August 1953.
5. AOR of Oct. 1953.
6. Stebbins, *U.S. in World Affairs, 1953* (New York, 1954), p. 425; AOR for Dec. 1953.
7. AOR for Jan., Feb., and Oct. 1954.
8. AOR for Mar., Apr., May and July 1954.
9. Polls of May, July, and Sept. 1954.
10. AOR for Aug., Sept., and Dec. 1954.
11. AOR for Sept. and Nov. 1954.
12. AOR for Jan., Feb., Mar., and May 3, 1955.
13. AOR for June 1955.
14. AOR for Aug. 1 and Sept. 2, 1955.
15. Ibid.; N.O.R.C. polls ##376, 379, and 390.
16. AOR for July 1, Aug. 1, and Sept. 29, 1955.
17. AOR of Sept. 2, 1955.
18. AOR of Oct. 5, 1955.
19. N.O.R.C. polls ##366 and 378; AOR of Oct. 11, 1955.
20. AOR for Oct. 11 and Nov. 1, 1955.
21. AOR of Dec. 2, 1955.
22. AOR for Jan. 3 and Feb. 2, 1956.
23. AOR for May 2 and Aug. 2, 1956.
24. AOR for Sept. 4 and Nov. 2, 1956.
25. AOR of Dec. 3, 1956.
26. AOR for Nov. 1950 and Oct. and Nov. 1951.
27. AOR for Jan. and Feb. 1952.
28. AOR of Oct. 1952 (poll); AOR for Aug. 18 and Sept. 9, 1953.
29. AOR of Nov. 25, 1953.
30. AOR for June 1954.
31. AOR of Nov. 22, 1954.
32. AOR of Sept. 23, 1955.
33. AOR of Dec. 23, 1955.
34. AOR of Jan. 23, 1956.

35. AOR for Feb. 2 and Mar. 20, 1956.
36. AOR of Mar. 2 and 30, 1956.
37. AOR for June 28 and Sept. 4, 1956.
38. AOR of Aug. 2, 1956.
39. AOR of Aug. 14, 1956.
40. AOR of Sept. 4, 1956.
41. AOR of Oct. 2, 1956.
42. AOR of Dec. 3, 1956.
43. AOR for June 29, 1953 and June 10, 1954.
44. Hollis Barber, *U.S. in World Affairs, 1955* (New York, 1956), p. 306, note 37; AOR of June 24, 1955, June 4, 1959, Apr. 4, 1960.
45. AOR of April 30, 1955.
46. Richard P. Stebbins, *U.S. in World Affairs, 1953* (New York, 1954), p. 97; AOR of July 6, 1955.
47. AOR for June 14 and Aug. 5, 1954.
48. Barber, op. cit., p. 243; AOR for Jan. 17 and Mar. 4, 1955.
49. AOR of June 8, 1955.
50. AOR for Jan. and Feb. 1953.
51. AOR for May and July 1953.
52. AOR for Apr., Aug., and Dec. 1954.
53. AOR for Feb. and May 3, 1955.
54. AOR for Jan. 3 and Feb. 1956.
55. AOR for Mar. 2 and June 1, 1956.
56. AOR of Oct. 2, 1956.

X
EISENHOWER'S SECOND TERM (1957–1958)

Pres. Eisenhower's second inaugural address was received with all the approval and appreciation which commentators had accorded his first four years as national leader. The general public, having resoundingly reelected him to office gave a 74% vote of confidence for the handling of foreign affairs to "the present officials in Washington" (19% expressed disapproval, 7% gave no opinion). Moreover, press commentators strongly supported the Administration.[1]

The next two years witnessed many foreign affairs developments. The Middle East, quiet after announcement of the Eisenhower Doctrine, flared up again in the Lebanon crisis. Relations with China raised continual questions, climaxed by another Quemoy crisis. Talk of arms control tinged European relations and UN sessions; but sputnik and the subsequent Soviet challenges were the biggest developments of all.

Eisenhower Doctrine

Strong public support was forthcoming when the Administration requested Congressional backing for the Eisenhower Doctrine, i.e., stand-by economic and military authority to counter any Communist attacks in the Middle East which might occur as a sequel to the war of the previous year. Proponents conceded that the Doctrine did not cover all problems of the area, but stressed that it was a "necessary first step" toward "stabilizing" the region for an attempt to deal with the problems of Suez and Palestine. A Gallup Poll reported 70% approval of the economic component of the Doctrine, 53% for sending military supplies to build up the armies of friendly countries in the area, and 50%-to-34% approval of a "U.S. promise to send our armed forces if Russian troops attack these countries." A proposal that UN forces should patrol the Israeli-Egyptian demarcation line won nearly unanimous approval in public comment; but editors were divided on Israel's demands that her withdrawal from Aqaba and Gaza be conditioned on UN "guarantees" against Egyptian "harassment."[2]

Impatient about Congressional "dawdling" over the Eisenhower Doctrine, commentators cheered when favorable action was taken in March. Many were gratified over the defeat of attempts to hamper the President's authority respecting economic aid; editors felt that Congressional modification of the requested language would nevertheless permit him to accomplish what he had in mind. A few, like the Indianapolis Star, remained opposed to the Doctrine, and hoped that the "bruises" inflicted by Congress would be powerful "deterrents to another such squeeze play." Many editors felt that the Congressional resolution was a "fitting response" to the new Soviet "propagandistic" call for Middle East agreements. Commentators were generally agreed that the Soviet proposal of a ban on all arms shipments to the area was too "one-sided" for serious consideration.[3]

In the Israeli-Egyptian impasse, commentators applauded U.S. leadership in offering peaceful support for Israel's rights to innocent passage through the Gulf of Aqaba and in supporting the presence of UN forces to prevent Gaza's use as a base for Egyptian attack. But some also upheld Israel's reluctance to rely on the "blind faith" of U.S. promises; and some "nationalist" sources objected to the U.S. offer "to do for Israel what the UN should do for it" (e.g., N.Y. News, Chi. Tribune, Hearst papers). A similar mixed response followed Pres. Eisenhower's call for Israeli compliance with UN withdrawal requests (Feb. 17) and the President's radio-TV appeal of Feb. 20. Most sources maintained that Israel had been given all the guarantees possible until her "defiance" of the UN had ended. But Israeli sympathizers protested that no similar "pressure" had been applied to Egypt, Russia, or India when they "defied" UN directives.[4]

Even sharper debate waxed on the Administration's position that the U.S. might consider sanctions if Israel's continued occupation of Gaza and Sharm el Sheik led the UN to invoke such measures. The heavy Congressional protest against any consideration of sanctions was led by a number of Republican Senators. When Israel did withdraw from the Gaza and Aqaba areas, some commentators felt that the U.S. should see to it that Egypt prevented renewed raids on Israel from Gaza, and that Egypt permitted Israeli navigation in the Gulf of Aqaba. According to a March poll, 70% held that the U.S. should "work mostly through the United Nations" in dealing with the "trouble between Israel and Egypt;" while 15% thought we should handle these problems "mostly by ourselves." Following the Hammarskjold-Nasser talks on the Suez Canal, some editors were optimistic but others were critical, demanding the complete divorcement of the Canal from domestic Egyptian politics (e.g., N.Y. Times and Herald Tribune, Edw. Murrow).[5]

U.S. moves to bolster King Hussein in Jordan were strongly endorsed by the majority of commentators; they saw the U.S. statement of concern for the independence and integrity of Jordan, and dispatch of the Sixth Fleet to the Eastern Mediterranean, as moves by a great power "in defense of its own vital interests" (e.g., Ex-Pres. Truman, Hearst papers). Some questioned whether the Jordan "internal situation" really came under the purview of the Eisenhower

Doctrine, but the proposal to grant $10 million in economic aid to Jordan was cautiously approved. A few strongly protested the action in the Jordan affair as "again barging into the middle of a foreign crisis" (Chi. Tribune, Chi. News). While numerous editors were critical of inadequate handling of relations with Nasser, 50% of the general public voiced satisfaction with "the way Eisenhower and Secretary Dulles have handled the Israel-Egypt problem." The critics felt that Nasser was exercising too much control over the Suez Canal and the Gulf of Aqaba.[6]

By the end of May several commentators were writing of "improvement" in the Middle Eastern picture, and claiming that a "large share" of the improvement was attributable to U.S. actions and policies. The stabilization of Jordan, and the agreement between Saudi Arabia and Iraq, were regarded as encouraging. Ambassador (former Congressman) Richards' trip to explain the Eisenhower Doctrine to Middle East nations stirred considerable American comment; most concluded that "something was accomplished, if not as much as may have been hoped for." Some, however, stressed that the U.S. failed to secure statements of solidarity, in opposition to Soviet policies, from Middle Eastern states which had not already committed themselves to the Western side.[7]

According to a May Poll, Americans were much more likely to blame Egypt (40%) than Israel (12%) for "the trouble between the two countries;" but 15% blamed both nations, and 33% gave no opinion. In evaluating U.S. policy, 56% said it had been "about right" in "dealing with Israel," 19% said the U.S. had "not been tough enough," and 9% said "too tough" (16% no opinion). On dealings with Egypt, only 41% called U.S. policy "about right," while as many as 42% said we had "not been tough enough." When the U.S. joined the military committee of the Baghdad Pact, editors remarked that "it was about time," although some criticized America's "puzzling attitude" toward the Pact itself (e.g., Dallas News, Milwaukee Journal).[8]

China

The U.S. prohibition on travel to Communist China by American newsmen in 1957 was almost unanimously condemned by the press, which deplored the "threat" of punitive action to be taken against any person defying the "ban." Editors and critical Senators contended that the ban had failed in its alleged primary aim of ameliorating the lot of American prisoners in China. The State Department's position was that travelers ought to have passports, and that these could not be utilized in countries not recognized by the U.S. A "deal" in which the U.S. would let its newsmen visit China in exchange for release of the 10 American prisoners held by Peking was advocated by several prominent Democratic Senators as well as by various editors. A March poll found that 65% felt that "our government should allow American reporters to visit China."[9]

Meanwhile, a few American editorial voices had been raised in favor of less rigid opposition to a UN seat for Peking. John Cowles (Des Moines Register) wrote that Americans should realize that "an overwhelming proportion of the Asian countries . . . want Red China admitted;" and the Washington Post recommended a "two-China policy" that would respect the rights of Formosa. Earlier, the Boston Herald had regretted the rigidity of both 1956 party platforms on our relations with Peking (also Prov. Journal, New Republic). Most papers, however, had supported the firmness of the platform pledges against letting Peking "shoot its way" into the UN—especially while it remained so "unrepentant" about its aggression (e.g., N.Y. Times, Scripps-Howard, Saturday Evening Post).[10]

However, some movement on the issue of trade with China was evident. A speech by Henry Ford II, advocating relaxation of some allied restrictions on trade with China, attracted much favorable comment asking "serious consideration" of the proposal. Several commentators also said that our allies should be allowed to engage in "non-strategic" trade with Communist China, and our own traders, too. Among the general public, in 1956 a majority had registered willingness to permit non-strategic trade with the Soviet Union (63% to 32%); but in the case of China a March 1957 poll reported a majority (55%) disapproving a change in U.S. regulations "to permit American businessmen to sell goods to Communist China," even if such trade did not "include war materials" (35% did approve; 10% gave no opinion).[11]

Criticism of the State Department for not permitting U.S. newsmen to go to mainland China continued. Sec. Dulles' proposal that American news agencies hire foreigners to cover the news from Red China was severely criticized by editors, publishers, and some Congressmen. Press people were somewhat encouraged when the State Department invited news media representatives to discuss the problem of U.S. news coverage of Red China; but the Department's "trial formula" turned out to be far from satisfactory to the overwhelming proportion of the nation's press. Only a few saw "some merit" in the Department's "limited approach to removing its paper curtain." Others felt that "any compromise which restricts news coverage to certain agencies or publications, or limits the tenure of their stay, gives the State Department control over the assignment of foreign correspondents." Said William R. Hearst, Jr.: "The notion that foreign coverage by the American press comes under State Department supervision should be abandoned by Sec. Dulles." Some critics cited a Gallup Poll showing that a majority of Americans (57%) were in favor of having U.S. newsmen visit Red China.[12]

The broad question of how the American people viewed their overseas representatives was partially answered by a poll in the spring of 1957 which reported that 70% now said that U.S. ambassadors were "doing a good job of representing the U.S. to other countries" (62% with no criticism, 8% with qualifications). Although this polling question differed from earlier queries, it seems likely that four years of approval for the "Washington officials handling foreign policy" was rubbing off on the ambassadors. Only 5% of the respondents said that the emissaries were doing a "poor job." Those who were critical or offered reservations were asked: "In what way are the ambassadors not doing a good job?" Replies alleged that we are misunderstood overseas, fail to show our goals, or antagonize the people; others stressed that the ambassadors were political appointees or wealthy men, rather than qualified professional officers.[13]

Violent anti-American demonstrations in Taipei at this time shocked Congress and the press, and led many to call for a thorough review of U.S. policy toward China. Commentators agreed that the U.S. was probably over-staffed not only in Taiwan, but elsewhere; they felt that this "irritant" should be reduced. However, the suggestion of cutting economic and military aid was strongly rebutted by the supporters of Chiang Kai-shek who said such reductions were just what the Chinese Communists wanted.[14]

A San Francisco address by Sec. Dulles, reaffirming U.S. policy toward China and "cogently explaining" the reasons for it, was welcomed by editors from coast to coast, who had been troubled by the "concerted effort to stimulate debate on a more lenient" policy (e.g., Time, Newsweek). Some others were gratified by the Secretary's indication that the U.S. would "shift to a more affirmative line when, as and if the Communists change for the better." Some voices continued to advocate trade with mainland China; but the opposition replied in strength, including a group of 175 business leaders headed by Charles Edison of McGraw-Edison and Admiral Moreel of Jones & Laughlin Steel Co.[15]

Acceptance by some American youths attending the Moscow Youth Festival of an official invitation to visit Peking precipitated a flurry of debate in the American press. Commentators tended to view the American youths as "unwise" to accept the Peking invitations, but Acting Secretary Herter's letter declaring stern punishment for violation of the terms under which their passports had been issued provoked more criticism than support. Mr. Herter's letter was approved by some (e.g., Houston Post); but the critics said it played directly into the hands of the Peking propagandists by "casting Uncle

Sam in the role of the Big Bad Wolf ordering harsh punishment for what most of the world will take as a typical youngster's prank." Some editors declared that the Department's "stiff-necked" attitude about contacts with China would continue to create problems until it was modified or abandoned.[16]

On August 22 the Department modified its press ban and permitted 24 news-gathering agencies to station one representative each in Communist China for a limited period. Initially this news was highly gratifying to the media representatives, although they were disappointed by the "limited" and "experimental" character of the arrangement. When Peking injected the reciprocity issue into the controversy, the frustrated press directed a blast of criticism not only at Peking for "reneging" on its original invitation, but at the State Department for "bungling" the whole problem from the start, and for attaching "provocative" conditions to its relaxation of the news ban which "practically guaranteed" that Peking would reject them.[17]

Chou En-lai's proposal of an "even exchange" to solve the issue of "journalistic" reciprocity was unacceptable to some editors who saw it as another transparent attempt to maneuver the U.S. closer to recognition. Sen. Bridges (R-NH) warned: "We cannot afford to be forced into any reciprocal agreement." At the same time some commentators concluded that the U.S. was actually taking a "more flexible" attitude toward China, citing the Department's decision to consider entry applications from qualified newsmen and athletes, and its decision to "deal gently" with the 42 American youths who traveled to China in defiance of this Government's wishes. For the most part, these decisions had won commendation from the press, which approved of "giving offenders a second chance" if they had no intention to commit a new violation. When the United Nations General Assembly voted to postpone debate on the seating of Communist China, a few commentators suggested that the U.S. employ the year gained thereby to puzzle out the answers to basic questions in our relations with China, several urging consideration of the "two Chinas" solution.[18]

Europe; Arms

Americans welcomed the Macmillan government in succession to that of Anthony Eden, and also the improved prospects for unity in Western Europe. Skepticism about Soviet willingness to agree to any effective arms limitation also continued strong, although some counseled that the U.S. should expand its disarmament proposals to include an offer for mutual troop withdrawals from Central Europe (e.g., Sen. Humphrey, Geo. Kennan).[19]

In the spring of 1957 when Mr. Stassen and his U.S. delegation joined the other negotiators at the Disarmament subcommittee conference in London, press comment ranged from pessimistic to cautiously hopeful. No one expected a broad conclusive agreement to be reached, but there was hope of agreeing on some steps in that direction. Editors saw a challenge to the Soviet Union, and a good propaganda move, in the U.S.-British announcement at Bermuda of willingness to give the UN advance notice of future nuclear tests, and to permit international observation of such tests "if Russia would do the same." But the Washington Post was critical of U.S. "propaganda maneuvering" at a time when the world was in danger of destruction by poisoning as a result of the tests, if not of pulverization.[20]

In some quarters mistrust of Russia's negotiating role was strong (e.g., N.Y. News, Wilmington News). The Soviet proposal of April 30, which included aerial inspection of wide areas in the Soviet Union and western United States was regarded as "too one-sided," but some commentators thought it could serve as a basis for negotiations. Agreement by Messrs. Eisenhower and Adenauer that no action taken in the field of disarmament would "prejudice" German reunification, and Bonn's consequent support of efforts to reach a limited arms control agreement, were appreciated by commenting editors. The debate on ratification of the statute of the International Atomic Energy Agency also took into consideration the arms control effort, with proponents saying that establishment of an adequate inspection system could be a prelude to international inspection of nuclear weapons, while opponents said agency-furnished material could be adapted for military use by Communist (and other) countries.[21]

In June, for the first time in a decade of UN negotiations, commentators felt they saw some real prospect of breaking the disarmament deadlock, when Zorin included acceptance of inspection posts inside the U.S.S.R. as part of his June 14 proposal for a moratorium on nuclear testing. The majority of commentators thought Pres. Eisenhower was taking the right approach in promising "earnest and sympathetic study" of the proposal; and many thought a temporary suspension of tests would go a long way to ease worldwide fears of radioactive fallout. Some said the need for a first-step agreement was so urgent that they favored a ban on tests without a prior agreement to halt production of nuclear weapons or to limit conventional armaments (e.g., Boston Herald, Sen. Mansfield). But dubious editors questioned the possibility of effective inspection, and were almost gleeful over announcement that the U.S. was nearing development of a "clean bomb," virtually free of radioactive fallout (e.g., David Lawrence, Time). Several advocates of a first-step agreement were now dismayed by what they called the President's "retreat" from his earlier stand on test suspension.[22]

More debate developed over reports that the U.S. was tying reduction in force levels to progress on German reunification. Some felt that "lowering the shadow of the H-bomb" was the "primary problem" facing the world, and these opposed attaching "political conditions" to any first-step arms agreement. But others argued that any agreement would be likely to freeze the status quo and thus make political settlements more difficult (e.g., N.Y. Times); and "nationalist" press spokesmen insisted there could be no agreement with the Soviet Union until the Iron Curtain was removed and Soviet forces withdrawn from Eastern Europe (e.g., Cinci. Enquirer). Advocates of arms limitation hailed Senate ratification of IAEA, whereas Sen. Bricker had felt that "U.S. ratification would be an act of suicidal folly."[23]

U.S. efforts to produce agreement at the London talks were backed by commentators; they supported our "far-flung aerial and ground inspection plan," also the proposal of a two-year suspension of nuclear tests. These sound initiatives should at least improve America's propaganda position in the world, commentators said (e.g., Prov. Journal, C. S. Monitor). But cautious American hopes were dashed by Soviet negativism and Moscow's announcement of a long-range missile (ICBM). These developments were taken as evidence that Russia wanted no agreement, and as perhaps constituting part of a broader hardening of Soviet policy. The general reaction was that the U.S. should strengthen its defenses; yet some still held that the U.S. should keep the door open for disarmament, in case the Soviets turned cooperative. Greater concern was shown about the "psychological and political" implications of the Soviet ICBM than about its military implications; and some stressed that "wise use of economic and political power" was as necessary as added military strength.[24]

Sec. Dulles' reaffirmation of U.S. arms policy before the UNGA (Sept. 19) was supported by most of those commenting, although a few said he should have indicated willingness to accept a cessation of nuclear weapons testing. Gromyko's speech was taken as added evidence of Soviet intransigence, and the New York Times concluded that the U.S. should undertake to "strengthen our will and our power to resist new Soviet aggression."[25]

Discussion of Soviet relations included some references to Eastern Europe. Earlier, a proposal to admit another 75,000 Hungarian refugees by Sen. McCarthy (R-Wis) received several endorsements; but others contended that America had already borne its full share of the burden and said further admissions should be tapered off (e.g., C. S. Monitor, Sen. Mundt). When Congress acted a few months later, editors were disappointed by the restrictions incorporated in the new general immigration law, but they resignedly endorsed the "quarter-loaf" measure. One feature commentators had hoped for was permanent status for the Hungarians who had been admitted as parolees; but editors were gratified that the new law did eliminate the "mortgage" feature on country quotas.[26]

Sputnik and After

Soviet launching of an earth satellite in October sparked a huge volume of editorial comment, much of it reflecting grave concern about the relative position of the United States in the field of scientific research in general, and missile achievement in particular. Everyone felt that the Soviet Union had also made a great propaganda gain; many saw an urgent need for counterbalancing action by the U.S., some suggesting a "crash" program comparable to the Manhattan atomic project. The Soviet achievement would serve a useful purpose, commentators said, if it shattered American complacency.[27]

According to the Gallup Poll, nearly half (49%) of the general public believed that the Soviet Union "is moving ahead of the U.S. in the development of missiles and long distance rockets;" 32% said No to this query (19% gave no opinion). Gallup added that, in a special poll of Washingtonians and Chicagoans, 43% called the Soviet satellite "A serious blow to U.S. prestige;" but 46% said No. These respondents agreed (61%) that the "next great advancement of this nature" would be by the U.S.; they also felt (61%) that the "earth satellite is more likely to be used for good purposes" than for bad purposes.[28]

Launching of a second Soviet satellite in early November gave fresh stimulus to calls for U.S. action. Pres. Eisenhower's November 7 speech drew a mixed reception: a number of newspapers termed it "reassuring;" but a few press and radio commentators and Democratic political leaders were rather sharply critical, saying the speech was not so candid or inspiring as it should have been. A second presidential speech (Nov. 13) drew a similar mixed verdict. A sense of urgency in this crisis was expressed especially by some Democratic Senators and editors (e.g., Symington; Louisville Courier-Journal); it was also voiced by some Republican spokesmen (Javits; N.Y. Herald Tribune). In both parties some conservative spokesmen tended to minimize the current danger, and to adhere to rigid governmental economy and a balanced budget—sputnik or no sputnik.[29]

News of Pres. Eisenhower's illness (Nov. 25) evoked immediate anxiety over his disability at a "particularly critical time." The U.S. must offer vigorous leadership, it was felt, in developing the free world's response to the Soviet gains in the "sputnik era." Adlai Stevenson's acceptance of a consultative role in shaping a program for the NATO "summit" meeting evoked widespread approval, as it was "signally desirable" that the U.S. show a posture of unity in foreign policy.[30]

Moscow's post-sputnik diplomacy was thought to be a real threat in many parts of the world, as commentators pointed to Khrushchev's statements to Wm. Randolph Hearst, Jr. and the "peace manifesto" issued at the close of the 40th anniversary celebration of the Bolshevik revolution. Americans were urged to "take literally" these "blueprints" of how Moscow planned to achieve world conquest (e.g., Hearst papers, Phila. Inquirer). Although it was generally considered unlikely that the Soviet Union would "loose its new weapons of mutual destructive power" upon the world, many saw great danger in the possibility that the Soviets would use their missiles to "blackmail" their way to a cold war victory. Some editors counseled the West to neglect no genuine opportunity to negotiate peaceful coexistence; but most of them concluded that a summit meeting could not be fruitful in the foreseeable future. They were disposed to postpone a summit until the Soviet Union offered "deeds, deeds, deeds" to prove it meant to use such a meeting as more than a propaganda platform (e.g., Boston Herald, Wash. Star). At the same time there was vocal support for "going ahead with whatever exchanges" the Russians would agree to.[31]

At the December NATO meeting in Paris the allies reached an agreement on the construction of missile bases in Europe, although its "vagueness" was scored by critics who desired "more positive" action. Commentators noted a shift in emphasis during the Paris meeting–from the strictly military functions of the alliance to its political and diplomatic potentialities. Some said the U.S. had "bowed" to European sentiment for another try at negotiations with the Soviet Union before making a final commitment to accept U.S. intermediate-range missiles. It was also true that the rising pressure for negotiations which was heard in Europe found increasing echoes in the U.S. press (e.g., Wash. Post, Des Moines Register).[32]

1958 Soviet Challenge

As 1958 opened, the Soviet "challenge" to the free world remained the dominant concern in American public discussion. There was uneasiness and concern about the future of the Western alliance under the double impact of Soviet development of missile power and the Kremlin's persistent "peace" propaganda. It was generally agreed that the U.S. should accelerate its efforts in missilery, but also show its constant willingness to enter talks with the Soviets which offered any promise of reducing world tensions–if only to demonstrate that it was they, rather than we, who were obstructing the peace. A minority, however, were troubled by the reluctance of our allies to provide missile bases and, fearing that the West would be negotiating from weakness in any talks with the Soviets, stressed that the time was not right for such talks.[33]

Indeed, there was general agreement that there was little hope of any substantial agreement on arms control in the immediate future, particularly in view of the Soviet Union's steadfast refusal to accept inspection. When Chairman Bulganin put forward the Rapacki proposal for a "denuclearized zone" in Central Europe, Walter Lippmann and others favored careful diplomatic exploration of the idea. Critics rejected the proposal on grounds that such a nuclear ban in West Germany would "cripple U.S. forces there" and compel U.S. withdrawal from the area (e.g., U.S. News).

Launching of the U.S. earth satellite, Explorer, on Jan. 31, 1958 was viewed by some as improving the prospects for US-USSR negotiations, a subject which was claiming voluminous discussion. Pres. Eisenhower's State of the Union message was widely hailed as a "sober assessment" and "inspiring in its enlightened challenge" to the Communist world; and a number praised his emphasis on meeting the Soviets with more effective U.S. aid and trade measures. Similarly, the President's reply to Bulganin's letter was welcomed because of its "new tone" and "greater flexibility" in understanding other points of view, but particularly for its "challenging," concrete proposals–especially that calling for "peaceful" development of outer space.[34]

Meanwhile, a vigorous debate arose over former Amb. Kennan's suggestion of some military "disengagement" by mutual withdrawal of U.S. and Russian troops from Central Europe, with Germany becoming "neutral" and "disarmed." Prompt rejection of the Kennan thesis was registered by ex-Pres. Truman, Dean Acheson, James Conant, and a majority of commenting editors. They felt that only the presence of U.S. troops had kept Western Europe from sharing the fate of Eastern Europe, and pointed out that Russian troops would withdraw only to the Polish border whereas U.S. troops would withdraw across the Atlantic Ocean. But there was some support in the House of Representatives for a modified "disengagement" plan, including a demilitarized zone from the Rhine to the Russian border, but with some U.S. forces remaining on the Continent (Reuss, D-Wis; Boyle, D-Ill).[35]

A new U.S.-Soviet agreement on exchange of persons–the "first bilateral agreement" with the U.S.S.R. since World War II–was supported as a "good beginning" in improving mutual understanding by leaders of the press and Congress, although some added that the pact's significance "could easily be overestimated." "Nationalist" critics were doubtful that the agreement on radio and TV exchanges would make it any easier for the U.S. to reach the Russian people.[36]

The State Department's decision to revive the science attache program was welcomed by editors who thought this "wise restoration" would enable us to "keep closer check on foreign scientific advances," and to show the world we "do not think entirely in military terms" (Milwaukee Journal, Wash. Star).[37]

After the launching of a U.S. earth satellite several writers suggested that the United Nations should control outer space, or that the UN should develop a program for space exploration and control. The only practical way to confine the use of outer space to nonmilitary purposes, said the Des Moines Register, "would be to turn its control over to the United Nations." The St. Louis Post-Dispatch asked: "Who can deny that the UN would indeed be the proper agency to coordinate the research, approve the program, and supervise what undoubtedly would be mankind's biggest adventure?" Some suggested that the U.S. take the lead in advocating such a program (e.g., Ernest Lindley, Sen. Lyndon Johnson, Fed. of Amn. Scientists).[38]

When Moscow proposed an agreement to ban the use of outer space for military purposes, and linked it with the elimination of foreign military bases (Mar. 15), editors tended to regard it as a propaganda move; some termed it a propaganda "victory." As usual, several spokesmen felt that the U.S. should give more than a simple negative answer; Sens. Johnson and Mansfield urged that the U.S. go to the UN with a proposal for space control.[39]

More concrete discussion of possible agenda topics in future negotiations with the Soviet Union—whether at the summit or not—was stirred by suggestions in Premier Bulganin's letter to Pres. Eisenhower. Popular support for increased U.S.-Russian trade was shown by a Gallup Poll; commentators were less inclined to demand an increase, but they backed the Administration's decision to meet the Soviet challenge in aid and trade. The Gallup Poll also showed approval for suspending nuclear tests for a 2–3 year period (49% to 36%); the editors mostly backed the U.S. position of conditioning test suspension on a suspension of producing fissionable materials for military purposes.[40]

Discussion of possible "disengagement" continued, with few advocating total American disengagement from Europe, but some suggesting various forms of limited disengagement in Central Europe which might break the deadlocks on the issues of Germany and disarmament, and hold out hope of easing Moscow's grip on Eastern Europe. Most discussed was the Rapacki plan; it was deemed "unacceptable" by the great majority of commentators. These felt that a denuclearized zone embracing Poland, Czechoslovakia and the two Germanys would leave the West "defenseless," and did not provide for the withdrawal of the Red Army from the area. Still, some editors thought Rapacki's idea could form the basis for a reasonable compromise. The Gallup Poll found willingness, 50% vs. 30%, for the U.S. and its Western allies to "keep all atomic and hydrogen weapons out of West Germany if the Russians keep them out of Eastern Europe."[41]

By an even larger margin, 62% to 29%, the Gallup respondents upheld a proposal "to set up an aerial and ground inspection system extending 500 miles either side of the Iron Curtain as a measure against surprise attacks." This approval of inspection was in line with current public comment; but it stood in contrast to the disapproval which earlier polls had found for Pres. Eisenhower's "open skies" idea for aerial photographic inspection of the U.S. and Soviet Union. Least appealing of the five "Bulganin suggestions" tested by the Gallup Poll was the proposal to "thin out" the armed forces stationed in Central Europe. By a margin of 44% to 41%, respondents did favor reduction in the "number of troops based on our side of the Iron Curtain, if Russia reduces the number of troops on her side." Little attention was given to this idea in editorial columns.[42]

Meanwhile, arrangements with our allies were improving. Commentators supported the Anglo-American missile agreement which provided for placing U.S. nuclear weapons on British soil, but required a joint decision by the two governments for launching them. This "satisfactory" solution of the control problem, however, might not persuade the other NATO peoples to accept American missiles, said the Providence Journal, "unless we can demonstrate an equal determination to resume the search for an arms control agreement."[43]

At this point Khrushchev assumed the premiership in place of Bulganin, and the Kremlin pushed its drive for a summit meeting on disarmament, as the U.S. maintained its insistence on advance preparation of a summit agenda to include the German and satellite issues. This position was endorsed in public comment, yet some feared that the Russians were outsmarting the Americans in their appeal to world opinion and said that the U.S. should make its true concern for peace more evident. As the Philadelphia Inquirer defined the difference between the U.S. and Soviet positions, "the gap is between Russia's interest in the surface appearance of a summit meeting and the American interest in what such a meeting could accomplish."[44]

The Kremlin's announcement of a unilateral suspension of nuclear weapons tests was widely regarded as an insincere move, but a significant propaganda triumph for the Russians. Some editors feared that the U.S. had lost the opportunity to negotiate effectively for inspection, but inspection was believed to be essential to a meaningful stoppage of tests. A number suggested that U.S. action was still imperative, Speaker Rayburn advocating prompt preparation for a summit conference, and saying we cannot allow the Russians to create the impression that they are "the peace people of the world." A number of commentators feared that the Soviet announcement would provide a fresh fillip to the flagging campaign in Britain to "ban-the-bomb" from the allied arsenal.[45]

By the beginning of May editors believed that the U.S. was in a much improved world position vis-a-vis the Soviet Union, chiefly as a result of its positive response to Soviet charges regarding U.S. Arctic flights. This reversal of U.S. and Russian positions before world opinion followed Moscow's taking to the UN Security Council its charge that the U.S. was endangering world peace by the SAC flights on which American planes carrying nuclear bombs regularly flew toward the Soviet Union border and then returned to their home bases.[46] The charge was generally believed to have been made for propaganda purposes, and editors endorsed the U.S. position of welcoming UN debate on the subject. The Chicago Tribune saw the Kremlin's move as "designed to place the U.S. on the defensive and to force this country reluctantly to agree to a 'summit' meeting on Soviet terms" (similarly, N.Y. Times). By "wisely welcoming UN consideration of the protest," said the Providence Journal, "we demonstrated an understanding of the fears and hopes of mankind that we have always shown." Ambassador Lodge "turned the tables on Russia by demolishing" the Soviet charges, said the Newark News; and the U.S. program for Arctic inspection was widely welcomed as a positive move. "Our government has come out with an easy-to-understand proposal that makes this nation look good to every friend of peace," said the Kansas City Times.[47]

The Soviet Union's withdrawal of its resolution against the U.S., and its veto of the U.S. proposal, combined to explode the Soviet pretensions. The veto must "shake even the most naive believer in the Kremlin's claim that it seeks only a lessening of world tensions," said the Scripps-Howard editorial. These events also considerably reduced the pressure for a summit meeting.[48]

The NATO meeting of mid-April was encouraging to commentators for its "strong display of solidarity" on doubling NATO's ground forces and reinforcing its nuclear retaliatory power with American missiles. Editors also backed the Administration's request for legislation permitting the divulging of secret atomic information to our NATO allies; but several members of Congress feared that such dispersal of secrets might broaden the arms race. The Washington Post favored the legislative changes, but it stressed the need for "utmost delicacy and discretion" in administering the amended law.[49]

Soviet Economic Challenge

The sweeping Soviet offer, at the Asian-African Solidarity Conference in Cairo, of large-scale technical aid caused a number of supporters of the Mutual Security Program to perceive a "Soviet economic challenge" at least as grave as the military one. Many called for American "leadership" and "new programs" of U.S. assistance; and they were gratified by Vice President Nixon's speech warning that the Soviet challenge required a "manysided effort" on our part, including increased foreign aid and further reduction of trade barriers. But the ever-active aid opponents insisted that the answer to a scientific breakthrough like sputnik was "not to be found by circling the globe willy-nilly with more foreign aid dollars."[50]

Advocates of tariff reduction had taken a dim view of the concessions to protectionists incorporated in the Administration's trade bill of 1957, especially the proposal to let the President–under "escape clause" procedures–raise tariffs up to 50% above the 1934 tariff rates. Pres. Eisenhower's rejection, at the end of 1956, of a Tariff Commission recommendation for an increase in the fish tariff had received backing in most editorial comment. It was generally felt that maintaining the economic strength of allies that sent us fish (e.g., Iceland) was too important to permit the U.S. fishing industry an overriding voice in this aspect of foreign policy.[51]

Administration efforts to raise the tariff on lead and zinc, in the summer of 1957, stirred up a storm of editorial oppositon, and Congress failed to enact the raises. In late 1957 the Administration's announcement that it would seek a 5-year extension of the Reciprocal Trade Agreements Act expiring on June 30, 1958 was warmly welcomed by the great majority of commentators and organization spokesmen discussing it. They saw a need to increase trade to strengthen the economies of the free world, and to meet the challenge of sputnik and Communism. They also stressed keeping the friendship of our allies and promoting greater prosperity at home. Opponents, in Congress and out, argued that increased imports add to unemployment, that reciprocity had not in fact been achieved, and that the rights of Congress had been usurped.[52]

In 1958 the Soviet Union's stepped-up drive for trade and aid throughout the world was seen by editors as adding impetus to the Administration's campaign to extend the Reciprocal Trade Agreements Act. The Russo-German trade pact, said Felix Morley, should provide an object lesson to those who opposed liberalization of our trade policy, for "it's impossible to discourage expansion of German trade with their Communist neighbors unless we are prepared to offer alternate markets." Editors expressed their usual support for renewal, but the protectionist forces refused to support a program which would "liquidate vital American industries."[53]

Pres. Eisenhower's "vigorous campaign" in behalf of the Reciprocal Trade Agreements bill was credited for House passage of the measure, including its 5-year extension. Spokesmen for the textile industry, however, urged the Senate to "tighten" the bill and to limit extension to two or three years. The final compromise on a 4-year renewal was accepted by editors as permitting "meaningful negotiations" with the European Economic Community, and also assuring Canada and Latin America that the U.S. would assume greater leadership in world trade. Editors also welcomed the U.S. efforts which gave "a new lease on life" to GATT.[54]

Editors also manifested a comparable interest in developing our aid in response to the Soviet challenge. The report of the Fairless Committee, which adjudged the Mutual Security Program "successful" and held its continuance essential for defense of the free world, was supported by a majority of those commenting. Some questioned the report's recommendation of "priority" for military aid, citing the "closer look" at economic development by the Eric Johnston committee, and its "basic philosophy" that U.S. aid to underdeveloped countries should be "separated" from military containment tactics.[55]

Sec. Dulles' proposal to separate economic from military aid, and to place the latter in the defense budget, was commended by many editors. They also liked Dulles' proposal to set up an economic development fund on a "long-range" basis. Although a minority of editors and Congressmen condemned the new "giveaway plan" (e.g., Los Angeles Times, Scripps-Howard papers), a number of organizations telegraphed their support to the White House (e.g., National Grange, Natl. Ccl. of Churches, Gen. Fed. of Women's Clubs). A May opinion poll showed 81% in favor of continuing "economic aid to countries that have agreed to stand with us against Communist aggression." Also, half of the respondents said they were willing to "spend four billions" on aid for the next year, whereas 37% called that figure "too much." Less than half were willing to send aid to such non-allies as Poland and India. The ultimate action of the Congress in cutting Mutual Security funds from 4.4 billion to 3.4 billion was deplored by a majority. But the Scripps-Howard papers contended that Congress had voted more money than "can be spent prudently or otherwise."[56]

In 1958 much favorable comment was accorded the Washington bipartisan conference of business and organization leaders, which Eric Johnston called at the invitation of Pres. Eisenhower, to consider ways of increasing public understanding of the Mutual Security Program. But publisher John S. Knight scored "the outmoded notion you can defeat Communism with dollars." Some others maintained that such foreign policy issues had been magnified by the sputniks, "possibly out of all semblance of their true proportion."[57]

A State Department report, "outlining the fast developing Soviet economic assistance program," sparked much editorial comment favorable to the MSP. Commentators welcomed statements by the Rockefeller panel and Adlai Stevenson emphasizing the "economic interdependence of the free world;" and the "deep cuts" made by the House Committee, especially the reduction in the Development Loan Fund, were deplored by many (e.g., Wash. Star, N.Y. Times). Final passage of MSP in August was welcomed as a "victory" for the Administration, despite the DLF cuts. The press carried much favorable discussion of "regional" aid for the less developed countries, and expressed considerable satisfaction with U.S. contributions to the Colombo Plan. Pres. Eisenhower's appointment of the Draper Committee to "critically appraise" the MSP was also thought to be appropriate.[58]

The President's 1959 MSP message to Congress evoked the usual majority support among editors. Several also endorsed Sen. John Kennedy's proposals for a "generous enlargement" of the Development Loan Fund and for an "immediate study of India's development needs." In March several editors upheld the Draper Committee's recommendation of $400 million additional military assistance, particularly "if it goes to NATO," in view of the Berlin situation. On the other hand, the Citizens Foreign Aid Committee of long-time aid opponents recommended a "50 percent slash" in funds and "an end to all foreign aid within three years." Nevertheless, Sen. Fulbright's proposals accentuating long-range economic aid and playing down military aid in developing countries were often endorsed. The balance-of-payments situation was stressed by some in Congress' appropriation of 3.2 billions for Mutual Security instead of the requested 3.9 billions.[59]

The President's 1960 MSP message evoked the usual editorial applause. Some also hailed the World Bank's completion of the IDA Charter. But critics continued to deplore this "big and growing racket;" the Wall St. Journal called MSP "the chief cause of our seriously adverse balance of payments." But the Administration's plan for a new Organization for Economic Cooperation and Development to "coordinate the vast financial and trade potential" of the West was promptly endorsed by editors. Some added that our allies should give us real help in supplying economic aid to needy nations.[60]

Anti-American Demonstrations

The mood of general gratification in the spring of 1958 after the Copenhagen NATO meeting, marked by allied solidarity, was rudely shattered by the developments of May 13, when Vice President

Nixon was stoned in Venezuela and American libraries were attacked in Beirut, Algeria and Paris. Press critics scored Pres. Eisenhower and Sec. Dulles for failing to offer vigorous leadership in countering the new Soviet round-the-world challenges. Some editors agreed with Sec. Dulles that American global policies were basically sound; but the governmental crisis in France, threatening the whole continental defense program, far overshadowed Moscow's "favorable reply" to the President's proposal that U.S. and Soviet technical experts meet to discuss means of enforcing any agreement on nuclear testing.[61]

Editors felt that the attack on Vice Pres. Nixon and his party at Caracas demonstrated that U.S.-Latin American relations were even more dangerously strained than had been feared. Many saw the "U.S. debacle in South America" as a complex tale of U.S. disinterest, misunderstanding, neglect, inconsiderate economic policies, and undue identification with dictators. Some stressed the role of a "vocal and violent Communist minority," while others felt that Communists alone could not be blamed for the "highly exploitable conditions." Mr. Nixon's own recommendations for future policy were thought worthy of consideration: avoidance of policies which give the impression of favoring "the governing elite;" and extending to "dictators only a handshake and to democratic leaders an embrace." The Chicago Tribune, however, posed the question of how the State Department could "use a slide-rule and say whether a government was entitled to 100, 90, or 70 percent support." The public dispatch of U.S. forces to the Caribbean to protect the Vice Presidential party stirred much concern—with a greater number of spokesmen thinking the move offered Moscow a propaganda ploy, than regarded it as a justifiable precaution.[62]

Opponents of foreign aid saw in the attacks "the failure of dollar diplomacy." But many editors expressed gratification that, by approving further Mutual Security help for Latin America, the House of Representatives repudiated the "neo-isolationists" who favored lashing back at the whole world for the sins of a few. Editors supported the Senate Foreign Relations Committee for its "substantial" approval of the economic and military assistance asked by the President.[63]

Lebanon

A "new test" of America's ability to "preserve some influence" in the Middle East came with the violent anti-U.S. demonstrations in Beirut, and the spectacle of "massive interference from outside" Lebanon against the Chamoun government. Most commentators attributed the turmoil to "Nasserism plus Communism," and the Scripps-Howard papers said: "This is not the voice of the Lebanese government or people, but is part of a deliberate campaign by enemies" of Lebanon. Some saw the Lebanese outbursts as "our reward" for adopting a "softer approach" toward Nasser (e.g., Max Lerner).[64]

U.S. action in sending "police weapons" to Beirut and "alerting" the Sixth Fleet received some approval, and several said Washington "should go as far as it can" to support the Lebanese government. But the consensus was that Beirut did not present a clear case under the Eisenhower Doctrine against Communist activity in the area. Indeed, the majority of those commenting concluded that the U.S. should support Beirut "primarily through the UN." Before Lebanon appealed to the UN a Scripps-Howard editorial said that if the UN cannot protect Lebanon, the U.S., "preferably with Britain—may have to. That is all the more reason the United Nations should be given the chance to meet its responsibility first." Similarly, the St. Louis Post-Dispatch asserted: "Unilateral intervention surely can be only a last resort. Preservation of Lebanese sovereignty obviously is the concern of the United Nations." The Providence Journal was pleased with U.S. action vis-a-vis Lebanon, saying: "To have refused their pleas for assistance—to have relied exclusively on a Lebanese protest in the UN would have been to destroy the whole Eisenhower Doctrine and leave the remaining Arab leaders no choice but to come to terms with Nasser." The Security Council's decision to send groups of observers to Lebanon was believed to have eased the danger that Lebanon might become another Korea (e.g., N.Y. Times).[65]

But the Iraq revolt on July 14 was regarded as a serious blow to the West (e.g., N.Y. Herald Tribune, Louisville Courier-Journal). Nevertheless, editorial comment on July 15 tended to be cautious re U.S. policy, with some advocating dispatch of a UN emergency force (e.g., Boston Herald, N.Y. Post, Milwaukee Journal). Some, like the Wall St. Journal, flatly said "it would be foolhardy for the U.S. now to rush into armed intervention either directly or through the United Nations."[66]

When the U.S. did respond to Lebanon's plea by sending U.S. Marines to that country, the reaction in the U.S. was mixed; but it was predominantly favorable. Supporting editors noted that the crisis was "so acute and the necessity for dealing with it in a positive manner so urgent that the U.S. could not sit by waiting for United Nations action that might be delayed for days by Soviet obstruction—or not come at all" (Phila. Inquirer). The Washington Post added that "Washington has attempted a rescue operation as a self-appointed advance agent of the UN." Indeed, there was a considerable feeling that U.S. maintenance of troops in Lebanon should be terminated as soon as possible (e.g., C. S. Monitor, N.Y. Times).[67]

On the other hand, a number of newspapers were either critical of the decision to send troops, or highly dubious about it (e.g., Chicago News, Chicago Tribune, N.Y. Post, Walter Lippmann, Sens. Cooper and Mansfield). "We are staking American lives," said the St. Louis Globe-Democrat, "on a power policy that is not too clear and may be found on the wrong side of history's fence."

The majority of the general public, however, supported the Marine landings; and an even larger majority was in favor of dispatching a UN force to prevent outside interference in Lebanon. The Gallup Poll found 59% approving "U.S. action in sending troops into Lebanon," 27% disapproving, and 14% giving no opinion. "What the U.S. is trying to do in the Near East" was upheld by a similar ratio (56% to 26%). The idea of the UN "sending an Emergency Force into Lebanon" was backed by as many as 79%.[68]

When the Soviet Union proposed a summit conference "within three days" to consider Middle East problems, estimates of its probable utility ranged widely. Although few actually opposed such a meeting, its prospects were not generally estimated very highly; and editors felt that the U.S. reply should not be "simply negative." Pres. Eisenhower's idea that such a conference, if held, should be within the framework of the United Nations won approval from many sources (e.g., Hearst and Scripps-Howard papers).[69]

Pres. Eisenhower's address to the special UNGA session on the Mideast (Aug. 13), setting out a 6-point program for Middle Eastern progress and development, was strongly endorsed by a majority of those commenting. Several were pleased with the positive program instead of an indictment of Soviet policies; these editors contrasted the President's address with Gromyko's "repetition of the old Soviet propaganda line." Some, however, viewed the idea that the UN monitor "inflammatory" radio broadcasts as abridging the freedom of speech. Sharply critical, the Wall St. Journal saw the President as opening a "Pandora's box" in upholding the U.S. right to intervene militarily in defense of small nations.[70]

The UNGA concluded its special session by unanimous adoption of the "Arab" resolution which called upon the Secretary-General to negotiate the "early withdrawal" of Western forces in the area. The U.S. announced its intention of bringing out the Marines in October if there were no further difficulties. They came out on schedule, and commentators applauded the "pledged departure."[71] The Lebanon crisis stimulated discussion in the U.S. of enforcement measures appropriate for international crises; and the Senate passed a resolution calling for a permanent UN police force. A majority of those commenting supported such a force, but some doubted the practicality of attempting it (e.g., Phila. Inquirer, Des Moines Register, Minneapolis Tribune). The St. Paul Pioneer Press said such a world force would not be practicable as long as the Soviet Union was unwilling to cooperate.[72]

Arms Talks

Meetings of U.S. and Soviet technical experts in Geneva were making some progress in fields related to arms control. The delegates reached agreement upon the major methods of detecting nuclear explosions; and commentators were encouraged by Khrushchev's proposal of technical talks on the prevention of surprise attacks. Agreement of East-West scientists on a detection system to spot nuclear test-ban violations prompted Time magazine to say that the "main accomplishment" of the conference was Communist acceptance of the feasibility of inspection; on the other hand, the West would henceforth be under "increased pressure" to stop its testing. Some, however, continued to oppose any suspension of testing, saying that testing was greatly to our military advantage (e.g., N.Y. Mirror, Wall St. Journal).[73]

Pres. Eisenhower's proposal of a 1-year U.S. suspension of nuclear tests, though, was approved by a majority of editors, some stating their hope that this could be "a step toward nuclear peace," if there were effective inspection. To Quincy Howe (ABN) and others, this "radical change" in U.S. foreign policy was wise; and "cause for mild hope" was seen in Soviet acceptance of negotiations, although many commentators remained skeptical of the outcome in view of recent Soviet propaganda and the continuing uncertainty about whether Moscow would actually permit Western inspection posts within the Soviet Union. A Roper poll reported that 58% agreed "we should form an agreement with Russia to stop bomb testing," provided a system of international inspection was established; but 31% maintained "it is imperative that we continue testing nuclear bombs, whatever Russia does" (11% gave no opinion).[74]

The Second International Conference on the Peaceful Uses of Atomic Energy (Sept. 1-13) won appreciative comment; its greatest accomplishment was thought to be the breaking down of secrecy requirements, which was expected to speed progress toward utilization of hydrogen power (e.g., Wall St. Journal, Houston Post).[75]

Amb. Lodge told the American Legion convention, during this period, that the U.S. would propose to UNGA a program for international cooperation in the field of outer space. The news was welcome to many editors, the Chicago Sun-Times interpreting it as "one more challenge to Russia to work in harness with the U.S. for the betterment of mankind." Some cautioned that the program "be spelled out in meticulous detail in the UN so that the American people . . . (can) determine what guarantees it contains against a Russian planetary double-cross" (Hearst papers). Sen. Lyndon Johnson's subsequent appearance at the UN was widely applauded as demonstrating the breadth of U.S. support for the proposal.[76]

So long as American Marines remained in Lebanon editors continued to discuss the establishment of a UN police force. Some editors favored a force composed of men from smaller countries; others would have added volunteers from the larger countries. Secretary-General Hammarskjold declared that a standing force would be of little value, but he suggested that acceptance of principles providing a "framework for later operations" could be helpful.[77]

As the number of UN members steadily increased—now 81—editors were aware that the U.S. was finding it increasingly difficult to have its way in the world organization. Some saw danger of a rising public demand for U.S. withdrawal (e.g., Detroit Free Press); the Des Moines Register saw the U.S. needing to "cock its ear more and more intently to the sounds of world opinion—not a bad thing for the U.S. or the rest of the world." The Worcester Telegram hoped for the "gradual elimination of blocs in the UN," with each member voting its own way on each issue.[78]

Establishment of a disarmament commission composed of all members of the General Assembly was viewed critically; editors thought this body too large to accomplish much. Those desirous of suspending nuclear tests were dismayed when the Soviet Union resumed its testing (Oct. 1), and later refused to join the U.S. and Britain in a 1-year suspension. Prospects for the Geneva conference on testing were naturally dimmed; and some feared that the Soviets were impressing the world with their grandiose proposals, despite their unwillingness to agree to the steps necessary to make any sort of disarmament practical (e.g., Phila. Bulletin). But editors persisted in their hopes, and said the U.S. must make every effort to reach a reasonable agreement despite Soviet intransigence.[79]

Quemoy (Again)

Following secret talks with Khrushchev, Mao Tse-tung in late August launched his "unprecedented" bombardment of the offshore islands, setting off a concerned discussion in America. Editors agreed that the Quemoy islands were of slight military significance, but they differed as to whether their practical value warranted U.S. participation in their defense. Many commended Sec. Dulles' "forthright warning" to Peking that an attempt to seize Quemoy and Matsu would be a "threat to peace" in the area; they felt that we must "show clearly that we are prepared to fight," since it would be "humiliating for this country to back down" (e.g., Boston Herald, N.Y. Times and Herald Tribune).[80]

Another group, however, argued against attempting to defend the islands, even though this course would "enhance the propaganda triumph of Peiping's bluff-calling act" (e.g., Louisville Courier-Journal, Walter Lippmann, Sen. Morse). Some in each group felt that "our China policy weakens rather than strengthens us;" but on the recurring issue of seating Peking at the UN preponderant editorial opinion, expressed Congressional opinion, and popular opinion remained strongly opposed to "admitting bloody-handed Red China."[81]

Throughout September discussion of the Quemoy issue continued with deep division on "risking a war" to keep the offshore islands out of Communist hands. Yet opinion remained virtually unanimous on abiding by the U.S. commitment to defend Taiwan and the Pescadores against Communist attack. The Administration's resolve to make a "firm stand" against Communist aggression on Quemoy was endorsed by ex-Pres. Truman, the American Legion, and a substantial segment of the press. On the other hand, some Republican Senators (Cooper, Javits) joined a large number of Democratic Senators and commentators who were convinced the islands were "not worth the shedding of American blood," and stressed that these islands had always been considered geographically and historically a part of the Chinese mainland.[82]

The Administration's stress on its desire to settle the dispute through negotiations was generally approved; the President's statement that it doesn't pay to "appease aggressors" was also endorsed. A number advocated demilitarization and neutralization of the offshore isles, despite Taiwan's objections. Some thought the UN should try to settle the issue; and a Gallup Poll found a majority agreeing to the proposition that the U.S. "work out a solution in the UN before we get more involved in a military way."

By the end of October commentators were exasperated by the on-again, off-again bombardment of Quemoy, but they were relieved that the danger of the U.S. "being dragged into war" appeared to be reduced. Much importance was attached to Sec. Dulles' visit to Taipei, and to Chiang Kai-shek's statement in their joint communique that the use of force would not be the principal means he would use to carry out "his sacred mission of restoring freedom to the people on the mainland." Also noting Chiang's agreement to a gradual reduction in garrisons on the offshore islands, editors tended to agree with the Scripps-Howard editorial stating that "Sec. Dulles has taken the first preliminary but indispensable step toward getting America disentangled from the offshore islands and building the groundwork for a long-range policy of maintaining Formosa as a free China."[83]

Some, however, agreed with the New York Times that in allowing any Nationalist troops to remain on Quemoy the Administration left the situation basically unchanged–including the possibility of U.S. involvement in war with China. The continued decline in the "crisis atmosphere" over Quemoy prompted further tributes to the Administration for its "stand firm" policy; but the critics remained dissatisfied and felt that the danger of accidental war over Quemoy continued. To a substantial segment of opinion U.S. and UN recognition of Red China was "now only a question of time" (e.g., World Order Conf. of Natl. Ccl. of Churches); but such stands were swiftly and sharply opposed by leading individuals and newspapers.[84]

Reference Notes

1. AOR of Feb. 4, 1957.
2. Ibid.
3. AOR for Mar. and Apr. 1957.
4. AOR of Mar. 4, 1957.
5. AOR of Apr. 4, 1957.
6. AOR of May 3, 1957.
7. AOR of June 3, 1957.
8. AOR for June 3 and July 3, 1957.
9. AOR for Feb. 4, Mar. 4 and May 3, 1957.
10. AOR for Feb. 15 and Sept. 13, 1956; Mar. 4, 1957.
11. AOR of Mar. 4, 1957.
12. AOR for June 3 and Aug. 2, 1957.
13. N.O.R.C. poll #404, Apr. 26, 1957.
14. AOR of June 3, 1957.
15. AOR of Aug. 2, 1957.
16. AOR of Sept. 3, 1957.
17. Ibid.
18. AOR of Oct. 2, 1957.
19. AOR of Feb. 4, 1957.
20. AOR of Apr. 4, 1957.
21. AOR of June 3, 1957.
22. AOR of July 3, 1957.
23. Ibid.
24. AOR of Sept. 3, 1957.
25. AOR of Oct. 2, 1957.
26. AOR for May 3 and Sept. 6, 1957.
27. AOR of Nov. 1, 1957.
28. Ibid.
29. AOR of Dec. 4, 1957.
30. AOR for Nov. 1 and Dec. 4, 1957.
31. AOR of Dec. 4, 1957.
32. AOR of Jan. 3, 1958.
33. Ibid.
34. AOR of Feb. 3, 1958.
35. Ibid.
36. AOR for Feb. 3 and Mar. 3, 1958.
37. Ibid.
38. AOR of Feb. 15, 1958.
39. AOR of Apr. 3, 1958.
40. AOR of Mar. 3, 1958.

41. Ibid.
42. Ibid.
43. Ibid.
44. AOR of Apr. 3, 1958.
45. Ibid.
46. Stebbins, Richard P., *U.S. in World Affairs, 1958*, pp. 54-57.
47. AOR of May 16, 1958.
48. Ibid.
49. AOR of May 5, 1958.
50. AOR of Jan. 3, 1958.
51. AOR of Jan. 4, 1957.
52. AOR for Sept. 6 and Dec. 9, 1957.
53. AOR of May 5, 1958.
54. AOR for July 3, Aug. 5, Sept. 2, Nov. 3, 1958.
55. AOR of Apr. 4, 1957.
56. AOR for May 3, June 3, July 3, Aug. 2, Sept. 3, 1957.
57. AOR for Feb. 3 and Mar. 3, 1958.
58. AOR for July 3, Sept. 2, Dec. 3, 1958.
59. AOR for Mar. 2, Apr. 3, May 22, Aug. 4, Sept. 4, 1959.
60. AOR for Mar. 4 and Apr. 20, 1960.
61. AOR for June 3, 1958.
62. Ibid.
63. Ibid.
64. Ibid.
65. AOR of June 15, 1958.
66. AOR of July 25, 1958.
67. Ibid.
68. Ibid.
69. AOR for Aug. 5 and 24, 1958.
70. AOR of Sept. 2, 1958.
71. AOR of Nov. 3, 1958.
72. AOR of Aug. 24, 1958.
73. AOR for Aug. 5 and Sept. 2, 1958.
74. AOR for Sept. 2 and Oct. 2, 1958.
75. AOR for Sept. 16 and Oct. 2, 1958.
76. AOR for Sept. 16 and Dec. 15, 1958.
77. AOR for Oct. 15 and Nov. 15, 1958.
78. AOR of Nov. 15, 1958.
79. AOR for Nov. 3, Dec. 3 and 12, 1958, Jan. 2, 1959.
80. AOR of Sept. 2, 1958.
81. Ibid.
82. AOR of Oct. 2, 1958.
83. AOR of Nov. 3, 1958.
84. AOR for Dec. 3, 1958 and Feb. 2, 1959.

XI
CHALLENGES CONTINUE (1959–1960)

Moscow's addition of Berlin as a subject for propaganda campaigns prompted many commentators to stress the global character of the Communist challenge in 1959. Editors cited not only the rapid succession of high-pressure efforts involving the Middle East, the Chinese offshore islands, and Berlin, but also Soviet obstructionism at the two Geneva conferences (nuclear tests, surprise attacks), the firings upon U.S. planes, Khrushchev's boasts about rising production in the Soviet Union, and the far-flung competition in proffering aid to less-developed countries.[1] The final two years of Eisenhower's second term witnessed fewer crises in the Middle East and Far East than did the preceding biennium; but they included the extension of the Communist challenge to Africa and the United Nations. Castro came to power in Cuba. Khrushchev was the outstanding figure of this period: visiting the U.S., collapsing the Paris summit, and attending the UN General Assembly.

Berlin

In response to Khrushchev's "ultimatum" on Berlin (Nov. 10) commentators pointed to "only one merit," the time limit permitting a six-month continuation of the status quo in Berlin. This breathing-spell, it was felt, should give Western policy-makers the opportunity to work out a "coordinated policy." The stand taken by American editors was unanimous and unequivocal: the U.S. must not, under any circumstances, abandon Berlin to the Communists—as would result under Khrushchev's proposal to end the four-power controls and make West Berlin a "demilitarized, free city."[2]

On this issue of saving Berlin there was no division among the editors, or between the major political parties, as there had been over Quemoy and Matsu. The Government's firm determination to stay in Berlin, to refuse to deal directly with the East German "puppet regime," and to reject any unilateral Soviet action ending the four-power control of Berlin—was thoroughly supported. A number surmised that Khrushchev's Berlin proposal was really aimed at the reunification and neutralization of Germany. Accordingly, some advocated that the West renew its demand for free elections in both parts of Germany, and that the new German government be free to choose its own foreign policy (e.g., Wall St. Journal, Ernest Lindley, N.Y. Herald Tribune). Others, however, felt that the West must respond with something more than a restatement of familiar positions, suggesting the proposal of some form of "disengagement" and a "demilitarized buffer zone" in Central Europe (e.g., St. Louis Post-Dispatch, Edw. Murrow). Walter Lippmann's view that "confederation" might provide a "realistic and reasonable" solution was shared by the Louisville Courier-Journal.[3]

1959 was expected by commentators to be a year of "supreme challenge," with the "time-bomb" of Berlin as the main crisis, but others continuing in the Middle East and Asia (Quemoy). They felt the outlook was better than in 1958 because the U.S. had overcome the initial lag in rocketry and Western Europe had been strengthened by France's resurgence under de Gaulle and by establishment of the French-German partnership. The visits to the Soviet Union of Adlai Stevenson and Hubert Humphrey were thought to serve a useful purpose by increasing public understanding of what goes on in the Soviet Union. Similarly, scheduling of a visit to the U.S. by Deputy Premier Mikoyan was welcomed as likely to advance Soviet understanding of America.[4]

In the new year the U.S. policy on Berlin, to "fight if necessary," continued to be strongly backed by press and public. At the same time the West's renewed offer to discuss the problems of German unification and European security was also welcomed. Some were disappointed that the NATO allies stuck to the "old formulae," instead of offering counterproposals for easing the situation in Berlin and Germany that "might stand a chance of acceptance" by the Soviets (e.g., Wash. Post).[5]

The January visit by Anastas Mikoyan was deemed not to have justified either advance fears or hopes. Editors supported the U.S. rejection of current Soviet terms for expanded Soviet trade, yet most continued to see value in the exchange of visits by leaders and specialists. Few were opposed to ordinary trade, but commentators continued to voice opposition to trade in strategic goods. Some Congressmen and others registered opposition to Mikoyan's visit, but most commentators endorsed Pres. Eisenhower's admonition that the visitor be treated with typical American "courtesy."[6]

Berlin was the chief issue discussed in connection with Mikoyan's visit; and while editors felt that "nothing of substance was changed," there was considerable feeling that the visit had produced "a subtle change in the diplomatic climate." Commentators cited Mikoyan's suggestion that the May 27 "deadline" on Berlin was flexible and could be extended if East-West negotiations were under way by then; also mentioned was Sec. Dulles' observation that free elections were not necessarily the only way to unify Germany. Some journals, however, were vigorously opposed to any modification of our long-standing position of free all-German elections as a prerequisite to unification (e.g., N.Y. Times, San Diego Union).[7]

Castro

As events in Cuba moved toward the New Year's Day victory of Fidel Castro, and the departure of Pres. Batista, editors viewed the increasing violence "on our doorstep" with deep concern but gave overwhelming approval to the U.S. policy of keeping "hands off." Even to "protect the many billion American dollars invested in Cuba," the U.S. should not intervene—lest such action create ill will throughout Latin America and give the Communists "grounds for charging imperialism" (e.g., N.Y. Times, Toledo Blade). There was keen apprehension about the future under Castro, whose rebel forces had kidnapped U.S. citizens. The prevailing impression was that Communism would gain strength in Cuba only if the chaos continued.[8]

News from Cuba of peremptory military trials and mass executions aroused deep misgivings as to the true nature of the Castro regime, but to the majority of editors "prospects for a decent government still seemed favorable." Despite the "bloody turn of events," commentators continued to endorse the U.S. "hands off" policy. Comment on Dr. Milton Eisenhower's recommendations for future relations with other American republics showed gratification that the tone throughout was one of "partnership founded on understanding and candor."[9]

Premier Castro continued to receive editorial assurances of American "friendlines," but his tour of the U.S. produced little evidence of greater freedom in Cuba or of progress there toward stated goals. Cuba's "ambiguous" role in the "invasion" of Panama disturbed numerous editors. The "speed and unanimity" with which all members of the OAS rallied to Panama's aid when it was attacked by "invaders" was regarded by many as the "most heartening development" for hemispheric peace in years. Virtually all of those commenting "thoroughly approved" of the U.S. decision to "put itself at the disposal of the OAS" for whatever action it deemed necessary to quell the "invasion" of Panama. Few suggested that the U.S. unilaterally send arms and destroyers, even though many stressed that America's vital interest in the Canal gave us a "special interest" in supporting the legitimate government.[10]

From Dulles to Herter

Word of Sec. Dulles' enforced withdrawal from active direction of American foreign policy, for reasons of health, came at a time when there was continuing concern over the possibility of a "military showdown" over Berlin. Among the numerous high tributes to Mr. Dulles, the Secretary's "unique" contribution in handling allied strategy on the Berlin-German issue was mentioned by many; and commentators took considerable comfort from the fact that on his last mission to Europe he had succeeded in welding a common allied policy, proposing a Foreign Ministers meeting on all aspects of the German problem, while still firmly rejecting the Soviet ultimatum on Berlin. For the future, editors emphasized that the top echelon of the State Department–Messrs. Herter, Dillon, and Murphy–constituted a "strong team" which was thoroughly familiar with Mr. Dulles' views.[11]

But Chairman Khrushchev's public rejection of Western terms for a Foreign Ministers conference (Feb. 24)–in the midst of Prime Minister Macmillan's "goodwill mission" to Moscow–cast a pall of gloom over the prospects for a negotiated settlement. Khrushchev's repetition of his intention to turn over the Berlin access routes to the East Germans, and to sign a separate peace treaty with the Pankow regime, heightened the tensions of a tense time. To leave Khrushchev with "no uncertainty whatever" that the Allied right to access to Berlin could not be compromised, some called for Congress to pass a joint resolution supporting the President's firm stand.[12]

Various "Stalinist" speeches at the Communist Party Congress, and the U.S. disclosure of evidence that the Russians deliberately shot down an American transport plane over Armenia, appeared to dim hopes for lessened tension and improved relations. But at the Party Congress Khrushchev also issued a "back-handed" invitation to Pres. Eisenhower to visit the Soviet Union. The President's "cool" reply was regarded as appropriate by most editors; they were glad he made it plain that the "Soviet leaders would have to mend their ways" before he could consider accepting (San Diego Union). Others were pleased that the President refrained from taking any "door-slamming position;" and some suggested that it would not be appropriate for Vice President Nixon to make the trip instead of the President (e.g., Business Week, Walter Lippmann). An early February Gallup Poll had found a plurality in favor of Nixon's going to Russia "to return Russian Deputy Prime Minister Mikoyan's visit."[13]

Another Gallup Poll dealt with Russian trade and found a majority in favor of the U.S. and Soviet Union working out "a business arrangement to buy and sell MORE goods to each other." The 55% figure in February matched the degree of approval which had been recorded in 1955 at the time of the Geneva summit; and it marked an increase from the 50% approval reported in June 1957.

Pres. Eisenhower's TV speech of March 16 focused attention on efforts at negotiation, and his reaffirmation of our rights in Berlin received overwhelming support from Congress, the press, and the public. Gallup reported that the great majority felt that the U.S.–along with Britain and France–should keep its forces in Berlin "even at the risk of war." Gallup also reported public willingness to see the crisis "turned over" to the UN, expressed by a majority of the 78% who had "heard or read about" the Berlin problem. This sentiment in favor of UN handling, however, was appreciably less than had been registered during the crisis over Quemoy. By the beginning of April it seemed that the public anxiety over Berlin had measurably diminished, in view of the scheduling of a Foreign Ministers conference in May.[14]

While the Soviet-Western "tug-of-war over Berlin" continued, some observers voiced concern lest a flare-up in Asia confront the U.S. with a "dual crisis" (e.g., Sen. Jackson). Some who had long been worried about Quemoy renewed their urgings that the U.S. withdraw from any responsibility for the defense of "these exposed and generally unprofitable positions" (Prov. Journal). The revolt in Tibet against Communist oppression stirred sympathy for the Tibetans and sharp criticism of Red China for its ruthless suppression of a "supposed religious and political autonomy;" but few thought that the U.S. or free world could go beyond expressions of indignation. A few did think the Tibetan case should be brought before the UN. A number noted that the "rape of Tibet" had provided foes of a UN seat for Peking with potent ammunition.[15]

As Sec. Herter started out on his first major diplomatic mission—the Paris meeting of Western Foreign Ministers—editors were concerned about "serious divergencies" in the Western camp. Hence, the "complete agreement" which developed at Paris was warmly welcomed, even though there was little expectation that the Soviets would accept the agreed package, with its insistence on progressive German reunification based ultimately on free elections. Some observers thought it unwise of the West to insist on terms which it knew the Russians would reject (Walter Lippman, Wash. Post).[16]

Having vigorously rejected the Soviet attempt to impose a lid on allied air flights in the Berlin air corridor, the great majority of U.S. Congressmen and commentators upheld our government's determination to fly at any altitude. A few urged the U.S. not to exercise its right just then, so as not to appear "provocative" on the eve of the East-West negotiations.

At this point, a Western initiative in the nuclear test talks received editorial approval: a plan for a first-step ban on atmospheric and underwater nuclear tests. The plan would "curb the fall-out peril," and also permit "practice in at least partial measures of control." The Soviet rebuff of the Western move led some to expect "no progress" before a summit meeting.[17]

Pres. Eisenhower's decision to send Vice President Nixon to Moscow to open the American National Exhibition on July 25 was hailed as "eminently sensible," and ex-Pres. Truman felt that if, during Nixon's visit, Soviet Premier Khrushchev indicated a desire to visit

Washington, such an invitation "should be encouraged" (similarly, Phila. Inquirer). Support for the East-West exchange program continued to be expressed by a sizable majority.[18]

Sec. Herter's presentation of the West's peace plan at the Geneva Foreign Ministers meeting, including the Soviet Union, was highly praised; but a limited accord on Berlin, paving the way to the summit, was the most that observers expected to result. Commentators noted that the Western package peace plan was so "reasonable" that it made a favorable impression abroad as well as at home. Sec. Herter was also commended for two statements to Gromyko: his private notice to the Soviet ambassador that the U.S. would never attend a summit meeting under "duress;" and his stern rebuke to Gromyko to cease his "name-calling and slandering" of the West.[19]

U.S.-Soviet Relations; Europe

Amid speculation that Khrushchev might come to America for a summit meeting, a majority of commenting editors favored inviting the Communist Party Secretary to "see the real America;" but there was virtual unanimity that a Big Four summit meeting would have to be justified by adequate progress at the Geneva meeting of Foreign Ministers. A minority were sharply critical of "naive elements" in the U.S. who would give Russia world stature by having Pres. Eisenhower take the Communist leader "unto his official bosom" (e.g., David Lawrence, Nashville Banner). A July Gallup Poll found 50% in favor and 36% opposed to inviting Khrushchev (14% no opinion). For standing up to Khrushchev in the Moscow "kitchen colloquy" Vice President Nixon was highly praised, and also for telling the Russian and Polish people of America's strength and determination to uphold freedom.[20]

Belief that the West had gone as far as it could at Geneva, in making concessions to the Soviets, was virtually unanimous in comment on Sec. Herter's interim report, and after the long conference was concluded. Mr. Gromyko's insistence on tying a Berlin agreement to the establishment of an all-German committee to discuss Germany's future was regarded as "too high a price" to pay for an agreed document. In fact, some thought that the West had "gone too far" in proposing a 5-year continuation of the existing Berlin status without explicit definition of Western access rights.

But the anxiety with which many had contemplated Geneva's aftermath (e.g., new harassments in Berlin) subsided with the news that Chairman Khrushchev and Pres. Eisenhower had agreed to exchange visits. A number felt that the projected U.S.-Soviet talks offered advantages over a 4-power summit meeting, some saying that the pressure of a summit to produce tangible results might lead to "damaging Western concessions." Those who feared that the forthcoming bilateral talks might lead to deals "behind our allies' backs" were pleased that Pres. Eisenhower's plan to go to Europe to consult with our "principal allies" should allay any such misgivings.[21]

In August American commentators were deeply moved by the outpouring of popular affection and enthusiasm which greeted Pres. Eisenhower on his "triumphal tour" of Europe. The warmth and spontaneity of the President's reception in London, Bonn and Paris surpassed all expectations, observers agreed. The surge of feeling was deemed to be for "Eisenhower, the man of peace," and many perceived also a basic acceptance of the President's ability to deal with Khrushchev. Americans were cautioned not to expect any "dramatic" results from the projected talks; and Europeans voiced confidence that there would be no "deals" against their interests. Sensing "a deliberate change of U.S. diplomatic strategy," Walter Lippmann said: "We have backed away" from a show-down over Berlin into a "round of popular diplomacy" which draws its energy from the "popular feeling everywhere that a nuclear war must be avoided."[22]

All during the summer editors continued to express their strong support of the negotiations for a test ban accord; and the President's "wise" decision to extend the suspension of U.S. weapons tests until the end of the year was also welcomed. A number hoped that the whole question of atomic controls would be tackled in the forthcoming Big Two talks.

Concern that Communism was making "dangerous strides" in Castro's Cuba was widely expressed this summer, with some advocating U.S. steps to stop it (e.g., Omaha World-Herald). Others discounted charges that Castro was Communist. Earlier, American editors had expressed considerable sympathy for Cuba's aims at land reform; but they tended to feel now that the implementation was extortionate and opposed to the true interests of the people. Most also agreed with the U.S. note informing Castro that his agrarian reform plan did not "meet the test of fair compensation" (e.g., N.Y. Herald Tribune, Des Moines Register).[23]

China; Indochina

The need for changing U.S. policy toward China was stressed by Sen. Engle (D-Cal.) in 1959; but he made it clear he wasn't advocating U.S. recognition nor UN seating of Peking. Several Congressmen agreed with some of Engle's "middle ground suggestions" (non-strategic trade, exchange of newsmen, Peking's participation in any nuclear test ban agreement); but opponents of any change were also vocal. When the State Department validated the passports of Vincent Sheean and Averell Harriman to Red China as journalists, editorial comment was mixed—with some favoring a statement welcoming Chinese correspondents on a basis of equality with American correspondents.[24]

Warm congratulations were extended to Viet-Nam on its 5th anniversary for its good use of its freedom and for the "striking progress" made with U.S. aid. New Communist aggressions in the Far East heightened skepticism about the outcome of the forthcoming Khrushchev talks. China's application of military pressure along the 2,000-mile border from Laos to India (Ladakh) was thought to herald a "new period of tension in the Far East." Observers also saw "grave international complications" in the large-scale penetration of the Laotian frontier by Communist insurgents from North Viet-Nam, and they expressed fear that "another Korea" was in the making. As one editor put it, "every such demarche is a test case, and the free world cannot afford to lose any of them" (Boston Herald; similarly, N.Y. Times). Hence, the U.S. decision to airlift supplies to the Laos government, and grant additional "modest" aid in enlarging its forces, was warmly welcomed. Still, the great preference among commentators was for the dispatch of UN observers to the trouble spots who would report back to the UN.[25]

Khrushchev Visit

News and comment on Chairman Khrushchev's visit to America were tremendous in magnitude—on TV and radio and in the press. The Soviet moon-shot on the eve of the visitor's arrival sparked some editorial concern about how propagandistic was the trip's purpose, but the Soviet scientific achievement was ungrudgingly acknowledged. Khrushchev's initial speech (at the National Press Club) appeared to editors to confirm the advance expectation that the trip could produce little in substantive achievement, as it gave slight indication of a willingness to budge from previously stated positions. In fact, the Gallup Poll reported that only 13% expected a "great deal" of progress to flow from the Eisenhower-Khrushchev exchange of visits, 31% expected "some" progress, and 38% anticipated "little or no" progress.[26]

The polite, but restrained, conduct of the welcoming street crowds in Washington and New York was seen as evidence of a public determination not to be "taken in" by "Soviet smiles." Although the Russian leader drew considerable criticism at various points on his tour, the general editorial image was that of a very shrewd and formidable figure. His repeated assertions that "we will bury you" prompted numerous editorial rejoinders. At the end of the visit most commentators regarded the Camp David talks as beneficial, although all took a "wait-and-see" attitude pending further negotiations. According to James Reston, the general view in Washington was that the main result was that "it produced agreement to talk some more," which was not considered an inconsequential achievement. A majority of the public (52%) concluded that the visit had been "a good thing," and only 19% called it "a bad thing," according to a Gallup Poll taken shortly before the Camp David conversations. Some critics of the Khrushchev invitation, however, argued that the visitor had gained much publicity and prestige without any corresponding advantage to "our side" (e.g., Sens. Capehart, R; Dodd, D).[27]

Editors regarded as very helpful the specific agreement to reopen negotiations on the Berlin issue without any set "time limit." This was also viewed as removing a "major obstacle" to a summit conference. Chairman Khrushchev's disarmament address to the UNGA (Sept. 18) was received as a "propaganda bombshell." According to the New York Times, the Communist leader produced "a propaganda mountain and a disarmament mouse;" but the Washington Star warned that his speech could be "used effectively in many parts of the world." At the same time, a number of editors and political leaders advocated careful consideration of the arms proposals (e.g., Adlai Stevenson, Sen. Wiley; C.S. Monitor).[28]

The visit produced little in the way of more fruitful trade relations, both because of slight U.S. interest in anything the Russians had to sell, and because the Camp David talks offered little assurance Moscow was more ready to trade "by world community ground rules." An extension of credit was "unthinkable" to commentators who recalled the repudiation of the Czarist debts and the failure to settle the lend-lease account. A number agreed with Eric Ridder and the New York Herald Tribune that "an unfreezing of the cold war would have to precede any expanded trade relationship."[29]

When Pres. de Gaulle proposed that the East-West summit not be scheduled before the spring, in order to give the West time to work out allied differences before meeting the Soviets, there was general agreement in American comment. Official agreement on a meeting of the Western Big Four in Paris in mid-December was welcomed. So was British Prime Minister Macmillan's reelection; editors were pleased that the same team would be participating in the forthcoming negotiations, rather than the Labourites with their inclination toward disengagement in Central Europe, neutralization of Germany, and unilateral nuclear disarmament.[30]

Khrushchev's October visit to Peking interested Americans. They were pleased to see that the Soviet leader kept his promise to Eisenhower to counsel his Chinese allies to try negotiations, rather than force, in settling international disputes. But some saw a "loophole" for Red China in Khrushchev's statement that Marxism continued to recognize "liberating, just wars." Some felt that this "Red-made loophole" was the probable impetus for statements by Herter and other officials stating that the U.S. would hold the USSR responsible "to a very real degree" for any Chinese aggression–in Taiwan or elsewhere. The predominant reaction was favorable to this "doctrine of partial responsibility" (e.g., N.Y. Herald Tribune, Phila. Inquirer); a minority questioned the accuracy or wisdom of the doctrine (e.g., Walter Lippmann, St. Louis Post-Dispatch).[31]

The UN Security Council vote in September to dispatch a fact-finding team to Laos was warmly welcomed by commentators, and many felt that the UN Committee's presence would introduce a stabilizing element into the "very firm policy" Sec. Herter exemplified in his UN pledge to protect Laos; but collective action–rather than unilateral–was hoped for.[32]

Interlude (Asian Trip)

The time between Khrushchev's departure and the scheduled spring summit in Paris was marked by Pres. Eisenhower's Asian trip and new concern about Cuba. Renewal in November of the cultural exchange agreement with the Soviet Union was welcomed as one of the most hopeful auguries of friendlier U.S.-Soviet relations. At the same time, "competition with Communism" was regarded by many, in view of Khrushchev's U.S. speeches, as "the most important question in American life today" (C.S. Monitor, Wall St. Journal).[33]

Pres. Eisenhower's "December Odyssey" to India, Afghanistan, the Middle East and Europe was acclaimed as a "magnificent mission," and Americans were gratified at the re-discovery of good will for the U.S. on three continents. Many said the President had added "great moral force to the cause of the West in dealing with the East" (Edw. Folliard; Time magazine). Commentators also applauded Mr. Eisenhower's emphasis on the continued need for overseas investment and aid. A few felt that the "idealistic aspect" of his journey was "tarnished" by the stop in Spain, although they acknowledged the necessity of dealing with "unpalatable foreign regimes" (e.g., Denver Post, Chi. Sun-Times).[34]

Although the Mid-East had been relatively quiet, there had been earlier concern about Israeli-Egyptian relations. The United Arab Republic's barring of Suez Canal passage to Israeli cargoes–the detention of a Danish freighter bound for the Far East–prompted some editors to insist that the time had come for the great powers "to stand with Israel in defense of law and the pledged word" (e.g., Milwaukee Journal, Christian Century). Some were dissatisfied by U.S. failure to "deal strongly with Nasser" (N.Y. Post).[35]

During the UNGA session in the fall a number of commentators supported Israel's rejection of Arab "hints" that the blockade of

Israeli ships and cargoes was linked to the Arab refugee problem. Some felt that the U.S. was morally obligated to press the Israeli cause, "supported by international law" (Cincinnati Enquirer, N.Y. Times); some others suggested that the Arabs and Israelis should "seriously negotiate" the possibility of exchanging some Israeli assistance to the refugees for free canal transit (C.S. Monitor, Boston Herald).[36]

Observers divided sharply on the year-end decision of the World Bank to grant Cairo a $56-million loan for widening and deepening the Suez Canal, without requiring Egypt to end the exclusion of Israeli ships and cargoes. There continued to be editorial agreement that the Suez seaway should be truly open to all nations. In January the preponderant opinion welcomed Soviet construction of the Aswan Dam, despite the "unfortunate background of its financing," in the belief that this would "stabilize" the UAR and be "a factor in preserving peace" (e.g., Houston Chronicle, Wash. Post).[37]

Suspicions about Castro's activities reappeared in the summer of 1959. Discussing reports of further Latin American invasions linked to Castro, editors rejected Castro's "implications that the U.S. had any part in Cuban invasion plots" as "so much hot air." Despite pessimism about Cuba's future, many reiterated that it was "clearly not America's duty to intervene." Collective action was understood to offer the only practicable means of restraint.[38]

Concern about Cuba rose in October, when Amb. Bonsal expressed U.S. "shock and amazement" at Castro's charge that the U.S. "tolerated" American-based hostile flights over Cuba. Many felt that Castro was using the U.S. as a "whipping-boy" to divert attention from the discontent in Cuba. Commentators felt that the U.S. had "plenty of reason for the gravest concern over the direction the Cuban revolution was taking" (e.g., N.Y. Times, St. Louis Post-Dispatch). Nevertheless, several editors held that the U.S. should take "firm and immediate steps to insure that there was no recurrence" of the use of American shores as a base for operations directed at Cuba (e.g., Wash. Star, Balt. Sun). These also felt that the U.S. had "acted wisely" in asking the OAS Peace Committee to investigate Castro's allegations. But many felt that "setting out to punish him," as by cutting off sugar imports, would help Castro "fan his flames of hatred" and injure the still pro-American Cuban people. Yet, a number felt that "in the long run . . . we would not accept a Communist satellite in Cuba" (Sat. Eve. Post, N.Y. Times, N.Y. Mirror).[39]

For its significant decision to invite Khrushchev to an East-West summit, the Paris meeting of Western leaders with Pres. Eisenhower was applauded; also for the plan to hold a "series" of summit meetings which would permit "a cautious and gradual process of East-West accommodation," and avoid "grandiose showdowns" (Walter

Lippmann). The "unresolved" Franco-American differences over NATO integration also stirred much concerned comment; it was hoped that Pres. de Gaulle's April visit to Washington would result in important "fence-mending" prior to the summit meeting. Although hopes for the nuclear test ban talks didn't reach a high level of optimism, most felt that these talks should continue as long as there was any hope of agreement, and so should the more or less informal suspension of tests by the Soviet Union and the U.S. When Pres. Eisenhower announced that the U.S. would feel free to resume testing after the end of the year, but would not test without advance notice, the editorial comment was predominantly favorable.[40]

Paris Summit

Americans looked forward to the May meeting with Khrushchev in Paris, and felt that this engagement would keep the Russians "on their good behavior" until then. Yet skepticism continued as to the possibility of reaching any significant agreements at that time. Critics held that the Western position was seriously weakened by the lag of the U.S. behind the Soviet Union in the space-missile race (e.g., Democratic presidential aspirants Johnson, Kennedy, Symington); they also noted that Soviet "obduracy" had required breaking off the January lend-lease talks. There was gratification that Eisenhower's State of the Union message "practically doubled" the budget request for space development. But commentators were disquieted by Khrushchev's revival of his "threat" to sign a separate peace treaty with East Germany, thus suggesting the possibility of a new blockade of Berlin.[41]

France's atomic blast at this juncture evoked more misgivings than "hurrahs." Many feared that the arrival of a "fourth" atomic power would greatly complicate the "already complex" negotiations at Geneva. The current U.S. proposal of a test ban exempting small underground explosions was widely commended by editors, as a "realistic" answer to a difficult problem, now further complicated by the French. Although some favored amending existing law to share nuclear information with France, most felt that France did not yet qualify for such aid. On the broader question of sharing custody of American nuclear weapons with "reliable allies" (as suggested by Pres. Eisenhower), Congressional opinion continued to be predominantly hostile.

In February renewed Soviet threats about Berlin sparked considerable comment, with editors promptly approving the West's resumption of high altitude flights into Berlin at a time when Khrushchev was apparently "testing" Western resolve about Berlin in advance of the Paris summit meeting scheduled for May. At the same time, refusal of the U.S. to admit East German sports writers to cover the Winter Olympics provoked considerable criticism, the critics contending that the Department's ban had provided more anti-American ammunition than "the banned sports writers would ever invent." But editors found much to commend in Sec. Herter's warning against "over-optimism" regarding the Paris summit, since Soviet statesmen appeared to rule out any Berlin-German agreement except on "unacceptable" Soviet terms.[42]

As the date for the Paris summit approached, many commentators were encouraged to see a "narrowing" gap between Western and Soviet positions on a test ban. Editors cautiously welcomed the Eisenhower-Macmillan proposals which provided for a short moratorium on small underground tests in connection with an inspection-tight treaty banning larger tests (e.g., N.Y. Times and Herald Tribune). Others feared that the West was in danger of settling for inspection terms that would not prevent Soviet violations (e.g., Boston Herald), and urged the need for continued underground testing (e.g., Wash. Star, ex-Pres. Truman). In April a number of editors concluded that the 10-nation disarmament conference in Geneva had reached a deadlock, and that the Soviets were to blame.[43]

Collapse of the Paris summit on May 16 was greeted with shock and dismay. The Big Four leaders arrived in Paris under "unpromising circumstances," produced by the Soviet downing of an American "spy plane," but few commentators were prepared for the "brutal" manner in which Mr. Khrushchev wrecked the conference. Since Pres. Eisenhower had already met the main Soviet complaint, by giving assurances that aerial flights over the U.S.S.R. would not be resumed, many now concluded that Khrushchev had come to Paris intent on "scuttling" the summit. American and Western commentators favorably contrasted Pres. Eisenhower's dignified rebuff of Khrushchev's demands with the Russian leader's "fantastic tirades." Still, a number were inclined to fault the Administration for the "mishandling" of the U-2 incident and welcomed investigation by the Senate Foreign Relations Committee. Some felt that the risks to the U.S. world position of a U-2 flight on the eve of the summit had exceeded the potential intelligence gains (e.g., Louisville Courier-Journal; Walter Lippmann); and a number agreed with Chairman Fulbright that it was a mistake for Pres. Eisenhower publicly to associate himself with espionage acts (Wash. Star). Others, however, upheld the "presidential candor" (e.g., N.Y. Herald Tribune).[44]

A number concluded that "summitry is a basically faulty" diplomatic technique, agreeing with George Kennan that we "should look very, very carefully before we submit the prestige of the President of the United States again to what has happened in Paris." But editors also agreed with the Baltimore Sun that the worst mistake we could have made as a result of the collapsed summit would have been to "slam the door" on future negotiations with the Soviets. In his May 25 report to the nation, Pres. Eisenhower insisted on continued "businesslike dealings" with the Russians; this received strong endorsement from press and Congress. When the USSR took the U-2 affair to the UN Security Council, many welcomed this opportunity for a UN discussion of the subject; and the Security Council's 7-to-2 rejection of the Soviet complaint was regarded by many as a "moral victory as well as a numerical one" (Hearst press, Balt. Sun). The fresh wave of Kremlin threats and defamation tended to emphasize the continuing menace of a "surprise attack." However, commentators also felt that reconnaissance by U-2 planes was being made obsolete by observation satellites; and some suggested that these "aerial scouts" should be put at the service of the UN (e.g., St. Louis Post-Dispatch, C.S. Monitor). Some regretted that the U.S. announcement of a resumption of underground nuclear tests came so soon after the U-2 disclosure, but there was general editorial approval of these tests as a part of a wise program of detection research.[45]

"Public opinion is clearly aware that things have gone wrong in the conduct of American foreign policy in the last two months," declared Erwin Canham; and a number concluded that personal diplomacy "is a practice of dubious value which presents more hazards than hopes" (Scripps-Howard papers). Others maintained that presidential visits abroad could still be useful, provided they were carried out "at the proper times and were not overdone" (New Orleans Times-Picayune).[46]

Arms Talk

In early June the 10-nation disarmament conference in Geneva resumed, with the Soviets presenting a "new" or "reshuffled" plan which commentators agreed was not acceptable. But a considerable number held that it should be given "careful study," and possibly amended to make it acceptable. Although the Soviet bloc soon walked out of the conference, many editors felt that continued negotiation was desirable. A few, however, urged a radically different U.S. approach, which would regard maintenance of deterrent power as a stabilizing force, and not as something to be done away with under careful inspection (e.g., Henry A. Kissinger, Walter Lippmann).[47]

Those hoping for a nuclear test ban were discouraged by the Soviet Union's withdrawal of its experts' offer to conduct non-nuclear explosions in Russia as part of a joint East-West research program, and Moscow's rejection of U.S. safeguards against cheating in U.S. tests. A number of alternatives were suggested by editors in hope of meeting Soviet objections; but other spokesmen warned that the Communist "propaganda drive" for a test ban be "firmly rejected" and underground testing be resumed as "essential" to Western security (Sen. Goldwater, Fortune, Hearst papers).[48]

Completion of a multilateral treaty on the Antarctic, which would quiet territorial claims in the interest of preventing clashes over the polar continent, was hailed by a number of editors. Some saw in ratification a "golden opportunity" to commit the Soviet Union to international inspection in Antarctica and to establish a precedent for international cooperation in outer space (e.g., Dayton News, Wash. Post). Opponents of the treaty objected to placing the "seal of free world recognition on the Soviet presence in Antarctica," and to giving insufficient weight to U.S. territorial claims (e.g., Columbus Dispatch, Sen. Gruening, D-Alaska).[49]

The emerging pattern of Soviet cold war "opened up two huge new theaters of East-West conflict"–Latin America and Africa–said Business Week, while at the same time "threatening trouble in older theaters–Berlin, Italy, Iran, Southeast Asia and Japan." Editors believed that one factor in the timing of the global offensive was a desire to take advantage of the presidential election period. According to the New York Herald Tribune, the "exceptional fury" of Moscow's threats indicated that the Kremlin felt the time suitable for a "truly prodigious effort to crack the Western nerve." Commentators discerned two major Soviet goals: 1, to isolate America from its allies and from the world's neutrals; 2, to break up the system of U.S. overseas bases. A number saw a danger of war through Soviet miscalculation; and they welcomed Prime Minister Macmillan's letter to Khrushchev warning against the danger of misunderstanding American determination to stand firm, and also Sec. Herter's press conference to the same effect.[50]

Comment on the foreign policy planks of the 1960 political platforms stressed their similarity. The Democrats placed their emphasis on a new approach to the uncommitted and underdeveloped countries of Africa and Asia; while the Republicans focused on the need to contain Communism. Both parties were firmly against Communism, of course, and in favor of military preparedness, opposed to recognition of Communist China, and pledged to encourage settlement of Arab-Israeli differences, and generally take a pro-Israel line. Both platforms supported continuation of foreign aid, and favored ending nuclear testing when adequate safeguards could be agreed upon. Some "nationalist" newspapers found fault with the Democratic platform for "leaving the way open for a quick change of signals" if Peking showed signs of "greater respect for international obligations" (e.g., Columbus Dispatch, Chi. Tribune).[51]

The Soviet shooting down of a U.S. RB-47 reconnaissance plane over the Barents Sea in the neighborhood of Soviet territory drew widespread public comment. Although the Kremlin's call for prompt consideration by the UN Security Council was often adjudged a propaganda move, editors were ready to have the UN air the case. They believed that the U.S. won a considerable victory in the Security Council's 9-to-2 rejection of the Soviet charges against the U.S., and in Soviet unwillingness to submit its case to an impartial tribunal as the USSR vetoed a US proposal for an international investigation. Some papers which felt that the U.S. had a good case nevertheless expressed some misgivings about the wisdom of flights so close to the Soviet border (e.g., Wash. Star, Youngstown Vindicator).[52]

Far East; Latin America

The re-elections, in early 1960, of Chiang Kai-shek in Taiwan and Syngman Rhee in South Korea were gratifying to editors because these leaders were determined anti-Communists; but the elections themselves were regarded as far from democratic in character. When the Korean elections were followed by riot and bloodshed, and the U.S. administered a "rebuke" to the Rhee government, Pres. Rhee resigned and American editors expressed strong approval of the "vigorous line the U.S. had taken." There was widespread agreement that because of the "great stake" the U.S. had in Korea it couldn't "avoid responsibility" for the future of the republic it had helped to create at so great a cost in American lives and money. Editors felt that the U.S. had broken its unfortunate policy of neutrality toward dictators, and Time magazine welcomed the new policy of speaking up to "errant friends as well as enemies when their conduct—even though internal—offends the basic principles for which the U.S. stands" (also Hearst press, Prov. Journal). Several, however, did oppose such "blatant interference by the U.S." (e.g., David Lawrence), or charged the U.S. with a "double standard" in dealing with Franco and Castro (e.g., Los Angeles Times, N.Y. News).[53]

In early 1960 a report by the Rockefeller Brothers Fund urged "full reporting by Americans" in mainland China; the report halted just short of proposing diplomatic recognition and UN seating of Peking. A number of commentators also called for a "more flexible" U.S. policy toward China (e.g., Walter Lippmann, Phila. Bulletin).[54]

In Japan the Paris summit debacle was followed by mass demonstrations against the U.S.-Japanese security treaty, and Pres. Eisenhower's plan to visit occasioned great concern in the Administration and in the press. But the convening in Washington of a SEATO conference was an occasion for warmly welcoming the representatives of the Organization. The American pledges of full support, voiced by the President, Vice President, and Sec. Herter, were received as providing a welcome policy of "firmness without belligerence" in the wake of the Khrushchev-Malinovsky threats. Editors hailed also "history's biggest grain deal" between the U.S. and India, a number counting the deal a "happy climax" to Pres. Eisenhower's India visit.[55]

The President's summer trip to the Orient became controversial. His "massive" receptions in Manila, Taipei, and Seoul were heartening tokens of Asian goodwill, virtually all agreed; but these demonstrations were overshadowed by the developing crisis in Japan and the fact that the President's visit to Japan had to be canceled. However, some emphasized that although China "spent a fortune to kill the U.S.-Japan security treaty," it became law in both countries (N.Y. Times). The Hearst papers concluded: "We think the successes stack up encouragingly against the one big defeat." But some held that it was "dangerous self-deception" to blame the Japanese incident on the Communists alone (e.g., James Reston, Des Moines Register).[56]

Announcement in early 1960, that Pres. Eisenhower would work in a visit to four Latin American countries before the Paris summit, was welcomed by editors because they were deeply "worried" about Fidel Castro's continuing attacks on the U.S., and the unease in Panama despite U.S. agreement to permit Panama to fly its flag alongside the American flag over the Canal Zone. At the same time, Congressional and editorial comment reflected "thorough sympathy" with the President's adherence to a policy of non-intervention in Cuba's internal affairs. Eisenhower's actual journey was viewed as "another great triumph" for the President and a "spectacular success" in improving the climate of relations with our neighbors. A number advocated increased economic aid for the Hemisphere.[57]

Anger and resentment over Castro's "implied charges" that the U.S. was "involved" in a munitions ship explosion in Havana were manifested in editorial comment on Sec. Herter's firm rejection of the "baseless" charges. Still, only a minority said it was "time the U.S. took a big stick to Castro;" the majority felt that for the time being the U.S. had no choice but to "wait for time to do what diplomatic exchanges and economic pressure cannot do" (e.g., Honolulu Star-Bulletin, Life). Nevertheless an increasing number "hoped that we had a good stiff policy in readiness" in the event that anti-American elements gained ground in Cuba. When Cuban patrol vessels fired on a U.S. submarine, editors accused Castro of manufacturing "the Sea Poacher incident to take advantage of the American spy-plane debacle;" they felt that the U.S. was "thoroughly justified in demanding an explanation and in making it plain" that any attack upon an American vessel would be vigorously repulsed (e.g., Phila. Inquirer). They also felt the President should be empowered "to take timely action as our national security required," as in the matter of sugar quotas.[58]

The Chilean earthquake disaster received nationwide attention, and the speed of U.S. rescue and relief efforts was widely applauded. When "violations of human rights" in the Dominican Republic were strongly denounced by the OAS, many editors approved this "realistic modification" of the "sacrosanct doctrine" of non-intervention. Some, however, expressed concern lest the Trujillo regime collapse and be followed by "a new eruption of Castroism." Cuba, many urged, should become the next object of investigation by the Inter-American Peace Committee, and the U.S. memorandum setting forth Castro's provocations was heartily endorsed.[59]

Three significant July moves by Pres. Eisenhower respecting Latin America received whole-hearted support: a "big cut" in Cuba's sugar quota; a warning to Khrushchev that a Soviet threat to Latin America would be firmly met under the Monroe Doctrine; and a "big new aid program for our southern neighbors." Many editors supporting the rebuff to Khrushchev emphasized their belief that "the force to frustrate Communism should be the OAS. For sudden, unilateral moves, no matter how valid in law or international morality, could backfire on us" (Dayton News, similarly St. Louis Post-Dispatch, Denver Post, Louisville Courier-Journal). Some others feared that the OAS was "venturing into a quicksand" in putting Castro on its agenda, lest the task wreck "the otherwise successful regional system" (Wash. Post). The anti-Communist resolution adopted at San Jose by the OAS Foreign Ministers won editorial praise as a "diplomatic victory for the U.S." Commentators felt that the Declaration preserved hemispheric solidarity against Communist infiltration "to the maximum extent possible;" they added that the "instrument for dealing with Castro," if necessary, had been forged when the republics agreed on sanctions against Trujillo for violating the principles of non-intervention.[60]

The Act of Bogota, adopted in September, was approved as offering a program under which the people and governments of Latin America would develop "outstanding programs of social and economic progress," with the $500 million U.S. aid effort underwriting a scattering of pilot projects designed to produce immediate improvement in living standards. To the New York Herald Tribune, following through on Under Secretary Dillon's call for cooperative action meant "large U.S. public investments in agriculture, in housing, and in established industry," and permitting the recipient countries to "administer these investments in their own way." Some, however, felt that the U.S. should have Latin America's assurance of cooperation and reforms before any money was appropriated (e.g., Scripps-Howard papers).[61]

Africa; UN

The "rampaging insurrection" of the Congolese army, and the inability of the Republic of the Congo under Kasavubu and Lumumba to halt it, prompted wide public approval of United Nations efforts to bring order out of chaos. Citing the UN's dispatch of troops, its preparations for economic and administrative aid, and the "sterling efforts" of the Secretary-General, the Providence Journal declared: "The world has had reason to feel profoundly grateful" to the UN (similarly, Scripps-Howard papers, Christian Century).[62]

There was unanimous agreement that the U.S. showed "wisdom and restraint" in declining to send troops to the Congo; and there was also agreement that Soviet military units should not be allowed to enter the Congo. In general, observers praised the UN decision to rely principally on units from the other African states. They also strongly endorsed "large-scale U.S. technical and economic assistance" for the Congo, "channeled through the UN." They welcomed Premier Lumumba, and made him aware of "America's disinterested goodwill toward the Congo" (San Francisco Chronicle). Yet there were some dissents to heavy U.S. aid, for fear that the Soviet Union would "follow suite" (Wall St. Journal, Chicago News). Most commentators felt it was in the interest of the West to woo Premier Tshombe's Katanga back into the Congo Republic; but a few "nationalist" sources felt Tshombe should be encouraged in his call for a federation of anti-Communist African nations. As other new African states emerged (Somali, Malagasy, Mali), editors felt that the new nations had "great potential," and that the U.S. should supply assistance to stabilize them.[63]

Hammarskjold's original aim of moving UN forces into Katanga despite Tshombe's opposition was endorsed by the American press; and so was his subsequent decision to obtain a Security Council review of his mandate. When the Security Council rejected Lumumba's Soviet-backed challenge to UN operations in the Congo there was widespread applause; and most commentators were content for the time being with continuation of Hammarskjold's course of non-interference in Congolese internal disputes, and leaving such matters as the status of Katanga for political resolution. Americans looked hopefully upon the gathering in late August of eleven African delegates from nearby states to discuss African unity; but the delegates—and American commentators—were shocked by Premier Lumumba's oratorical outbursts. The New York Herald Tribune concluded that the independent delegates could "help the Congo—indeed, they must do so if the future of all Africa is not to be jeopardized by the creation of a Soviet satellite in the ruins of what might have been a thriving free state." Sizable support was accorded the Administration request for $100 million to meet unexpected UN expenses in the Congo; but "nationalist" sources solidly opposed the idea of "paying the expenses of trying to rescue Lumumba from the disorders of his own creation" (N.Y. News, Sen. Bridges).[64]

The Soviet proposal of a disarmament conference of all UN members was regarded as a propaganda move rather than progress toward disarmament; and the UN Disarmament Commission's call for resumption of great-power disarmament talks was interpreted by some as a rebuke to the Soviet Union (N.Y. Times, Milwaukee Journal). A number of American dailies approved the U.S. proposal that the USSR and US transfer matching amounts of enriched uranium to peaceful uses (Hearst papers and others); but the Soviet Union instantly rejected the proposal. On the subject of a nuclear test ban, observers doubted that much could be resolved at Geneva before the next U.S. president took office; but most felt that the effort would be carried on then. The Soviet offer of three annual inspections on Russian soil was generally regarded as "pitifully inadequate" (e.g., Des Moines Register, Wash. Star). Long-time test-ban skeptics supported Dr. Teller's call for immediate resumption of underground testing.[65]

The 70–0 vote in the special GA session endorsing the Secretary-General's handling of the Congo crisis was warmly applauded as a significant victory for Hammarskjold and the UN, for the "non-committed bloc" of members, and for U.S. policy on the Congo. Some editors saw "special significance" in the demonstration that the newly-independent African states "will not be used as pawns of Moscow" (e.g., N.Y. Herald Tribune, Balt. Sun). Joseph Alsop commented that if it hadn't been for Col. Mobutu's coup, the UNGA outcome "would have been very different." American commentators were hopeful that Mobutu, having ousted Soviet and satellite technicians and aides, could build a stable government.[66]

Announcement by the Soviet Union and its bloc that they would make no contributions to the heavy UN costs in the Congo provoked strong editorial denunciations, most commentators seeing this move as part of the Communist "attempt to weaken the UN." Some called on the organization to use all devices at its command to collect "this just debt from the deadbeat Communist members" (e.g., Chi. News, St. Louis Post-Dispatch). The Providence Journal commented that U.S. willingness to pay more than its "fair share" of these expenses would have to be based on realization that the UN can do such jobs "to better effect than could the U.S. alone, and probably at less actual cost."[67]

Chairman Khrushchev's proposal that the office of Secretary-General be trifurcated, and his accompanying attack on Hammarskjold, were promptly denounced as a "wrecking operation" and a move to obtain a Soviet veto in the Secretary-General's office (e.g., Los Angeles Times, Kansas City Times). Less concern was aroused by Khrushchev's suggestion that the UN headquarters be moved to another country; more editors seemed cool to the idea than approved it.[68]

The "narrow margin" by which the UN voted against placing the China representation issue on the agenda "should give the U.S. pause," many commentators said, some stressing that a "doctrine of universality" had set in. Editors generally conceded that the U.S. should prepare an "alternative" policy to meet the developing situation, but many felt that the U.S. should simply hold its ground. When five "neutrals" at the UNGA (including Tito, Nasser, Nehru) introduced a resolution calling on Pres. Eisenhower and Chairman Khrushchev to hold a summit meeting in the interests of "peace," American comment was heavily critical of the idea and its sponsors as "unrealistic." Pres. Eisenhower's rejection was fully endorsed by most of those commenting on it.[69]

As the 1960 presidential campaign warmed up, the agreement of Vice President Nixon and Sen. Kennedy to avoid an "unprepared" summit meeting, and also to defend Berlin against any attempted Communist take-over, was widely approved in comment across the country. In fact, Richard Stebbins, in his assessment of the campaign, said that "its most significant feature may well have been its revelation of the extent to which American foreign policy had in fact become a bipartisan enterprise. The main outlines of the national policy as it had developed since World War II were unequivocally endorsed on both sides." Stebbins added that both candidates did repeatedly recognize that "there would be room for increased vigor and imagination in the conduct of American foreign policy in the coming years."[70]

Summary

The last years of Eisenhower's presidency found the American public firm in its support of the United Nations, approving fresh manifestations in the Congo of the organization's efforts to bring about peace by the use of force, and resisting Soviet attacks to dilute the Secretary-General's power by creation of a troika. Americans were also willing to follow their govenrment's lead (although on a modest scale) in extending U.S. programs of economic aid to the new nations in Africa.

In these years (1959-60) there were no major crises in the life of

NATO or SEATO or the Rio Pact; but the American public maintained support for these collective security agreements. Sec. Herter carried on the Dulles policies, and Khrushchev allowed the Berlin crisis to simmer down. Movement toward detente with the Soviets was perhaps perceptible at Camp David in 1959; but certainly it ceased at Paris in 1960. Americans still wanted to limit nuclear arms and nuclear explosions; but they were unwilling to settle for mere promises in place of proper inspection safeguards. With reference to Communist China, perhaps some American voices were speaking up more about the need for realistic decisions to acknowledge each other's existence; but there was no indication of any major change of attitude on the part of the general public.

While in Latin America there was no occasion to invoke the Rio Pact, there was talk of using the OAS to restrain Cuban or Cuban-inspired attempts to upset Latin American governments. But Americans demonstrated a profound restraint; despite many anti-American acts by the Castro regime, they firmly opposed any U.S. effort to intervene in Cuba by force.

Pres. Eisenhower's administrations demonstrated that the replacement of an isolationist policy by an activist foregin policy was not a temporary shift, executed by a four-term president and his Democratic successor. In addition to Ike's active recourse to the United Nations and his maintenance of military alliances and foreign aid, the Eisenhower Doctrine (dispatching U.S. Marines to Lebanon) marked an extension of the scope of American activism. Americans were happy that the Marines returned from Lebanon; but, having elected and re-elected Eisenhower on the Republican ticket, they gave clear support to all the elements of America's active role throughout his presidencies.

Reference Notes

1. AOR of Dec. 3, 1958.
2. Ibid.
3. Ibid.
4. AOR of Jan. 2, 1959.
5. Ibid.
6. AOR of Feb. 2, 1959.
7. Ibid.
8. Ibid.
9. Ibid.
10. AOR for Apr. 3 and May 4, 1959.
11. AOR for Mar. 2, 1959.
12. Ibid.
13. Ibid.
14. AOR of Apr. 3, 1959.
15. AOR of Apr. 3 and May 4, 1959.
16. Ibid.

17. AOR of May 4, 1959.
18. Ibid.
19. AOR of June 4, 1959.
20. AOR of Aug. 4, 1959.
21. Ibid.
22. AOR of Sept. 4, 1959.
23. AOR of July 2 and Aug. 4, 1959.
24. AOR of June 4, 1959.
25. AOR of Aug. 4 and Sept. 4, 1959.
26. AOR of Oct. 2, 1959.
27. Ibid.
28. Ibid.
29. Ibid.
30. AOR of Nov. 2, 1959.
31. Ibid.
32. AOR of Oct. 2, 1959.
33. AOR of Dec. 2, 1959.
34. AOR of Jan. 4, 1960.
35. AOR of July 2, 1959.
36. AOR for Oct. 2 and Nov. 2, 1959.
37. AOR of Jan. 2 and Feb. 2, 1960.
38. AOR of Sept. 4, 1959.
39. AOR of Dec. 2, 1959 and Jan. 4, 1960.
40. AOR of Jan. 4, 1960.
41. AOR of Feb. 2, 1960.
42. AOR for Mar. 4 and Apr. 4, 1960.
43. AOR of May 4, 1960.
44. AOR of June 6, 1960.
45. Ibid.
46. AOR of July 3, 1960.
47. AOR of July 5, 1960.
48. Ibid.
49. Ibid.
50. AOR of Aug. 1, 1960.
51. Ibid.
52. Ibid.
53. AOR for May 4, 1960.
54. AOR of Jan. 4, 1960.
55. AOR of June 3, 1960.
56. AOR of July 5, 1960.
57. AOR of Feb. 2 and Mar. 4, 1960.
58. AOR for Apr. 4, May 4, and June 3, 1960.
59. AOR of July 5, 1960.
60. AOR for Aug. 1 and Sept. 2, 1960.
61. AOR of Oct. 3, 1960.
62. AOR of Aug. 1, 1960.
63. AOR of Sept. 2, 1960.
64. Ibid.
65. Ibid.
66. Ibid.
67. AOR of Nov. 1, 1960.
68. AOR of Oct. 15, 1960.
69. AOR of Oct. 15 and Nov. 15, 1960.
70. AOR of Nov. 1, 1960; Richard P. Stebbins, *U.S. in World Affairs, 1960*, pp. 51–52.

XII

KENNEDY ENTERS; PROBLEMS CONTINUE (1961)

Editors and political leaders of both major parties hailed the experience and the ability of the new President's foreign policy team: Secretary of State Dean Rusk, Under Secretary Chester Bowles, UN Ambassador Adlai Stevenson. Pres. Kennedy's inaugural address won general acclaim. James Reston said approval stretched from the "Conservative Republicans to the Communists in Moscow;" David Lawrence emphasized the President's eloquent support of "traditional (American) principles" in foreign policy. The young president set an activist course when he pledged that "we shall pay any price, bear any burden, meet any hardship, support any friend, oppose any foe to assure the survival and the success of liberty." Still, most commentators found the keynote of the inaugural in Kennedy's appeal to the Kremlin for fresh efforts to ease the Cold War; Erwin Canham said the address "did definitely reopen the door that was shut by the U-2 incident." Editors were encouraged by Moscow's release of the RB-47 survivors whose plane had been shot down over the Barents Sea in the previous summer; but immediate improvement in relations was not expected. Editors added that Pres. Kennedy's State of the Union message "set aside any doubts about 'softness' toward tyranny, Communist or otherwise" (e.g., N.Y. Herald Tribune, Wash. Post).[1]

American commentators mentioned an array of problems for the new team: balance of payments, the Congo, relations with China; but they stressed two areas of U.S.-Soviet relations posing especially "severe tests": Berlin and Laos. Then suddenly came the Bay of Pigs fiasco, to pose a problem unexpected by public and press.

Bay of Pigs

Keen and almost universal regret greeted the failure of the anti-Castro forces in their attack at the Bay of Pigs, but there was sustained approval of the U.S. positions enunciated by Pres. Kennedy. There was little tendency, however, to pass a critical judgment on the new President because of the military failure. The two major Kennedy principles which won sustained support from press and public were: 1, No U.S. military forces should participate in an anti-Castro effort; 2, the sympathies of Americans are wholly with those endeavoring to restore freedom in Cuba. Kennedy's reply to a threatening message from Khrushchev was applauded for its firm declaration that Soviet force applied in this Hemisphere would be met with counter-force. Popular "approval" of the President shot up from 72% (in March) to 83% (early May), as often happens after a President takes vigorous action; but it should be noted that on the specific question of "handling the situation in Cuba" approval was only 61% (disapproval was 15%).

Earlier some had criticized the Eisenhower Administration for breaking relations with Cuba only 17 days before Inauguration Day; but it was widely felt the the U.S. had been "provoked beyond the point of endurance." Two state opinion polls showed heavy support for the break: Iowa Poll, 73% to 10% in favor; Minnesota Poll, 76% to 11%. The Minnesota Poll found 2% of its respondents with a "favorable" impression of Premier Castro, 91% an "unfavorable" impression (7% no opinion). The minority opposed to the break had argued: "We should try to be friendly." Pres. Kennedy's offer of assistance to refugees from the Castro regime was approved by commentators as making clear that we regarded the Cuban people as "our friends and allies."[2] Dr. Gallup reported continuing opposition to the use of U.S. troops to "overthrow Castro," also readiness to "end all trade" with Castro's Cuba, but a close division of opinion on whether the U.S. should aid the anti-Castro forces by "money and war materials."[3]

Pres. Kennedy's announcement of his intention to rally the American republics to act in concert on Cuba met with general approval, even though some questioned whether the OAS could act effectively. A number also applauded the action of a House Appropriations subcommittee in supporting "every last dime" of the Administration's hemispheric aid program request, these editors saying that demands for social reform are the only kind of intervention that "can permanently succeed in Latin America" (e.g., N.Y. Times, Ralph McGill). Some observers, however, called for drastic action against Castro, suggesting a blockade or material support for his opponents (e.g., Sen. Keating, N.Y. Mirror).[4]

Later, the idea of obtaining freedom for 1200 Castro prisoners taken in the abortive invasion at the Bay of Pigs, in exchange for 500 tractors, was "distasteful" to most; but the majority saw it as a "humanitarian gesture" we must make. There were some vigorous objections to any "deal" which would strengthen Castro. Some also criticized the Administration for maintaining an "official distance" between the White House and the rescue undertaking led by Walter Reuther, Mrs. Roosevelt, and Dr. Milton Eisenhower (e.g., Chi. Tribune, ex-Pres. Truman). But the predominant view was that the advantage of "showing up Castro's cynicism"—equating two men to one tractor—would outweigh the manifest ransom connotations. When Castro subsequently sought to raise his ransom demand, it was widely agreed that the Tractors for Freedom Committee "took the only reasonable position" in rejecting it; but those who had been critical from the outset tended to stress "the futility of trying to do business with a dictator" (e.g., Wash. Star, Chi. News). Several hoped that the U.S. would "redouble its efforts to exert pressures on Castro" (e.g., N.Y. News, Milwaukee Journal).[5]

Adlai Stevenson's Latin American tour in June received comment favorable to the Ambassador's theme that "nothing short of partnership" can do the "great task" there, and concluded that the tour rendered a "major service" to hemispheric progress and solidarity. News of the assassination of the Dominican Republic's Rafael Trujillo brought no editorial regrets over the passing of his regime; but commentators urged that the U.S. identify itself with Dominican groups seeking to build a regime of social reform. These editors were encouraged by the prompt Dominican response to an OAS request that a fact-finding committee visit the republic. Referring to suggestions of U.S. military intervention, the Atlanta Constitution declared that "the propaganda backlash at this stage would be disastrous" (also Scripps-Howard papers). A significant number, however, held that although the OAS "should take on the job initially," the U.S. must be prepared to take whatever "positive steps" are necessary to insure that the Dominican Republic should not come under Communist control (e.g., N.Y. News, Cinci. Enquirer, Sen. Keating).[6]

Europe; Berlin

Pres. Kennedy's announcement of warm support for NATO was seconded in editorial comment, although some added that the U.S. is "entitled to expect adequate reciprocal loyalty" from our European allies who lagged behind in their proportionate contributions to NATO defenses. Some appreciated, however, West Germany's agreement to help out in dealing with foreign aid and balance-of-payments questions. Pres. de Gaulle's attitude toward military integration for NATO seemed more unbending. Prompt ratification of the convention establishing the Organization for Economic Cooperation and Development was urged by most editors and by some Congressional and trade group spokesmen; but traditional protectionist advocates opposed OECD as a "glorified GATT and a master Marshall Plan rolled into one" (Rep. Moore, R-W.Va.).[7]

Pres. Kennedy's meeting with Prime Minister Macmillan was welcomed as advancing the President's project of "reinvigorating" the Atlantic alliance. The equally cordial meeting with Chancellor Adenauer was thought additionally valuable in stressing Kennedy's "unequivocal" policies on the defense of West Berlin and West Germany. "Real gains" for the Western alliance were seen in Kennedy's subsequent visit to de Gaulle.[8]

But it was a "bleak day" for the U.S., in the American press, when Maj. Gagarin flew around the earth to become the "first man in space." Editors urged the U.S. to "get going" with the aim of surpassing the Russians, although some pointed out that the "pre-eminent position" of the U.S. in the world of science was not won by success in a single field, but on "virtually every scientific front in the catalogue" (e.g., Wall St. Journal, Chi. American).[9]

The President's announcement that he would meet Chairman Khrushchev in Vienna aroused widespread misgivings, along with some determined belief that the talks could be useful. The critical editors tended to be dubious about summit diplomacy, especially at this time when developments at the Bay of Pigs and in Laos placed the U.S. at a disadvantage. However, there was general rejoicing over Commander Shepard's space flight (May 5), even if it did not encircle the globe; and some felt that it could be helpful for Kennedy and Khrushchev to "size up" each other promptly, and for Kennedy to warn the Soviet leader of U.S. "firmness" (e.g., N.Y. Times, San Diego Union).[10]

Pres. Kennedy's TV report on his European trip (June 6) was widely appreciated; but as Moscow disclosed its post-Vienna attitude on critical issues commentators registered mounting concern. The "somber" TV report was commended for its realism and frankness. The Milwaukee Journal declared: "It was good for the American people to be talked to frankly, with no pulling of punches, no false assurances, no hiding of grim facts." Kennedy's "call to work and to win" should have the support of the American people, said the Chicago News. The Scripps-Howard editorial held that the trip would have been useful if the President convinced the country that "the Soviets are playing for keeps." The Chicago Tribune asserted that the renewal of Russian threats to Berlin "showed how futile" the trip really was.[11]

The "militant" tone in which the Soviet leader couched his threats to sign a separate peace treaty with East Germany by the end of the year led to general acceptance of the idea that "this time" Khrushchev meant to carry through such unilateral action. It was also widely noted that East German Communist chief Ulbricht left little doubt as to what this move portended for West Berlin's lifelines and the people's freedom. A mounting chorus of Congressmen, editors, and organization spokesmen called on the Administration to prepare to meet this "grim" prospect with all appropriate means, including military action.[12]

Several positive suggestions were made; and the mood against any U.S. "back-down" was forcefully shown in the storm of criticism which greeted Sen. Mansfield's suggestion that a "third way" be sought out of the deadlock on Berlin. Instead, commentators proposed: immediate strengthening of the U.S. defense effort; partial mobilization of reserves; an intensified air alert; reinforcement of the Berlin garrison; recall of military dependents in Europe; strengthening of NATO's conventional arms. However, some editors agreed with Walter Lippmann's plan that the West take the initiative in proposing negotiations with the object of attaining an "improved" status for West Berlin by frankly acknowledging the de facto division of Germany (e.g., St. Louis Post-Dispatch, New Republic).[13]

The lack of progress in the nuclear test ban negotiations was also a source of frustration. Earlier, all had agreed that the Soviet demand for a three-man inspection commission, with Soviet veto power, would make a "complete mockery" of inspection. Some commentators bluntly called for a resumption of testing by the U.S., while others stressed the serious consequences of failure to reach agreement on a workable test ban, including the adverse consequences in world opinion. But the Washington Star maintained: If U.S. "security is as imperiled as many experts fear, the U.S. ought to stop kowtowing to ill-informed international opinion and resume nuclear testing forthwith."[14]

Meanwhile, the Administration's proposal of a U.S. disarmament agency was promptly approved by most commentators; and Pres. Kennedy's UN address was said to mark the dramatic emergence of the U.S. as "the world leader for disarmament" (Scripps-Howard papers.)[15]

Laos; China

In his first "test of wills" with Khrushchev, that over Laos, editors felt that Pres. Kennedy faced up to the crisis with "great coolness and style." Bipartisan support was expressed for a firm U.S.-free world position. Commentators agreed that a neutral Laos was an admirable goal; nevertheless some asked whether a coalition government which included Communists could remain neutral. Others expressed concern over neighboring South Viet-Nam, saying that it—rather than Laos—was the primary target in the Communist drive for Southeast Asia.[16]

In May the Administration was confronted with a "cruel choice" in Laos: intervene militarily and risk expanded conflict; or, "abandon Laos," a move which would deal a "serious blow to American prestige." Most commentators counseled against intervention (e.g., Gen. Eisenhower, Scripps-Howard papers); but others felt there would be no end to Communist take-overs until the "free nations show some backbone" (e.g., Houston Chronicle), and accordingly urged a "get tough" policy (e.g., Wm. R. Hearst, Jr.). Despite the Kennedy-Khrushchev agreement in Vienna on the desirability of a cease-fire in Laos, the objective of a "truly neutral" Laos seemed more remote to observers than ever. These cited the prompt Communist seizure of Padong within a few hours of the Vienna agreement. Former Vice President Nixon and others protested that the U.S. "talked big" about Laos but "backed down when the chips were down." Some saw real danger that "world opinion will swing to the view that the U.S. is retreating before Communist aggression" (Jos. Alsop, Denver Post).[17]

The impending "neutralist settlement" in Laos, commentators said, was "bound to heighten the Communist peril to South Viet-Nam," which many regarded as of "even higher strategic importance" than Laos (e.g., Time, U.S. News & World Report). Editors were gratified by Pres. Ngo Dinh Diem's re-election, as a "rebuff to Communist terrorists," yet some were concerned about the "slow pace" of political reform there. Nevertheless, there was prompt endorsement of Diem's appeal for increased U.S. aid, in view of the grave danger from developments in Laos (e.g., N.Y. Herald Tribune, Kansas City Times). Observers felt that the pledges made by Vice President Johnson to South Viet-Nam on his Far East tour should strengthen the Republic's position in its fight against Communist subversion (e.g., N.Y. Times, St. Louis Post-Dispatch). But some remarked that no amount of military aid is "worth anything" if it is used to "shore up governments out of sympathy with the people we hope to defend" (e.g., Sen. Fulbright, C.S. Monitor).[18]

Encouragement about the outlook for South Viet-Nam was expressed by commentators who concluded that U.S. military training had helped the South Vietnamese army in its biggest battle against the Communists since the end of the Indochina war. Life magazine advocated "increased U.S. economic aid to back Pres. Diem's effective land reform by distributing more land to the tenant farmers." Time's cover story asserted that the U.S. "has made a major decision: South Viet-Nam must be defended at all costs. Given resolve, hard work and the cooperation of Communist fighter Diem, the U.S. hoped it was not too late."[19]

There had been disappointment in the spring over Peking's rejection of U.S. efforts to use the Warsaw ambassadorial talks to achieve a lessening of tensions between the countries. All agreed that Peking's conditions for improved relations were "impossible"—we couldn't "surrender" our commitments to the Republic of China in order to secure such relaxation. The "Warsaw rebuff" convinced observers that Peking did not really desire a UN seat. American popular opposition to seating Peking had changed little since 1955, according to the Gallup Poll: 67% against in 1955, 64% against in 1961. But there was a measurable shift on the issue of U.S. acceptance of majority UN decision on this question: in 1961 59% were prepared to "go along with" such a decision, whereas in 1955 53% said they were opposed to doing so.[20]

Reports of a "new U.S. approach" to the China problem now stirred up an intensive effort to mobilize American opinion against such "softening." Former Vice Pres. Nixon called upon Pres. Kennedy to "shoot down" the "trial balloon suggesting two Chinas in the UN;" but Nixon did not agree with the Young Republicans who favored termination of U.S. aid to the UN and "serious consideration" of U.S. withdrawal in case Peking were seated there. Some others, however, welcomed the idea of changes in U.S. China policy (e.g., Dayton News, St. Louis Post-Dispatch). A poll of its local committees by the Council on Foreign Relations found the 650 members closely divided on seating Peking in the UN: 45% were "favorably inclined," but 46% were "definitely opposed" and 4% were "unfavorably inclined."[21]

To prevent any "softening" of the U.S. position on China, an extensive effort was mounted in August which resulted in House passage (391-to-0) of a resolution opposing U.S. or UN diplomatic recognition of the Communist government. Some doubted the vigor with which the U.S. would press its opposition to Red China's seating at the UN; and editors counseled that "vigorous U.S. leadership" was going to be needed "if the UN is not to capitulate to Peiping's bullying" (N.Y. Herald Tribune). In similar vein editors applauded the U.S. decision to terminate the talks which had contemplated the possibility of recognizing Outer Mongolia. Most commentators hailed Pres. Kennedy's Oct. 19 statement that this country "firmly opposes the entry of Chinese Communists into the UN or any of its components." Former Vice Pres. Nixon added his belief that "no less than the survival of the UN itself" was now at stake. Some, however, reaffirmed their conviction that the tide of events was "inexorably ending the UN policy of quarantine" (N.Y. Post).[22]

The General Assembly voting in 1961 was highly gratifying to most commentators in upholding the U.S. resolution designating the China representation issue as "an important question" (thus requiring a two-thirds vote for official action), and in voting down the Soviet proposal to seat Peking in Nationalist China's place. Still, most commentators added that the U.S. "cannot afford complacency" about the 1961 vote; and supporters of the "two Chinas" solution urged U.S. policy-makers to shape their advance planning to achieve that result. In the end, said the Washington Post, "the geographic entity that is Formosa, and that which is continental China, both must be in a UN that is fully representative."[23]

With the Laos negotiations stalled, and the cease-fire precarious, Pres. Kennedy in September had voiced his concern over the "smoldering coals of war in Southeast Asia." Commentators shared the

President's feelings, and they were "shocked" at the successes gained by Viet Cong guerrillas in South Viet-Nam. The Providence Journal concluded that South Viet-Nam would "remain a nation under siege until the loyalty of the Vietnamese people to their government becomes strong enough to submerge their fear of Communists."[24]

The President's decision to send Gen. Maxwell Taylor to Saigon for an "across-the-board" assessment of the military, economic, and political situation in South Viet-Nam was welcomed. Some saw this move as a way of "advising Moscow the U.S. isn't becoming preoccupied by the Berlin crisis" (e.g., David Lawrence), and of showing increasing readiness to use force in Southeast Asia (e.g., Newsweek, Time). Of the fighting in the jungles of South Viet-Nam, the Los Angeles Times said: "If the tide of Communist empire cannot be stopped in Southeast Asia, it may never be stopped again." But several editors noted Gen. Taylor's statement that it was "far from certain whether the dispatch of American troops is what the situation calls for." Also, virtually all were favorably inclined toward the view that American troops could perform a useful role in communications, logistics and training in South Viet-Nam.[25]

Berlin Wall

Considerable public "worry about the chances of a world war breaking out in which atomic bombs would be used" was reported by the Gallup Poll on July 14: "very worried," 15% of men, 27% of women; "fairly worried," 36% of men, 38% of women. But the fact that the leaders on both sides of the Berlin dispute coupled their stepped-up military measures with a willingness to "talk" engendered hope that a "perilous showdown" might be avoided through resort to diplomacy.[26]

The "instant, galvanic" response of the Congress to Pres. Kennedy's address to the nation on July 25 meant that there could be "no reason for Mr. Khrushchev to miscalculate" U.S. intentions regarding Berlin, editors asserted. Public opinion polls also showed steady popular support, around 80%, for measures insisting upon allied rights in Berlin, as had been the case in the tug-of-war a dozen years before. But editors often said: "We still arm to parley."

Construction of the Berlin Wall and the "illegal sealing" of the East-West Berlin border on Aug. 13 were viewed with grave concern. Initially seen as something of a "propaganda triumph" for the West, the Wall came to be regarded by many as undermining the Western position in West Berlin, because of allied acquiescence in the border closure. It was generally agreed that the "most ominous" threat so far was continued in Moscow's Aug. 23 note challenging the inviolability of the West's air access to Berlin, and implying Soviet interference with those air routes. The swift and solemn U.S. warning to Moscow–that any interference would be regarded as an "aggressive act" for which the Soviet Union would bear "full responsibility"–evoked unanimous editorial approval. Soviet Major Titov's circling of the earth at this point was deemed "a propaganda sledgehammer of tremendous weight," and some feared that the space victory might increase Khrushchev's self-confidence to the point "where he would make some dangerous move." Despite Vice Pres. Johnson's "morale-building" visit to Berlin, a number of observers voiced deep doubts about the city's future viability; they saw it as an "isolated outpost," its communications to the West "under constant threat," and the city subject to "slow economic anemia." Some members of Congress thought it might be helpful to bring the UN into the picture; but few expected any support for the Western position from the current meeting of neutralist leaders in Belgrade.[27]

Berlin was prominent in Pres. Kennedy's address to the UNGA which won editorial praise for its eloquent expression of America's "firm but not provocative" position. The speech also voiced U.S. support for a vigorous Secretary-General–rather than a "troika"–as well as American opposition to seating Peking. To the many editors applauding the President's "masterful" address, his remarks left no room for doubt concerning the American resolve to defend our basic rights in Berlin; and the speech won overwhelming bipartisan support in Congress. At the same time, the President's statement that we were "committed to no rigid formula" and Gen. Clay's remarks in Berlin regarding acceptance of the "reality" of the two Germanys were interpreted by some as foreshadowing a compromise settlement. Some said Clay's remarks about the possibility of "de facto" recognition of East Germany bordered on "appeasement" (e.g., Chi. Tribune, Wall St. Journal). To head off further cries of "appeasement," some urged the President to undertake a program of educating the country on the need for "honorable compromise" (e.g., TRB in New Republic; Rep. Green, D-Ore.).[28]

There was disappointment in October over the failure of the Gromyko-Kennedy talks to lead to "reasonable" Berlin negotiations, but there was satisfaction with U.S. insistence "at bayonet point" on the right of American civilian representatives to cross into East Berlin unimpeded. To a good many it seemed that the U.S. had scored a point in obliging the Russians to demonstrate their responsibility for East Berlin by sending in Soviet tanks, contending that the presence of Russian armor exploded the "myth" of Pankow's sovereignty. For some Khrushchev's latest pronouncements confirmed the wisdom of Pres. de Gaulle's contention that the West should simply "sit tight" and refuse to negotiate until the Soviets came up with some constructive suggestions (e.g., N.Y. News).[29]

On Oct. 17 Khrushchev announced that he no longer regarded Dec. 31 as a "dead-line" for a Berlin settlement. As Richard Stebbins points out, the U.S. had by then achieved a "considerable all-around strengthening of the nation's defense capabilities," and had since Kennedy's July 25 speech brought up Army and Air Force strength in Europe to nearly 300,000. Four days after Khrushchev's statement Deputy Defense Secretary Gilpatric announced that the U.S. had developed a "second strike capability which is at least as extensive as what the Soviets can deliver by striking first. Therefore, we are confident that the Soviets will not provoke a major conflict." After Chancellor Adenauer's re-election the Kennedy Administration, in deference to West German "sensibilities," shelved consideration of such projects as "disengagement" or a thinning-out of troops in Central Europe.[30]

Nuclear Testing

In September Soviet insistence upon going ahead with atmospheric nuclear tests was considered an ominous development. When Pres. Kennedy's renewed appeal to the Soviet Union to join in immediate agreement with Britain and America to end such testing failed, the U.S. resumption of underground testing was approved as a necessary step by a majority of those commenting. Khrushchev's announcement at the Communist Party Congress that a 50-megaton bomb would be exploded in the atmosphere led to intensified American editorial criticism of the grave danger from fallout. It also "killed all present hopes for effective arms control," the Kansas City Times declared.[31]

The Soviet series of atmospheric tests accentuated mistrust of the Russians and spread the conviction that the U.S. must test in the atmosphere if U.S. security made such action desirable. Some commentators were already convinced that the U.S. should go ahead (e.g., Columbus (Ohio) Dispatch, Richard Nixon). The Gallup Poll showed a close division of opinion on resumption. The U.S.-British proposal to the Soviets that test ban talks be resumed was followed by a mixed editorial reaction; when the Russians accepted there was much skepticism about the end result, but a number favored negotiation anyhow (e.g., Wash. Post, N.Y. Herald Tribune). The majority shared the attitude of the Scripps-Howard papers, that the State Department had reacted properly. "It says we are willing to resume the talks—but we reserve the right to carry out . . . whatever tests are deemed vital to our national security." With negotiations resumed at Geneva, the Soviets proposed a ban without international controls; and this drew no approval in American comment.[32]

Africa; UN

Reports that a new plan for the Congo was being prepared by the Kennedy Administration found commentators divided on the wisdom of this plan, which called for the disarming of all the Congolese troops and administration of the country by all political elements, including Lumumba. However, editors were agreed in approving the U.S. stand at the UN against Soviet moves in the Congo and against Soviet efforts to restrain Secretary-General Hammarskjold. Strong endorsement was accorded the Security Council's 9-to-0 adoption of a resolution empowering the Secretary-General to prevent "widespread civil war"–by force, if necessary. Some who welcomed the new resolution noted that it presented problems as well as opportunities: where to obtain the new troops needed to compensate for some withdrawals, and how to deal with the continuing opposition by armed Congolese.[33]

In April, the refusal of the Soviet Union and France to help pay for the UN's Congo mission drew sharp criticism; and the "revolutionary" U.S. decision favoring a UN inquiry into Portugal's Angola was strongly endorsed by most of those commenting (e.g., Des Moines Register, Hearst and Scripps-Howard papers), although several underscored their concern about possible harmful effects on NATO. The New York News asked what help the Angola natives could give us "comparable to the Azores." Some commentators chastised the U.S. for "voting with Russia" (e.g., Trohan of Chi. Tribune). A majority supported the Security Council vote of June 9 condemning Portugal's policies in Angola, saying that the U.S. "took the right course" in deciding to "move in line with its anti-colonial convictions and traditions, even at the risk of embarrassing an ally" (e.g., Milwaukee Journal, N.Y. Times, Time).[34]

The UNGA's rejection of economic sanctions against the Union of South Africa was applauded by most of those commenting; but these papers did approve of the "milder approach" to the apartheid issue later adopted by the UNGA, that of inviting member states to consider what "separate and collective actions" of other types could be taken. However, several papers did oppose any action as "intervention in the domestic concerns" of a member nation (e.g., Wash. Star, New Orleans Times-Picayune).[35]

Americans were not happy about the UN record on Africa. Indeed, many American commentators were dubious about the UN policy which Secretary-General Hammarskjold was seeking to implement at the time of his tragic death in Africa. On the Sept. 13 UN military action against Katanga Province, the weight of public reaction was sharply critical. To the critics, the aims of preventing civil strife between Katanga and Leopoldville, and of forcing Tshombe to dismiss his mercenary soldiers, did not warrant the "setting of this precedent of an 'agressor' UN" (St. Paul Pioneer Press, Denver Post). The critics of UN policy also directed considerable fire at U.S. support for it; and some who had been initially sympathetic to the UN action felt, after seeing the magnitude of Katanga resistance, that the U.S. "should have no further part" in the coercive policy (Scripps-Howard; N.Y. Times).[36]

Continuing refusal by France and the Soviet Union to pay their assessed shares of the cost of UN operations in the Congo further weakened the position of the UN. Also, the General Assembly's censure of a policy speech by South African foreign minister Louw aroused a storm of criticism in the U.S. against this African-led interference with the right "freely to express" his government's position. Traditional critics of the UN reiterated their condemnations (e.g., Chi. Tribune, Cinci. Enquirer); but in most cases apprehension about the future of the world organization was not accompanied by hostility. Positive support for the United Nations at this time was given by the American Bar Association, religious organizations, organized labor, the American Veterans Committee, and women's organizations.[37]

Election of U Thant as Secretary-General was welcomed by many, and seen as auguring well for the future; but some "nationalist" sources tended to see him as too much of a "neutral against us" (e.g., Phoenix Gazette, Charleston News & Courier). As debate over Congo policy continued, some editors were very disturbed by mounting indications that the world organization was in a grave period of decline. Large numbers of UN members had failed to pay their assessments; and particularly caustic comment was directed toward the Soviet Union's plea of poverty in answer to a proposed assessment for the regular UN budget. The N.Y. Times believed that the U.S. "should try to strengthen the UN, even though we could no longer control it." But Secretary-General Thant's suggestion that the UN float a bond issue to liquidate its debt drew a generally cool reception, commentators saying: This would not solve the problem, the UN had no assets, and the likeliest purchaser of the unsecured obligations would be the United States.[38]

Aid & Trade

When Pres. Kennedy asked Congress to grant increased Executive "discretion" about extending aid to Eastern European countries, there was a mixed editorial reaction. Some noted that our aid had kept Yugoslavia out of the Soviet orbit (e.g., Milwaukee Journal, Worcester Telegram); others argued that loans and grants to a nation such as Poland prolonged the sway of Communism everywhere (e.g., Manchester Union Leader, Indianapolis Star). The President's comprehensive foreign aid message to Congress was favorably received by a majority of those commenting; but his request for a 5-year authorization, including borrowing authority, immediately became controversial. Aid supporters pointed out that it was hard for us to urge far-reaching reforms to receiving countries if we could offer aid only on an annual basis (e.g., Business Week, N.Y. Herald Tribune); but retention of effective Congressional control over aid funds was favored by many (e.g., Wall St. Journal, Scripps-Howard papers).[39]

In the June discussion of Pres. Kennedy's $4.8 billion aid request, support came from many newspapers and organizations (e.g., N.Y. Times, Christian Century, AFL-CIO, U.S. Council of the International Chamber of Commerce). Substantial cuts were urged by the U.S. Chamber of Commerce, American Farm Bureau Fed. and Wall St. Journal. Congressional debate resulted in a compromise, permitting 5-year commitment subject to annual appropriation, but not permitting "back-door financing" by the Treasury Department. Editors seemed to accept this result after the prolonged debate; yet most of the comment disapproved the "meat-axe slashes" which were voted by the House Appropriations Committee. But much of the House cut was agreed to by the conference committee and became law.[40]

The Inter-American conference at Punta del Este in August was hailed by editors in all parts of the country, and the Charter signed there was applauded as holding new promise for the "oppressed masses of Latin America." Many praised Pres. Kennedy for showing the "link between these needs and our own interests" and for proposing the Alliance for Progress. The Houston Chronicle warned: "If the Western nations do not pull Latin America out of the bog, the Communists will." Commentators were somewhat cautious as to expectations, agreeing that "fulfillment of a noble purpose depends mainly on the people of Latin America" (C.S. Monitor). Some added that the Alliance "will require firmness and understanding on the part of the U.S." as well (Milwaukee Journal). The Denver Post bluntly asked: "Will Congress back (Mr. Dillon's) pledges with the required appropriations?"[41]

Indeed, in early 1962 when Pres. Kennedy proposed a $4.9 billion program for foreign aid he received the backing of a majority of commentators, but some demanded "deep slashes" (e.g., Scripps-Howard papers) and others felt that the start of the Alliance for Progress had been disappointing. These had hoped that the Foreign Ministers at Punta del Este could produce some sort of collective diplomatic and economic sanctions against Castro's Cuban government (e.g., Gov. Rockefeller, Detroit Free Press). But the majority stressed the gains at Punta del Este, and most agreed that the effort should continue. Reports that Sec. Rusk had linked the amount of U.S. aid under the Alliance with the firmness of a country's action against Castro were approved by some (Hearst and Scripps-Howard papers), but others were opposed to using aid as a "stick" (N.Y. Herald Tribune, Mrs. Roosevelt).[42]

Debate over trade policy reappeared in May 1961 with the demands of American textile manufacturers for relief from "ruinous" Japanese competition. A number of Congressmen agreed, but several editors were prompted to stress the benefits of existing U.S. tariff policies, and to emphasize Japan's efforts to become an economic partner in the free world and to assist in Asian development, and pointed out that Japan had bought $2 billion of goods from America (e.g., Des Moines Register, Scripps-Howard papers).[43]

In the autumn a speech by Under Secretary Ball evoked widespread approval for a trade program affording the Government substantially broader and more flexible bargaining power. Most supporters cited the challenge in a new trading world of the prospering European Economic Community (e.g., Houston Post, N.Y. Times). Labor support came from George Meany and from the Intnl. Assn. of Machinists. Some of the "nationalist" papers advocated freer trade; but the Hearst papers were conspicuous for their sharp opposition to giving the Executive Branch "virtually dictatorial power to abolish the remnants of our protective tariff system." But most editors agreed with Mr. Ball that the item-by-item tariff reductions authorized by existing legislation were "hopelessly inadequate;" and many also agreed with Ball's thought that during the transition to freer trade "we may have to provide substantial government assistance to injured domestic industries."[44]

In his 1962 State of the Union message Pres. Kennedy gave much attention to his proposed Trade Expansion Bill; this was enthusiastically supported by the overwhelming majority of those commenting. The accords reached in Brussels for a common farm policy for the EEC, and for reciprocal tariff cutting between the EEC and the U.S. were hailed by many editors. Leaders of business, farming, and labor joined in supporting the new trade program (Henry Ford II, Homer Brinkley, Andrew Biemiller); but there was some opposition, too, in these categories (e.g., Natl. Fed. of Independent Business; Textile and pottery workers). In the summer the House passed the Trade Expansion Bill amid wide acclaim.[45]

Summary

Controversy with Castro continued after the Bay of Pigs episode, but the public supported the increasing U.S. attention to the rest of

Latin America as provided in the Punta del Este Charter and the Alliance for Progress. After Kennedy's Vienna meeting with Khrushchev, public opinion approved the U.S. steps in the continuing tension over Laos and Berlin. The public upheld the strong moves to defend allied rights in Berlin and Khrushchev, after erection of the Berlin Wall, relinquished his "dead-line" for a Berlin settlement. American sentiment was divided over the UN-U.S. policy for the Congo, but there was unity on opposing Soviet expansionism in Africa and Soviet efforts to undermine the position of the UN Secretary-General.

Although Laos could not be settled, editors approved U.S. efforts to assist the neighboring republic of South Viet-Nam. Strong popular opposition to the People's Republic of China persisted, and commentators were gratified by the UN resolution upholding the U.S. position on seating Peking; but some editors felt that the U.S. needed to plan for the inevitable time when Peking would have the requisite votes in the General Assembly. The Kennedy Administration had weathered its first year in foreign affairs, and public approval of the Kennedy presidency was higher than at the start (77% vs. 69%).

Reference Notes

1. AOR of Feb. 2, 1961.
2. AOR of Feb. 2 and Mar. 3, 1961.
3. AOR of May 4, 1961.
4. Ibid.
5. AOR of July 4, 1961.
6. Ibid.
7. AOR of Mar. 3, 1961.
8. AOR of May 4 and July 4, 1961.
9. AOR of May 4, 1961.
10. AOR of June 2, 1961.
11. Ibid.
12. AOR of July 3, 1961.
13. Ibid.
14. AOR of May 4 and July 3, 1961.
15. AOR of Aug. 4, 1961.
16. AOR of Apr. 3, 1961.
17. AOR of May 4 and June 2, 1961.
18. AOR of May 4, June 2, and July 3, 1961.
19. AOR of Aug. 4, 1961.
20. AOR of Apr. 3, 1961.
21. AOR of July 3, 1961.
22. AOR for Sept. 4, Nov. 2, and Dec. 15, 1961.
23. AOR of Jan 3, 1962.
24. AOR of Oct. 2, 1961.
25. AOR of Nov. 2, 1961.
26. AOR of Aug. 4, 1961.
27. AOR of Sept. 5, 1961.

28. AOR of Oct. 2, 1961.
29. AOR of Nov. 2, 1961.
30. Stebbins, R. P., *U.S. in World Affairs, 1961* (New York, 1962), p. 53; AOR of Dec. 1, 1961.
31. AOR for Oct. 2 and Nov. 2, 1961.
32. AOR of Dec. 1, 1961.
33. AOR of Mar. 3, 1961.
34. AOR for Apr. 3 and July 3, 1961.
35. AOR of May 4, 1961.
36. AOR of Oct. 2, 1961.
37. AOR of Nov. 2, 1961.
38. AOR for Dec. 1 and 15, 1961.
39. AOR for Mar. 3 and Apr. 3, 1961.
40. AOR for July 3 and Sept. 5, 1961.
41. AOR of Sept. 3, 1961.
42. AOR for Feb. 2, Mar. 2, Apr. 3, and May 2, 1962.
43. AOR of May 4, 1961.
44. AOR for Dec. 1, 1961 and Aug. 3, 1962.
45. AOR of Feb. 2, 1962.

XIII

BEFORE AND AFTER CUBAN CRISIS (1962–1963)

As the New Year of 1962 opened, it was the general consensus that some of the "steam" had gone out of the Berlin crisis; and the mid-January pullbacks of U.S. and Soviet tanks from the sector border were further encouraging. Still, commentators said that the basic situation remained unchanged, that the "menace" and the diplomatic "impasse" continued. Some editors therefore urged the West to continue to press for a negotiated settlement, rather than accept a "tacit" agreement to put up with the existing situation (e.g., Walter Lippman, N.Y. Post).[1]

Events of the next two years were to highlight the "menace" via the Cuban missile crisis (Oct. 1962), and also to witness the Soviet-American agreement on the Test Ban Treaty of 1963. Also during this biennium important questions arose in Viet-Nam and in the UN. The early collapse of the Geneva test ban talks was widely attributed to Soviet refusal to engage in "give-and-take." The result was viewed as an added reason for the U.S. to go ahead with atmospheric testing. A Gallup Poll showed the general public still closely divided on this issue (46% resume; 43% not resume).[2]

Soviet Relations; Europe

Behind a "facade of seemingly conciliatory gestures," the Kremlin was perceived as creating a "new crisis" over Berlin by challenging Western air access. The fact that the allied response was so "prompt" and "unanimously firm" against the Soviet demands for "exclusive" use of the air corridors at stated times, was a matter of deep satisfaction to many. Similarly, Sec. Rusk's "fast brush-off" of Khrushchev's proposals for an 18-nation "summit" meeting on disarmament was approved by the New York News; and the courteous rejections embodied in the President's replies were upheld by many. Editors agreed that preliminary progress should precede a summit meeting. After Col. Glenn's successful flight, Khrushchev's suggestion of U.S.-Soviet cooperation in outer space exploration was greeted with considerable skepticism, as chiefly a propaganda ploy. Nevertheless, cooperation was favored if Khrushchev was actually ready for cooperation.[3]

In March Soviet radar-jamming and "saturation" flights along the Berlin air corridors posed a danger of serious collisions, but press opinion was unanimous that the vital air links must remain open. Some, in fact, urged stronger retaliatory measures (e.g., Phila. Bulletin, Scripps-Howard papers). Soviet rejection at Geneva of an internationally inspected nuclear test ban was disappointing, even if expected; but a number felt that negotiation was still important. Pres. Kennedy received widespread applause when he announced that the U.S. would resume atmospheric testing in late April unless international agreement on a ban was reached earlier. The Gallup Poll now reported 66% in favor of resumption, and 25% opposed (9% no opinion). But editors maintained that testing should be ended as soon as possible–preferably by international agreement. The U.S. disarmament proposals presented on April 18 were supported, although many deemed it unlikely that they would result in any agreement.[4]

A crisis in European relations appeared in mid-May, with the great majority of commentators unequivocally supporting Pres. Kennedy's "Atlantic" concept over Pres. de Gaulle's design for a Continental Europe largely independent of the U.S. and Britain. Editors also applauded Kennedy's insistence that so long as we bore the ultimate responsibility for Europe's defense, we should continue to participate in the great diplomatic decisions. The President's determination to keep talking with the Soviets about Berlin was also strongly upheld. Many resented Chancellor Adenauer's "veto" of an American plan for a 13-nation control body to manage the Berlin access problem, but a number also had their doubts about the U.S. Berlin proposal. All were relieved when Sec. Rusk "patched up" relations with Bonn in June.[5]

The President's July 4 speech, calling for a "concrete Atlantic partnership," was very favorably received–as was his firm position on Berlin, despite the deadlocked Soviet-American talks. While a few feared that the President envisaged an "Atlantic Union," the majority refused to believe he had espoused a superstate, and commended him for preparing the country "to act in step with history." Some said a partnership of equals would require ultimate modification of existing U.S. control of nuclear weapons on allied soil; and some saw a need for Europe to contribute a bigger share for the conventional defense of Europe and for economic aid to the less-developed areas.[6]

The Soviet Union's tandem orbiting of two cosmonauts in August stimulated a rich wave of praise for Soviet scientists and technicians. Editors agreed with Pres. Kennedy in saluting the twin space shot as an "exceptional technical feat;" but it quickly became apparent that the Soviets, as in the case of the first sputnik, intended to use their achievement to exert new military-political pressure on the West in Berlin. This expectation triggered some critical questioning as to the adequacy of the U.S. space program; but for many the contrast between the Soviet "triumph" in space and Russia's "oppressive" earthly behavior was paramount. Acts of Communist "brutality" at the Berlin Wall produced intense feelings of outrage over Communist "inhumanity," and many American editors shared the West Berliners' indignation at the inaction of American authorities to prevent or alleviate tragic events at the Berlin Wall. When the Russian command in East Berlin was taken up by an East German officer, editors upheld the "properly firm" joint response by the allies.[7]

At Geneva, the U.S. proposal of an uninspected ban on nuclear weapons testing in the atmosphere, under water, and in outer space produced a divided reaction at home. Supporters agreed with the Administration that scientific progress had now made it quite possible to detect tests at a distance through instruments under U.S. control (e.g., N.Y. Herald Tribune, C.S. Monitor). But opponents insisted that "fool-proof inspection" was "an indispensable ingredient in any pact with our sworn enemy" (e.g., Chi. American, Hearst papers). In any event, pessimism about an agreement remained predominant.[8]

United Nations

At the beginning of 1962 grave concern about the UN, and its prospects, continued—with considerable debate on the proposed U.S. purchase of $100 million of UN bonds. Prompt opposition was registered by some Congressmen and editors (e.g., Chi. Tribune, Portland Oregonian); but others increasingly approved the idea, saying that the purchase was essential to the effective life of the UN (e.g., Chi. News, Phila. Inquirer, Wash. Post). The Gallup Poll reported 83% of Americans calling it "very important" that the U.S. "try to make the United Nations a success," 9% calling it "fairly important," and 4% "not so important." The minority favoring U.S. withdrawal declined from 12% in 1951 to 5% in 1962.[9]

The Middle East conflict came to the surface again in April when the U.S. and Britain backed a UN Security Council resolution censuring Israel's raids into Syria. American editors were divided. Some said "this rebuke was deserved" (e.g., Wash. Star, Balt. Sun); but others complained that the resolution represented "less than even-handed justice" (e.g., N.Y. Times, Wash. Post, Phila. Inquirer). A more decisive UN policy in the Congo, to overcome Tshombe's separatism, was put into effect in 1962, at the urging of the Secretary-General and the U.S. In his *To Move A Nation*, Roger Hilsman points out that there was an "important difference" in the situation from 1961 when a forceful UN policy lacked support; now, after the "months in which a patient and reasonable" effort to bring Tshombe around had failed, many came to share the frustration of the UN and the "New Africa" group in the State Department. These activist officers "conducted an educational campaign on Capitol Hill and among the press" and even the general public, producing a climate of opinion more favorable to the economic pressure and UN military action which resulted in Tshombe's capitulation in Jan. 1963.[10]

Viet-Nam

Agreement by South Viet-Nam and the U.S. on a joint 11-point socio-economic program for the Republic was viewed as encouraging, although some said it was "still a gamble" whether the necessary reforms could be carried out "in time" (Kansas City Times). There was general appreciation of the possibility that as more Americans assumed tasks which moved them to the fighting fronts, the risk of U.S. casualties would rise. But virtually no one suggested that the U.S. "alter our course" in Southeast Asia. Sen. Ellender (D-La.) was one exception; he proposed that unless we received financial and military help from our allies we "should consider a gradual withdrawal of assistance." But others urged sending "more military hardware" plus "training in how to use it" (Scripps-Howard papers).[11]

On relations with mainland China, editors offered little support either for dispatching grain to Peking (in view of its attitude toward the U.S.), or for supporting Chiang Kai-shek's "invasion plan." On the other hand, observers saw the U.S. taking a "fateful decision" in further expanding the American role in the "subterranean" Viet-Nam war, thus "irrevocably drawing a cold war battle line" in a strategic area. When Attorney-General Kennedy said in Pakistan that "we are going to win" in South Viet-Nam, he was applauded by the San Diego Union, Kansas City Star, and former Vice Pres. Nixon. Similarly "optimistic" statements were made by Asst. Sec. of State Harriman and Defense Sec. McNamara; and some editors said that Peking's outcry against U.S. aid to Saigon was "eloquent testimony" to its effectiveness.[12]

At the same time, the voluminous discussion of Viet-Nam brought out the widespread conviction that the Administration should be thoroughly "candid" about U.S. involvement (e.g., N.Y. Times, St. Louis Post-Dispatch). A few complained that the "pattern exists for slipping into full-scale war without public discussion or Congressional decision" (Chi. Tribune), or said that the President "faces a large order" in "selling" Americans on a war which might be lengthy and costly (Doris Fleeson, Wash. Post). Still, at the end of February no one was asking for a "re-examination" of the U.S. commitment in Viet-Nam, and the press and TV were presenting at some length, pictorially and verbally, the scope of the U.S. operation in Southeast Asia. Life, for example, had a 12-page spread on "The Far-off War We have Decided To Win."[13]

In May, Asian crises came to the fore, and Pres. Kennedy dispatched U.S. combat troops to Thailand to be on hand in the event that the deteriorating situation in Laos should flow over the border. This action brought the U.S. "very close to the brink," but observers felt that not to have honored our commitment to our SEATO ally would have left our Asian friends in doubt, and given the Communists dangerous illusions about our determination to implement our security arrangements. At the same time, editors preferred to have no Americans committed to combat in Laos, and would have felt reassured if our SEATO allies had sent substantial rather than token aid to Thailand.[14]

Pres. Kennedy's statement (6/27) of U.S. policy in the Taiwan Strait was widely approved. Some liked the continuing "ambiguity," others approved his making it "clear that he would oppose a Communist attack on the off-shores, just as he would oppose Nationalist China's use of the islands for invasion of the mainland" (e.g., N.Y. Herald Tribune, Phila. Inquirer). As in previous off-shores crises, a number said that "when the heat is off," the U.S. should "liquidate the very dangerous commitment in the islands" (e.g., St. Louis Post-Dispatch). In Viet-Nam some saw noticeable improvements, despite the "fumbled command and bureaucratic fog" in Saigon; but Robert Elegant saw it as a "testing ground, not only of the Communists' strength, but also of the American will to fight a protracted, inglorious and probably inconclusive war" (in New Leader).[15]

The growing American casualty list in Viet-Nam provoked concerned comment; and the news reports from correspondents prompted a number of troubled observers to ask: "How well is the U.S. venture going there?" The disturbing picture of an "uncooperative" Diem government clashed with Defense Sec. McNamara's professed encouragement over progress. Sen. Smith (R-Me.) felt that the Administration was either "misleading itself with bootstrap optimism, or is deliberately misrepresenting the actual facts to the American people" (also C.S. Monitor).[16]

Cuba and Missile Crisis

American commentators warmly welcomed the unanimous agreement at Punta del Este on the "incompatibility" of Cuba's Marxist-Leninist regime with the hemispheric system, but many were disappointed over the abstention of six large Latin American governments on the resolution excluding the Castro government from participating in the inter-American system. The imposition of a U.S. embargo on trade with Cuba—except for medicines and food for the Cuban people—was endorsed by virtually all of those commenting. When Fidel Castro offered to ransom for $62 million the rebels taken in the abortive Cuban invasion attempt, editors denounced this "despicable blackmail" effort. They said the U.S. should not place barriers to payments by private groups, but the Government should remain aloof.[17]

During August rising concern was expressed in some quarters about the reported entry of 5,000 Soviet technicians into Cuba, and the apparent inactivity of the U.S. Administration in the face of this development. Even accepting Pres. Kennedy's view that there was no evidence of a "troop" landing, said the Washington Star, "the possibility remains" that "technicians" could serve as guardians of a Cuban "Communist outpost." Some, who saw the Monroe Doctrine "being openly flouted," urged a strong "U.S. countermove" (e.g., David Lawrence, Hearst papers); but Arthur Krock thought that a U.S. naval patrol to block Red arms shipments to Cuba would be preferable. Several journals approved the Administration's "resisting the clamor" for direct intervention (e.g., N.Y. Times, Wash. Post). According to the Denver Post, "the times call for waiting and seeing, not shooting or even aiming."[18]

September witnessed increasing editorial discussions of Cuba, as reports of a Soviet arms build-up on the island continued; and from Berlin came reported developments cooler than those on Cuba. Differences of editorial opinion over Cuban policy became stronger, with Administration supporters praising the President for "keeping his nerve and his head," and welcoming his statements on U.S. determination to prevent establishment of an "offensive" Cuban base which could threaten the U.S. and other hemisphere countries. But the critics inveighed against America's "public display of cowardice" (Indianapolis Star) or "failure to do its duty" (e.g., San Diego Union, Sen. Goldwater). To the Dallas News, the President–in his "timid course"–was "about the only American unwilling to face the realities of the Cuban situation." With the midterm elections approaching, some editors cautioned the critics against "playing politics with Cuba" (e.g., Dayton News).[19]

A Congressional resolution endorsed the use of "whatever means may be necessary" to prevent Communist aggression or subversion based upon Cuba. A number applauded the resolution as "bolstering the President," and for providing for action through the OAS, while reserving to the U.S. unilateral action if necessary. It charted a course "both constructive and flexible," said the Chicago News. To the Hearst and Scripps-Howard papers the resolution "assumed the initiative for the U.S.–and high time." But most of the Cuba policy critics assailed the resolution's "weakness," asserting that it "recognizes and accepts the Soviet presence" in the Caribbean (e.g., N.Y. News). The resolution authorizing the President to call up 150,000 reservists was approved, although some felt it was of "strictly psychological value."[20]

Soviet announcement of plans to build a "fishing base" in Havana Bay sparked new anger and concern, as editors said this could change the danger of Cuba under Communism into "an actual rather than a potential threat." The point of broadest agreement in the Cuba discussion was the conclusion that "greater cooperation should be forthcoming" from America's NATO and OAS allies.

During October debate continued as to the extent and seriousness of the Soviet build-up in Cuba; and tension mounted. When Pres. Kennedy addressed the Nation (Oct. 22), the outpouring of expressions of support left no doubt of the overwhelming popular approval of his firm stand on the build-up of offensive Soviet weapons in Cuba. It was recognized by the public that the U.S. was facing the possibility of nuclear war, but the public comment reflected willingness to take the risk. The President's action was considered relatively restrained—"not so drastic as many Americans would like to take," said the New York Times. The President's "patience in waiting for incontrovertible evidence of establishment of an offensive base "has greatly strengthened our position," said the Baltimore Sun. The President's plan of a graduated response, starting with a partial blockade, or "quarantine," received general approval.[21]

Editors warmly welcomed the support given to the U.S. blockade by the Organization of American States and by some of our European allies. When Khrushchev gave an indication that he might be willing to negotiate, this prospect was welcomed; but there was general agreement that the Soviet build-up in Cuba must be removed. The eventual news that Khrushchev was willing to dismantle the missile complex was greeted with elation tinged by caution. A few contended that the U.S. goal must be the overthrow of the Castro regime.

As the situation developed there was particular satisfaction with Pres. Kennedy's insistence on verified withdrawal of offensive missiles and bombers. "We and our hemispheric neighbors must have unmistakable proof that all offensive arms have actually been shipped back to the Soviet Union," said the Kansas City Star, which added that as long as Castro "declines to admit international inspectors, we retain full liberty to take any countermeasures necessary to assure the safety of the Western Hemisphere." This was a widely-held view; and Castro's five conditions for permitting UN on-site verification of the removal of offensive weapons met a general rebuff. The crisis seemed to have passed the acute stage by the end of November. As Business Week said, "The U.S.-Soviet confrontation in Cuba virtually ended when the Kennedy Administration favored a backdown on the bomber issue."[22]

Pres. Kennedy's Nov. 20 press conference drew great praise for the Administration's policies which dealt with the crisis so successfully, especially Mr. Kennedy's combination of firmness and restraint. Many wished to see progress now toward an arms agreement, and there was widespread agreement on the need for effective inspection or verification. Editors felt that the Cuban crisis offered proof that U.S. insistence on verification was justified, and they wondered how far Khrushchev's assurance that international inspectors could enter the Soviet Union might lead.[23]

Crisis Aftermath

Despite the Cuban crisis, the October newsmagazines could report: "More and more the military aid program in South Viet-Nam is becoming a shooting war between Red guerrillas and U.S. personnel." The introduction of rocket-armed helicopters and other modern weapons prompted the Philadelphia Inquirer to stress the difficulty, "or perhaps the impossibility, of drawing a line between an advisory role and actual fighting support for the South Vietnamese." There was criticism of the "unnecessary fiction" that Americans are in Viet-Nam as "non-combatants," and of a policy which "has obscured from the public too much of the progress of a war to which we are now fully committed" (e.g., N.Y. Times, Cleve. Plain Dealer). The Providence Journal said: "This clear and present conflict deserves more of our national attention." The contemporary optimism is indicated by this sentence of Harold Martin from Saigon, "We can meet and best the Communist insurgents in Viet-Nam as we have done in Greece and the Philippines."[24]

Commentators were gratified that Berlin had remained on the back burner during the Cuban crisis; but they could not refrain from commenting on China's unexpected attack on India. Support for U.S. aid to India came from press and public; a Gallup Poll found about 6 out of 10 respondents saying "the U.S. should help India in her plight." The UNGA vote against seating Peking was very welcome, although expected in view of the attack on India.[25]

Many felt that the U.S. had emerged from the Cuban missile crisis with its prestige greatly enhanced, and the American leader "far more confident of his ability" to deal with dangerous situations abroad. The expectation that the U.S. would be "more assertive in world affairs from now on" was heightened by Pres. Kennedy's TV interview of Dec. 17, in which he showed a "clear, balanced and practical" grasp of the Communist danger, on the one hand, and the danger of nuclear war on the other (e.g., Balt. Sun). In contrast, the USSR and the "much-touted monolithic Communist bloc" were seen as beset by internal dissension which might bode a change of historic importance.[26]

Liberation of the Cuban prisoners just before Christmas dominated press and TV attention at the close of the year. This ransoming of Cubans captured at the Bay of Pigs, for $53 million of food and medical supplies provided by private sources, was welcomed by some editors (e.g., Milwaukee Journal, Hearst papers), and accepted by others in view of U.S. responsibility for the invasion attempt (e.g., C.S. Monitor, Wall St. Journal). Several stressed that the "leftist Castro regime" remained in place, "with all its dangers of hidden weaponry and subversion of the Americas" (Scripps-Howard); and it was generally agreed that the U.S. was not bound by any "no-Cuba-invasion" pledge until the Soviet commitment to on-site inspection of Cuban missile bases was honored. Some were disturbed by indications that Pres. Kennedy would accept photographic surveillance of the Cuban missile sites instead of on-site inspection (John S. Knight). The Minnesota Poll, which had reported 78% calling the Castro government a "serious threat" in September, now found (Dec.) the threat termed "quite serious" by 23% and "fairly serious" by 32%, while 40% called it "not too serious" (in this category were 54% of the men, but only 26% of the women).[27]

After Khrushchev's speech acknowledging America's "nuclear teeth," Pres. Kennedy's State of the Union message was felt to have balanced "the right note of optimism" with the "right note of caution" (e.g., Chi. News, Life). A sizable group, however, found the President's appraisal "too good to be quite true," citing especially the troubled state of the Western alliance and the "far from solved" problem of Cuba (e.g., N.Y. Times, Chi. Tribune). But there was no recurrence of the editorial fear (before Oct. 22) that Khrushchev was miscalculating U.S. intentions and determination.[28]

Europe; NATO

Pres. de Gaulle's announcement that France was vetoing Britain's entry into the Common Market came as a considerable shock to most American editors, who concluded that France had delivered a "serious setback" to both European unity and Atlantic solidarity. Most commentators continued to uphold Pres. Kennedy's design for a broad Atlantic partnership embracing both trade and military matters; they favored positive steps to draw the other five members of the Common Market into closer relations with Britain (and the U.S.), while leaving an "open chair" for eventual French occupancy.[29]

In early 1963 considerable press comment was devoted to the multilateral nuclear force which had been proposed for NATO. A number expressed uncertainty and doubt about the feasibility of the force at all, or showed hesitation over the new plan to substitute surface ships for atomic submarines. Commentators commonly included among their reasons for skepticism the opposition of members of the

Joint Congressional Committee on Atomic Energy to any attempt to relinquish U.S. control over the nuclear weapons in a NATO force. Long-time supporters of the project refused to be discouraged by the complexity of the task, and stressed the need for pressing negotiations with our European allies (e.g., N.Y. Times, Los Angeles Times, Time).[30]

As Amb. Merchant completed the first round of talks in Europe, press assessments ranged from "dismal failure" to "qualified success." Writing in The Reporter, Henry A. Kissinger saw as preferable to the multilateral plan, an autonomous European nuclear force based upon the British and French programs, which could then be coordinated with the U.S. force. Gov. Rockefeller and Mr. Nixon urged Congress to amend atomic legislation to permit nuclear sharing with our allies so that they might construct their own force, free from a U.S. veto; but Congressional sentiment seemed squarely opposed to such a change.[31]

A Gallup Poll of March 10 showed that the cumulation of Pres. de Gaulle's oppositions to U.S. policies in Europe and elsewhere had reached the point where a plurality of Americans said France was "*not* a dependable ally of the U.S." (35% v. 32%, with 33% giving no opinion). Among the college-educated the plurality deeming France "not dependable" was 47% vs. 36%; but those having a grammar-school education remained more trustful (31% vs. 28%, with 41% no opinion). Majorities continued (Mar. 13) to regard as "dependable allies," Great Britain (63%) and West Germany (58%).

Pres. Kennedy, on his European trip, spoke of a "more closely unified Atlantic deterrent," but the prospective European partners (particularly Chancellor Adenauer) favored postponement of the multilateral force. While press commentators suspected that deferment of MLF meant "ultimate interment," Sec. Rusk discussed the plan in detail in a speech before the Virginia Bar Association. Journalists speculated that with a test-ban agreement being discussed with the Soviets, the U.S. would not push MLF in deference to Moscow's opposition to giving "the Germans a finger on the nuclear trigger."[32]

While there were doubts about "personal diplomacy," Pres. Kennedy's June trip to Europe, and the "tumultuous" welcome accorded him in Germany, swayed a sizable segment of opinion to strong approval. The President's "eloquent" statements, reiterating the theme of Atlantic interdependence and U.S. determination to defend freedom while working for a lessening of tensions, were gratifying to many commentators. Some, however, continued to criticize such "personal diplomacy."[33]

At this time a Roper proposition, that the UN alone cannot keep the peace, "so we must have strong ties with other countries in addition," was agreed to by as many as 74%. Also in public comment support for the basic concept and commitment embodied in the North Atlantic Treaty continued, in 1963, to be virtually unanimous. At the same time, some editors and Congressmen stressed the failure of our European allies to "do their share" in the mutual defense effort (and in foreign aid). Pres. de Gaulle's attitude toward NATO, and his antipathy to Anglo-Saxon defense ideas, were not appreciated by most American commentators; but some had long anticipated what the Saturday Evening Post called the "revolt of Europe" against "American hegemony." These thought it inevitable that, as Europe recovered its economic and political self-confidence, it would seek to adjust the disparity in influence between itself and the American "nuclear giant." The NATO agreement at Ottawa, to give Europe a greater sense of participation in Western nuclear defenses, was approved by American editors although they conceded that the "unnamed" allied nuclear force would do little to enlarge the Europeans' actual role in the defense of Europe.[34]

A Roper survey of opinion, taken after the President's European trip, found continuing majority approval of the alliance, with as many as 79% agreeing to the Roper proposition, "We are more certain to remain a strong and democratic country if we continue our alliances with other countries." Despite the contemporary disarray among the allies, or perhaps because of it, one-third (32%) said we "should form even closer ties with the countries of Western Europe," and another third (34%) favored "maintaining ties of about the same degree of closeness as now" (28% gave no opinion). Only 6% said we should "pull back from our ties as soon as possible."

Another round of MLF discussions with our European partners took place in the autumn, with some former skeptics believing MLF was "here to stay," despite the serious doubts about the feasibility of the plan on both military and political grounds. Press discussion was extensive; and Moscow's renewed criticism of MLF reinforced the objections of the critics, whereas Soviet hostility was good reason for some editors to endorse the project (e.g., Hearst papers). Time magazine called MLF a "thin disguise for continued U.S. nuclear monopoly of the West."[35]

Credibility and Popular Opinion

Questions about the credibility of the Administration were most insistent and persistent with reference to Cuba—in view of the necessary curbing of information during the crisis and Cuba's subsequent refusal to permit any on-site inspection. Some felt that reports of Administration "management" of the news during the crisis had clouded the Administration's credibility (e.g., Boston Herald, Chi. Tribune). In the months which followed there was some diminution in popular satisfaction with "the way the Kennedy Administration has been handling the Cuba situation in recent weeks": Feb., 56% satisfied, 28% dissatisfied; March, 52% to 33%; April, 49% to 29%. But few thought it would improve things if "the U.S. should send our armed forces into Cuba to help overthrow Castro." Only 20% agreed with that proposition (in Feb.).[36]

Reports of a "humiliating and costly defeat" for South Vietnamese forces and their U.S. advisors at Ap Bac prompted many to express their concern about the U.S. commitment there and their feeling that much information "was being kept from the American people" about the U.S. role there (e.g., Wash. Star). Some declared that, "unless we can bring about effective reforms in the present regime (in Saigon), it is useless to continue to throw away American lives on a losing cause" (Prov. Journal, Wall St. Journal). Others, however, felt that we must not be "driven ignominiously from Vietnam, where we have committed so much prestige, interest and treasure and are beginning tangibly to commit our blood" (Sulzberger in N.Y. Times).[37]

On the issue of a policy of "managed news," a Minnesota Poll indicated that Republicans were unhappy; but a majority of Minnesotans (56%) felt that the Kennedy Administration was doing a "good" or "excellent" job "when it comes to informing the American people about what the government is doing in foreign affairs." One third (34%) assessed the job as "just fair," but only 6% termed it "rather poor." But among the Minnesota Republicans sampled, a majority (59%) rated the Administration as either "just fair" or "rather poor" on informing the public. A Gallup Poll, published Feb. 6, reported that nationwide the Democrats now held "a substantial edge over the GOP" on the question, "Which political party do you think would be more likely to keep the U.S. out of war?" (32% Democratic; 23% Republican; 20% no difference; 25% no opinion). The Gallup release referred to the Democrats' gain in being regarded as "the party of peace" as "one of the important side-effects of the peaceful resolution of the Cuba crisis."[38]

In this year of the Freedom March on Washington, polls inquired about the differences in foreign policy attitudes of "whites" and "non-whites." Breakdowns of a dozen Gallup questions by these categories showed that both groups registered "satisfaction" over the handling of foreign affairs and of relations with Cuba; but there was greater satisfaction on the part of the "non-whites" (76%) than of the "whites" (63%) with "the way Pres. Kennedy was handling our foreign policy." On all the polling questions, the "non-whites" gave a larger proportion of "no opinion" answers, probably reflecting their smaller degree of familiarity with foreign policy questions. (At least 62% gave no opinion as to whether Britain or France or Germany could be counted as "dependable friends" of the U.S.) Also, the 1960 census reported that white Americans had 10.9 median years of schooling, whereas the non-whites had only 8.2 median years.[39]

In the case of policy toward Cuba, the colored respondents were also more approving (69% vs. 54% for the whites), and they were less approving of the idea of invading Cuba (15% vs. 21% for the whites). The most striking contrast in the views of the two racial groups was on an "expectation" question: "Looking ahead to 1970, which country do you think will be the greater threat to world peace—Russia or Communist China?"

	All Respondents	Whites	Non-whites
Russia	34%	33%	44%
Communist China	47	50	21
No opinion	19	17	35

It would be interesting to know whether the "non-conformist" sentiment of the "non-whites," that the Russians would present the greater threat, could be attributed to the lesser attention that these respondents presumably gave to current discussions of world affairs, or to a feeling that the non-white Chinese were less likely to threaten world peace—or to some other factor.[40]

The principle of foreign aid was favored in a Gallup Poll of Feb. 3 by nearly a 2-to-1 margin among those expressing an opinion; and that popular support was greater in 1963 than it had been in 1958. Leading newspapers also gave considerable support to the aid program, although some of these supporters referred to the program as "unpopular" with the American people. According to Gallup, the proportion saying that "in general, I am *for* foreign aid" rose from 51% in 1958 to 58% in 1963; and those saying they were "against foreign aid" declined from 33% to 30%. Regionally, support ranged from 60% in the East to 55% in the South; and there was majority support in all three major political groups: Democrats, 59%; Republicans, 54%; Independents, 61%. Dr. Gallup added that there was "criticism of certain aspects" of the aid program; and some commentators termed the Alliance for Progress a "failure" and also questioned the size of the aid appropriations.[41]

In April comment the goals of the Alliance continued to be endorsed by the majority of editors; and a number contended that the joint declaration by Pres. Kennedy and Central American presidents at San Jose in March advanced the implementation of these goals. Several "nationalist" sources, dubious about the Alliance's "socialist" and reform objectives, also expressed disappointment that the Presidents' meeting stressed economic rather than military measures against Castro.[42]

Test Ban Treaty

Developments during the first half of 1963 suggested that, after all, some improvements in U.S.-Soviet relations might follow the Cuban missile crisis. Publication in January of an exchange of letters between Pres. Kennedy and Chairman Khrushchev, disclosing Khrushchev's willingness to accept the principle of on-site inspection, aroused varying degrees of cautious optimism. A little later the Soviets expressed willingness to open negotiations on a direct communication link ("hot line") between Moscow and Washington. Editors welcomed this development which they felt could help to prevent an accidental war.[43]

At a press conference in May Pres. Kennedy referred to the so far unsuccessful efforts to reach an agreement banning nuclear tests, and said: "Perhaps the genie is out of the bottle." The New York Herald Tribune declared: "Someone will *have* to put the genie back into the bottle," for "if there is no agreement . . . the world must gird itself for another round of ever-expanding tests." Many agreed that the U.S. should take steps to maintain nuclear weapons superiority. On June 10 Pres. Kennedy gave his American University address, including his appeal for an easing of cold war tensions and specifically a proposal for a ban on nuclear testing. According to the Providence Journal, this was "an initiative for peace which it should be difficult for reasonable men in the Kremlin to ignore;" and many applauded the President's move. The skeptics, as usual, underscored their mistrust of the Soviets.[44]

Then came Chairman Khrushchev's East Berlin speech (July 2), in which he expressed agreement with an earlier Kennedy-Macmillan proposal banning tests in the atmosphere, under water, and in space, but permitting underground tests which produced no international fallout. While commentators continued to debate the wisdom of accepting such a limited test ban, Louis Harris published a poll showing little outright opposition to a test-ban agreement. Seven out of ten respondents were in favor, said Harris, but "the number who would support a test-ban settlement" were divided "between those who feel we should bend any and all efforts toward this end" (47%), and those who "insist that varying safeguards be strictly observed" (26%). Outright opposition came from 17% (10% "weren't sure").[45]

The rather sudden materialization of a limited test-ban treaty (signed at Moscow Aug. 2)—after years of routine "talks" about banning nuclear tests—came at a time when the Gallup Poll had reported that "Racial Strife Replaces Russia As Top Worry of American Public." Dr. Gallup noted that concern about "international problems (Cuba, Berlin, etc.)" had dropped from 65% to 35% in April.

The early 1960s had witnessed an increasing amount of public attention to domestic racial matters, despite the fact that the Cuban missile crisis was a major international event, and that Prof. Klingberg's hypothesized "period of extroversion" would be continuing until 1966 or 1967. Indeed, the Gallup Poll reported that "racial" questions were regarded as "most important," among those facing the country, in October 1963, July and October 1964, and April 1965. In some in-between months international problems resumed their customary primacy; and after April 1965 the Viet-Nam war and other international topics reigned supreme.[46]

After signing of the limited test-ban treaty the President asked the Senate to give unequivocal backing to this "first concrete result of 18 years of effort by the U.S. to impose limits on the nuclear arms race." Although many citizens had displayed sustained concern about "nuclear fallout," there had been relatively little discussion acquainting the whole public with the full consequences of a ban on nuclear tests. Some editors were worried about the military results of the treaty, or about making any agreement with the Soviets. But a majority of outstanding newspapers were prepared to accept whatever "risks" might be involved in treaty ratification, and a number hoped to conserve the momentum of this "first step." Several thought it a worthwhile objective simply to remove the threat of nuclear fallout.[47]

During a month of Senate hearings and debate on the treaty it was widely expected that it would receive eventual approval; but many were fearful lest the Senate adopt "reservations" or "understandings" which could vitiate the pact or materially reduce its significance. Editorial discussion of the suggestions made by Gen. Eisenhower and Sen. Goldwater showed deep basic approval of the treaty. Editors agreed with Eisenhower that it must be clear that the U.S. would be free to use nuclear weapons in case it was attacked; but most felt that the treaty was clear-cut on this point, or that any clarification should not require re-negotiation of the pact or its re-signature by the scores of nations which had already signed it. Goldwater's proposal to condition approval of the test-ban treaty upon Soviet withdrawal from Cuba was promptly rejected by editors and Senators of both parties.[48]

A number of editors did feel it was helpful for Pres. Kennedy to give the Senate explicit answers to questions about future U.S. testing and defense policies. Many leaders of organizations voiced approval of the treaty, including Protestant, Catholic, and Jewish leaders (who issued a statement through the American Association for the United Nations) and ad hoc groups of businessmen and of scientists. The American Legion, unlike the Veterans of Foreign Wars, passed a resolution of approval—although this resolution included opposition to any future disarmament treaty not containing ironclad safeguards against cheating.

Substantial majority approval of the treaty was shown by several public opinion polls (Gallup, Harris, Minnesota). On Sept. 16 the Harris Survey reported 81% in favor of ratification–a considerable increase from the 52% who had registered approval in July; only 8% were opposed, and 11% gave "qualified approval." The persistent opponents of the treaty stressed their distrust of the Soviet Union and of the Kennedy Administration's "appeasing" tendencies (e.g., Chi. Tribune, N.Y. News, San Diego Union). Khrushchev's proposal of a non-aggression treaty between the NATO and Warsaw Pact powers met with strong opposition which extended well beyond the hardened "anti-Communists." Some editors expressed willingness to consider the idea of a simple declaration of non-aggressive intent, reaffirming the principles of the UN Charter, provided this agreement included specific Soviet guarantees of West Berlin and the access routes (e.g., Kansas City Times, St. Louis Post-Dispatch).[49]

Senate ratification of the treaty by a large vote, 81 to 9 (on Sept. 24), was welcomed by a large majority of editors, many of whom regarded it as a sound "first step." There was no particular concentration on a "next step," but editors applauded Pres. Kennedy's address to the UNGA as a reasonable move toward peace, avowing an exploration of every possibility in the direction of reducing East-West conflict. The agreement in principle–by the U.S., British, and Soviet Foreign Ministers–to ban nuclear weapons in Outer Space was welcomed; but a number expressed agreement with the New York Herald Tribune that it was "at most an agreement not to do what nobody particularly wants to do."[50]

UN General Assembly

The General Assembly vote against the seating of Communist China (Oct. 21) drew a great deal of American editorial approval, as usual. Said the Philadelphia Inquirer: "To confer upon Peking Communists the trappings of respectability would be to encourage their atrocities against mankind." Still, a number shared the doubts of the Milwaukee Journal which said that "in time our policy on Communist China will have to be reassessed. . . . A fifth to a quarter of mankind can't be quarantined forever." The New York Times urged "two Chinas" in the UN as the "logical" and "inevitable" solution.[51]

The treatment accorded Amb. Adlai Stevenson at a Dallas observance of United Nations Day, where he was roughed up and spat upon by a group of anti-UN people, was a reminder to editors that such emotional opposition persisted. The event prompted a spate of indignant comment from all parts of the country and reaffirmations of support for the UN. One of the first acts of Pres. Johnson, after his accession to the presidency, was to journey to New York to address the UNGA "as a sign of the respect and regard in which the world organization is held by the U.S. and its new President" (N.Y. Post). A November Gallup Poll indicated that only 8 out of every 100 Americans favored U.S. withdrawal from the UN (compared to 5% in 1962). A Roper poll on attitudes toward international organization found that they were remarkably similar to those expressed in 1953 in response to the same questions, with a majority upholding our working through the United Nations, whereas only 11% gave top preference to world government, and 6% to a union of democratic governments. It is interesting to note that opposition to the proposals for greater federation was higher among the young (21 to 34 yrs.) and the college-educated. Among the young 47% rejected a combined NATO nation which would give "interchangeable rights of citizenship," and 55% of the college-educated did likewise.[52]

The American public gave sustained support to Pres. Kennedy's major foreign policy leads, with strong backing for his firm position on the Soviet challenge in the Cuban missile crisis, and also for his achievement of an agreement with the Soviets in the test ban treaty. Less discussion was devoted to the Administration's steps toward greater U.S. involvement in the Viet-Nam fighting, but these were upheld by most commenting editors and a majority of the general public. The Administration did not win Congressional approval for some of its desired changes in foreign aid, but the public continued to voice approval of the principle, including the Alliance for Progress. It also welcomed Congressional enactment of the Trade Expansion Act of 1962. In his inaugural address Pres. Kennedy gave as ample a pledge as any of his predecessors to maintain an active U.S. policy in behalf of freedom; and in the Cuban missile crisis he placed the U.S. in an activist role. Throughout his term popular support for an activist policy remained strong, with no backward step toward isolationism.

Reference Notes

1. AOR of Feb. 2, 1962.
2. Ibid.
3. AOR of Mar. 2, 1962.
4. AOR for Apr. 3 and May 2, 1962.
5. AOR for June 1 and July 3, 1962.
6. AOR of Aug. 3, 1962.
7. AOR of Sept. 6, 1962.
8. Ibid.
9. AOR of Feb. 2 and Mar. 2, 1962.
10. Hilsman, Roger, *To Move A Nation* (Garden City, 1967), pp. 256–262; AOR of May 2, 1962.

11. AOR of Feb. 2, 1962.
12. AOR of Mar. 2, 1962.
13. AOR for Mar. 2 and Apr. 3, 1962.
14. AOR of June 1, 1962.
15. AOR of July 3, 1962.
16. AOR of Aug. 3, 1962.
17. AOR for Feb. 2, Mar. 2, May 2 and July 3, 1962.
18. AOR of Sept. 6, 1962.
19. AOR of Oct. 2, 1962.
20. Ibid.
21. AOR of Nov. 2, 1962.
22. AOR of Dec. 3, 1962.
23. Ibid.
24. AOR for Nov. 2 and Dec. 3, 1962.
25. AOR of Dec. 3, 1962.
26. AOR of Jan. 2, 1963.
27. Ibid.
28. AOR for Feb. 1 and 8, 1963.
29. AOR of Feb. 8, 1963.
30. AOR of Mar. 14, 1963.
31. AOR for Mar. 29 and May 14, 1963.
32. AOR for June 28 and July 19, 1963.
33. AOR of July 1, 1963.
34. AOR of May 31, 1963.
35. AOR of Nov. 7, 1963.
36. AOR of June 27, 1963.
37. AOR of Feb. 1, 1963.
38. AOR of Feb. 8, 1963.
39. AOR of June 27, 1963.
40. Ibid.
41. AOR of Feb. 8, 1963.
42. AOR of Apr. 18, 1963.
43. AOR for Feb. 1 and Apr. 18, 1963.
44. AOR for May 15 and June 15, 1963.
45. AOR of July 15, 1963.
46. See Vol. III of *The Gallup Poll.*
47. Richard P. Stebbins, *U.S. in World Affairs, 1963* (New York, 1964), p. 26; AOR of Aug. 23, 1963.
48. AOR of Sept. 16, 1963.
49. Ibid.
50. AOR of Oct. 15, 1963.
51. AOR of Nov. 15, 1963.
52. AOR of Dec. 15, 1963.

XIV

LBJ "CONTINUES" (1963-1965)

Pres. Lyndon Johnson's emphasis upon continuity of policy, at home and abroad, was warmly welcomed in editorial comment. The President's address at the UN General Assembly (Dec. 17) was deeply appreciated in America; and the St. Louis Post-Dispatch said this "splendid address" must have sounded to the delegates "like a direct sequel" to Pres. Kennedy's American University speech in June. To the New York Herald Tribune, the President seemed to have "soberly and thoughtfully executed a public rededication of the U.S. to what its goals have been all along." The Milwaukee Journal observed that "the world saw and heard the continuity of our government." Through his "conciliatory tone," said the Scripps-Howard papers, Pres. Johnson "has established himself firmly in a position of leadership for world peace."[1]

The level of public concern about foreign affairs, it will be recalled, was lower than for several years; and observers speculated that 1964 would usher in a period of relative calm in East-West relations, with perhaps a substantial broadening of cooperation—particularly in the fields of cultural contacts and trade with the Communist bloc. Chances of major progress in disarmament were not regarded as bright; but at least the U.S. was advancing practical proposals for consideration at the Geneva disarmament conference. If the chances of a world conflagration were less, there was still concern that the U.S. remained engaged in a "hot" war in South Viet-Nam (see following chapter); and in de Gaulle's Europe NATO was seen as in a state of "disarray." In Latin America two crises flared up to plague the Johnson Administration: in Panama and the Dominican Republic.[2]

Panama

Rioting in Panama broke out on Jan. 9, 1964, endured for three days and a half, and resulted in over 20 deaths, including some American soldiers. The immediate issue was the right to fly the Panamanian flag over a high school in the Canal Zone; but it was generally recognized that the Panamanians felt that they were not being fairly treated by the U.S.—despite the fact that the terms of the 1903 treaty had been improved in 1936 and 1955. Virtually all commentators opposed Panama's call for termination of U.S. control of the Canal; but some felt that we should deal sympathetically with Panama's grievances.

Many observers wondered about a Communist role in the rioting in Panama; and Sen. Goldwater thought he saw "Cuba's hand in this mess." But Goldwater was among those suggesting that an increase in rental payments to Panama "might be a solution." A number of editors emphasized that "some revision of the 1903 Canal Zone treaty is inevitable" (e.g., Minneapolis Star, N.Y. Times, Wash. Post). Some suggested internationalizing the Canal, perhaps under the OAS or UN; others advocated joint U.S.-Panama control. But some newspapers denounced the idea of any treaty revision, the Chicago Tribune terming "unwise and unnecessary" the steps taken by Presidents Eisenhower and Kennedy to acknowledge some Panamanian "titular sovereignty" in the Canal Zone. There was also much speculation about constructing another canal, perhaps through Mexico or Nicaragua, perhaps a sea-level canal.[3]

As Panama continued to insist on a U.S. advance commitment to re-negotiate the basic treaty, attitudes ranged from agreement with Panama (The Nation) to Rep. Pepper's position backing his Miami American Legion Post's demand for Presidential rescission of the order permitting the two flags. The largest group of editors appeared to back the U.S. position of willingness to consider changes requested by Panama—but not under threat. These editors felt that some of Panama's complaints were reasonable (e.g., annual rental payments; some voice in Canal management; labor policy). Some newspapers called upon the U.S. to give a fuller explanation of the situation to the public (e.g., N.Y. Times, Charlotte Observer). Several others felt that past concessions by the U.S. had merely "fed Panamanian jingoism" (e.g., St. Louis Globe-Democrat). "Maybe we have been too friendly," said the Port Huron (Mich.) Times-Herald; "if the Marines are needed, send them." The general public appeared to be less ready for treaty changes than the editors. In a Gallup Poll (Feb. 12), 64% said they "had followed the discussion between the U.S. and Panama over the Canal Zone." A plurality (45% of the answering group—29% of the total sample) said that the U.S. should maintain a "firm" policy, make no concessions. The Minnesota Poll reported that 71% thought it was "fair" to Panama "for the U.S. to be able to rent and manage the Canal Zone for all time, as the treaty provides." A majority (52%) also approved the idea of building a "new, larger canal."[4]

Asia

France's recognition of Peking in early 1964 prompted many commentators to say this move would lead to the seating of Peking in the UN; a majority of those commenting disagreed with the idea that it was time to alter U.S. policy. A Gallup Poll (Feb. 14) reported that popular opinion had become more hostile to seating Peking than it had been in October 1961, opposition rising from 65% to 71%. There was even a plurality (44% to 42%) in favor of "not going along with a UN decision to seat Peking."[5]

In Saigon Pres. Diem had been assassinated in the same month as Pres. Kennedy. His successor, Gen. Minh, had received aid from the U.S.; but he was ousted in January by a coup establishing Gen. Khanh. American observers were disappointed that the "post-coup period" was going badly; they felt that the idea of Saigon negotiating a peace from its weakened position was "out of the question." And the U.S. had too much at stake, in men, material and prestige to countenance the idea of negotiating at that time. South Viet-Nam "must be held if the area is to remain free," said the Baltimore Sun, and "the American people may as well understand" now that its land "will not be secured quickly or cheaply."[6]

On the general handling of foreign affairs, the Gallup Poll reported (Feb. 23) majority approval of "the way Pres. Johnson is handling our foreign policy"–Democrats, 71%; Independents, 58%; and Republicans 47% vs. 20% disapproving. However, the New York Times found it "frightening" to observe "U.S. vulnerability to challenge from the weakest nations, like Cuba and Panama, and the danger of escalating from a local commitment to a nuclear war, as in Viet-Nam." Still, only a few commentators called for withdrawal from Indochina "before it is too late" (Sen. Morse, publisher John S. Knight). A much larger number agreed that we must "stand firm" on our commitment to assist South Viet-Nam, because the role of the U.S. as world leader of the cause of freedom was "squarely on the line" in the Mekong Delta. "The American people have the stamina to stay with the Viet-Nam war until the Vietnamese are able to handle their own problems," said the New York News and others.[7]

By the end of February 1964 unhappiness about the course of the fighting in Viet-Nam had increased. Some editors said the U.S. should exert a much greater effort in manpower and money, including South Vietnamese air strikes at the "privileged sanctuaries" in North Viet-Nam. Some others advocated a "political settlement" which might offer a "face-saving" way out of a "difficult" situation. A call for clarification of U.S. policy was raised by some after Sec. McNamara declared that our troops would leave at the end of 1965 regardless of how the war was going; and Pres. Johnson said: "We will not pull out because we are not willing to yield that part of the world to Communism."[8]

In May misgivings about the war increased with: 1, charges by American servicemen that Vietnamese officers lacked "the will to win;" 2, the tepid response of our SEATO allies to America's call for "more flags" in South Viet-Nam; and 3, the deterioration of the situation in Saigon. Still, there were few calls for "withdrawal" or a "negotiated settlement." Like it or not, most felt "we are in this too deep to allow a Communist takeover." There was also widespread belief that we must improve our military position before attempting a political solution. At this point, a Gallup Poll reported only 37% saying they had been "following developments in South Viet-Nam;" these "aware" people were fairly closely divided: 16% saying the U.S. was "doing as well as could be expected," and 17% saying "we are handling affairs badly." Many commentators were calling on the government to "give out more of the real facts" about the war. In a Gallup Poll on the "most important problems facing this country" (May 20), the "racial problem" and "international problems" each received 41% of the respondents' votes. The basic editorial support for U.S. aims in Indochina did not prevent a widespread feeling of frustration about the war, despite the special high-level conference in Honolulu on June 1. Some hoped that the UN decision to send an inspection team to the Cambodian-Vietnamese border would open the whole Southeast Asian conflict to UN "scrutiny" and involvement."[9]

Presidential Year

Developments in the Republican contest for the presidential nomination drew Amb. Henry Cabot Lodge back to the U.S.; and he was succeeded by Gen. Maxwell Taylor, whom the press acknowledged as having had intimate experience with Viet-Nam. As early as February, Pres. Johnson had felt impelled to strike out against the "alarmists" who criticized U.S. foreign policy "weakness" in Viet-Nam, Cuba, Panama, China, and elsewhere. Republican spokesmen were prominent among these critics, including Sen. Goldwater, Governors Rockefeller, Romney and Scranton, and former Vice President Nixon. Said Nixon: "It is difficult to name any place in the world where the U.S. is not being blackmailed, threatened, insulted, or kicked around by some pipsqueak dictator." Some writers countered that the Republicans "must also tell the voters how they would straighten out the mess" (John O'Brien in Phila. Inquirer, Chalmers Roberts in Wash. Post).[10]

The appointments of Gen. Taylor and U. Alexis Johnson to the top posts in the American Embassy at Saigon won bipartisan support; but some Senators saw these appointments as regrettably auguring "an expansion of the war" (e.g., Dirksen, Ellender). Although former Amb. Lodge did not see Viet-Nam as an appropriate issue for the Republican platform, Sen. Goldwater did; and he had the backing of Rockefeller, Scranton, and platform chairman Laird in attacking "indecision and vacillation" over Viet-Nam. A group of House Republicans led by Rep. Ford also challenged Lodge's position on

Viet-Nam; and they attacked Democratic performance during the Cuban missile crisis as the "most flagrant breach of the Monroe Doctrine in history." A second group of 45 Republican Representatives, which did not prefer Goldwater for the presidency, nevertheless echoed Goldwater's attack on "news management" to "conceal the facts (about Asia) from the American people." This "moderate" group also urged that the Republican platform reaffirm support for the UN, support mutual relaxation of trade barriers, and endorse disarmament proposals having "enforceable safeguards."[11]

The Republicans' nomination of Sen. Goldwater aroused deep editorial dismay in view of the Senator's "militancy" and "irresponsibility." Also distressed over the foreign policy planks of the platform, commentators felt that Goldwater's election "would edge this country away from its allies and toward a direct military confrontation with its enemies" (N.Y. Times). The failure of the "Goldwater" platform to reassert Presidential control over the Pentagon's use of nuclear weapons contributed to the decision of several Republican "moderates" to withhold support from Goldwater's candidacy (e.g., Sens. Javits and Keating, Rep. Lindsay). On the other hand, "nationalist" spokesmen applauded Goldwater's foreign policy stands as "charting a coherent course away from appeasement" (e.g., N.Y. Times, Chi. Tribune, Indianapolis Star). Some others disagreed with parts of Goldwater's foreign policy, but approved his "firmer line toward Communists" (e.g., Hearst papers, Wall St. Journal).[12]

Soon after the Republican Convention Pres. Johnson told Congress and the nation of attacks against U.S. vessels in the Gulf of Tonkin. Republicans and Democrats joined in giving overwhelming support to the Congressional resolution making clear that American opinion stood behind U.S. commitments in Southeast Asia, whatever the cost might be. On August 7 the resolution was adopted, authorizing the President to "repel any armed attack against the forces of the U.S. and to prevent further aggression," by a House vote of 416 to 0 and a Senate vote of 88 to 2. However, one school of thought stressed the need for restraint in responding to the Communist challenge, citing the possibility of involvement in a land war with Communist China (e.g., Walter Lippmann, St. Louis Post-Dispatch). Another group, including some Democrats, shared Goldwater's view that Pres. Johnson "had not gone far enough" in his moves against North Viet-Nam (e.g., Sen. Dodd, D-Conn.; N.Y. News).[13]

A "lull in the cold war" with the Soviet Union was marked by signature in Moscow of the treaty authorizing an exchange of consulates outside the capital cities. Goldwater denounced the consular convention as a "secret treaty" with "our enemies," but the pact was welcomed by the press as marking another "important step toward more normal relations" with the Soviet Union after the test-ban treaty (e.g., Kansas City Times, Phila. Inquirer, Wash. Post).[14] In his keynote speech at the Democratic Convention, Sen. Pastore attacked Goldwater for suggesting that authority to order an atomic attack might be shared by the President with a military commander. Pastore added that the key issue in the presidential campaign was "whose finger should be on the nuclear trigger." The majority of the press on this point sided with the Administration against Goldwater. When the Harris Survey inquired about which presidential nominee was the better man to "work for peace in the world," the vote favored Johnson 72% to 28%.[15]

The Johnson Administration's retaliatory action ("limited response") against North Viet-Nam's second attack on U.S. destroyers on the high seas in the Gulf of Tonkin received overwhelming support from the press, Congress, labor and veterans organizations; and the political differences of this presidential year were submerged. Virtually no one agreed with Sen. Morse's charge that the U.S. was as much to blame for the current crisis as Hanoi was; Sen. Aiken (R-Vt.) said: "We are supporting the President to a man, and those of us who felt it was unwise to expand the war hope we were wrong." A Harris Survey, taken after the air strike against the North Viet-Nam PT-boat bases, reported: "Fully 85% of the American people stand solidly behind Pres. Johnson's Viet-Nam action," and "only 3% opposed it on the ground that it would lead to atom war." Nevertheless, there were some Congressional and press misgivings about the growing U.S. involvement. Some Senators mentioned their fear that the Congressional Resolution would allow the President to decide "on his own" to send American troops to fight a land war in Asia; but they didn't vote against the Resolution (e.g., Sens. Morton, R-Ky., Fulbright, D-Ark.). The New York Times regretted that the Resolution failed to incorporate more of the temperate "no rashness, no wider war" language of the message from the President.[16]

Another "mysterious encounter" on Sept. 18 led Administration critics to suggest that the Administration "needs to do some more talking–especially about future policy in the Tonkin Gulf" (e.g., Chi. News, Los Angeles Times). Later some commentators held that a change in U.S. policy in Viet-Nam was urgently required in view of the fact that existing policy was "getting us nowhere." Still, editors seemed less positive than before about their prescriptions for future action: some favoring dispatch of additional U.S. forces, or strikes against supply routes and North Viet-Nam, while a few renewed their advocacy of negotiations for a "neutralized" South Viet-Nam. Yet almost all of those commenting voiced opposition to any U.S. withdrawal.[17]

As the campaign progressed, Republicans continued to stress the inadequacy of Administration policies not only on Viet-Nam, but also on Cuba and NATO. Democrats defended the Administration's decisions. When Khrushchev was succeeded by Brezhnev and Kosygin, when Labor defeated the Conservative government in Britain, and when China touched off its first nuclear explosion, Republicans again criticized the U.S. response in political campaign fashion. The Republicans also revived charges of Communists in the State Department, saying 150 employees had been cleared to "deal with secret matters without waiting for a full field investigation," and that Otto Otepka had been persecuted for daring "to tell the truth about lax security practices" in the State Department.[18]

The re-election of Pres. Johnson was seen by the press as a "victory for moderation" (Hearst newspapers) and a rejection of "the hipshot, the easy answer, the ultimatum" (Balt. Sun). It was also viewed as a vote for "continuity rather than radical change." According to Walter Lippmann, the result was to "beat and crush a rebellion against the established and accepted line of domestic and foreign policy." But ahead editors saw difficult problems, mentioning especially Viet-Nam and differences within the NATO alliance.[19]

The Gallup Poll now reported that about 7 out of every 10 Americans said they were following developments in South Viet-Nam; and among these one half said we were "handling affairs there badly." A plurality of Democrats said the U.S. was "doing as well as could be expected;" but the "doing badly" verdict was returned by 60% of Independents and 67% of Republicans. Dr. Gallup recommended an information program by the government "such as followed the Cuba missile buildup." Another Saigon governmental crisis in December prompted the Hearst papers to headline their editorial: "We've had it!" Citing Gen. Khanh's suggestion that "the Yankee pack up and go home," the editorial said: "That might not be a bad idea," adding that the U.S. could move to "friendly, stable Thailand." The Scripps-Howard papers expressed a similar feeling of exasperation; but there was no real reversal of editorial support for the U.S. government.[20]

NATO

The "disarray" of NATO in 1964 was felt by commentators to be symptomatic of two great changes that had taken place since NATO was born 15 years earlier: renewal of the political and economic strength of its European members; and relaxation of Soviet military pressure. It was also rather generally agreed that Pres. de Gaulle's policy of withdrawing French participation in the "integrated" military plan had created the greatest "cloud" over NATO's future. Some optimism about the Multilateral Force (MLF) was generated early in 1964 when five NATO nations decided to join the U.S. in an experimental operation of a U.S. destroyer (West Germany, Britain,

Italy, Greece, Turkey). A report by the Critical Issues Council of the Republican Citizens Committee, written by Gen. Norstad, advocated a "true share" for European members in the process by which nuclear decisions were reached in NATO; but candidate Goldwater called the "polyglot navy" a "sop, not a solution," of the NATO nuclear problem.[21]

After the election, Pres. de Gaulle's newly-vocal hostility to the MLF led to U.S. postponement of the program in the interest of avoiding a showdown. This met with editorial approval, since some felt that not only the fate of MLF was at stake, but the future of NATO, the EEC, and the Kennedy Round of trade negotiations. Sen. Keating (R-N.Y.) urged reconsideration of the whole MLF project, which he said "had grown almost surreptitiously, without full Congressional authorization, without open hearings, and without any clear national understanding of what is going on." A number concluded that Sec. Rusk had staked out a "wise position" for the U.S. by leaving it up to the British and European members to try to work out a compromise on some sort of joint force (e.g., N.Y. Herald Tribune, Scripps-Howard papers).[22]

Trade and Aid

Trade policy was important in 1964, with the first UNCTAD meeting (UN Conference on Trade and Development, March-April) and the opening of the Kennedy Round of GATT talks (May), both in Geneva. Commentators agreed that Under Secretary Ball, in presenting the U.S. position, had given good advice to the assembled developing nations, as he stressed their need to attract capital investment and to practice self-help. The New York News was happy to be able to applaud a State Department spokesman; and another journal said that "dissatisfaction with foreign aid at home" had forced Ball to set a "new tone, one of bluntness instead of generosity" (No. Virginia Sun). About half of those commenting wished that the U.S. had been more responsive to the needs of developing countries. "Should the West fail to listen," said the Kansas City Times, "the Communist nations will." Openly critical, the Washington Post felt that in failing to offer a more generous and positive view, "this country has lost the first round in what could become an ugly and fruitless struggle for the political allegiance of the 'have-not' nations" (similarly, C.S. Monitor.).[23]

French proposals were seen as more responsive; and it was feared the Soviets would make gains at the conference. The desire of poorer countries for commodity agreements setting a floor for prices of raw materials important to their livelihood was regarded as impractical by some editors who cited the coffee agreement (e.g., Phila. Bulletin,

Chi. Tribune). Some were disappointed that the conference adjourned without "concrete" economic results; but a number saw a gain in the resolution calling upon the UN to set up a permanent 55-member Trade and Development Board (e.g., Milwaukee Journal, Business Week). Some were gratified also by the apparent failure of the Soviet Union to emerge as the champion of the "poor" countries. Several agreed that if the "surprising" unity displayed by the poor countries persisted, "a new political force has entered the world . . . neither capitalist nor socialist" (John Allan May in C.S. Monitor; Commonweal, Time).[24]

In May the Kennedy Round of negotiations opened in Geneva, anticipated ever since enactment of the 1962 Trade Expansion Act. Hardly anyone appeared to feel that Kennedy Round success was certain, yet almost all felt that the effort was very much worth undertaking; and many anticipated a significant agreement. Appreciation was expressed for the U.S. team led by Amb. Herter; and Crosby Noyes said the U.S. had avoided the "greatest error of American postwar diplomacy: firm commitment of American prestige to goals which may be unobtainable" (in Wash. Star).[25]

East-West trade had become an important discussion topic in the autumn of 1963 when it became known that Canada was selling $500 million of wheat to the Soviet Union. Whereas a year earlier sentiment seemed strongly opposed to such trade, the Canadian sale stirred envy—or annoyance that the U.S. was being by-passed. In Congress, and in agricultural and business circles, there developed a demand for letting down the barriers to East-West trade. The prospect that the U.S. might work off its burdensome farm surpluses, while easing its balance-of-payments problems, was tempting to a number of "conservative" as well as "liberal" spokesmen; though a vocal minority remained opposed to any "trading with our enemies."[26]

By the end of 1963 Congress had passed an act permitting wheat sales on credit to the Soviet Union, although the House had twice passed the bill with restrictions on the extension of credit. Most commentators applauded the final version as supporting "the President's power to conduct foreign policy" as provided in the Constitution. While the Kansas City Times frankly preferred "cash on the barrel-head," Wm. R. Hearst, Jr. cited an Export-Import Bank official as saying that "the Red Bloc's payment record is 'impeccable'." But several "nationalist" spokesmen did regret "subsidizing these sales of foodstuff to Communists determined to enslave us all" (N.Y. News). No contemporary poll was taken on the extension of credit; but both Gallup and Harris reported a majority (57%, 54%) in favor of "selling wheat to the Russians."[27]

U.S. permission for grain trading with the Soviet Union prompted the opponents to redouble their demands for U.S. moves to prevent our allies from selling goods to Castro Cuba. But when the U.S. on Feb. 18 announced that it had terminated military aid to three countries trading with Cuba (Britain, France, Yugoslavia), the predominant editorial reaction was unfavorable. Critics contended that the punitive measures hurt the three countries "only in the most picayunish way, and Fidel Castro not at all" (Balt. Sun, Chi. News and Tribune). But this implementation of the Congressional ban on trading with Castro drew praise from some legislators and journals (e.g., Hearst and Scripps-Howard chains). Several business journals, however, warned against attempting to make reprisals against the trade of other countries for political reasons, pointing out that we were exporting far more to Britain and Western Europe than these countries sold here.[28]

On April 25 Pres. Johnson stated his willingness to consider proposals for expanded trade with Communist countries; this was welcomed by many (e.g., N.Y. Times, Cleve. Plain Dealer, New Republic). Business leaders spoke up for an easing of restrictions on non-strategic trade with Eastern Europe; but neither they nor most editors favored easing the trade embargo against Cuba and Communist China. (Exceptions were David Rockefeller and Cyrus Eaton.) "Very possibly," said the Kansas City Times, "we have moved into a stage of post-war history in which such trade would have the double purpose of strengthening the free world's economy and of weakening the Communist world's diplomacy." Yet a large part of the business community remained opposed to long-term credits to Communist countries, which would amount to our financing "some part of the Soviet economy's growth" (Los Angeles Times). Some others opposed all trade with Communist nations, agreeing with Sen. Lausche that trading with Red governments was tantamount to telling the world "we've gone to bed with the Communists."[29]

The Rumanian-American trade accord in June found a majority of editors supporting this "major step" toward Pres. Johnson's goal of "building bridges" to Eastern Europe. The editorials welcomed the expanded market for the U.S. and the potential political gain in reducing Rumania's dependence on Moscow (e.g., Wall St. Journal, Milwaukee Journal). But the minority remained vocal in its opposition; the New York News denounced the deal for letting Rumania get oil refineries, industrial plants, possibly a nuclear reactor—all on "easy credit." Some others cited Rumania's pledge to permit any nuclear reactor to be inspected by the International Atomic Energy Agency (Wash. Star, Newsweek). Before the end of the year business interest in expanded trade was shown by the visit to Moscow of 92 American executives, a resolution by the Foreign Trade Council, and a survey of exporters, bankers and economists by the Senate Foreign

Relations Committee. Much of the press was sympathetic; but traditional opponents of East-West trade stood their ground.[30]

In the summer of 1965 the Firestone Company abandoned its plan to build a synthetic rubber plant in Rumania after "anti-Communist pickets" at Firestone outlets in America urged the public to boycott all Firestone products. This decision prompted Sen. Fulbright to call upon the Executive Branch to display greater firmness in resisting "irresponsible pressures" from private groups and businesses upon U.S. foreign policy. The Boston Herald called it "shocking that the State Department should sit idly by" while an American industrial firm was smeared as "Red" for following a policy already enunciated by the President himself (also St. Louis Post-Dispatch). Several editors specifically supported East-West trade; but the activities of the right-wing demonstrators were upheld by the Chicago Tribune and Wm. F. Buckley, Jr.[31]

In 1964 Pres. Johnson enjoyed phenomenal success in securing from Congress legislation on his domestic goals, perhaps partly because of a feeling that Congress had let Pres. Kennedy down on his legislative program. Similarly, as Prof. Davids points out, Congress "approved a foreign aid bill that was remarkably close to the administration's request." Pres. Johnson had lowered the aid request to $3.4 billion, and even the usually successful efforts of Rep. Passman failed to reduce the eventual act to less than $3.3 billion for economic and military aid. The deep cuts of 1963 had been strongly criticized by a substantial majority of commenting newspapers (e.g., Boston Herald, Chi. News, Kansas City Times).[32]

A mail poll taken by a highly reputable market research organization (Feb. 1964) found that 93% of its respondents favored some sort of aid program—only 7% favored its elimination. An increase in amount was favored by 7%, 22% declared for the "same amount," and a majority (64%) wanted the amount reduced. Queried on various propositions, 73% agreed that the "aid program is morally right," 65% said "it has helped countries develop their own economies;" 50% agreed that "it has helped check Communism;" but a plurality disagreed that it had "increased respect for the U.S. among recipients" (46% to 42%), and as many as 62% agreed that "there has been corrupt use of aid funds."[33]

Editors approved when the House, reversing itself, appropriated funds for the International Development Association, as commentators emphasized that other countries would contribute $1.40 to the IDA for every dollar put up by the U.S. When the Foreign Affairs Committee approved the Administration's request without reduction, editors welcomed this noteworthy achievement (Wall St. Journal, Wash. Star); but some organizations continued to demand cuts (U.S.

Chamber of Commerce, Amn. Farm Bureau Fed.). The full amount was advocated by ex-Pres. Eisenhower, Gen. Clay, and the AFL-CIO.[34]

In 1965 Pres. Johnson sent Congress an aid proposal of $3.338 billion. Editors noted the comparative smallness of the request and tended to express their approval (e.g., N.Y. Times, Detroit Free Press); some thought it was too small (e.g., Wash. Post, Atlanta Constitution). However, a number were strongly convinced that aid to countries headed by such "anti-American" leaders as Nasser and Sukarno did not serve U.S. interests (e.g., Wash. Star, Columbus Dispatch). But the Christian Science Monitor felt that "in the long run we can be sure that humanitarian help to Egypt's poor will not be overlooked in Cairo." According to the Boston Herald, "Almost everybody is dissatisfied with one aspect or another of foreign aid as it is now administered, but almost everybody also agrees that some kind of foreign aid is both desirable and necessary." When the President signed the aid bill in October he noted that the small cut of 7%, compared with his original request, reflected the "unusual scrutiny given the measure by both the administration and Congress."[35]

China

On October 16, 1964 the People's Republic of China detonated an atomic device and called for a "global" summit conference to discuss the prohibition of nuclear weapons. A fortnight earlier Sec. Rusk had forecast the Chinese development, and thereby touched off a considerable discussion. Commentators expected a big jump in prestige for Communist China, with primarily Asiatic impact. Discussing implications for U.S. policy, editors took two chief lines: 1, urging a stronger effort for international control of nuclear weapons and for better relations with Communist China; and 2, an undertaking to provide protection for Asian countries.

A considerable shift in popular opinion had been disclosed by Gallup Polls over a 3-year period when they inquired whether Soviet Russia or Communist China was "the greater threat to world peace."

	China Greater Threat	Russia Greater Threat	No opinion
1961–March	32%	49%	19%
1963–March	47	34	19
1964–May	56	27	17
1964–Nov.	59	20	21

The change which followed the Chinese nuclear blast in October was very much less than that after the Cuban missile crisis of October

1962. In his interviews with newspaper editors and TV-radio executives, A. T. Steele also found that these key people, even more than the general public, overwhelmingly regarded China as the "greater long-range danger to the U.S."[36]

France's recognition of Peking earlier in the year prompted some journals to ask the U.S. to "begin a series of steps which would gradually lead to U.S. recognition" (e.g., N.Y. Times; Cleve. Plain Dealer, San Francisco Chronicle). Often the call was for "holding open the door to China just as we have to Russia" (Commonweal). Editorial opinion had long favored the exchange of newsmen with Communist China; and a 1964 poll by the Survey Research Center (Univ. of Michigan–taken for the Council on Foreign Relations) found a majority of the public taking the same stand. The SRC poll asked for opinions on five possible presidential initiatives in our relations with China, with results as indicated in the following table (the five questions were not asked of the 28% who had indicated they were not aware that "most of China" was under "communist government").[37]

Attitudes Toward Certain Presidential Initiatives re PRC

Suppose President Suggested:	Favor Idea	Oppose Idea	Neither	Unaware most of China is Red	Total
A. Visits (e.g., Newsmen)	53%	11%	8%	28%	100%
B. Exchange ambassadors	37	24	11	28	100
C. Talk over, try to agree	51	14	7	28	100
D. Selling things like wheat	31	34	7	28	100
E. Let Red China sit in UN	22	38	12	28	100

In addition to exchanging newsmen, a majority favored "talking over problems of Asia with Communist China and trying to come to some agreements with them." At this time Amb. Alexis Johnson was holding talks in Warsaw from time to time with China's Amb. Wang in an effort to settle some bilateral problems (such as Americans held in Chinese prisons).[38]

But this poll showed only 22% in favor of seating Peking in the United Nations. Similarly, Gallup Polls showed only a minority in favor, although opposition had diminished appreciably in the 14 years since the Korean War broke out. But the SRC poll, like others,

	Should seat Peking in UN	Should Not do so	No Opinion
1950 (before Korean War)	11%	58%	31%
1954	8	79	13
1955	10	67	23
1961 (March)	20	64	16
1964 (Feb.)	15	71	14
1964 (Nov.)	20	57	23

showed clear support (54% of total sample) for America's staying in the UN in case Peking were seated.

Latin America; Dominican Crisis (1965)

The "anniversary riots" in Panama on Jan. 9, 1965 sparked little additional comment on the major policy issues involved there. Editors continued to support the U.S. policy of renegotiating the treaty with Panama. In a representative comment the San Diego Union declared: "The immediate and vital question is what kind of a new treaty the U.S. can negotiate with Panama without endangering its own security." A few added that the old canal treaty "must in simple justice be rewritten to meet many of Panama's demands."[39]

When the U.S. Marines landed in the Dominican Republic at the end of April 1965, the initial editorial comment was predominantly favorable. The majority view, expressed by the Scripps-Howard papers, was the hope that the presence of U.S. troops would "exert a stabilizing influence . . . among our friends in the Caribbean," as well as protect U.S. citizens and other foreign nationals. Several agreed with the Chicago Tribune in regarding "the loud howls from Havana about the intervention" as an indication that the rebellion in the Dominican Republic was "probably a mask for an attempted take-over by Castro's agents." The Washington Star said the U.S. "has an obligation to see to it that Trujillo, the dictator, is not replaced by another Castro-style dictator." Statements by Congressmen were similar.[40]

But the New York Times was critical of a political mission for the Marines. The Times said it was valid for the Marines to land and protect Americans and evacuate those desiring to leave–but not to extend their stay. The Washington Post, recalling Pres. Wilson's use of Marines in the Dominican Republic and the dictatorship of Trujillo that followed, said: "Certainly either the OAS itself or the UN would appear preferable to the U.S. Marine diplomacy of 1916." According to Joseph Kraft, the "chief danger" was not a "Communist or Castroite take-over," but that the U.S. would "emerge from the crisis, to its disadvantage all around the world, as the sponsor or seeming sponsor of yet another corrupt, repressive, militaristic government." Kraft suggested that the U.S. associate itself as much as possible with the OAS. Several others said OAS action was desirable. The New York Herald Tribune felt it would be preferable if the U.S. "did not have to intervene unilaterally," but the OAS was "not yet capable of acting swiftly to deal with a situation of this kind."[41]

As the intervention continued, editorial approval of the role of the Marines in protecting the lives and property of U.S. citizens continued to receive the approval of the overwhelming majority of American newspapers—the New York Times and the Chicago Sun-Times no less than the New York News and the Los Angeles Times. Endorsement of the use of U.S. armed forces to prevent a Communist take-over was not unanimous, but it was widespread (e.g., Chi. News, Wall St. Journal, Walter Lippmann). Most editors advocated OAS action also; and some thought it urgent "to transfer to the OAS full responsibility for obtaining a cease-fire and establishing a government of reconciliation" (N.Y. Post, Milwaukee Journal, Denver Post). Perhaps most critical was the New York Times, when it said that the U.S. "gives the appearance of heading toward the unenviable, self-righteous and self-defeating position of world policeman." As the unfavorable foreign reaction to the U.S. move became known, some American editors expressed concern. "If the net effect of the President's action is to leave anti-democratic forces in power," said the St. Louis Post-Dispatch, Latin Americans will be convinced that we are engaged in "the gunboat diplomacy which was supposed to be a relic of the past." The Los Angeles Times said that Pres. Johnson must now "move with equal vigor to alleviate the grave damage to our relations with other nations." According to the Louisville Courier-Journal, "the new Johnson policy seems to line us up against all changes in Latin America, the moment the cry of Communism is raised."[42]

Discussion of the Dominican crisis continued as the fighting continued; and among the strong supporters of U.S. policy were Bishop Reuben Miller (pres., Natl. Ccl. of Churches) and George Meany (AFL-CIO). "This sort of gunboat diplomacy" was praised by Sen. Goldwater. Drew Pearson reported that "a private Oliver Quayle survey shows that 69 percent of Americans approve" the dispatch of the U.S. Marines to the Dominican Republic, with 16% disapproving (15% no opinion). Although the OAS adopted a resolution providing for an Inter-American Peace Force, and Gen. Panasco Alrim of Brazil arrived with 1250 men to join smaller groups from a few other countries, American discussion of Dominican affairs in May became predominantly critical. The press charged that U.S. policy was confused and hampered by diplomatic blunders; and official claims of a policy of strict neutrality toward the embattled Dominican factions were contradicted by news reports in leading journals which charged that the U.S. was tied to the junta.[43]

Pres. Johnson, in his June 1 press conference statements, made a good case for his Dominican policy, editors said. A Hearst editorial said the President "persuasively rebutted those who have been calling the action in Vietnam and the Dominican Republic menacing manifestations of imperialism." The New York Times, however, still found the contradictions between statements and facts "bewildering." In the upshot, several commentators suggested that the key test of U.S. policy would be whether or not the Dominicans emerged with a popular government. Sec. Rusk was seen as "eager to see constitutional government restored" (Wash. Post). A U.S. policy shift, from backing of the junta to establishing a more popular government, was reported by some (e.g., Savile Davis in C.S. Monitor). On June 2 the Gallup Poll reported that when the "nearly 80%" of the public who were aware of the Dominican crisis were asked about the sending of troops, 76% gave favorable replies, and only 17% "unfavorable." By mid-June it was felt that the Dominican crisis had eased; there was hope that the 3-man OAS committee could bring peace by establishing an acceptable government committed to democratic elections. The U.S. Marines were withdrawn, although U.S. army troops remained as a large part of the International Peace Force. The role of the OAS in the crisis received general approval. The Los Angeles Times felt that much of the "criticism and confusion have grown from the administration's own tendencies toward excessive secrecy and occasional lack of candor; this nation's actions in Vietnam and the Dominican Republic have been honorable and defensible" (similarly, Time magazine).[44]

As the Dominican debate simmered down in the autumn, Sen. Fulbright won attention by raising again the question of long-range U.S. policy in Latin American relations. Commonweal summarized the unanswered question in this fashion: "If we so over-react to the presence of those Communists who will inevitably accompany almost every Latin American revolution, can the U.S. ever hope to do anything but support oligarchies and military dictatorships?" The strong supporters of the prompt U.S. intervention maintained their original opinions. Some of the former critics of U.S. policy, however, tended to view U.S. Dominican policy more favorably. The Washington Post, for example, said: "It probably has done no harm, and perhaps has done some good, to demonstrate that the U.S. will not tolerate the imposition of another Castro regime." The Des Moines Register said there may have been mistakes in the beginning, but later U.S. policy was successful, "nearly non-violent," and the "American force was quickly absorbed" in an OAS force. The ultimate action of the U.S., said the St. Louis Post-Dispatch, "deserves great respect," it "finally used its influence in a way which Sen. Fulbright suggested, to establish a provisional government looking toward free elections."[45]

Immigration and Travel

Basic changes in our immigration legislation were proposed by the Johnson administration in early 1965 and they received prompt approval from the great majority of commenting newspapers. A few editors were uncertain about the wisdom of increasing the annual total of immigrants; but virtually all supported repeal of the "national origins" provisions. The existing "discrimination" in favor of Northern Europe, and against such countries as Greece and Italy was frequently set forth and condemned. Adoption of the new admissions criteria, stressing personal skills and family relationships, was regarded as an important step forward. These editorial attitudes represented considerable change in sentiment since 1953 when the idea of scrapping the "national origins" provisions failed to win much support. Richard Stebbins remarked that the new law, which had been "recommended by four successive postwar Presidents, could be regarded as a counterpart to the progressive elimination of legalized race discrimination within the U.S."[46]

Later in the year Fidel Castro made an offer to allow some Cubans to emigrate to the U.S. if they wished to. There was considerable discussion as to why the offer was made, whether Castro was seeking to dump his aged and sick on the U.S., or what; but opposition to the U.S. policy of welcoming refugees was expressed by very few of the many who commented. A Hearst editorial said: "No finer, or more timely, verification could have been had of the liberal intent of the new immigration law, signed under the Statue of Liberty, than the President's avowal that our gates are open to Cubans who desire to flee to freedom." The ultimate arrangement (Nov. 6) for the airlift of Cuban emigrants, with priority given to those having close relatives in the U.S., and the exclusion of men of military age, was considered an imperfect agreement. But the New York Times said that this "accord on refugees, limited as it is," would be beneficial if it became the "precursor of other moves to ease tensions between Havana and Washington."[47]

The Supreme Court's decision (6 to 3) upholding the powers of the Secretary of State (in *Zemel v. Rusk*) to refuse to validate passports for particular areas—in this case Cuba—met with the approval of a majority of commenting editors. They agreed that restriction of travel is a power necessary to the proper conduct of foreign relations and the protection of citizens. Some urged that the Department exercise this power with care; and felt that this had been done with reference to Cuban travel. A few agreed with the dissenting justices and urged greater freedom of travel, including an easing of the ban on travel to Cuba (e.g., Prov. Journal, The Reporter). The Des Moines Register said it "thoroughly agreed" with Mr. Justice Douglas who "thought that Americans should be allowed to visit Communist countries in order to understand them."[48]

Arms; UN

Although public discussion of arms control had subsided, the Harris Survey in the spring of 1965 reported that a majority of Americans (60%) continued to favor a "new agreement with the Russians for control of underground atomic testing;" 27% were opposed and 13% "not sure." Communist China's explosion of a second nuclear device aroused considerable concern; editors resumed their advocacy of controls to prevent the proliferation of nuclear weapons. Sen. Robert Kennedy was applauded for his rebuke to the Administration for not going faster in its efforts to control the spread of such weapons.[49]

NATO's nuclear problem, it was hoped, was alleviated by Sec. McNamara's proposal to the NATO defense ministers of a special committee to study the extension of allied participation in planning the use of nuclear forces (e.g., Boston Herald, Scripps-Howard papers). Some were favorable to the idea of an Atlantic Nuclear Force (e.g., N.Y. Times). The Milwaukee Journal conceded that the experiment with the U.S.S. Ricketts demonstrated that mixed manning "does work;" but the Journal favored dropping the nuclear fleet concept, holding that a "supplementary nuclear force is no longer needed because of the growth of our own nuclear missile power." Some others likewise counseled NATO to give up the MLF and move on to "a more practical and beneficial method of joint planning and control."[50]

During 1965 American opinion of France had worsened, as de Gaulle's opposition to U.S. policies grew, respecting Viet-Nam as well as European topics. A Gallup Poll found 43% with "unfavorable" opinions of Pres. de Gaulle vs. 32% expressing "favorable" opinions. In the following year, the Gallup Poll (July 8, 1966) reported a clear majority (56%) regarding France as "not a dependable ally;" among the college-educated 66% took that stand. Even in early 1968, when the Gallup Poll asked respondents to rate a score of countries, France was rated "favorably" by only 49%, as contrasted with 75% for West Germany, 85% for Great Britain, and 94% for Canada.

As for U.S. clashes with the Soviet Union, Richard Stebbins remarked that in 1965, "for the first time since World War II, the

Soviet Union appeared to have lost the initiative on the international scene."[51]

For many months American editors had backed the U.S. effort in the United Nations to enforce Article 19 of the UN Charter, which provides that member countries which are two years in arrears on their UN payments shall lose their votes in the General Assembly. This financial issue was complicated by the conflict among members over paying peace-keeping assessments. Referring to the Soviet Union's obstinacy on this matter, the New York Times said that the preceding year at the UN had demonstrated that the organization "cannot be strengthened by the effort to force a major power to pay for peace-keeping activities of which it has disapproved." After the U.S. dropped its fight for the application of Article 19, a number of editors saw a weakening of the UN as a result (e.g., Chi. News, Los Angeles Times, Scripps-Howard). The New York Herald Tribune saw "the collapse of collective financial responsibility at the UN;" and the Baltimore Sun asserted that the Soviet Union had "succeeded in crippling the UN peacekeeping authority." But another school of editorial thought saw the U.S. acting wisely in a "long over-due acceptance of reality and recognition of our own self-interest" (Prov. Journal, C.S. Monitor, Hearst papers). The Cincinnati Enquirer said the U.S. decision "eliminates the threat that America might some day find herself obliged to finance moves contrary to her vital interest."[52]

Summary

In 1963-64 Americans supported Pres. Johnson in his aim to continue the policies of Pres. Kennedy. The public upheld the President's successful appeals to Congress for the Gulf of Tonkin resolution, implementation of the Trade Expansion Act, and foreign aid appropriations; and it rebuffed Sen. Goldwater's plan to step up the Viet-Nam war. But it maintained its hostility toward Communist China. Pres. Johnson, confronted with fresh crises in Panama and the Dominican Republic, took actions which restored order and won majority approval from the American public—including his use of the Marines in the Dominican Republic.

Reference Notes

1. AOR of Jan. 14, 1964.
2. AOR of Jan. 10 and Feb. 14, 1964.
3. AOR for Jan. 13 and 24, 1964.
4. AOR of Mar. 10, 1964.
5. AOR of Feb. 14, 1964.
6. AOR of Jan. 10, 1964.

7. AOR for Feb. 1964.
8. AOR of Feb. 27, 1964.
9. AOR for May 21 and 27, June 9 and 16, 1964.
10. AOR of Feb. 19, 1964.
11. AOR for June 26 and July 2, 1964.
12. AOR of Aug. 14, 1964.
13. Ibid.
14. AOR of June 3, 1964.
15. AOR for Aug. 28 and Sept. 16, 1964.
16. AOR for Aug. 6 and 12, 1964.
17. AOR for Sept. 30 and Nov. 10, 1964.
18. AOR for Oct. 26 and 30, 1964.
19. AOR of Nov. 6, 1964.
20. AOR for Dec. 3 and 30, 1964.
21. AOR for May 27 and Aug. 5, 1964.
22. AOR for Nov. 19, 1964 and Jan. 13, 1965.
23. AOR of Apr. 3, 1964.
24. AOR of June 30, 1964.
25. AOR of May 26, 1964.
26. AOR of Sept. 27, 1963.
27. AOR of Jan. 2, 1964.
28. AOR of Feb. 28, 1964.
29. AOR of May 1, 1964.
30. AOR for June 12 and Dec. 23, 1964.
31. AOR of Aug. 6, 1965.
32. Davids, Jules, *U.S. in World Affairs, 1964* (New York, 1965), p. 8; AOR of Feb. 3, 1964.
33. AOR of Apr. 21, 1964.
34. AOR for June 3 and July 1, 1964.
35. AOR for Jan. 6, Feb. 2, Mar. 18, Sept. 1, 1965; Stebbins, Richard, *U.S. in World Affairs, 1965* (New York, 1966), p. 309.
36. Steele, A. T., *The American People and China* (New York, 1966), p. 61.
37. AOR of Dec. 14, 1964.
38. Steele, op. cit., p. 275.
39. AOR of Jan. 22, 1965.
40. AOR of Apr. 30, 1965.
41. Ibid.
42. AOR of May 6, 1965.
43. AOR for May 19 and 27, 1965.
44. AOR for June 4 and 17, 1965.
45. AOR for Oct. 1 and Nov. 15, 1965.
46. AOR of Feb. 8, 1965; Stebbins, op. cit., p. 298.
47. AOR of Nov. 10, 1965.
48. AOR of Aug. 24, 1965.
49. AOR for Apr. 15, May 17, July 9, Aug. 12, 1965.
50. AOR for June 11 and Dec. 7, 1965.
51. Stebbins, op. cit., p. 143.
52. AOR of Sept. 13, 1965.

Part Three

MODIFYING FOREIGN POLICIES (1968–1975)

XV

VIET-NAM WAR: OTHER TOPICS (1965–1968)

1965 marked a significant change in America's role in Viet-Nam. Viet Cong attacks on Feb. 7 on the American installations at Pleiku moved the U.S. Administration promptly, and for the first time, to unleash U.S. air strikes against North Viet-Nam. American opinion rallied strongly to the Government's decision to respond to the Communist "test of U.S. political will and purpose" in South Viet-Nam.

Throughout Pres. Johnson's elected term of office Viet-Nam remained the central focus of U.S. foreign policy. In addition to the Dominican crisis in 1965 (see preceding chapter), the Indochina war was complicated by the conflict in Asia among Pakistan, India, and the People's Republic of China. The warfare against North Viet-Nam was escalated in 1967. The Arab-Israeli war of that year complicated U.S. relations with the Soviet Union and led to Pres. Johnson's Glassboro meetings with Premier Kosygin. The Tet offensive in 1968 precipitated fateful decisions about the war and Pres. Johnson's future.

In 1965 support for the U.S. retaliation against Viet Cong areas in North Viet-Nam came from leaders of both parties and from editors, some of whom had various reservations about the U.S. commitment in Viet-Nam. Some supported the action in hopes that it would bring the Communists to the negotiating table; others hoped that additional U.S. military measures would promptly follow. "U.S. air and sea power should be used to stop further movements of men and supplies to the Viet Cong," Richard Nixon declared. Only a few said the President had made a "grievous mistake" (Sen. Gruening, D-Alaska; Comm. for a Sane Nuclear Policy). The Wall St. Journal warned that the "American people should not be led, reprisal by reprisal, into an expanded war without a clearer idea of the ultimate purpose and the chance of winning."[1]

As second thoughts were registered, both "hawks" and "doves" complained that "retaliation by itself is no policy." David Lawrence doubted that "limited U.S. air strikes on North Viet-Nam will persuade the Communists that we mean business, and intend to defend South Viet-Nam successfully." According to the St. Louis Post-Dispatch, "the new exchange of strikes simply emphasizes the bankruptcy of American policy; our basic purpose ought to be to disengage from a fruitless conflict by seeking a political settlement." The Gallup Poll reported that 91% of the public had heard or read about the developments in Viet-Nam, and 67% of these expressed approvai of the U.S. actions; 64% said we should "continue present efforts" in Viet-Nam (even at the "risk of nuclear war," according to 31% of the total).[2]

Issuance of a U.S. White Paper on Viet-Nam in March 1965 elicited the editorial support of a clear majority; but advocates of "negotiations" said the document did not "stand up" against critical examination. Some still called for a statement by the President; but Walter Lippmann and others supported the "wisdom of Presidential silence." In reply to the minority demand for "negotiations," Congressmen replied that "there is no evidence of intent on the part of our adversaries thus far to arrive at any kind of honorable solution" (Sens. Cannon, D-Nev., Harris, D-Okla.). Deployment of U.S. Marines in Viet-Nam, regarded as an "escalation" of the war, was welcomed by the majority, but viewed with some apprehension by the minority seeking a political settlement "before it is too late." Suporters of U.S. policy expressed dissatisfaction with the reluctance of free world nations to participate in this "very important confrontation," and their continuing trade with Hanoi—especially France.[3]

Johns Hopkins Address

Pres. Johnson's April 17 address at Johns Hopkins University was welcomed as both "an overture to the North Vietnamese," in its offer of unconditional discussions, and a "cram course" on the realities for the American people. Sen. Mansfield said: "The door is open to a bonafide settlement which will permit the people of Viet-Nam to live in peace and freedom;" but some Republicans were concerned lest the overtures to North Viet-Nam be construed as signs of lessening American determination to bring the struggle to a successful end (e.g., Sens. Dirksen and Hickenlooper). Pres. Johnson's offer of $1 billion in U.S. aid to regional development in Southeast Asia was deemed very large but acceptable. "That's a lot of money," said the Scripps-Howard editorial, "but it's cheap compared to the price of war, in lives lost on both sides as well as dollars spent for bombs and guns and rockets" (also Phila. Inquirer, others). Among the doubters, Sen. Carlson (R-Kan.) said: "My hope is that we can reduce foreign aid expenditures, rather than expand them." There was general agreement that it was now up to Hanoi whether there would be an era of peaceful development or a period of tragic devastation.[4]

While the majority continued to feel that the Administration's position on Viet-Nam was just, Sen. Fulbright suggested a temporary cessation in the bombing of North Viet-Nam to enhance the chances for peace talks. Considerable press and TV attention was also given to "peace marchers" and student demonstrators in Washington and elsewhere who were calling for an end to the fighting. Some supported the Fulbright suggestion (e.g., N.Y. Post, Milwaukee Journal);

but a number of others agreed with Secretaries Rusk and McNamara that this was "not the time to let up pressures" (Boston Herald, Hearst papers). The demonstrators were deplored in most press comment, as simply counseling that the U.S. "turn tail and run;" but James Reston maintained that it would be irresponsible for U.S. officials not to take seriously the current campus "revolt" and take steps to counter it.[5]

Despite urgent attention to the Dominican crisis, Congress gave a swift and overwhelming response to Pres. Johnson's appeal for $700,000,000 in extra funds–mostly for Viet-Nam. The Harris Survey in four 1965 polls found an American plurality favoring the "middle course" of "holding the line" in Viet-Nam over the two proffered alternatives of "carrying the war into North Viet-Nam," and "negotiating a settlement with the Communists and getting out now." Here are the four polling results:

	Feb.	**March**	**Early April**	**Late April**
Hold the line	40%	46%	48%	43%
Negotiate; get out	23	35	31	28
Carry war to North	13	12	17	20
Not sure	24	7	4	9
	100%	100%	100%	100%

As the no-opinion group diminished, each of the more extreme alternatives gained some support, so that the hold-the-line group in the middle was flanked by two sizable and contradictory minorities. Harris also inquired into attitudes toward the "present government running South-Vietnam," finding that 49% expressed "no confidence" in it, or only a "little," while 18% voiced "some" or "a lot" of confidence in it (33% gave no opinion).[6]

During May those advocating and demonstrating for "negotiations now" continued to be very active, promoting a nationwide discussion of U.S. policy on Viet-Nam. Editorial supporters of U.S. policy approved the bombing of North Viet-Nam, the policy of barring conference representatives for the Viet Cong, and also the Government's policy of sending briefing teams to college campuses to present the Government's case at teach-ins. On the other hand, the New York Times said "it would not be necessary to commandeer TV circuits and to send numerous officials on speaking tours" if the Government would permit "free access to officials" and enable "a free press on its own to inform the nation" (similarly, Chi. News, Des Moines Register). A Gallup Poll (May 16) reported that a majority (59%) said that "we should continue to bomb North Viet-Nam," and only 21% said that "we should stop" (20% gave no opinion).[7]

Pres. Johnson's TV address of May 13 was almost universally praised, some editors stressing renewal of the offer of unconditional discussions, or the temporary cessation (May 13–17) of the bombing of the North, or the proposal for regional economic development (including the Asian Development Bank). The bombing suspension was welcomed by several editors and opposed by none. The national teach-in held in Washington on May 15, and relayed to many college campuses by radio, elicited voluminous editorial comment, most of which was favorable to the idea of responsible debate between academic and Government spokesmen. The preponderant view was that events showed it wasn't true that "the Communists would like to end the terrorism and killing, if only we gave them a decent chance."[8]

As editors declared there was "no alternative," the U.S. steadily built up its military forces in Viet-Nam during the summer. A Gallup Poll (released June 9) showed that the minority favoring termination of U.S. military action continued to number about a quarter (26%) of the general public, whereas a larger total would either "continue the present policy" (20%) or "increase our military action" (21%). "Looking ahead five years," only 13% expected Viet-Nam to have a "Communist government," 32% foresaw a "neutralist government," and 22% a "pro-U.S. government" (33% didn't guess). At a Madison Square Garden rally June 8, sponsored by SANE and groups of students, clergymen, and labor spokesmen, some 18,000 persons participated as opponents of U.S. policy, although not united on what policy should follow. Another Gallup Poll, on the "most important problem facing this country today," reported Viet-Nam tied for first place with civil rights—23% each.[9]

In late June 1965 a Harris Survey reported 62% registering over-all approval of Pres. Johnson's "handling of Viet-Nam," with larger majorities feeling that "Asia will go Communist if we don't stand firm in Viet-Nam" (79%) and supporting "unconditional negotiations" (73%). Harris found 59% backing the retaliatory bombings of the North, and a plurality (47%) in favor of sending more troops (Republicans 48%; Democrats 47%; Independents 48%). The Johnson billion-dollar regional aid program was favored 42% vs. 35%. A Minnesota Poll (July 4) reported about the same attitudes as in March 1964 and April 1965, when respondents were asked to decide between "sending more aid" to Viet-Nam (71%), and "pulling out" (16%). Some organization stands of this period are of interest. The United Church of Christ adopted a resolution commending Pres. Johnson's willingness to discuss peace; the Southern Christian Leadership Conference called for U.S. troop withdrawal from Viet-Nam and the Dominican Republic. But at an NAACP meeting Roy Wilkins counseled against mixing civil rights and peace.[10]

When it was claimed that the U.S. "can't win," the Philadelphia

Bulletin retorted that there was no proof "that the most powerful nation in the world must play for a tie in Southeast Asia." Reappointment of Henry Cabot Lodge as ambassador in Saigon was approved in most comment; and editors voiced strong support of Pres. Johnson's position on Viet-Nam. When Rep. Gerald Ford proposed the prompt bombing of missile sites, if placed around Hanoi by the Soviet Union, there was less press approval than disapproval, the editors supporting the President's effort to "hold down the pace of escalation" (N.Y. Times). Instead, several spokesmen advocated establishing a series of "unconquerable U.S. beachheads" in South Viet-Nam, to which our troops could pull back, providing a "basis of influence while a new order of things in Asia is being negotiated" (e.g., Walter Lippmann, N.Y. Times).[11]

Of the 50 State Governors, 48 were reported as backing Pres. Johnson's plans for defending South Viet-Nam and for attaining a peaceful settlement. In August former Pres. Eisenhower stated that his commitment to Viet-Nam as President had been economic rather than military, and added that he supported Pres. Johnson's current policy. Most of those commenting tended to minimize "what happened twelve years ago," but considered it important that Eisenhower "put himself unequivocally on record as backing the Johnson policies in Viet-Nam" (e.g., Wash. Star, Milwaukee Journal). A Gallup release (Aug. 27) reported that opposition to Viet-Nam policy was "not concentrated in any single population group," such as the "intellectuals of the country." Republicans expressed approval by a margin of 46% to 35%. These polling results were of particular interest because the publicity accorded the critics, through teach-ins and paid advertisements, had been so considerable as to cause doubts about the public support for the President. The dissent was real enough, but it tended to obscure the fact that the bulk of the public was giving quiet support to the nation's policy. In September the Harris Survey also reported approval of the President's handling of Viet-Nam (66% to 34% among those expressing their opinions).[12]

Asian Impacts

Other Asian events had some impact on attitudes toward Viet-Nam at this time. In September 1965 the possibility of conflict between India and Pakistan over Kashmir loomed on the international horizon, and American editors were gravely concerned. Some saw a threat of world war. Many called for action by the UN Security Council to damp down the conflict; a number also asserted that American and Soviet interests were similar in this case, and that the two nations should exert pressure toward ending the conflict. Some noted that the U.S. had supplied arms to both combatants, and suggested that this fact didn't help our world "image" (Chi. Tribune). The Wall St. Journal thought the U.S. should "exercise more discretion in the dispensing of military aid and tie much tighter strings on the purpose of its deployment." Achievement of a cease-fire agreement between India and Pakistan through the United Nations brought a sense of relief, and editors approved the U.S. role in working through the UN.[13]

Communist China's ultimatum to India heightened concern, and commentators felt that the U.S. and Soviet Union had now an even greater common interest in trying to restrain China, as well as other parties to the conflict. Peking's ultimatum was seen by many as a fresh demonstration of Communist China's threat to Southeast Asia. "By standing in Viet-Nam," said the Minneapolis Tribune, "we hoped to save other countries from being engulfed by the Red tide; now that danger seems greater than ever before" (similarly, St. Louis Post-Dispatch, Chi. Tribune).[14]

Sen. Robert Kennedy's speech on the nuclear proliferation problem (Oct. 13) rekindled public discussion which earlier had been aroused by the nuclear blasts set off by the People's Republic of China. Kennedy's specific suggestion was to invite the PRC to participate in the international effort to halt the spread of nuclear weapons; and most commenting editors commended this proposal. Although most deemed China unlikely to respond, they welcomed Kennedy's suggestion as a stimulus to U.S. policy which they considered too rigid or unimaginative. "The State Department has scoffed at the Senator's proposal," said the Providence Journal, "but the weight of reason is all with Mr. Kennedy." The New York Herald Tribune, however, noted that "many serious minded men in many capitals" had been pressing Communist China to join the Geneva talks, but "Peking is no more interested than Paris in nuclear disarmament or control."[15]

Meanwhile, polls agreed in showing some decline in popular antipathy to the seating of Peking in the United Nations, although a plurality still opposed that step. Louis Harris pointed out that "admission of China to the UN was opposed in 1965 by 61% to 21%; this was a softening from the 73% to 10% margin of opposition just a year earlier. A year later the public would oppose admission for China by only 51% to 30% . . . The major impelling reason for the softening of the traditional hard-line view toward China could be found in the 49% to 35% plurality who wanted to see the U.S. and China negotiate a nuclear test-ban treaty."[16]

1965 Peace Offensive

At this time, "Anti-Vietnam war pickets" were prominent enough for the Harris Survey to ask its respondents to evaluate their role;

68% said the pickets were "more harmful than helpful to American life," 5% found them "more helpful," and 27% said that they "didn't matter much one way or the other." The Progressive magazine, long opposed to U.S. policy in Viet-Nam, announced a change of heart and applauded the "Johnson Administration's peace offensive." Former Sen. Goldwater was reported by the press as expecting the Viet-Nam war to be "over in two or three months," and Richard Nixon was quoted as seeing the U.S. "winning the war" soon.[17]

In mid-October U.S. policy was attacked at rallies and parades staged in 50 cities across America and overseas; and in some areas there were attempts to interfere with military and Selective Service operations. Editors upheld the right to demonstrate, but most of them also defended U.S. policy in Viet-Nam. In the ensuing weeks these editors were gratified by counter-demonstrations in many areas, a "ground-swell of patriotism" involving petitions, rallies, parades, and blood-bank contributions. Declarations by organized labor and by student groups also attested their support of U.S. policy.[18]

In November a Gallup Poll reported on whether respondents would be "more inclined or less inclined" to vote for a Congressional candidate who advocated "sending a great many more men to Viet-nam." Now 46% were "more inclined" to send more men, only 31% "less inclined." The same Gallup respondents also backed (68%) a Congressional candidate who "said that we should try harder to reach a compromise peace settlement." The war protesters held a big demonstration in Washington on Nov. 27, which reportedly mustered 50,000 marchers; the dominant tone was relatively restrained, with the signs requesting "Stop the Bombing" and "Supervised Cease-fire." A full-page advertisement was taken in the Washington Post by the "Faculty and Associates of San Francisco Bay Area Universities and Colleges" which also stressed "Stop the Bombing." In the nation as a whole Harris found that 71% favored continuation of the fighting "until we can negotiate on our own terms."[19]

Along with policy support, several editors expressed sharp criticism of the Government's information policy, the Boston Herald saying: "We have been subjected to alternating reassurances and warnings, which is confusing, and given too little information, which is worrisome" (similarly, Louisville Courier-Journal). Said the Wall St. Journal: "As the war widens and worsens, it seems more necessary than ever to provide an adequate accounting to the people." The Washington Star urged the President to "tell the people that we are engaged in a major war, and invoke in this country the measures which are necessary to fight such a war."[20]

CBS News asked the Opinion Research Corporation to take a comprehensive poll on issues related to Viet-Nam; it was released Dec. 14. In addition to showing majority support for U.S. policy in

Viet-Nam, it inquired about what a U.S. victory there should mean. Offered three alternatives, 38% favored a "settlement which would create conditions for free elections in Viet-Nam," 31% chose "destroying once and for all the Communist war-making potential in that part of the world," and 13% chose "unconditional surrender of the enemy forces fighting in South Viet-Nam" (13% gave no opinion). Respondents were also asked to choose among three alternatives what our country's future policy should be:

45% said "we should use force if necessary to stop the spread of Communism any place in the world;"
36% said "We should consider each Communist threat separately;"
12% said "We should not consider it our responsibility to protect the world from Communism;"
7% gave no opinion.

The U.S. "peace offensive" at Christmas-time 1965 was overwhelmingly approved by American editors as an effort to demonstrate through international diplomacy the American desire to bring the Viet-Nam war to a negotiated settlement. It was anticipated that the failure of Hanoi to accept the overtures would mean a resumption of intense fighting. The Harris Survey reported that the bombing pause, intended to achieve a cease-fire, was approved by a margin of 59% to 33%.[21]

1966: War, PRC; UN

In his 1966 State of the Union message, Pres. Johnson included his thinking about Viet-Nam. Noting that many countries relied upon America for protection, the President stressed that to "yield to force in Viet-Nam" would "undermine the independence of many lands and would whet the appetite of aggression." The U.S. would then "have to fight in one land, and then we would have to fight in another—or abandon much of Asia to the domination of Communists." Editorial approval for Mr. Johnson's firm statement on Viet-Nam came from the Hearst press and also the St. Louis Post-Dispatch; and Sen. Dirksen's TV reply for the Republicans was also welcomed for its support of Viet-Nam policy.[22]

A mail poll of Congress on Viet-Nam by U.S. News & World Report (Jan. 31) reached 237 Representatives and 35 Senators, most of whom felt that if no truce resulted from the bombing pause that we "should hit Viet-Nam harder." Indeed, a majority said "North Viet-Nam should be bombed into submission if necessary to win" (155 Representatives vs. 45; 16 Sens. vs. 13). The Washington Star spoke calmly of a possible increase to 500,000 in U.S. troops there; but many other voices spoke out against such escalation. By this time Sens. Fulbright and Aiken had joined Morse and Gruening in their criticism of Viet-Nam policy. When the U.S. resumed its bombing, it also moved to inscribe the conflict on the agenda of the UN Security Council; some hoped the result would be setting up a Geneva conference. Editors approved the conference at Honolulu to which Pres. Johnson flew to meet South Vietnamese leaders; some stressed the resulting socio-economic program, others the military build-up. At this point Walter Lippmann disassociated himself from U.S. policy, saying: "It is our duty to search for a wiser alternative" than a U.S. policy of "unlimited war."[23]

In order to encourage Communist agreement to peace talks, Sen. Robert Kennedy suggested that the U.S. agree to the admission of the Viet Cong to a "share of power and responsibility" in the government of South Viet-Nam. This proposal of a coalition government sparked editorial dissents. The "U.S. has no legal or moral right to barter away" the right of the Vietnamese people to "a government of their own choice" in order "to cover its own convenient withdrawal," said the Washington Post. The New York Herald Tribune added that the "more encouragement" the peace bloc gets from Americans of Mr. Kennedy's standing, "the more Hanoi is encouraged to hold out for total victory." A Harris Survey reported that 2 out of 3 Americans continued to voice support for U.S. policy in Viet-Nam, with 73% approving the decision to end the bombing "pause." But polls showed substantial opposition to bombing "big cities" or "population centers," or "bombing the Chinese mainland," or using "atomic ground weapons in Viet-Nam."[24]

"Peace marchers" reappeared in March, with the New York parade claiming a participation of 21,800. Most commenting editors were critical, especially of the effect of the marches on our military personnel in Viet-Nam. But several editors reiterated their advocacy of peace negotiations. In a TV appearance Rep. Ford (R-Mich.) suggested a "ceiling" on the number of U.S. ground troops in Viet-Nam until American "sea and air power is more fully utilized" in that theater. The House Republican leader added that Richard Nixon was speaking for himself only in calling for the bombing of military targets in the port of Haiphong. However, a comprehensive poll taken for NBC News by National Analysts, Inc. reported (Apr. 2) substantial American support for major U.S. policies. Thus, the bombing of North Viet-Nam was approved by 78%; and 71% held that the President is "doing enough to achieve peace" (20% said "not enough").[25]

In the May 15 Voters March on Washington, some 11,000 persons participated. Among the total population, approval of "the way Pres.

Johnson is handling the situation in Viet-Nam" declined from 54% in April to 41% in June; but approval still exceeded disapproval (37%). Another Gallup question disclosed that a plurality (49%) continued to say the U.S. "did *not* make a mistake in sending troops to fight in Viet-Nam." The proportion calling this policy a "mistake" rose from 25% in March to 36% in the poll released June 3. According to Walter Lippmann, the doves were "quite right in complaining that in spite of all the peace gestures the President never has made a genuine realistic move to bring about a negotiated settlement." Lippmann called for a ceiling on our military forces in Viet-Nam also an unequivocal U.S. decision to withdraw eventually from the mainland of Asia.[26]

Considerable discussion was devoted in the summer of 1966 to the U.S. bombing of oil depots near Hanoi and Haiphong; the great majority of editors viewed the actions as "justifiable escalation" of the war. Louis Harris reported that, after the bombing actions, approval of the President's "handling of the war" increased to 54% from the June figure of 42%. Once again the assembled U.S. governors voted (49-to-1) a resolution backing up U.S. servicemen on their mission in Viet-Nam. After the oil bombings several foreign governments (especially Prime Ministers Gandhi and Wilson while in Moscow) sought to achieve a settlement of the war, or at least a cease-fire. Editors welcomed these moves which were in accord with the U.S. policy of "negotiations without conditions." Some scholars and churchmen, however, were critical of the Administration for passing up numerous alleged opportunities for peaceful discussions about settlement. According to the Baltimore Sun, "if the authors (of the Citizens White Paper) are wrong, they should be refuted by evidence."[27]

In the continuing discussion on whether the U.S. should escalate its military operations in Viet-Nam, a number called for increased forces (Hanson Baldwin, Barry Goldwater, Richard Nixon, N.Y. News, Chi. Sun-Times). On the other hand, a halt in the build-up was urged by the New York Times, Boston Globe, and 27 Southeast Asia specialists. Henry Kissinger called for concentration on creating "secure zones" in South Viet-Nam. Reports that Hanoi planned to place on trial captured U.S. aviators as "war criminals," since the U.S. had not declared war, created universal concern. Aside from being unjust, editors said, such a trial would engender strong popular demands for retaliatory attacks upon North Viet-Nam, and would "sweep away any possibility of the peace negotiations so sincerely desired by the President and the American people" (Louisville Courier-Journal). There was general agreement with the Washington Post's view that "the President took the right tack in inviting Hanoi to discuss under Red Cross auspices the treatment of prisoners in Viet-Nam."[28]

1966 Election (South Viet-Nam)

When Premier Ky of South Viet-Nam advocated an invasion of North Viet-Nam, all American comment was hostile to this idea, and editors reaffirmed their support of the limited U.S. objectives in the war, and their desire to minimize a confrontation with Communist China. Newsweek published a Harris Survey on basic policy for Viet-Nam, reporting that "69% of the people polled indicated that they are firmly committed to the U.S. presence in Viet-Nam, even though they expect the war to 'last a long time'."[29]

The Sept. 11 elections in South Viet-Nam occasioned a great volume of press comment which viewed the elections as a resounding defeat for the Communists' claims to represent the people, and as a significant "start" toward representative government for the South Vietnamese. To David Lawrence this was "perhaps the most remarkable election in modern history," proving that the idealism of Americans in defending Vietnamese self-government was soundly based. Several newspapers critical of U.S. Viet-Nam policy concurred in calling the election a success (e.g., N.Y. Times, St. Louis Post-Dispatch). A few hoped the election results might hasten a negotiated settlement; but most stressed Hanoi's obduracy.[30]

Amb. Goldberg's Sept. 22 address to the UN General Assembly was widely acclaimed as "the most constructive foundation yet put forward by any major power for a negotiated end of the conflict" (N.Y. Times). The Times was pleased that Goldberg had "opened the way for affirmative action on all three points of U Thant's plea." Some, however, urged prompt cessation of U.S. bombing (Sen. Fulbright, St. Louis Post-Dispatch); but Richard Nixon called for repudiation of the bombing offer, saying we must not surrender "our greatest military advantage today." Still, James Reston felt able to say that the President "now has behind him a much more united country." Polls pointed in the same direction.[31]

In October much comment looked forward to the Manila meeting of Asian leaders and Pres. Johnson's visit to six Far Eastern nations. The President declared himself "very disappointed" with the results of the "pacification" program in South Viet-Nam and hoped to develop a more "effective" program at the Manila meeting. Richard Nixon held that the conference could be meaningful if Johnson seized the opportunity to hammer out with our Asian allies a "Pacific Charter" similar to that drawn up by Roosevelt and Churchill for the Atlantic. The actual Manila Manifesto was judged by its pledge to withdraw U.S. and allied troops from South Viet-Nam in six months, provided North Vietnamese forces left. The Manifesto was promptly approved by the Washington Post, Philadelphia Inquirer and Wall St. Journal, the latter saying that the conference left the impression of "reasonable men trying to find a way out of a tortuous conflict."[32]

Meanwhile, the Harris Survey had measured a decline in popular support for escalation of the Viet-Nam war. From the 60% approval of escalation in July after the oil bombing, the figure declined to 52% in September, and down to 44% in mid-October, when 56% favored de-escalation of the war. At the same time, pollster John Kraft reported that Pres. Johnson's popularity on handling Viet-Nam "soared while he was touring the Far East." In late October he had positive ratings from 63%, compared to 55% in August. Congressional Quarterly reported a poll giving the views of members of Congress on basic U.S. policy in Viet-Nam: 313 members of Senate and House (58.5%) were in favor; 26.4% wanted more decisive military action, and 15.1% favored a de-emphasis on the conflict and increased emphasis on peace talks.[33]

The Congressional election registered Republican gains over the 1964 presidential election time; but commentators agreed that "no change" was registered on U.S. policy on Viet-Nam. In fact, Wm. R. Hearst, Jr. pointed out that Richard Nixon "warned our enemies not to interpret the GOP surge as any repudiation of the Johnson administration" on this point. Ted Knap reported that among 34 candidates backed as "war opponents," only the 9 incumbents were elected; the other 25 were defeated.[34]

Amid hopes for another Christmas truce, as urged by the Pope, there arose increased discussion of the "credibility gap," particularly with reference to the Administration's response to the U Thant peace feelers of 1964-65 (e.g., Walter Lippmann, Wash. Star). Some criticized the Administration and its statements about the bombing of Hanoi: whether it had struck "downtown Hanoi" or near the "edge of the city limits" (N.Y. Times, Wall St. Journal).[35]

1967 Escalation

Pres. Johnson's State of the Union message evoked a fresh flock of endorsements of U.S. policy on Viet-Nam; it also brought renewed criticism from the minority which had been giving priority to the need for negotiations. The policy of bombing North Viet-Nam also continued under debate. Protest advertisements continued to appear in the press, with the Ad Hoc Faculty Committee taking another full page in the New York Times, and a group of 300 architects and planners sponsoring a smaller one. A unilateral bombing halt was opposed by twice as many newspapers as advocated one. According to a Harris Survey (released Feb. 12), 67% expressed approval of the bombing of military targets in North Viet-Nam. The Gallup Poll, seeking popular reaction to U Thant's 3-part program for settling the Viet-Nam conflict found a close division of opinion on this rather complex issue. The package question involved: 1, ending unilaterally the bombing of North Viet-Nam; 2, reducing our military activities there; and 3, entering into talks with the Viet Cong as well as the North Vietnamese. Forty percent favored acceptance of the package; 41% rejected it; 19% gave no opinion. It wasn't immediately clear how much the replies to this 3-barrelled question meant a change in the long-time popular willingness to see a negotiated settlement of the war; but apparently the proposed specific concessions to the North Vietnamese reduced the normal approval of "negotiations."[36]

With news of peace moves by Pope Paul, and by Prime Minister Wilson with Premier Kosygin, still in the air, many editors expressed dismay at the resumption of bombing in North Viet-Nam without any statement except the President's terse word that there was "no alternative." Others felt that the U.S. was right to resume the bombings, but expressed regret and resignation over this development. When the U.S. also "escalated" the warfare in Viet-Nam by laying mines in North Vietnamese waterways, by artillery shelling across the Demilitarized Zone, and by increased naval bombardment, the predominant view was to stress that Hanoi had refused to respond during three truces, and that "the new steps are simply part of 'doing the job' " (Scripps-Howard papers). The minority regretted that the escalation would probably reduce the chances for improving U.S.-Russian relations and for peace talks. But several agreed with Sen. Byrd (D-Va.) when he said: "If Russia really wants peace, there is a clear and simply way to prove it–stop supplying war material to North Viet-Nam."[37]

Newsweek carried a Harris Survey which stressed that, although there was now a margin of disapproval of Pres. Johnson's "handling of the war," the "bulk of American opinion on the war forms a broad middle ground"–not fitting into either the "dove" or "hawk" categories. Harris said 12% opposed U.S. policy on "dove" grounds, favoring "either de-escalation, a retreat into enclaves or complete withdrawal;" and 18% opposed U.S. policy on "hawk" grounds, favoring "more escalation, moving the ground fighting to North Viet-Nam, or bombing Chinese airfield sanctuaries." In the middle, Harris saw a majority desire "to end the war without selling out to the Communists," and it was not regarded as "selling out" to treat with the Viet Cong, to see a government which would include Communists, or to create a neutralist South Viet-Nam. The Gallup Poll, when it repeated its "mistake" question, found a majority asserting that it was "not a mistake" to send troops (52%–up from 48% in Sept. 1966).[38]

Continuing press support for basic Viet-Nam policy was shown in editorials condemning the current protests and demonstrations. When Sen. Kennedy renewed his attack by proposing another bombing halt and a 3-stage plan for negotiations, he was supported by only 5 out of 23 commenting newspapers–the five all being long-time advocates of a U.S. bombing halt (Chi. Sun-Times, Detroit Free Press, N.Y. Post, N.Y. Times, St. Louis Post-Dispatch). Among the 18 papers critical of Kennedy's proposal were the Hearst and Scripps-Howard chains; and the Los Angeles Times questioned the judgment of Kennedy and U Thant in attacking U.S. policies at a time when "contacts with the North Vietnamese are in a very delicate phase." A Harris Survey (March 13) reported that 63% opposed stopping the bombing.[39]

Publication on March 21 of an exchange of letters between Pres. Johnson and Ho Chi Minh prompted considerable comment, with most editors strongly upholding the President's position, although some critics persisted in condemning the Administration for not trying hard enough to obtain negotiations. The majority said Pres. Johnson had "gone more than halfway" in his pursuit of peace (N.Y. World-Journal-Tribune); and Ho has "publicly slammed the door on peace negotiations based on any honorable terms" (Newsday). The President's naming of Amb. Bunker to the Saigon post was widely and warmly welcomed, though the Boston Globe saw "serious doubts as to whether the greatest mediator on earth could accomplish anything now." Opinion on the President's trip to Guam divided along the usual lines. There was some approval for the new South Vietnamese constitution; but the Christian Science Monitor said, "the most disheartening aspect of the whole South Vietnamese situation may well be that 13 months after Honolulu, no real start has yet been made on bringing about that 'social revolution' which is an absolute must if South Viet-Nam's freedom and independence are to be secured."[40]

The March 28 announcement that the U.S. had accepted U Thant's 3-point proposal for peace negotiations was approved by an overwhelming majority; and the New York Times thought it "safe to say the U.S., its allies and South Viet-Nam would be willing to stop the fighting once there were agreement on the details of the cease-fire." The Scripps-Howard papers said, "U Thant has revised his plan for the better;" and others said Ho Chi Minh's rejection of it made it clear who was responsible for continuing the fighting. U Thant's subsequent advocacy of a unilateral cease-fire prompted relatively little comment–chiefly negative.[41]

Still, a Minnesota Poll of this period found considerable tolerance for dissent from U.S. policy when 52% of its respondents said they would have "no objection if a high-school teacher told his classes that he personally felt the U.S. should not be fighting in Viet-Nam." Almost as many (46%) said they would have objections. Among the college-educated, 64% said they didn't object; 33% said they did. Yet, after the April 15 protest marches (125,000 in New York; 50,000 in San Francisco) strong criticism was registered by almost all of those commenting in the press. Editors also applauded Gen. Westmoreland's criticism of the dissenters in his address to the Associated Press, also his statement that the men and women under his command had "earned the unified support of the American people."[42]

Following the April increase in the bombing of North Viet-Nam, an analysis of the views of 33 outstanding newspapers had this result: 24 approving, 9 calling for reduced or terminated bombing. Nine papers which had formerly called for increased bombing now seemed content (e.g., Hearst and Scripps-Howard, Chi. Tribune); 7 papers said the U.S. should not halt the bombing without some reciprocal action from Hanoi (e.g., Wash. Star, Phila. Bulletin); 8 papers accepted the escalated bombing, but had some doubts (e.g., Balt. Sun, Wall St. Journal). Those still asking for a reduction included the New York Times and Boston Globe. A Harris Survey reported that 48% of a national cross section of blacks disagreed with Dr. Martin Luther King, Jr. in his strong opposition to the war: 25% agreed, and 27% gave no opinion.[43]

Mid-East; East-West Trade

The surge of discussion of the Mid-East crisis in late May reduced the volume of comment on Viet-Nam. Editors agreed that two crises were harder to handle than one; but there was little suggestion that the Arab-Israeli conflict should mean any change in U.S. policy on Viet-Nam. A few newspapers hoped that the possible four-power talks (U.S., USSR, Britain, France) could advance "peace both in Asia and the Mid-East." A Gallup Poll of this period (released May 28, 1967) shed some light on the Viet-Nam attitudes of college students, many of whom had been popularly identified with antiwar demonstrators. After surveying 1,098 representative college students, Gallup reported that 49% considered themselves "hawks" (56% of men, 38% of women) and only 35% called themselves "doves" (30% of men, 42% of women).[44]

In the continuing foreign policy discussion, several commentators discussed why so many Viet-Nam "doves" were Mid-East "hawks." Americans belonging in this category tended to stress the greater significance of the Mid-East area to the United States. Clayton

Fritchey said that, "unlike Viet-Nam, the Arab-Israeli conflict does seriously involve the national interest of the U.S., and our commitments to maintain peace in the area could not be more binding" (similarly, Des Moines Register, Balt. Sun). But Wm. R. Hearst, Jr. countered those who saw a more important obligation in the Middle East, saying that "their strong urgings are complicated by personal sentiments," and adding: "We have a present commitment that surpasses all others," our obligation "not to betray the more than 10,000 Americans killed thus far in Viet-Nam." Bruce Biossat remarked that "many U.S. liberals like to separate the dictators of this world according to their professed social goals," readily branding Nasser as a "tyrant" but "so persuaded of the rightness of Ho's social cause that they can ignore almost totally the terror by which he lives."[45]

Public comment in June on Viet-Nam increased in volume, although not to the level which obtained before the Mid-East crisis. A Gallup Poll (June 18) on expectations as to the ultimate outcome in Viet-Nam found only 15% expecting all-out victory for the U.S. and South Viet-Nam; a majority predicted a "compromise peace settlement." As to the government in Saigon, Dr. Gallup said that only one person in four thought that a strong enough government could be developed in South Viet-Nam "to withstand Communist pressures," in case the U.S. made peace with the North and withdrew its troops.[46]

When Pres. Johnson met Premier Kosygin at Glassboro editors hoped that they might move toward a negotiated settlement of Viet-Nam, as well as the Mid-East. But at Glassboro there were no tangible results. Earlier, in 1966 and 1967, Pres. Johnson had requested a change in U.S. tariff legislation governing relations with certain Communist countries of Eastern Europe which would have given the Chief Executive limited authority to extend the benefits of "most-favored-nation" treatment to these countries. Aside from some of the "nationalist" newspapers, editorial sentiment was favorable to this kind of "bridge-building" to the Communist countries. Support for liberalization of our nonstrategic trade with Eastern Europe came not only from the Washington Post and St. Louis Post-Dispatch, but from the Detroit News and the Hearst chain and the U.S. Chamber of Commerce, which had always been wary about closer ties with Communist countries. In addition to benefiting our businessmen, said the New York Times, establishment of "improved relations with the Soviet Union and Eastern Europe (would) provide safeguards against expansion of the (Viet-Nam) conflict into a general world war." Some papers were fearful that the Communist countries would not make adequate concessions in return for U.S. concessions. Thus the Scripps-Howard papers said: "It's about time Poland starts working on its end of the bridge." Outright opposition was limited to a few papers and Republican members of Congress. The Chicago Tribune found it an "anomaly that, while fighting Communists in Asia, the President hopes to cozy up to the Western species" (similarly, N.Y. News, Indianapolis Star).[47]

Escalation Considered

Editors often coupled the racial riots in American cities with the Viet-Nam war as the two most urgent problems confronting the nation; some stressed the greater importance of the "security of the stockade" (Wash. Post), whereas the Denver Post declared: "What happens in our urban ghettos will affect the future of the U.S. more profoundly than what happens in Viet-Nam." A number of editors continued to oppose escalation of the war.[48]

In July a plurality of the general public continued to hold that the war in Viet-Nam was "not a mistake" (48% to 41%), according to the Gallup Poll; but respondents also opposed large-scale escalation. Gallup reported (July 30) on popular reactions to a proposal to "send 100,000 more U.S. troops in addition to the 465,000 already there": 49% against this increase; 40% in favor (11% gave no opinion). Those in favor of the escalation held that added troops were "needed to win;" opponents held that enough troops were present to "do the job" and that additional U.S. forces would not help. A Harris Survey reported opposition to sending another 100,000 troops by the margin of 61% to 29%; it also reported that approval for Administration handling of the war had "slumped from 47% to 33%."[49]

In August 1967 editorial debate was heavy on the issue of extending the bombing and on the arrangements for elections in the South. When Sec. Rusk confirmed that at Glassboro Premier Kosygin told Pres. Johnson that peace talks could begin if the U.S. unconditionally stopped its bombing, the New York Post renewed its appeal for such a halt (also Marquis Childs). Bombing advocates continued to call for "massive pressure" on Hanoi (e.g., Richard Nixon), and opponents stressed the risk of war with China and the hope for negotiations if the bombing were halted.[50]

Before the September 3 election date for South Viet-Nam most editors had become sympathetic to the election and to Pres. Johnson's dispatch of a score of U.S. observers; the idea that the election would be a "fraud" was rejected by the great majority of editors. After the event, commentators praised the 83% turnout and accepted the observers' report that the election was reasonably fair and free. Many said that the legitimacy of the Thieu-Ky government was important and that it augured well; but some past critics of U.S. policy minimized the significance of the election (e.g., Sens. Robert Kennedy and Morse). In the bombing debate editors were 2-to-1 in opposing expansion of U.S. bombing–thus rejecting the recommendation of a Senate subcommittee. A typical comment was that of the Minneapolis Star, which found the Stennis committee report "dangerous on two grounds: it forgets that the war must be won in the South, and ignores dangers of becoming involved in a deeper war." On the other hand, newspapers of "nationalist" outlook tended to agree with the subcommittee in wanting action to compel the North to give in (e.g., N.Y. News, Chi. Tribune, San Diego Union).[51]

Pres. Johnson's San Antonio speech (Sept. 29) prompted a number of editors to reaffirm their strong support for U.S. policy on Viet-Nam, with several stressing the fairness of the President's offer to stop the bombing of North Viet-Nam. The President "backed up his contention that (the war) is a battle for the security of the U.S. and to avoid a third world war," said the Cleveland Plain Dealer in a representative comment. Some felt that Johnson had made it "a bit easier" for Hanoi to agree to peace talks by failing to specify any advance guarantees or gestures from Hanoi (e.g., Time magazine). Nevertheless, almost as many papers were disappointed (as approved) that there was "nothing new" in the speech to encourage the start of peace negotiations (e.g., N.Y. Times, St. Louis Post-Dispatch). In reply, the Scripps-Howard editorial asked: "What 'new' is there to offer an enemy who so persistently has rejected the present fair offer?" (similarly, Denver Post).[52]

Before long newspapers were headlining popular opposition to the President's "handling of the war," but Louis Harris declared: "For all the grimness which now envelops American attitudes about this war, a majority still support it," Harris giving a figure of 58%. Harris added: "Only 13% of the American people favor precipitate withdrawal to 'give it all up'." A Gallup Poll in early October found a majority (55%) wanting the U.S. to keep up military pressure until Hanoi agreed to reduce action and enter peace talks; but a plurality opposed letting the military escalate the war as it sees fit (increasing pressures, hitting Haiphong, using nuclear weapons)–48% vs. 42%.[53]

At a press conference (Oct. 12) Sec. Rusk made a vigorous counter-attack against the critics of U.S. policy on Viet-Nam, stirring considerable editorial comment. A number approved the Secretary's exposition of U.S. policy in terms of "national interest" (e.g., Wash. Star, Scripps-Howard); but a larger number of newspapers were critical, particularly dissenting from Mr. Rusk's emphasis upon the threat posed by Red China. According to James Reston, Sec. Rusk–"having failed to persuade the Administration's critics–is now trying to scare them." Some of the most ardent advocates of prompt "negotiations" saw in the press conference renewed evidence that the

U.S. was not engaged in a "genuine search for peace" (e.g., N.Y. Times, St. Louis Post-Dispatch).[54]

1968: Tet Offensive; Johnson Decisions

The course of Viet-Nam discussion was abruptly re-channeled in February by the Viet Cong's surprise Tet offensive. Editorial hopes for peace negotiations were supplanted by discussion of the need for sending more American troops to Viet-Nam. Escalation of U.S. forces to meet the new situation was urged by some Pentagon officials and by several voices in the press (e.g., Wash. Star. Jos. Alsop). But further military escalation was promptly opposed, among others, by Sen. Javits, George Kennan, and Business Executives Move For Vietnam Peace (1600 members). The New York Times remarked: "The question of reinforcements will look totally different if their purpose is to help achieve a settlement rather than to pursue the will-o-the-wisp of victory." In late February a plurality (49%) for the first time called it a "mistake" to send our troops to "fight in Viet-Nam" (41% still said "not a mistake").[55]

At this point the New Hampshire presidential primary election registered a surprisingly high vote for Sen. McCarthy of Minnesota (over 40% of the Democratic vote), which was commonly attributed to "voter frustration over the course of the war" (Scripps-Howard editorial). Next, the Senate Foreign Relations Committee held two days of nationally televised hearings featuring Sec. Rusk's defense of Viet-Nam policy and the doubts of Committee members. After the hearings Newsweek declared that "it seemed a fair assumption that the White House decision, however temporary, to send only a moderate number of additional troops was in large measure a response to mounting antiwar pressure from Capitol Hill."[56]

In his memoirs former Pres. Johnson said that in his own mind he had decided against an increase as large as 100,000 or 200,000 in U.S. forces in Viet-Nam before his March 31 TV broadcast.[57] In the TV broadcast Johnson announced four major decisions, of which the most unexpected was his decision not to accept renomination to the Presidency. This decision, Johnson has written, had long been planned and he felt that devotion of his energies to a campaign could work against his hopes for a Viet-Nam settlement. Commentators, however, tended to relate this decision to the New Hampshire primary's demonstration of considerable public dissent from the President's Viet-Nam policies. The three broadcast announcements about Viet-Nam were: 1, a stop to most of the bombing of North Viet-Nam; 2, an increase in the priority for aiding the South Vietnamese to fight more effectively for themselves; and 3, to provide a small increase in the U.S. forces in Viet-Nam (20,000 to 30,000 men). The former President has written that the decision on the military build-up rested in large measure upon a comprehensive canvass of the problem by an interdepartmental group of officials directed by Clark Clifford, the new Secretary of Defense. This decision was noteworthy because it marked the first occasion in the already long history of U.S.-Vietnam relations that it was decided to place a limit upon the commitment of U.S. resources to Saigon.[58]

It had been at a March meeting in Washington that a majority of the President's informal civilian advisers shifted their position from November's strong support for U.S. policy on Viet-Nam to advocacy of change (especially Dean Acheson, McGeorge Bundy, Douglas Dillon, Cyrus Vance). The basic goals of the U.S. in Viet-Nam continued to be accepted by a majority of the press and a majority of the public; but for the first time a majority of the people were saying that the cost–in terms of human sacrifice–was also an essential consideration. No longer was the goal to be pursued regardless of costs. This was clearly a turning-point in U.S. policy, as in American public opinion. Townsend Hoopes concluded that "when public opinion quickly endorsed (the President's) decisions and their implications, there was born a new policy of finite means which became in fundamental respects irreversible."[59]

A few days after the President's TV address the Gallup Poll asked: "Do you approve or disapprove of Pres. Johnson's decision to stop the bombing of North Viet-Nam?" and 64% said Yes; only 26% registered disapproval. From mid-February to May 1 the proportion of respondents describing themselves as "hawks" (i.e., "wanting to step up our military effort in Viet-Nam") diminished from 61% to 41%.[60]

On May 3, 1968 Pres. Johnson announced that peace talks with representatives of Hanoi would commence in Paris in a few days, with Ambs. Harriman and Vance heading the U.S. delegation. The news was warmly welcomed, although most added that the talks would be long and difficult. Several regarded the agreement to talk as a U.S. victory (e.g., Chi. News and Sun-Times). A Hearst editorial saw Hanoi's decision to talk as an acknowledgment that its troops were taking an "insufferable beating." The Harris Survey reported (June 3) that no less than 88% of Americans "really want to see a negotiated settlement," but most of them guessed that the process would take "a long time, even years." Harris added that a majority (52%) continued to oppose "our agreeing to give the Viet Cong–the Communists–some minimum representation in the South Vietnamese government."[61]

Intermittently, as the Paris talks continued, some voices in the press would call for full-scale resumption of U.S. bombing of the North, in view of the lack of progress in Paris; and some other voices would impatiently ask the U.S. to end all bombing of North Viet-Nam, or to make other moves for peace. The Administration's idea of reassuring Pres. Thieu of continuing U.S. support through a meeting of heads of government at Honolulu was approved by a number of editors (e.g., Balt. Sun, Denver Post); but afterwards others saw "little new or promising" in the Honolulu communique (e.g., Phila. Inquirer). The Scripps-Howard papers commented that "eventually a way must be found to include dissident elements in the governing structure of South Viet-Nam," because the Viet Cong would not settle for anything else.[62]

Fairly early in the presidential campaign year (June) the Gallup Poll asked: "Which of these two men—Richard Nixon or Hubert Humphrey—do you think can do a better job of dealing with the Viet-Nam war?" The result was: 41% Nixon, 41% Humphrey. After the party conventions commentators called the platforms of the two major parties substantially similar on Viet-Nam, although Republican candidates Nixon and Agnew continued to criticize the past conduct of the war by the Administration. Both Nixon and Humphrey vowed to end the Viet-Nam war.[63]

Pres. Johnson's election-eve TV broadcast won the approval of the great majority for its announcement of a complete bombing halt and the "understanding" with Hanoi that its forces would operate under certain restraints, and that representatives of the Thieu government and the National Liberation Front could join the Paris talks. About one-fourth of commenting newspapers were critical of the President's position, usually stressing doubts about the effect of a bombing halt. Louis Harris reported in Newsweek that the public backed the President's action by 2-to-1. President-elect Nixon's statement, backing the stance of the Johnson Administration on the Viet-Nam negotiations in Paris, was acclaimed by many newspapers as "a very large contribution to continuity."[64]

Summary

For four weary years (1965–68) the American public had hoped for a negotiated settlement of the Viet-Nam war, and had often backed escalation of the fighting to impel the North Vietnamese to the conference table. In the spring of 1968, however, the public signaled a halt to further substantial escalation of the number of U.S. troops in Viet-Nam. The war was not to be pursued regardless of costs. This was not a turn back toward isolationism; but it was a definite curb to the activism pursued under Presidents Roosevelt, Truman, Eisenhower and Kennedy. The public had called for a limit on the war, and the public hoped that Pres.-elect Nixon could carry the stalled Paris peace talks to completion.

Reference Notes

1. AOR of Feb. 8, 1965.
2. AOR for Feb. 11 and 16, 1965.
3. AOR for Mar. 4, 11 and 18, 1965.
4. AOR of Apr. 9, 1965.
5. AOR of Apr. 22, 1965.
6. AOR of May 6, 1965.
7. AOR for May 12 and 19, 1965.
8. AOR of May 19, 1965.
9. AOR for June 9 and 16, 1965.
10. AOR for July 1 and 8, 1965.
11. AOR for July 29 and Aug. 26, 1965.
12. AOR for July 29, Aug. 26, Sept. 2 and 16, 1965.
13. AOR for Sept. 10 and 24, 1965.
14. AOR for Sept. 23 and Oct. 8, 1965.
15. AOR of Oct. 22, 1965.
16. Harris, Louis, *Anguish of Change* (New York, 1973), pp. 251–52.
17. AOR for Sept. 30 and Oct. 7, 1965.
18. AOR for Oct. 22 and 28, Nov. 4 and 12, 1965.
19. AOR for Nov. 26, Dec. 2 and 9, 1965.
20. AOR for Dec. 9 and 16, 1965.
21. AOR of Jan. 7, 1966.
22. AOR for Jan. 14 and 20, 1966.
23. AOR for Jan. 28 and Feb. 11, 1966.
24. AOR for Feb. 25, Mar. 3 and 10, 1966.
25. AOR for Mar. 31, Apr. 6 and 7, 1966.
26. AOR for May 12 and 19, June 17, 1966.
27. AOR of July 14, 1966.
28. AOR for July 29 and Aug. 18, 1966.
29. AOR for Aug. 4 and 18, 1966.
30. AOR of Sept. 23, 1966.
31. AOR of Sept. 30, 1966.
32. AOR for Oct. 18 and 26, 1966.
33. AOR for Oct. 25, Nov. 3 and 4, 1966.
34. AOR for Nov. 10 and 17, 1966.
35. AOR for Dec. 15 and 22, 1966.
36. AOR for Jan. 12 and 26, Feb. 21, 1967.
37. AOR for Feb. 21 and Mar. 2, 1967.
38. Ibid.
39. AOR for Mar. 9 and 16, 1967.
40. AOR of Mar. 24, 1967.
41. AOR for Mar. 31 and Apr. 6, 1967.
42. AOR for Apr. 6, 20 and 28, 1967.
43. AOR for May 19 and 26, 1967.
44. AOR of June 1, 1967.
45. AOR of June 8, 1967.
46. AOR of June 22, 1967.
47. AOR for May 13, 1966 and Jan. 20, 1967.
48. AOR for June 29, July 27, Aug. 3, 1967.
49. AOR for Aug. 3 and 31, 1967.
50. Ibid.
51. AOR for Aug. 31, Sept. 7 and 14, 1967.
52. AOR of Oct. 20, 1967.

53. Ibid.
54. AOR of Oct. 25, 1967.
55. AOR for Feb. 27, Mar. 1 and 4, 1968.
56. AOR for Mar. 13 and 18, 1968.
57. Johnson, Lyndon B., *The Vantage Point* (New York, 1971), p. 365.
58. Johnson, op. cit., p. 402.
59. Hoopes, Townsend, *The Limits of Intervention* (New York, 1969), p. 223.
60. *The Gallup Poll*, Vol. III.
61. AOR for May 10 and June 6, 1968.
62. AOR of July 25, 1968.
63. AOR of Sept. 20, 1968.
64. AOR for Nov. 4 and 12, Dec. 2, 1968.

XVI

NIXON POLICIES (1969–1971)

Pres. Nixon, in a widely-approved campaign promise, had pledged to end the Viet-Nam war; but, while the Paris negotiations were grinding on without noticeable progress, the new President called public attention to our relations with Europe and our mutual defense problems. He himself undertook an official visit to Europe scarcely a month after his inauguration; and his subsequent trips to China and the Soviet Union were of even greater significance.

At all times the President and the people were conscious of the war in Viet-Nam, and always wishing that something would make it go away. Attitudes toward the war affected general attitudes about relations with other countries: Communist China, the Soviet Union, our allies, our trading partners, and the nations to which we sent foreign aid.

First Trips

Editors welcomed Nixon's European tour plans, and they tended to be modest in their expectations. "If he can merely establish rapport with his counterparts abroad and indicate his desire to work with them in a cooperative spirit," said the Denver Post, "his trip will be very much worthwhile." The Philadelphia Bulletin added that the "kind of fence-mending Mr. Nixon plans in Europe at the very least represents a welcome effort to give long-range perspective and balance to American foreign policy."[1]

Editors were particularly pleased that the President's first trip focused on a visit to NATO headquarters. The Scripps-Howard papers saw "three main tasks" for the President in Brussels: 1, to convince the Western Europeans of the special interest of the U.S. in their countries; 2, to declare an end to the preponderant U.S. influence over NATO and expect "correspondingly larger European contributions" to the alliance; and 3, to begin to move NATO forward toward being "an instrument for detente" as Mr. Nixon had suggested during his campaign. Others mentioning increased European contributions were the Los Angeles Times, Wall St. Journal, and Chicago Tribune. Others hoping that the planned discussions would afford a "basis for effective negotiations with the Soviet Union" included the New York Times and Denver Post. The Hearst papers declared that "Soviet Russia remains as the prime threat to stability," but this chain saw the "possibility of mutually beneficial accommodations."[2]

The European trip was adjudged by editors as a success in improving U.S. relations with Western Europe, and also improving the basis for later talks with the Soviets. Time magazine said the President had "laid a sound foundation for the 'new era of negotiation';" and a number felt that the "coming talks with Moscow" were "more important" than the Western European talks themselves (e.g., Boston Globe, Chi. Sun-Times, St. Louis Post-Dispatch). A few held that arms control talks with Moscow were so urgently needed that they thought the President mistaken in waiting to link such talks with progress on peace in Viet-Nam and the Middle East (e.g., N.Y. Times, Wash. Post).[3]

After the President's March 4 press conference, the Minneapolis Star applauded the President's recognition of limits on American power respecting European unity and American commitments to Spain and said: "This subtle difference in direction does not mark the beginning of a new isolationism," but of a more careful weighing of U.S. interests. Celebration of the 20th anniversary of NATO by a Washington meeting of the NATO Council in April was accompanied by considerable discussion of whether real agreements could be worked out with the Soviet Union. Comment after the meeting showed firm conviction that NATO was still needed, and that one of its goals should be seeking detente in Europe. Editors welcomed Pres. Nixon's suggestion that, under appropriate circumstances, the "fist" of NATO could become "a hand of friendship" to the Communist countries of Europe. The idea of pursuing bilateral talks, rather than a European conference, on security problems was upheld by most of those commenting. As the Newark News put it, "the possibility of reaching a sound detente in Europe lies in the slow, but positive, process of working out friendlier relations with nations on an individual basis." However, the New York Times commented on the slowness of the bilateral process and said that such "a lack of urgency is disappointing" (also St. Louis Post-Dispatch).[4]

Meanwhile, considerable debate developed on one specific measure requested by the President in the field of nuclear weapons, the Safeguard Anti-Ballistic-Missile system (ABM). In the spring of 1969 editorial discussions were very evenly divided, with ABM supporters feeling that some action to counter the Soviet nuclear moves was essential, or at least prudent (e.g., Hearst and Scripps-Howard papers, Denver Post). Many of these editors mentioned their hopes for atomic negotiations with the Soviets soon. Opponents often stressed the sizable military appropriations required for the ABM system; and some, citing the division of opinion among scientists, questioned the effectiveness of the proposed system (e.g., St. Louis Post-Dispatch, Atlanta Constitution, Minneapolis Tribune). Public opinion polls showed that many respondents "didn't understand the ABM very well," and that opinion was sometimes closely divided (Minn. Poll).

A Harris Survey found a considerable margin of approval (47% to 26%, with 27% unsure); approval was highest in the South and West, while heaviest opposition came from the big cities, Negroes, respondents under 30, and the college-educated. The favorable vote in Congress was very close.[5]

In the meantime Pres. Nixon's interest in trying to improve the Middle East situation was also welcomed. A Gallup Poll (Feb. 6) reported that as many as 63% of a nationwide sample thought that "another full-scale war between the Israelis and the Arabs is likely to occur during the next five years" (22% said "not likely"). Most commenting editors approved the idea of the Big Four nations (i.e., Britain, France, U.S., USSR) applying pressure for peace within the UN framework upon the Arab countries and Israel.[6]

Viet-Nam

In Paris the Viet-Nam negotiators reached agreement in January on procedures and held their first "substantive" meeting to include representatives of the Thieu government and the National Liberation Front (NLF). Some editors had called for a cease-fire as the next objective (e.g., Miami Herald, N.Y. Post); but the Philadelphia Bulletin said it would be a "serious error if the Paris meeting were to drift into a strictly military session." While some Senators maintained that the U.S. should start withdrawing troops without any "reciprocity" (Cranston, D-Cal; Hughes, D-Iowa), other commentators wanted to see progress on the political settlement first (e.g., Harsch in C.S. Monitor). The outbreak of enemy attacks in February aroused concern, but most editors agreed with Pres. Nixon in opposing precipitate action by the U.S. Some journals were pressing for withdrawal of 40,000 or 50,000 U.S. troops in the next few months (e.g., Life). The Gallup Poll found the general public rather divided as to the "next steps" in Viet-Nam: some saying, "Go all out" (25%), some saying the U.S. should let the South Vietnamese take over (21%), others saying we should stay in Viet-Nam until a cease-fire (15%), and the remainder giving other or no responses.[7]

Most Americans, according to a Time-Harris survey (May 2), still believed that the original U.S. commitment to South Viet-Nam was "justified." In fact, 56% called it "very important" that Hanoi and the Viet Cong should *not* take over South Viet-Nam. If, however, respondents had known that the Viet-Nam war "would last so long and cost so many lives," a definite majority (63%) said that they would have opposed it (26% would still have favored it). As things stood in 1969, did respondents think the war was "worth it"? Yes, said 50%; No, 37%. Although Americans had voted for a candidate who promised to end the war, it was evident that the people were willing to give him quite a bit of leeway on when, and how, to end it.

When the President issued his 8-point peace program (May 14) it received high praise; and editors were pleased to learn that Nixon would hold a meeting with Pres. Thieu on Midway Island, in view of South Viet-Nam's reluctance to agree to compromises in the Paris talks which seemed essential to a settlement. The Minneapolis Star "suspected" that Saigon did not feel ready to fulfill Pres. Nixon's pledge of "opportunity for full participation in the political life of South Viet-Nam by all political elements." A Scripps-Howard editorial noted that Nixon would have to abide by his pledge "not to impose a solution." The New York Times concluded that "Saigon has to be persuaded to accept, as Washington appears to have accepted, the realistic necessity for reasonable compromise." Some editors felt it essential that Saigon accept a coalition government, including representation for the NLF (e.g., N.Y. Post); but a Harris Survey reported that the idea elicited greater popular opposition (47%) than approval (26%)–even if the "Communists won a place as a result of free elections." Another Harris question asked about "bringing 50,000 American troops from Viet-Nam this year, if there has been no settlement of the war there." A plurality (49%) were in favor of this idea, with 55% in favor among Americans under 35, and 60% among black Americans.[8]

Pres. Nixon did, in fact, reduce the U.S. draft calls and begin the withdrawal of troops from Viet-Nam, as a part of his program of Vietnamization of the war. Announcement in September of a further withdrawal of 35,000 troops by December 15 was approved by a majority of commenting newspapers; but the minority of critical newspapers contended that more U.S. troops should be withdrawn more quickly. The idea of setting a final deadline for the withdrawal of all U.S. troops, however, was opposed by a sizable majority of commenting editors. The opposing editors usually agreed with the President that setting a deadline would tend to extend the war to that date, and would tend to encourage Hanoi simply to wait without making any bargaining offers. The Gallup Poll continued to report that a majority of Americans "approved the way Pres. Nixon is handling the situation in Viet-Nam"–52% vs. 32% in late September.[9]

On the campuses and elsewhere demonstrations for faster troop withdrawals, and for cutting loose from the foot-dragging Thieu regime, mounted in October and November with the so-called "moratoria," until Prof. Spanier could refer to them as "perhaps the most spontaneous and extensive demonstrations for peace in the nation's history."[10] Moratorium Day on Oct. 15 was approved as a constructive idea by a majority of commenting newspapers, although they continued to oppose setting a deadline for complete withdrawal of U.S. troops. The Gallup Poll (Oct. 12) reported that 57% of its national sample did approve of Sen. Goodell's (R-NY) idea of requiring total withdrawal by the end of 1970 (31% opposed this proposed legislation).

Pres. Nixon's November 3 speech on Viet-Nam won the approval of 3 out of 4 commenting newspapers. The Philadelphia Bulletin said it was "likely that Mr. Nixon earned, from most Americans, at least a little more time to follow his timetable." The Gallup Poll reported that approval of Nixon's handling of Viet-Nam had risen to 58%. The Harris Survey found 81% agreeing that the war demonstrators were "raising real questions which ought to be discussed and answered," yet it also reported a majority (60%) agreeing that Pres. Nixon is right to ask people "not to support anti-war protests because it hurts his chances of getting peace;" and a plurality (45% to 39%) "disagreed with the goals" of the demonstrators.[11]

The peace "mobilization" which brought some 250,000 demonstrators to the Washington Monument grounds on Nov. 15 made a favorable impression on most editors, the Baltimore Sun finding it "on the level of the Civil Rights March of 1963." Editors agreed with the President that the Paris talks were getting nowhere; but there were two schools of thought about what should happen next. Stressing concessions already made by the U.S., one group agreed with the Administration that the next move was up to Hanoi (e.g., Cleveland Plain Dealer, Chi. Tribune, Wall St. Journal). The other school stressed the importance of keeping the Paris talks going, and tended to feel that the U.S. should do something (e.g., N.Y. Times, Chi. News, C.S. Monitor). A Gallup Poll taken during the November mobilization found that popular approval of Pres. Nixon's handling of Viet-Nam had risen to 64%.[12]

Youth's Role

The role of youth in the demonstrations against the Viet-Nam war was so prominent, and so publicized that many Americans came to feel that attitudes toward the war were clearly geared to age—with older citizens supporting the war, and younger citizens opposing it. Such conclusions, however, are not borne out by analysis of a score of public opinion polls appearing from Feb. 1969 to April 1970. These polls sometimes showed differences of a few percentage-points in accord with the above-mentioned contemporary stereotype, but young people and old people often expressed similar views—with some increasing tendency in this direction. In 1966, for example, there had been a 9% difference between the "50 and over" age group and the 21-to-29 age group on the Gallup Poll question of whether the Viet-Nam war was a "mistake": 30% of the older respondents said Yes, 21% of the younger respondents. By Oct. 1969 majorities in both groups said Yes, but the differential between the age groups had declined to 5%; 63% in the older group said Yes, 58% in the younger group.[13]

American youths who were currently attending college were more unhappy about the war than were older citizens. According to a Nov. 1969 Gallup Poll, students were appreciably less approving of "the way Pres. Nixon is handling the situation in Viet-Nam" (although a plurality of the students actually approved the President's role). The Gallup findings also showed considerable variation in student opinion according to the geographical location of the college, as indicated in the following table.

	Approve Handling	**Disapprove Handling**	**No Opinion**
All students	50%	44%	6%
(All adults)	(64)	(25)	(11)
Colleges in:			
South	60	34	6
Midwest	52	43	5
Far West	50	42	8
East	36	58	6

Several observers also noted that approval of the war was greater on the part of students whose college studies were closely geared to vocational objectives, such as engineering or medicine, than among those seeking degrees in English, science, or law (e.g., Wm. R. Hearst, Jr.; State Dept. officers visiting college campuses).[14]

In three areas related to foreign policy (although one was not related to the war), polls clearly did show substantial differences in attitude linked to the age of the respondent: protest demonstrations; Ho Chi Minh; and space exploration. In late 1969 Louis Harris asked his respondents whether or not they "in general sympathized with the goals of the people who are demonstrating, marching and protesting against the war in Vietnam." Those under 30 did sympathize with the goals by a margin of 52% vs. 34%, whereas those 50 and over disagreed with the goals by a margin of 55% to 28%. After the death of Ho Chi Minh, the Minnesota Poll (October 12, 1969 release) asked respondents whether they thought "history will rate Ho favorably or unfavorably." The statewide verdict was unfavorable (53% vs. 32%); but those in the 21-to-29 age group foresaw a favorable verdict (52% to 34%). On attitudes toward space, polls by Gallup, Harris, and Minnesota all found greater appreciation among the young than among older respondents. The Minnesota Poll, for example, reported that 68% of respondents in their twenties felt that the U.S. had "gained a great deal" by placing men on the moon, whereas only 34% of those 60 or older saw "great gains" (58% in this group assessed the gains as "not too much").

It may be noted here that newspaper editors hailed Pres. Nixon's trip around the world, after the successful moon landing by U.S. astronauts, as a successful and worthwhile journey. The Houston Post remarked that American prestige, in the wake of the Apollo achievement, was probably "higher throughout the world than at any time since the start of the Viet-Nam war." Some of the editorials stressed their endorsement of the President's policy on Asia, the San Francisco Chronicle calling it a "hopeful message to carry around the world," i.e., that the U.S. is "in favor of landings on the moon and against the landing of troops in remote continents here below."[15]

Defense Pledges

Considerable discussion in early 1969 was devoted to the change in the mood of the American people about U.S. military commitments. Time magazine's report of a poll on which Time collaborated with Louis Harris created a stir because it pointed to rather severe limits upon U.S. defense commitments which were being currently imposed by the American public. This survey found Americans appreciably more willing to defend neighboring countries than those some distance away. Thus, if Canada "were invaded by outside Communist military forces," 79% would be willing to help defend–57% with military force, and an additional 22% would provide weapons or other forms of help. In the case of Mexico, the comparable figures were 76% and 52%; in the case of the Bahama Islands these figures were 63% and 43%. If Brazil were invaded by Communist military forces, 52% favored helping defend her, 34% by military force. For West Berlin the comparable figures were 64% and 26%, for West Germany, 59% and 38%, for Italy 42% and 27%.

In Asia pluralities were often favorable to helping defend our allies: South Korea, 51% and 32%; Philippines, 47% and 30%; Japan, 42% and 27%; Taiwan, 41% and 26%, Thailand, 40% and 32%. Willingness to send armed forces to Israel was the smallest out of 22 countries reported on, 9%; but willingness to provide some help was fairly high, 44%. Of course, there must always be a question of how well replies to hypothetical questions about the future will correspond to attitudes in the actual circumstances. The earlier responses of around 80% willing to defend West Berlin by military force may well have turned out to be too high; and it may well be that these 1969 replies showed less willingness than would exist in the event of an actual invasion. But there could be no question that these polling responses of the era after the American decision not to persist in Viet-Nam were appreciably lower—showed less willingness to use force to uphold our commitments to our allies than did the findings of polls a decade or two earlier.

Looking into the future, and assessing the wisdom of our commitments to the defense of other countries, 8% said they favored a larger role for the U.S., 34% wanted to reduce our commitments, and 51% said that "our present stance" was "as far as we should go." Thus a clear majority (51% plus 8%) were willing to sustain the current U.S. military role, whereas about one-third would have reduced that role. The Time-Harris survey also reported that a majority of the respondents (52%) said they thought a "third World War could be avoided" (32% said No). This expectation bolstered the Administration's efforts to create an era of negotiations; but many citizens still felt that the U.S. needed greater arms against the Soviets. At the same time, the Time-Harris survey reported that a majority (51%) deemed it "likely" that arms limitation would actually take place.

Nixon Doctrine

The presidential lowering of the U.S. "profile," particularly vis-a-vis Asia, was well received. Several editors welcomed the President's greater emphasis on U.S. aid for nation-building, on help to threatened nations in the form of arms and training assistance, and approval of military intervention only to combat external aggression. Some pointed up the fact that "considerable U.S. help will still be available to Asian nations," although the President "did not promise massive infusions of new aid" (San Diego Union, Denver Post). Said the Providence Journal: The U.S. will be "far more cautious in its commitment of aid; but its commitment to the balance of power there will remain."[16]

Sec. Rogers, in late 1969, sought to encourage steps toward a Middle East settlement by proposing guidelines to that end. Among the papers welcoming this move, the Chicago Sun-Times said that Rogers "made it clear that a reasonable basis for peace negotiation does exist and that the U.S. is neutral in its efforts to find peace." Out of the 47 newspapers in the Department's sample, 19 were favorable to the U.S. proposals, 14 were critical, 4 were non-committal, and 10 refrained from comment. The favorable papers felt that, despite the "fairness" of the proposals, there nevertheless was little prospect of reaching agreement. Some of the critics held that the proposals were impractical, that they wouldn't work; others asserted that the Rogers plan was "unfair" to Israel. The Kansas City Star complained that the U.S. proposals were "rather specific about what the Israelis should be expected to give up, but considerably less definite on the terms and guarantees of whatever peace they might expect to get in return."[17]

Pres. Nixon's summation of his foreign policy, sent to Congress on Feb. 18, 1970, was very well received by most of the press, for its comprehensiveness and its reasonableness. A number were pleased at the continuing emphasis on a policy of negotiation; "there isn't a syllable of Cold War rhetoric in the entire 40,000 words," said Roscoe and Geoffrey Drummond. Others supporting the message liked its firmness vis-a-vis the Soviet Union, a Hearst editorial saying that in each of the "four basic trouble areas–Vietnam, Middle East, arms control, and our own national defenses–it is Soviet Russia which is the prime complicating factor." Editors also appreciated Nixon's "intention to go on cutting back on America's involvement in the affairs of nations abroad and to seek partnership instead of domination" (C.S. Monitor). Criticism came from some who disagreed with the President on his ABM program or on Viet-Nam (e.g., Des Moines Register, N.Y. Times). The Louisville Courier-Journal conceded that there was much that was appealing in the President's message, but what was "hard to accept" was "the over-merchandizing of the product," the declaration that is is a "policy for the decade and a watershed in the life of the nation."[18]

In March 1970, as the withdrawal of U.S. forces from Viet-Nam continued, Pres. Nixon announced that U.S. "advisers" in Laos would help the Laotian forces counteract the use of Laotian territory by the North Vietnamese; he added that there were no plans for U.S. ground combat troops in Laos. Editors were closely divided about the wisdom of this Laos move. A slight majority of newspapers (19 out of 36) gave sympathy or support to the new move; but nearly half stressed their anxiety over the dangers for the U.S. in the Laos situation. A clear majority expressed dissatisfaction with the Administration's information activities respecting Laos, and saw the development of a "widening credibility gap" as a result of official statements. The Hearst papers, unlike the critics, did "not for a moment believe that Pres. Nixon may unwittingly be risking another Vietnam-type of combat involvement in Laos," but they were unhappy about the incompleteness of Administration statements on Laos–"the failure to level with the public on Laos." When respondents of the Minnesota Poll were offered three alternative policies for Laos, 40% favored "pulling out altogether," 39% approved "continued limited military assistance," and only 16% favored providing as much equipment and combat troops as might be "necessary to ensure independence" (5% gave no opinion). Also asked about U.S. information policy, 75% of the Minnesota respondents said that the "Administration is not telling as much as they should about U.S. involvement" in Laos.[19]

Editors approved the continuing withdrawal of U.S. forces from Viet-Nam; and a Gallup Poll reported (Mar. 15) the following division of opinion (in response to Gallup alternatives):

Withdraw all troops immediately	21%	46%
Withdraw all troops by end of 18 months	25%	
Withdraw troops but take as many years to do this as are needed to turn the war over to the South Vietnamese	38%	45%
Send more troops to Vietnam and step up the fighting	7%	

When Lon Nol succeeded Prince Sihanouk as head of Cambodia, editors offered the same advice as they had for Laos: no further military involvement for the U.S. The Baltimore Sun, in a representative editorial, stressed the "folly of risking a repeat performance in Laos or Cambodia," adding that possible gains could not offset the "direct costs in lives and money." As the Cambodian fighting continued, so did the division in American editorial opinion. An unusually large number of papers remained "on the fence," unable to approve–yet unwilling to condemn. They "hoped and prayed."[20]

Pres. Nixon's order, at the end of April, for U.S. and South Vietnamese troops to clean out the North Vietnamese "sanctuaries" in Cambodia led to a fresh wave of campus protests, which were even further heightened by the shooting and killing of four students in the protest at Kent State University in Ohio. On some campuses there were student "strikes" which effectively "shut down" the institutions in question. By June, however, among newspapers the division had returned to equality between supporters and critics; a consensus failed to develop.[21]

In Congress, as outside, discussion of the rate of U.S. troop withdrawals continued, as did efforts to set a deadline for the return of all troops. Sens. Hatfield and McGovern proposed the end of 1971 as the deadline; and the Harris Survey collected national opinion on this proposal. A plurality (44%) registered approval, while 35% said No (21% gave no opinion). But in answer to a different Harris question, nearly half continued to hold that the withdrawal rate was "about right," as indicated in the following table.

	Withdrawal About Right	**Too Slow**	**Too Fast**	**Unsure**
Oct. 1969	49%	29%	6%	16%
Apr. 1970	47	34	8	11
May 1970	45	27	13	15
July 1970	49	32	11	8

By autumn, the Philadelphia Inquirer (which had been critical of U.S. policy) said: "The fact is that Pres. Nixon's program for winding down the war and ending American involvement is working . . . The way is open to negotiate on realistic terms if the Communists are interested." Indeed, before the November Congressional elections it was widely felt that Pres. Nixon had de-fused Viet-Nam as an issue.[22]

China and Russia

Other significant opinion developments in the autumn of 1970 require mention. A Gallup Poll (Oct. 18 release) reported that the number of "Americans who favor admitting Communist China to the United Nations has reached the highest point recorded, although the proportion falls short of a plurality." In the national sample the figures still showed a sizable plurality against seating Peking–49% to 35%; but among college-educated respondents a majority (52%) approved Peking's participation in this poll taken prior to Canada's recognition of the People's Republic. In the total sample the proportion in favor had increased to 35% from 25% four years earlier (Oct. 1966). The earlier poll had also shown that "leaders" favored the seating of Peking by a 2-to-1 margin (64% to 32%), based upon a random sample of persons listed in Who's Who in America. The 1966 release had also reported that a majority "would favor" China's seating if that "would improve U.S.-Communist China relations" (55% to 30%).[23]

A survey of editorial opinion in this autumn of 1970 provided a striking contrast with an editorial roundup of 1964, when Communist China produced its first nuclear bomb and a majority opposed its seating in the United Nations. Now, out of 33 newspapers sampled, 26 (or 78%) espoused a "two-Chinas" solution as the best answer, i.e., "seat Peking but do not expel Taipei." The 1964 opposition included the Hearst and Scripps-Howard chains and several independent papers which in 1970 advocated a two-Chinas policy (e.g., Wash. Star, Kansas City Star, Los Angeles Times). Strong opposition to seating Peking still came in 1970 from the Chicago Tribune, Richmond Times-Dispatch, and St. Louis Globe-Democrat; and three other papers strongly hoped that Peking could be kept out once again (Boston Herald Traveler, Cinci. Enquirer, Dallas News). The great majority of the editors said it was "realistic" to expect that Peking would soon be seated in the UN, and that it would be "wise" for the U.S. to reconcile itself to this prospect. At the same time, these editors said, the U.S. must not permit expulsion of Taipei–usually mentioning the U.S. obligation to defend the Republic of China, and often adding that the Republic had been a loyal, cooperative member of the UN. Several editors pointed out that "neither

China" favored a "two-China" solution; but they felt it was better for the U.S. to promote a compromise than to "continue its negative stand" (Kansas City Star).[24]

Public interest in reaching agreements with the Soviet Union was strong in late 1970, according to the findings of a Harris Survey (published Oct. 10); and a majority (51%) judged it "possible for the U.S. and Russia to come to a long-term agreement to control wars in the world." A very large majority were in favor of a Kosygin-Nixon summit meeting (80% vs. 8%). When asked about reaching agreements in specific fields, as many as 69% said they favored a pact "limiting ABM systems," and larger majorities favored an agreement to expand trade (75%), and to provide for educational and cultural exchanges (79%).[25]

The most significant Soviet-American talks going on at the time were those on the limitation of nuclear weapons (SALT). In December editors were disappointed that three rounds of SALT talks in Helsinki and Vienna had failed to reach agreement, and feared that mutual mistrust was seriously hampering the negotiations. Most editors felt that these talks were very important to the U.S. and to the world; they felt that both participants had a "compelling interest in avoiding whatever would lead to a nuclear confrontation and the oppressive burden" of the arms race (Balt. Sun). Editors did remain cautiously optimistic that mutual interest would bring the negotiators together in the long run; and some were encouraged by the U.S.-Soviet agreements reached on space-docking and banning nuclear weapons from the ocean floor. As the Boston Globe phrased it, if the two powers can live together in space, "they will also find a way to live together on earth." But the continuing arms race seriously troubled some commentators. When Sec. Laird called for greater U.S. defense efforts to match recent Soviet build-ups, some wondered if that would not sound to the Russians "more like confrontation than negotiation" (e.g., Minneapolis Star). The New York News, however, was pleased that the U.S. was ahead in the over-all race and urged: "let's keep it that way" (also Scripps-Howard, Houston Post).[26]

Trade and Aid

Considerable discussion during 1970 was devoted to trade, as there were talks with Japan about restricting "voluntarily" its exports to the U.S. and Congress was developing a new trade act. Pres. Nixon had opposed U.S. import quotas as a general rule; but he had requested that an exception be made in the case of textiles. Most editors, however, were thoroughly against import quotas; in fact, 34 out of 38 newspapers advocated continuation of the liberal trade policy which the U.S. had now been pursuing for 36 years. "Reciprocity, rather than protectionism, should be the watchword," said the Philadelphia Inquirer; the Des Moines Register declared: "Import quotas are a device to make American consumers pay through the nose to support industries which cannot compete." The editors applauded Pres. Nixon's threat to veto a Christmas-tree tariff bill. Over half of the papers discussing trade policy specifically criticized Japanese trade policy; but only a few felt that the U.S. answer should be mandatory import quotas. The most formidable advocate of some continuing protection was the Hearst chain, but even its editorial said: "In general, we favor the lowering of international trade barriers; but it is a fact that the U.S. has done far more than its share." The Salt Lake City Tribune felt that a U.S. import quota would simply be "retaliating for practices it considers injurious."[27]

Pres. Nixon's Sept. 15 message to Congress on Foreign Assistance for the Seventies was well received by the press. Out of 21 commenting newspapers, 17 were sympathetic to the President's recommendations for a more effective program and felt that Congress "should consider them carefully." Among specific proposals, greatest support was accorded the idea of shifting as much aid as possible from bilateral to multilateral agencies, such as the World Bank. A number also favored the President's idea of separating military aid from economic and humanitarian aid. Nearly half of the editors specifically backed Nixon's recommendation that "the downward trend of U.S. contributions to the development process should be reversed."[28]

The New York Times, however, was disappointed that the President failed to endorse Lester Pearson's proposal that countries should devote 1% of their national production to aiding others. The Washington Post felt that the President should have opened the "epic struggle that will be necessary to educate the American people to its continuing responsibilities." A few, however, said the President was asking for too much (e.g., Wall St. Journal, Miami Herald, St. Louis Globe-Democrat).

By Nov. 18 Pres. Nixon decided to send Congress a "billion-dollar surprise package," asking appropriations for additional military assistance to a number of countries, the largest being $500 million for Israel, $155 million for Cambodia and $150 million for South Korea. In general, the editorial response was sympathetic; and a number promptly supported the appropriation for Israel. The aid to Cambodia was more controversial. It was supported explicitly by the Hearst and Scripps-Howard papers; others counseled "careful study" before enlarging our commitment to Cambodia (Balt. Sun), or conditioned their approval upon the adoption of safeguards against deeper U.S. involvement (Wash. Post). The St. Louis Post-Dispatch was flatly opposed to further aid to Cambodia.[29]

A great outburst of editorials followed the hijacking (in Sept.) of four commercial aircraft which were flown, with their passengers, from Europe to Jordan. Editors warmly applauded Pres. Nixon's initiative in proposing domestic and international measures to prevent further outrages of this sort. Sentiment was favorable to action by the United Nations (and the International Civil Aviation Organization) to promote international agreements against air piracy, but there was much skepticism that policing would actually be undertaken under these auspices. Over half of the newspapers advocated some sort of economic retaliation against countries too weak, or unwilling, to take action removing the current sanctuaries for hijackers. A number upheld the President's suggestion of withholding air service and landing rights from uncooperative countries. Many held, however, that pre-flight security measures offered the greatest promise as deterrents to would-be hijackers.[30]

1971

At the beginning of 1971 discussion of U.S. action in the Indochina war continued, with editorial debate on U.S. air action in Cambodia, in support of the successful campaign of South Vietnamese forces to regain Highway 4. A majority of commenting newspapers approved this action, although some of them were troubled by U.S. statements about Cambodia which they feared could "lead to another Viet-Nam." Expressing this same concern, a minority of editors opposed U.S. actions in Cambodia as "too risky."[31]

Considerable comment sympathetic to the Nixon Administration's foreign policy was stirred by the President's second Foreign Policy Report to Congress, and by his radio broadcast on the day of its publication (Feb. 25). Both the idea of an annual report and the substance of the 1971 policy in the various areas were received approvingly by the majority of commenting editors. The critical minority devoted most of their attention to criticism of Viet-Nam policy; but even those critics tended to support U.S. policy in most areas, and also Mr. Nixon's warning against under-involvement, as well as over-involvement, in world affairs. They agreed on the continuing danger in the Middle East and the President's emphasis on the need for a series of negotiations with the Soviet Union aimed at a "stable and just peace." Earlier, when Sen. Mansfield had again proposed the reduction of U.S. troops in Europe, a majority of editors backed Pres. Nixon's pledge *not* to reduce those troops unless there were agreement with the Soviet Union on a mutual reduction. While two-thirds of the newspapers across the country upheld the President, the minority declared themselves in favor of some immediate reduction (e.g., Wall St. Journal, St. Louis Post-Dispatch).[32]

At the same time editors did approve the President's policy of withdrawing troops from Viet-Nam, believing that he was doing the best that was possible under the circumstances. Not all of these approvers, however, shared Mr. Nixon's conclusion that Vietnamization was already a "success." The minority (29%) expressed clear disapproval of current policy, wanting the U.S. to set a definite date for full withdrawal or advocating additional U.S. actions which they felt would induce Hanoi to join in making peace. Nationwide opinion polls showed an increase in the majority (over 1970) favoring a Congressional resolution which would call for withdrawal of all troops from Viet-Nam "by the end of 1971." One of these polls, however, that by the Opinion Research Corporation, probed attitudes on withdrawal more deeply and reported that 55% would not favor withdrawal that soon, "if it meant a Communist takeover of South Viet-Nam;" and 75% would be opposed if withdrawal at that time "would threaten the lives or safety of U.S. POWs held by North Viet-Nam."[33]

There were other signs that thoughtful opinion was not in favor of immediate withdrawal. An article in the May issue of Fortune reported that among the nation's top business executives three-fourths felt that the U.S. must not withdraw "precipitately." Members of the American Historical Association put to a referendum a resolution calling for "immediate withdrawal from the war in Southeast Asia," with this result: For the resolution, 1,543; Against, 2,435.[34]

"Pentagon Papers"

Government officials in Washington were startled in July by the newspaper publication of secret documents on the development of the Viet-Nam war which were called "The Pentagon Papers." Lengthy transcripts appeared first in the New York Times; and extensive portions were published a little later by a number of other papers in various parts of the country. Government officials were distressed that these classified documents had been purloined from government archives, and that "confidential" memoranda were being spread in public print for the whole world to see. American newspapers, however, were editorially overwhelmingly of the belief that it was right and beneficial that these documents about the history of U.S. involvement in Viet-Nam be made so directly available to the American public. Among columnists and the general public opinion about the "Pentagon Papers" was less uniform. The editors were unimpressed by the Government's concern about "stolen" papers or the breaching of "confidentiality." In fact, a number of editors who approved Pres. Nixon's Viet-Nam policies agreed with their colleagues who said that the Government's efforts to prevent publication of the papers (as by seeking temporary injunctions against further publication) were actually widening the "credibility gap" between the Administration and the public (e.g., Wall St. Journal, Balt. Sun, Chi. Tribune, C.S. Monitor).[35]

Some columnists shared the attitude of the editors (e.g., Marquis Childs, Jos. Kraft), but a considerable number were critical of the project, holding that the published papers constituted a "slanted" selection which was "grievously misleading," and denying that Pres. Johnson and his Administration had sought to "deliberately deceive" the American people. This group included: Joseph and Stewart Alsop, Wm. F. Buckley, Jr., Kenneth Crawford, Roscoe Drummond, Evans & Novak, David Lawrence, and Wm. S. White. Among the general public, according to a Newsweek-commissioned poll by the Gallup Organization, a majority (56%) said that the press was "too quick to print classified information;" but a majority also held that the Government "tries to keep too much information secret from the public" (56%). More specifically, a plurality disapproved the Government's effort to keep the newspapers from "publishing material from a secret government history of how the U.S. got involved in the war in Viet-Nam (48% to 33%, with 19% giving no opinion). When the Gallup Poll undertook a poll for its own use–with interviewing two days after the Supreme Court had heard the case, but before the verdict was handed down–it found that as many as 45% of the national sample "had not heard or read about the articles first published in the New York Times about how we got involved in the Viet-Nam war." According to the Gallup release, 58% of the respondents said the newspapers "did the right thing in publishing these articles." If, however, the entire sample is taken as a base, the results would be: 45% hadn't heard; 32% said the newspapers did the right thing; 16% said they did the wrong thing; and 7% gave no opinion.[36]

Far East

When Sec. Rogers signed the treaty returning Okinawa to Japan (June 17, 1971), outright approval came from 17 of the 18 newspapers noted as commenting on the action. Some stressed past U.S. promises to return Okinawa; others saw a "shrewd investment in continued good relations" with Japan (e.g., Wash. Post). The lone dissenter, the St. Louis Globe-Democrat, asked the Senate to "make certain" that we can count on "full use" of the Okinawa bases in the future. The attitudes of the general public had changed considerably in a relatively short time: from 50% against "giving Okinawa back" in 1969 to 49% approval of the 1971 treaty (39% still opposed Okinawa's return). So there was still a contrast between the editors, strongly supporting the Administration, and the "average citizens" who hadn't yet registered a clear majority in favor of returning the island.[37]

The issue of seating the People's Republic of China in the United Nations was covered by three opinion polls published in May and June 1971. All three recorded a shift from plurality opposition to plurality approval. Louis Harris observed: "This reversal is one of the most dramatic shifts in American attitudes in recent times." The polling results indicated that the general public had now "caught up" with the attitudes of American editors. The following table of polling results indicates that the changes in popular opinion took place between October 1970 and May 1971.

	Admit Peking	Oppose	No Opinion
1968 Harris Survey	32%	54%	14%
1969 (Sep) Minnesota	42	50	8
1970 (Oct) Gallup Poll	35	49	16
1971 (May) Gallup Poll	45	38	17
1971 (May) Harris Survey	48	27	25
1971 (June) Minnesota	51	35	14

Noteworthy differences are revealed by the educational breakdowns of the May Gallup Poll; respondents who had attended college were 66% in favor of seating Peking; those with high-school education, 43% in favor; those with only grammar-school training, 27% in favor.[38]

Forty newspapers were noted as commenting on Sec. Rogers' Aug. 2 statement backing a UN seat for Peking and continuing support for Taipei as a UN member. As many as 33 papers approved the seating of Peking; only two were in flat opposition (Chi. Tribune, St. Louis Globe-Democrat). According to the Milwaukee Journal, "the overwhelming fact is that 800-million people and their government can no longer be barred from the forum of Nations." A sizable majority favored Taipei's retention of its seat in the UN; and several took no clear-cut position on this issue. Only one paper, Newsday, dissented from U.S. policy, saying: There is only one China . . . Support for an aged generalissimo with dated delusions is a belief in myths, not reality."[39]

Soviet Union

Evidences of a thaw in relations with the Soviet Union were also noted about this time. The May 20 announcement by the U.S. and Soviet Union that the SALT talks would next concentrate on limiting defensive weapons, but also agree on some measures to limit offensive weapons, was welcomed by the great majority of newspapers—30 out of 36 papers. Only 6 journals stressed their qualms or doubts about this new SALT agenda. This degree of consensus stood in marked contrast to the divisions in earlier comment, when some editors strongly urged an ABM-only agreement, while others insisted on limiting offensive weapons. Signs now that both parties to the SALT talks were willing to compromise were especially encouraging to some editors; others praised the Nixon administration for its "patience in securing the May 20 agreement."[40]

Louis Harris reported in July: "The demand from the American people that Washington explore and find ways of living in peace with leading communist nations has now grown to major proportions" (July 29, 1971). The table below indicates how a trend in this direction was visible before the 1968 election, but was slowed up in late 1968—at the time of the invasion of Czechoslovakia by the Soviet Union.

"Do you think it is possible for the United States and Russia to come to a long-term agreement in the world which will work, or do you feel it is not possible for that to happen?"

	July '68	**Aug. '68**	**Dec. '68**	**1970**	**1971**
Possible to happen	49%	34%	40%	51%	54%
Not possible	37	50	48	32	33
Not sure	14	16	12	17	13
	100%	100%	100%	100%	100%

Breakdowns of the replies to this "feasibility" question showed that in 1971 the young and the college-educated were significantly more optimistic than were the older and less-educated respondents.[41]

The Harris Survey had also explored, for some years, attitudes toward negotiations on several specific subjects. In 1963 only academic and artistic exchanges commanded as much public support as 70%; but half a dozen years later that degree of support was accorded other subjects: trade expansion, limitation of nuclear weapons (defensive and offensive), and joint exploration of the oceans. The following table brings together the proportion of respondents favoring "agreements between the U.S. and Russia" on various topics from 1963 to 1971. In 1971 Harris also found 71% supporting an agreement between U.S. and USSR on "mutual troop reductions in Eastern Europe." This popular support for troop reductions, and for the SALT negotiations as mentioned earlier, was parallelled by editorial opinion in leading American newspapers.

Proportions Favoring US-Russian Agreement on Stated Subjects

(Harris Surveys)	**1963**	**1968**	**1969**	**1970**	**1971**
Exchange Students, Artists	70%	–	79%	79%	80%
Expand Trade	54	–	74	75	76
Limit Atomic Weapons (Offensive & Defensive)	–	66%	72	69	72
Joint Exploration					
of Oceans	–	–	71	70	71
of Space	–	–	63	62	64

As discussion of SALT continued during the autumn weeks, editors paid considerable attention to Defense Department statements about Soviet military capacities and the military appropriations bills. Out of 19 editorials of this period, 13 were less worried about the current strategic position of the U.S. than about the costs and dangers inherent in the arms race; six did express primary concern about the threat of the Soviet arms buildup. The advocates of SALT tended to join the Wheeling Intelligencer in asking: "If it is still felt necessary to make or keep this the most powerful military power on earth, what hope is there of achieving a negotiated reduction in world armaments?" A Detroit Free Press editorial was entitled: "Missile Gap Rhetoric Is Familiar, Phony Refrain." Also, a Harris Survey reported (Aug. 25) that a plurality rejected the statement that "the defense of the U.S. is being endangered by cuts that have been made in our military research and development" programs.[42]

In the autumn of 1971 the ratio of papers emphasizing the need for arms control versus those stressing the danger of the Soviet strategic threat continued to be about 2-to-1. At this time also (often stimulated by the underground tests on Amchitka Island on Nov. 8) there appeared a significant number of editorials sympathetic to a complete ban on nuclear weapons tests. The December NATO meeting evoked considerable favorable discussion, with most editors applauding the agreement among certain European members to increase their combined NATO contributions to the extent of a billion dollars. A few nevertheless deemed this response to be inadequate (e.g., Dallas News, Kansas City Times). A substantial majority of editors gave sustained support to maintaining U.S. troops in Europe, rather than cutting down their numbers.[43]

Economic Policies

Despite the continuance of Viet-Nam as the most important issue "facing the nation" (Gallup release June 17), editors took time to discuss the Reciprocal Trade Agreements bill which died in the Senate at the termination of the 91st Congress. Editors were even more favorable to a liberal trade policy than they had been in 1970, with 39 out of 40 newspapers now taking this stand. The Wheeling Intelligencer was the only advocate of import quotas noted; the other 39 papers shared the Chicago Tribune's view that "free trade has proved immensely beneficial to everybody." At the same time, many editors expressed the hope that voluntary agreement between Japanese and American textile producers might succeed in deflating protectionist pressures and avoid any occasion for international retaliation. Pres. Nixon's emergency economic steps of August 1971, including the floating of the dollar and a temporary 10% import tax, were promptly applauded by representative newspapers across the country. Virtually all felt that letting the dollar float was necessary and that this step was a move toward international monetary equilibrium. Many made a point of asking that the import surcharge be rescinded as soon as possible, when revaluation of the dollar had been achieved. Editors in this group adhered to their basic belief in a liberal tariff policy, and were also fearful lest the U.S. precipitate a trade war.[44]

Pres. Nixon's foreign assistance proposals were received as sympathetically as usual by a majority of commenting editors. They approved the President's suggestions for improvement, including the idea of engaging more private support. They continued to support increased use of multilateral aid organizations, and separation of military aid. Questions about U.S. aid to particular countries were raised in 1971, namely Greece, Chile, and Pakistan. The House of Representatives approved a bill to end aid to the regime of the Greek colonels, unless the President certified to the "over-riding requirements of the security of the United States." About half of the commenting editors favored such a suspension of aid, holding that the U.S. should not aid a "military dictatorship" which ruled through "terror and torture." These writers rejected or ignored the contention that Greece is vital to the security of the U.S.; but the minority (about 30% of the total) stressed that Greece was a "linchpin" of NATO and a much-needed friend in the Mediterranean area. These saw denial of aid to Greece as a "vainglorious gesture" or an "ineffective moral sanction."[45]

When the House moved to suspend aid to Pakistan until the current turmoil in East Pakistan was resolved, this position was upheld by 2 out of 3 commenting papers. Majority spokesmen called it wrong for the U.S. to give aid to "barbarous acts of tyranny" against the East Pakistani who had been "subjected to almost incredible debasement" (Phila. Bulletin, Chi. News). This Pakistani question stirred more comment, and greater opposition, than did that of aiding Greece. Many editors praised U.S. efforts in behalf of emergency aid to the East Pakistani refugees. In the case of Chile nearly all editors felt that American companies (Anaconda and Kennecott) had been unjustly refused compensation when they were expropriated by the Allende government. Several papers favored U.S. countermeasures, such as cutting off aid; but the larger number counseled calmness and restraint. The Miami Herald said we might "alienate much of the hemisphere by turning to get-tough policies that will surely backfire."[46]

Defense Commitments–1971

At this time, while the U.S. was withdrawing troops from Indochina, a Harris Survey (Aug. 25) sounded current attitudes on willingness to go to war under various circumstances. Bluntly asking whether "it would be worth going to war again" in case of the Communist invasion of particular areas, Harris found that most respondents (95%) were ready to defend the U.S., and 77% to meet an invasion of Canada, but they were not ready to act in some other situations, including some covered by U.S. defense treaties. (See accompanying table.)

	Worth Going To War Again	Not Worth It	Not Sure
If U.S. were invaded	95%	2%	3%
If Canada were invaded	77	12	11
If Western Europe were invaded by Communists	47	31	22
If Communists invaded Australia	40	38	22
If West Berlin were taken over by the Russians	32	47	21
If Israel were going to be taken over by Egyptians supported by Russians	25	52	23
If South Korea were invaded by Communists	25	54	21
If Castro took over a country in Latin America	21	50	29
If Communist China were to invade Taiwan	18	58	24

The figures on West Berlin were quite different from those registered ten years earlier, when over 80% favored preventing a takeover during the crisis of the Kennedy administration; but these 1971 results were about the same as those found in 1969. Of course the 1971 figures could not be taken as an accurate prediction of future attitudes in future circumstances. Before World War II, for example, less than one-fourth of a nationwide sample said they "would be willing to fight or to have a member of your family fight in case the Philippines were attacked" (Fortune Poll, 1936). But the 1971 results certainly indicated less readiness to carry out defense pledges to other countries than existed at the time these pledges were given. However, Mr. Harris pointed out that the great majority of respondents (76%) agreed that "the threat of Russia and China is so great it is necessary for the U.S. to be ahead of anything in military research those Communist countries have."[47]

Another interesting Harris Survey of this period showed that Americans were feeling less confidence in their national institutions than they had had in earlier years, as well as less confidence in international institutions. From 1966 to 1971 the proportion having "a great deal of confidence" in Congress declined from 42% to 19%, and in "the military" from 62% to 27%. The 1971 figures for the Executive Branch of the Federal Government (23%) and for the Supreme Court (23%) were only slightly higher than those for Congress for "a great deal of confidence."[48]

Nevertheless, the public continued to approve Pres. Nixon as "working for peace in the world" (57% giving positive ratings) and for "handling relations with Russia" (52%) in the November 29 poll. Also pluralities favored his plans for summit meetings in Moscow (49%) and Peking (46%). The editors continued to be virtually unanimous in applauding the plans to visit China and Russia in the New Year. Referring to the President's campaign pledge to substitute an "age of negotiation" for an "era of confrontation," the Washington Star said that "he has richly fulfilled that promise in half a dozen respects."

On some presidential topics, however, popular opinion was less affirmative. On the President's handling of the Mideast 49% were negative (34% positive); and on his handling of "disarmament negotiations with Russia" the verdict was 47% negative to 33% positive, according to the Harris Survey. The popular judgment was most adverse on "winding down the Viet-Nam war," 51% to 32%. During the early and middle summer of 1971 pluralities had said that the pace of withdrawal was "about right." On this topic the press was more favorable, with over a third clearly favorable to the Administration, another third mixed in opinion, and nearly a third unhappy about the rate of returning our troops. The New York Times, for example, held that "Pres. Nixon's developing Vietnam strategy increases the risk of indefinite involvement in an unending Indochina war;" but the Hearst editorial maintained that the President, "carefully protecting his flank and honoring the nation's commitments, clearly is bringing our active participation to the earliest possible end."[49]

United Nations

Sec. Rogers' speech at the annual meeting of the UN General Assembly won approval from commenting editors; they particularly supported the U.S. on the seating of Peking and Taipei. The October 25 vote which seated Peking and expelled Taipei was almost universally called disappointing; and editors agreed that the U.S. must keep its obligations to the government on Taiwan. But most of those commenting rejected the counsel of those Congressmen who urged the U.S. to cut its financial support of the UN, the editors saying such a policy would be harmful to those U.S. interests which had led the U.S. to join the organization. A Gallup Poll shortly after the UNGA vote on China found a somewhat larger number of respondents saying the UN was "doing a poor job" (43%) than had given that verdict the year before (40%). The Harris Survey inquired whether the U.S. should alter its support to the United Nations; it found a plurality (45%) in favor of continuing (33%) or increasing (12%) "U.S. activity in the UN," with 38% in favor of reducing our support for the UN (30%) or of "getting out" of the organization (8%).[50]

Meanwhile, on the U.S. course vis-a-vis the Indo-Pakistan war, editors were more critical than approving. All commentators agreed that this was a tragic and unnecessary war, but a number criticized the U.S. for holding India "mainly to blame" for the outbreak of war. These papers laid greater stress upon the earlier repressive measures taken by the Government of Pakistan in East Pakistan (which resulted in an exodus of 9 or 10 million refugees into India) than upon India's methodical preparations for the military measures which she actually initiated. As the U.S. efforts to win Pakistani approval for Eastern autonomy became more widely known, there was some tendency to modify the harshness of earlier criticisms, but there was a continuing feeling that the U.S. had been too partial in "tilting toward Pakistan."

The greatest degree of popular agreement in judging events in South Asia was found in the 55% upholding this Harris Survey statement, "The people of East Pakistan should rule their own country, so getting their independence is a good thing." Many editors anticipated prompt U.S. recognition of Bangladesh; and several spoke out in favor of sending economic aid to the new country, although a few expressed opposition. One other issue related to the South Asian war stirred editorial discussion: Was the U.S. correct in sending a fleet to the Indian Ocean at this time? The commenting papers were nearly evenly divided, pro and con.[51]

Summary

During Pres. Nixon's first three years in office the American public backed his efforts to negotiate a settlement of the Viet-Nam war; but a vocal minority objected to his stepped-up military moves in Laos, Cambodia and North Viet-Nam–holding them to be counter-productive of peace. Pres. Nixon's distress about publication of the "Pentagon Papers" was not shared by most newspaper editors, but a majority of the general public agreed that the press was "too quick" to publish secret documents. But the general public appeared to be more willing than the editors to "water down" our defense commitments to other nations (aside from Canada and Mexico); most editors agreed with Pres. Nixon that it was appropriate for the U.S. to carry a "lower profile" in the world.

During these years there appeared a notable softening of hostility toward Communist China and the Soviet Union. A majority agreed that Peking should be seated in the United Nations; and editors and the general public increasingly favored agreements with Moscow to limit arms, expand trade, and increase exchanges of artists. The UN vote to expel Taipei tended to reduce somewhat popular appreciation of the United Nations. American opinion was divided on our role vis-a-vis the newer countries, in particular on our position on the Indo-Pakistan war.

Reference Notes

1. AOR of Feb. 14, 1969.
2. Ibid.
3. AOR of Mar. 20, 1969.
4. AOR for Mar. 20 and Apr. 8-12, 1969.
5. AOR of May 9, 1969.
6. AOR of Feb. 6, 1969.
7. AOR for Jan. 31, Mar. 14 and Apr. 1, 1969.
8. AOR of June 5, 1969.
9. AOR for Oct. 3 and 23, 1969.
10. Spanier, John W., *American Foreign Policy Since World War II* (Fourth Revised Edition, New York, 1971), p. 275.
11. AOR of Nov. 14, 1969.
12. AOR for Nov. 26 and Dec. 18, 1969.
13. AOR of May 20, 1970.
14. Ibid.
15. AOR of Aug. 21, 1969.
16. Ibid.
17. AOR of Jan. 29, 1970.

18. AOR of Mar. 4, 1970.
19. AOR of Mar. 30 and Apr. 10, 1970.
20. AOR for Apr. 10 and May 8, 1970.
21. AOR of June 10, 1970.
22. AOR of Oct. 9 and Nov. 10, 1970.
23. AOR of Oct. 21, 1970.
24. AOR of Feb. 16, 1971.
25. AOR of Oct. 20, 1970.
26. AOR of Dec. 18, 1970.
27. AOR of Aug. 21, 1970.
28. AOR of Oct. 16, 1970.
29. AOR of Nov. 25, 1970.
30. AOR of Oct. 5, 1970.
31. AOR of Jan. 26, 1971.
32. AOR for March 1971.
33. AOR for May 1971.
34. AOR for May 24 and June 9, 1971.
35. AOR for July 1971.
36. Ibid.
37. AOR for Aug. 1971.
38. AOR for July 1971.
39. AOR for Aug. 1971.
40. AOR of July 2, 1971.
41. AOR for Sept. 1971.
42. Ibid.
43. AOR for Oct. 31 and Dec. 3, 1971 and Jan. 1972.
44. AOR for May and Aug. 1971.
45. AOR for July and Aug. 1971.
46. AOR for Sept. and Oct. 1971.
47. AOR for Sept. 1971.
48. AOR for Nov. 1971.
49. AOR for December and Dec. 2, 1971.
50. AOR for Oct. and Nov. 1971.
51. AOR for Dec. 1971 and Jan. 1972.

XVII

VIET-NAM ACCORD—AND AFTER (1972-1973)

At the beginning of the election year of 1972 Pres. Nixon, who had promised in his 1968 campaign to end the war, issued a new plan for peace on Jan. 25 and revealed that the U.S. had already been engaged in secret negotiations with the North Vietnamese. The year 1972 was destined to include a dazzling summit meeting at Peking and another summit at Moscow, also enactment of a war powers bill, as well as the staging of a presidential campaign. In 1973 both Asian and European issues persisted, with global economic questions and the problem of Panama in addition.

On the 1972 Nixon proposals for Viet-Nam, many shared the view of the Houston Post when it said: "It should be reassuring to Americans to see with what persistence the President has pursued peace negotiations and explored every possible channel for arriving at an understanding with Hanoi." Three quarters of the commenting papers approved the new plan, terming it "fair" and "generous." These papers were not too sanguine about the actual prospects for a negotiated settlement; but the approving majority included many who as recently as October had been critical of U.S. plans for withdrawal from Viet-Nam. The New York Times was unusual in its hopefulness, saying: "For the first time in four years of effort the way seems open for serious negotiation of the peace settlement." A minority, however, felt that the new proposals were insufficient to gain a release of the POWs or to start genuine negotiations. When Sec. Rogers cautioned presidential candidates to exercise "responsibility" about attacking the President's peace proposals—lest they encourage Hanoi to hold out for easier terms, some editors who upheld the Nixon proposals spoke out in favor of wide debate on how to end the Viet-Nam war (e.g., Los Angeles Times, Scripps-Howard, Phila. Inquirer).[1]

The public shortly joined the press in approval of the President's "handling of the Viet-Nam situation," 52% to 39% (9% gave no opinion). The two chief reasons given by respondents for approval were the fact that troops were being withdrawn, and the feeling that the President was "doing the best he can under the circumstances." Disapprovers said: "The President isn't doing what he said he would." But people seemed to be definitely more favorable than they had been a couple months earlier.[2]

Another January statement by the President also won plaudits from the press: the U.S. policy concerning aid to nations which have expropriated American investments. Newspapers–including both the Hearst and Scripps-Howard chains–supported the U.S. position against extending bilateral or multilateral aid to countries expropriating American enterprises without offering reasonable compensation–except in cases of humanitarian need, or when the aid would nevertheless be in the U.S. interest. Some papers emphasized the "flexible"–rather than automatic–character of the U.S. prohibition. The Washington Post was unusual in criticizing the new policy, saying: "A meaner and more short-sighted policy would be hard to conceive."[3]

Some discussion of defense spending was sparked by Pres. Nixon's statement in his State of the Union message, that the U.S. would increase its expenditures for strategic weapons unless the Soviets agreed to limitations on such weapons at the SALT talks. Editors divided into two relatively equal categories: 1, those advocating a very hard look at all of the defense budget requests in hope of significant reductions; and 2, those favoring an increase in funds for strategic weapons–unless the SALT talks resulted in nuclear limitations. A majority were hopeful that SALT would obviate the need for added expenditures. Also, Pres. Nixon's 1972 foreign policy report once again drew favorable comment from most leading papers. "Mr. Nixon is turning away from the 'containment' of the Communists," said the Norfolk Virginian-Pilot, "and is seeking to adjust the fears of the Forties and Fifties to the realities of the Seventies." The New York News, which referred to the People's Republic of China as a "slave kingdom," was almost unique in expressing dismay over the prospect of change in U.S. policy toward China.[4]

Peking Summit

The President's much-anticipated journey to Peking was very heavily reported in the press and on TV; and the great majority of commenting editors agreed that the trip was definitely worthwhile–a good beginning. A few concluded that the U.S. had "sold out" Taiwan in the joint communique (Oakland Tribune, St. Louis Globe-Democrat); but many newspapers specifically denied any "sell-out" (including the Hearst and Scripps-Howard chains). Other papers which adjudged the trip's gains as dubious were more inclined to stress their feeling that Peking had not reformed, than to dwell on the U.S. stand on Taiwan.[5]

The general public also took a favorable view of the trip, according to a Gallup Poll taken during the week following the President's return. As many as 98% of the polling sample said they had heard or read about the China trip–"the highest awareness score for an event in the 37 years of the Gallup Poll's existence." Dr. Gallup also reported that the public now had a "far more favorable image" of the mainland Chinese than it had in 1966. In both years respondents were asked to select from a list of favorable and unfavorable adjectives to describe "the mainland Chinese." In 1966 "the total of negative terms used by the public outweighed the total of positive terms by the ratio of approximately 8-to-5. Today, in contrast, positive terms outweigh negative terms by more than 3-to-1." Dr. Gallup added that about one-fifth of the respondents still selected "Sly" (from 20% in 1966 to 19% in 1972).[6]

War Powers Act

Senate passage on April 13 of a War Powers bill (68-to-16) prompted comments from a large number of newspapers, of which about two-thirds were favorable. The approving editors generally believed that the bill, which sought to establish rules governing the use of U.S. armed forces in the absence of a declaration of war by Congress, would rectify an imbalance which had developed between the executive and legislative branches, and would return the power to declare war to its constitutionally-prescribed position. Many welcomed the act as an indication that Congress would not allow further erosion of its authority in this important area. "The bill seeks a restoration of both Constitutional and common sense balance," said the Minneapolis Star. The Baltimore Sun added: "The bill is useful as a 'never again' statement." Editors disapproving the bill feared that its enactment would unnecessarily restrict the President's ability to respond to crises. "What is potentially dangerous about the measure," said the Hearst papers, "is that it would block strong military action by the President in emergencies other than those specified" in the bill.[7]

On May 8 Pres. Nixon made another effort toward settling the Viet-Nam war; he offered new peace terms suggesting U.S. willingness to make further compromises and simultaneously announced the mining of all the ports of North Viet-Nam. The editorial response in leading papers was more questioning than approving the mining and the bombing of rail lines to China; these dubious editors felt that the new moves would be ineffective militarily, that they raised the possibility of global involvement, and also jeopardized the Moscow summit and the several agreements being readied for that occasion (e.g., C.S. Monitor, N.Y. Times, Scripps-Howard). Some of the papers critical of the new mining policy did approve the President's new peace terms (Scripps-Howard, Los Angeles Times). The mining was upheld by about one third, including the Hearst chain. Mining of the ports did appeal to the general public, according to the Harris Survey, which found 59% approving vs. 24% disapproving. Mr. Harris commented: "These results can be taken as a rallying of public opinion behind the President in a time of national crisis." Other questions in the Harris Survey showed "popular willingness to go a substantial distance toward compromise at the negotiation table." Respondents (60%) said they would be willing to see Thieu resign if that were "the only way we could get peace in Vietnam." A majority (51%) favored a "cease-fire stand-still" agreement; a plurality said they would let North Viet-Nam "keep the territory it now occupies" (44% to 38%).[8]

In the middle of 1972 William Watts and Lloyd Free prepared an important analysis of American opinion which they published in their *State of the Nation* (1973). For this purpose they commissioned a comprehensive Gallup Poll and were able to compare the 1972 results with those secured in 1964 and 1968 by the International Institute for Social Research. Public comment on Pres. Nixon's statement in Guam in 1969 had indicated that Americans favored some reduction in their international involvements; but it had remained unclear how far this change in sentiment had gone in practical terms. Watts and Free demonstrated that there was a definite decline from 1964 to 1972 in the degree of internationalist sentiment–but without any appreciable increase in truly isolationist sentiment. Respondents in each of the three surveys were divided into the five categories indicated in the following table.

	1964	**1968**	**1972**
Completely Internationalist	30%	25%	18%
Predominantly Internationalist	35	34	38
Mixed	27	32	35
Predominantly Isolationist	5	6	5
Completely Isolationist	3	3	4
	100%	100%	100%

While the numbers of "isolationists" remained almost static throughout this 8-year period, the numbers of "Complete Internationalists" were almost halved. The survey also included an over-all proposition with which 87% of the total sample expressed agreement. This was that the U.S. should "continue a major role internationally, but cut down on some of its responsibilities abroad."[9]

While Americans had not become isolationists, their concern about getting into another war was well brought out in the responses to the following statement: "The U.S. should maintain its dominant position as the world's most powerful nation at all costs, even going to the very brink of war, if necessary." Exactly one-half disagreed

(50%), 11% gave no opinion, and 39% agreed with the statement. Other questions in this poll permitted a pin-pointing of how this sentiment affected attitudes toward U.S. defense commitments in various parts of the world. The NATO commitment was regarded as real by more persons than recognized U.S. obligations in other parts of the world, although the NATO tie was honored by a much smaller proportion than the 80% or so who had said in the 1950s that they favored the NATO defense commitments. In 1972 a clear majority (52%) expressed agreement with this statement: "The U.S. should come to the defense of its major European allies with military force if any of them are attacked by Soviet Russia." About a third (32%) disagreed with the statement, and 16% gave no answer. By a fairly slim plurality, 43% to 40%, respondents agreed with the proposition that the U.S. should defend Japan "if it is attacked by Soviet Russia or Communist China." By a similar margin (46% to 43%) respondents favored taking "all necessary steps to prevent the spread of communism." Unlike some other polling inquiries which have been mentioned earlier, this survey did not ask about defending Canada, Berlin, or Israel.[10]

SALT; Moscow Summit

A couple European topics, bearing on U.S.-Soviet relations, received significant discussion in early 1972. When Sen. Fulbright suggested that Radio Free Europe and Radio Liberty "should take their rightful place in the graveyard of cold war relics," he was promptly disputed by many editors. Nineteen of 22 editorials urged that these two radio centers be kept on the air "because their main purpose is to give the people behind the Iron Curtain factual information" not available in the media controlled by their governments (e.g., Chi. News). The three papers which agreed with Sen. Fulbright referred to the two radio stations as propaganda outlets (Des Monies Register, Newsday, St. Louis Post-Dispatch). It may be added that the civil strife in Ireland gained some editorial attention, with each commenting paper urging that the U.S. avoid any form of "U.S. intervention" there.[11]

Pres. Nixon's trip to Iran, Poland, and the Soviet Union was appreciated by the public particularly for the summit talks in Moscow. Mr. Nixon's report to Congress (televised) was likewise admired, including his moderate over-all view of summit achievements and his acknowledgment that differences with the Russians continued. Editors hadn't expected "instant peace;" and they did find in the specific Soviet-American agreements a substantial "foundation for peace." Some expressed disappointment that a trade agreement had not been included; but editorial emphasis was placed on the accomplishments at Peking and Moscow, which commentators felt added up to a great step toward an era of "negotiation" instead of "confrontation." The press was very approving of the SALT agreements, with 38 out of 45 papers advocating prompt ratification of the treaty limiting ABM defenses, and Congressional approval of the 5-year executive agreement limiting some offensive weapons. Some editors regarded the SALT agreements, coming after those which prohibited bacteriological warfare and military use of the seabeds, as indicating substantial progress in the control of armaments; but others were disappointed that these agreements appeared to curb the arms race so little. The other 7 newspapers counseled waiting for a full discussion of the nuclear proposals before commending them (Chi. Tribune, Wall St. Journal).[12]

The Harris Survey, which had found 72% approval of the President's trip in advance, reported that a week after his return no fewer than 82% registered approval (11% voiced disapproval). In addition, Harris found 80% or greater approval for each of the several agreements (SALT, space cooperation, trade commission), and as much as 90% approval on health-medical cooperation and 92% on the anti-pollution pact. Asking specifically about the treaty limiting the manufacture of nuclear defensive missiles (ABM missiles), Harris reported approval from 80%, disapproval from only 12%. On another Harris trend question, the President's rating on "working for peace in the world" went up from 50% positive before the Moscow summit to 64% afterward. At the same time, when asked about the proposition that "the Cold War is probably over," a decisive majority disagreed—65% to 17%.

In the wake of the Moscow summit American editors expressed wonder and delight over successive announcements of substantial increases planned for American trade with the Soviet Union. The deal on feed grains ($750 million over 3 years) was widely appreciated as a boon for American farmers and transportation people; later reports said it would amount to nearly a billion dollars. Then came the wide-ranging contract of Occidental Petroleum Co., involving U.S. technology and Soviet raw materials over a 5-year period. The editors, with their long-time attachment to a liberal trade policy, emphasized that both countries would gain from these trade exchanges. Some added that "this deal with the wicked, tricky, atheistic communists has come just in time to sew up the conservative, God-fearing, anti-Communist farm belt for Pres. Nixon in November" (Detroit Free Press). The editors expected that a lend-lease settlement would have to precede any extension of major credits, or of "most-favored-nation" tariff treatment for the Soviet Union. But the Chicago News did remark that "the thought that the U.S. might one day be dependent on Russia for gas and oil is not very comforting." However, many felt that as trade soars, "mutual dependency should reduce the probability of war" (Canton Repository; similarly, New Orleans Times-Picayune, Milwaukee Journal).[13]

The summer's enthusiasm about the mounting Soviet purchases of American grains was somewhat modified as various questions were raised in connection with the sales. Sen. McGovern charged that the Administration's handling of the Soviet deal made possible huge windfall profits for the large grain exporters; a Harris poll reported a majority (53%) endorsing the Senator's effort to "expose the profits" of the grain dealers. Newspapers in Texas and Kansas thought it unfair that grain producers in that area had received much lower prices than the Dakota farmers whose wheat matured after the heavy Russian purchases had materially boosted the price. When the higher grain prices increased the cost of bread, additional questions were raised; but the greater number of newspapers continued to feel that the grain deals were beneficial to the U.S.–economically and politically. In Congress, however, where a general trade agreement with the Soviet Union was being considered, a number of members moved to condition Congressional approval of a trade agreement upon termination of the Soviet Union's high exit fees for emigrants. They referred particularly to the obstacles to the emigration of Jews desiring to emigrate to Israel. This debate was extended to the press, with some agreeing with the Congressional move, and some disagreeing and objecting to the linkage of an internal Soviet question to a bilateral trade agreement. Some editors agreed with Pres. Nixon in preferring to settle the issue by "quiet diplomacy."[14]

There was some disappointment that the Moscow summit failed to mark any progress toward settlement in Viet-Nam. A Harris Survey (June 12) included several hypothetical questions in an effort to clarify the public's requirements for peace there; it found a 3-point basis for settlement: 1, return of POWs; 2, a stand-still cease-fire; and 3, establishment in Saigon of a "neutral but non-Communist" government. On the prisoner issue, 75% favored "continuing our involvement in Vietnam until the prisoners are released;" only 13% would end our role "without assurances of the return of our men." In early July another Harris Survey inquired about people's preferences as between Pres. Nixon and Democratic contender Sen. McGovern on ending U.S. involvement in Viet-Nam: 52% were favorable to Nixon; 33% to McGovern; 15% "not sure." Yet sentiment was not completely favorable to Nixon, as seen by the results of a series of questions dealing with the President's performance on several foreign policy problems.[15]

	Positive	Negative	Not Sure
President's trip to China	70%	23%	7%
Handling Russian relations	68	25	7
Working for world peace	64	34	2
Handling Chinese relations	60	30	10
Handling Mid-East crisis	44	43	13
Handling Viet-Nam war	47	50	3

Election Campaign

In October Sen. McGovern outlined his plans for ending the Viet-Nam war. Press comment was sharply divided, with half of the editorials definitely opposed to his proposals as abandonment of our commitment to Saigon. The other half of the editorials were sympathetic to the Senator's plans to end the fighting; but some of these were uneasy about "walking out" on our ally and leaving Saigon without arms or funds. A little later the Administration announced its draft Viet-Nam settlement, winning the support of both erstwhile "doves" and "hawks" for producing as good a settlement as reasonably could be expected (e.g., Chi. Tribune, N.Y. Times). Several said that the draft incorporated the Administration's minimum objectives: honorable settlement, prisoner return, chance for Saigon Government. Some also referred approvingly to the stipulated role for the U.S., and some referred to the postwar reconstruction. The editors agreed with presidential assistant Kissinger that "peace was at hand." Then Pres. Thieu withheld his concurrence, and the settlement once more was in doubt.[16]

In accounting for Mr. Nixon's overwhelming electoral victory, editors generally emphasized that voters appreciated the President's achievements in foreign affairs and desired a continuation of the policy of negotiation toward an enduring peace (e.g., C.S. Monitor, N.Y. News). Some added that the voting outcome represented "more anti-McGovern than pro-Nixon sentiment;" and several declared that Sen. McGovern had "seriously misjudged the mood of America" (e.g., Balt. Sun, Phila. Inquirer). Most often election analysts referred to improved U.S. relations with Peking and Moscow, and the chances for continued improvement in the future.[17]

Post-election polls by Harris found that 82% of the respondents expected Pres. Nixon in his second term to "expand trade with Russia and China far beyond what it has ever been before;" and 76% expected him to "come to further major agreements with the Russians on arms control limitations." But, reacting to a third Harris proposition, only 37% said they expected Nixon to "establish a generation of peace." Meanwhile, the Harris Survey published its annual sounding of popular confidence in America's leadership–in the "people running" various institutions and professions. Mr. Harris reported "marginal progress" in popular confidence in the nation's leadership. Military leaders scored the greatest gain (from 27% to 35%) among those enjoying "a great deal of confidence," but Harris added that they were "still criticized by most of the college-educated, the young, and the blacks." Lesser gains were chalked up by the Supreme Court (from 25% to 28%), the Federal Executive Branch (from 23% to 27%), and by Congress (from 19% to 21%).[18]

United Nations

The long-anticipated United Nations conference on the Human Environment at Stockholm prompted considerable public comment–both hopeful and unhopeful. Some environmentalists regretted that the conference avoided such basic issues as war and depletion of non-renewable resources. Some others were dismayed at the intrusion of such political issues as apartheid, the current boycott by the European Communists, and the Chinese and Swedish attacks against U.S. actions in Viet-Nam. But "beneath the polemics," wrote Walter Sullivan in the New York Times, "there ran a groundswell of unanimity." The concrete recommendations to the UN General Assembly were welcomed editorially: the new UN mechanism of cooperation, the U.S.-proposed voluntary supporting fund, and many of the 200 specific recommendations. It was evident that the level of awareness among the world's governments had been raised; and some were particularly encouraged by Robert McNamara's statement that environmental standards could be met without adding prohibitively to development costs.[19]

Meanwhile, a vote in the U.S. House of Representatives for an immediate reduction in the U.S. share of the UN operating budget, from 31.5% to 25%, found favor with only 3 out of 22 commenting editors. Many were actually in favor of a reduction, but they agreed with the Scripps-Howard editorial stating that "the reduction should be done legally, through negotiations with other UN members, and gradually so it doesn't cripple the organization." According to the Denver Post, "America, instead of undercutting the UN, should be giving it firm and continued support." But the editorial minority, still angry about "free China's expulsion," favored even larger cuts in the U.S. contribution.[20]

The second veto ever cast by the United States in the Security Council was on a resolution condemning Israel for retaliatory raids across her national borders, but ignoring the terrorist killing of Israeli athletes at the Munich Olympics. The veto was strongly supported by 23 out of 24 commenting newspapers which agreed that the UN resolution was "one-sided." The lone dissenter, the Christian Science Monitor, agreed that the UN resolution was incomplete, but felt that the U.S. should "join in condemning an act of reprisal which can only perpetuate hatred and defer peace." Sec. Rogers, addressing the UNGA, asked for an international treaty for the prevention and punishment of acts of terrorism; he received the unanimous support of 25 newspaper editorials praising his "timely plea." Yet, over half of the editorials stressed the enormous political problems standing in the way of UN action, due to the opposition of Arab, African and Asian nations which believed such a treaty might be used against national liberation movements.[21]

When a little later Fidel Castro offered to negotiate with the U.S. a treaty to curb hijacking, American editors were eager to go ahead, and were encouraged by reports that the Swiss diplomats representing U.S. interests in Havana were making progress. Many editors acknowledged that the treaty must be reciprocal, and the U.S. would need to prosecute Cuban hijackers if Cuba were to prosecute hijackers from the U.S. Several, however, emphasized that the U.S. must not undertake to return Cuban refugees to Cuba. The Chicago News said a hijacking treaty "could be a first step toward the gradual normalization of relations, which is badly needed for hemisphere peace, security and progress."[22]

At the UN General Assembly the U.S. asked for a reduction in regular dues from 31.5% to 25%. Earlier, when the House of Representatives had brusquely resolved to execute this change, editorial opinion was strongly opposed. Now that the move was being made in legal and orderly fashion, most editors upheld the U.S. request which ultimately succeeded in New York. They applauded Amb. Bush's vigorous response to the Soviet attack on the U.S. proposal; and most papers also underscored Bush's statement contrasting U.S. voluntary contributions (amounting to 45% in that category) with the Soviet contributions (under 2%). Several called it "essential" that our voluntary contributions remain high (e.g., Wash. Post, N.Y. Times); but the Hearst papers favored Congressional action to limit U.S. voluntary contributions also to 25%.[23]

Chile's Pres. Allende won Third World applause at the UNGA when he attacked multi-national corporations and charged an "invisible blockade" with cutting Chile off from international financing in reprisal for Chile's expropriations. Most American editors rejected these charges–the Washington Post and New York Times, as well as the Wall St. Journal and New York News. In 1971 editors had expressed considerable sympathy for the Allende government and conceded its right to nationalize basic industries; but they felt that Anaconda and Kennecott had not been fairly compensated. Even so, commentators counseled U.S. calmness and restraint rather than retaliation. Now, in 1972, they attributed Chile's difficulties in international borrowing to the country's record on repaying past obligations and to current Chilean inflation, rather than to arbitrary decisions by the U.S. government and American corporations. Most editors shared the Minneapolis Star's conclusion: "Chile's woes are basically of Allende's own making." The New York Times added that the "Nixon Administration had wisely ignored ITT's appeal" for help in 1971 against the Allende government.[24]

In the middle of 1972 editors had hailed the "thaw" in relations between South Korea and North Korea as a real contribution to peace. Now in late 1972 editors were surprised and dismayed over Pres. Park's declaration of martial law in South Korea; they found it ironic that Park was justifying the imposition of martial law by saying it was needed to prepare the people for their new relations with the North. Most commentators specifically endorsed the State Department's public disapproval of Pres. Park's move. Some said that the U.S. "did not fight a costly 3-year war against Communism" in Korea in order to substitute "another form of totalitarianism" (Los Angeles Times, Kansas City Times). They also remarked the "disturbing resemblance" to recent moves in the Philippines, Thailand, South Viet-Nam, and Cambodia; some concluded that the "growing contempt for the democratic process (in Asia) may make it harder for the President to continue his doctrine of helping non-Communist Asian nations to defend themselves" (Scripps-Howard papers).[25]

Viet-Nam; Economic Policy

Commentators were glad that Pres. Nixon proceeded to work for a Viet-Nam settlement following the pre-election delay owing to the reluctance of the Thieu government. A number, however, criticized the bombing of North Viet-Nam; and some others would have preferred to leave the political fate of South Viet-Nam to the Vietnamese instead of the President's insistence on working for survival of the Thieu government. The Minnesota Poll in late December found a majority of Minnesotans opposed to the resumption of bombing. This poll also reported that a majority (51%) of Minnesotans said that Dr. Kissinger's "peace at hand" statement was made in order to "help the campaign," but 37% said that Kissinger was "sincere;" and 6% said he was both "sincere" and "helping the campaign" (6% gave no opinion). Pres. Nixon's Second Inaugural Address was well received by the press, and most editors agreed that the international situation was good and likely to get better. Three days later the President announced that an accord had been reached on Viet-Nam.[26]

Editorial opinion on the Viet-Nam agreement (signed at Paris Jan. 27) was unanimous in rejoicing over cessation of the killing and the promised return of POWs and of U.S. troops. Earlier critics and supporters of the U.S. war policy joined in hailing a time of thanksgiving, rather than of triumph. Many said the terms were "the best possible;" and half of those commenting specifically welcomed the prospect that South Viet-Nam now had a "reasonable chance" for survival. The Hearst papers and several others agreed that we had obtained "peace with honor;" and only a few disagreed (e.g., N.Y. Times, St. Louis Post-Dispatch). A number added that the most important "lesson" of Viet-Nam was to be found in national adoption of the Nixon Doctrine. Some papers which had been strongly critical of the war doubted that the 1973 terms were materially different from those which could have been obtained years earlier. The Viet-Nam accord called for U.S. aid in the reconstruction of both South and North Viet-Nam. Eighty percent of the commenting papers gave clear support to this commitment, often citing the pledges by Presidents Johnson and Nixon (including Hearst and Scripps-Howard chains).[27]

A Gallup Poll by telephone reported 80% "in general, satisfied with the Viet-Nam peace agreement reached;" and a majority (58%) felt that we were achieving a "peace with honor." At the same time, only 35% felt that "the peace agreement is likely to last." On the issue of bombing cities in North Viet-Nam, a majority (57%) agreed in saying that it "helped bring about the peace agreement." Yet, if North Viet-Nam were to try to "take over South Vietnam again . . . in the next few years after U.S. troops are withdrawn," only 17% said the U.S. should again bomb North Viet-Nam (71% said it should not do so).

Dr. Henry Kissinger's 1973 trip to the People's Republic of China, which resulted in an agreement calling for the exchange of official liaison offices was widely and warmly praised. Editors saw the agreement as a significant step toward the ultimate goal of full diplomatic relations and expected it to serve many useful purposes in the meantime. Some expressed surprise at the "miraculous pace" of the thawing process (Phila. Bulletin). The editors showered praise upon both Dr. Kissinger and Pres. Nixon. According to the Harris Survey, 65% gave positive ratings to the President on his "handling of relations with China;" 27% gave negative ratings (8% "not sure"). The President's efforts at building up the structure of peace and stability, said the Louisville Courier-Journal, might well earn him "a comfortable place in history." Many were concerned that the issue of Taiwan remained as an obstacle to a formal Sino-American relationship. Withdrawal of U.S. troops from Taiwan was urged by the Denver Post in order to reassure Peking that the U.S. looks forward to a peaceful settlement of the issue. A few cautioned against jilting a friend and ally (Chi. Tribune, N.Y. News).[28]

Happy as Americans were that our POWs and our soldiers had returned from Viet-Nam, and that U.S. ground combat there was over, they were nevertheless concerned about questions relating to the cease-fire and settlement. Two prominent issues were: the continued bombing over Cambodia; and reconstruction aid for Indochina. Public opinion polls showed popular sentiment opposed to both the bombing and the aid. But the editors hadn't given up their view that aiding North Viet-Nam could be of help to the U.S. and to the peace.[29]

On the bombing, a Harris Survey question explained that the U.S. was using B-52 bombers in Cambodia "because it is felt the peace in Vietnam is threatened," but a plurality expressed disapproval (49% to 33%). A Gallup Poll found greater disapproval (57% to 29%); and Gallup reported that 59% thought the bombing in Cambodia and Laos would "lead to our getting involved in Southeast Asia again with U.S. troops." On these two Gallup questions there was a sizable difference between the replies of Republicans and Democrats; but there was little partisan difference on a third Gallup question: "Do you think further military action in Southeast Asia should require a vote of approval by Congress, or not?" As many as 76% said Congressional approval should be required; only 13% said it should not be.[30]

In January American editors had upheld aid to Indochina, including Hanoi, as a legitimate part of the peace package; but the continuance of the fighting in Viet-Nam created unhappiness; and anger against the North Vietnamese was heightened by reports from returning POWs about their torture. Still, there didn't appear to be any rush of editors to reverse their earlier support for aid to Hanoi. The general public maintained its oppositon to aid. The Harris Survey reported 70% against aid to Hanoi in February–71% in March. Harris also found a switch from approval to disapproval on aid for rebuilding South Viet-Nam: 46% approval in February, 52% disapproval in March. The most frequently given argument against aiding Hanoi was the popular preference for "spending on social programs here at home."[31]

On June 13 in Paris the parties to the Viet-Nam agreement signed a second pact in hope that clarification of the political terms in the original peace agreement would result in a more genuine cessation of firing; but a majority of American editors were skeptical about its success because they saw the new accord as "essentially a retread of the Jan. 27 Paris Pact with all the weaknesses of that much-abused document" (N.Y. Times). According to the Cincinnati Enquirer, the "possibly fatal flaw" lay in the limitations upon the ability of Messrs. Kissinger and Tho "to force those terms upon the NLF and Saigon." Those who were guardedly optimistic about the new pact (about a third of those commenting) said the agreement might "stick" this time because the Vietnamese people "surely must suspect by now that 25 years of war are enough" (Miami Herald).[32]

Several editors discussing Dr. Kissinger's assertion of the U.S. right to go on bombing Cambodia, expressed the hope that Congress would delete the funds for this activity. In fact, continued bombing was opposed by 30 out of 33 commenting papers; they felt that massive bombing of civilians could not have a significant effect on actions by North Viet-Nam or Cambodia. Editors agreed that, in view of Congressional aversion, "economic aid to North Viet-Nam is an impossible dream" (Chi. Sun-Times, Hearst papers).[33]

Devaluation of the dollar on Feb. 12, and announcement of the Nixon Administration's trade legislation plans, were welcomed by editors as recognitions of economic realities. A number compared favorably Sec. Shultz's consultations with other governments, with the more unilateral moves which preceded the Smithsonian meeting of 1971 (e.g., Wash. Post, Los Angeles Times). Feeling that the 1973 gains from devaluation could prove inflationary, editors generally agreed that the U.S. must push ahead with its monetary and trade negotiations for more permanent arrangements for currency parity. The Nixon Administration's activity on the trade policy front was also welcomed, even though it was asking for legislation permitting a raising of tariffs (including quotas and surcharges), as well as lowering them (e.g., Chi. News, Hearst papers).[34]

In early 1973 both economic and political problems contributed to increased editorial attention to Europe. The scheduling of talks on troop reductions and SALT, as well as the expansion of the Common Market from six to nine members on New Year's Day, were among the developments which led editors to talk about 1973 as possibly "the year of Europe." As the Conference on Security and Cooperation in Europe opened at Helsinki (Jan. 15), American editors increasingly spoke of the importance of action there to improve the flow of people and ideas across European borders and particularly the Iron Curtain. Several were encouraged by Romania's "procedural protest" at Helsinki to "let the big powers know that the medium and small nations of Europe are going to be heard from" (e.g., Balt. Sun). The New York Times saw a possibility that the West might be able "to exact some lifting of Soviet-bloc barriers in return for the pledges of expanded trade and economic cooperation Moscow seeks." According to the Los Angeles Times, the "ultimate question is whether a security conference would be used, as Moscow wishes, to sanctify the division of Europe, or whether it will be used, as the West insists, to ease those divisions."[35]

In April Dr. Kissinger suggested a new Atlantic Charter to meet the circumstances of the 1970s. This idea, and related passages of

Pres. Nixon's State of the World message (May 3), were hailed by the press as timely. All did favor earnest efforts to improve our relations with the NATO nations and Japan. Most of these editors put themselves on record in favor of the President's proposals for trade reform (37 out of 38 commenting). Many acknowledged concern over the sweeping executive powers incorporated into the Trade Reform Bill, but conceded their necessity if the U.S. were to participate effectively in the negotiations scheduled to start in Tokyo in the autumn. Some said the trade proposals delivered the same policy message as Dr. Kissinger had, but in "much more substantial terms" (e.g., Wash. Post). As usual, some editors mentioned a need for NATO members to assume a much larger share of the burden of financing the military defense of Europe (e.g., Scripps-Howard and Hearst papers), and thus relieve our balance-of-payments deficit.[36]

Summit in the U.S.

Shortly before the Nixon-Brezhnev summit in the U.S. (June 18–25) the Gallup Poll reported that this was a time when Americans "are more favorably disposed toward the Soviet Union than at any time since World War II." Even in 1973, as the accompanying table indicates, only one-third of the general public actually held a "favorable" view of the Soviet Union; but Dr. Gallup declared that the "change in the public's attitude during the past two decades–especially since the McCarthy period–is unparallelled in the annals of public opinion polling." The April poll also found significant differences in attitude associated with both age and education.

	Favorable to USSR	(Highly Favorable)	Unfavorable to USSR	(Highly Unfavorable)
1954	5%	(1%)	88%	(75%)
1967	17	(2)	–	–
1973	34	(21)	57	(30)

Among respondents between 18 and 29, as many as 45% held favorable opinions of the USSR. A clear majority of college-educated respondents (51%) held favorable attitudes toward the Soviet Union, those with high-school backgrounds were 32% favorable, and those who had attended only grammar school were 27% favorable.

After the conclusion of Secretary Brezhnev's visit to the U.S. virtually all commentators felt that some worthwhile gains had been realized at the summit, even though a majority suspended judgment until pending negotiations had been concluded–especially on SALT and troop reductions. Only 4 out of 41 commenting papers emphasized their skepticism about the worth of the 1973 summit, and even these papers acknowledged at least temporary improvement in the relations of the superpowers (Hearst papers, Dallas News, N.Y. News).[37]

One journal frequently critical of the Administration voiced the views of many when it said: "The President deserves credit for helping change the stultifying U.S. posture toward the Soviet Union" and the "progress of last year at Moscow has now been consolidated" (St. Louis Post-Dispatch). The President's summit partner was also applauded for his position. The "surprise" Soviet-American agreement on seeking to avert nuclear war was called "toothless" by some; but some others felt it could contribute to a "climate of peace" (Phila. Bulletin). The majority held that actual progress on SALT, and on troop reductions, would be the real tests of the summit.

Editors lauding the benefits of the summit meeting often stressed the prospect of increased Soviet-American trade, and linked the outlook for detente directly to our "becoming economic partners." According to the Chicago Tribune, "if Mr. Brezhnev was conciliatory, it was because he needed to be so in order to acquire what his country badly needs from the U.S." Referring to reports that the U.S. might obtain oil and gas from the Soviet Union, the Wall St. Journal wondered "Whether U.S. money and resources could be more wisely employed to develop clean and efficient ways to use the vast American reserves of coal." The Milwaukee Journal commented that the grain agreement with Russia had been "underwritten by the American taxpayer in subsidies and higher food prices." That stalwart supporter of liberal trade policies, the Baltimore Sun, nevertheless declared: "There are good reasons for skepticism about the theory that the road to better relations among nations is paved with fat contracts and growing trade accounts."[38]

Panama

The UN Security Council meeting in Panama in March received considerable press attention; and the U.S. policy concerning Panama and the Canal was upheld by the great majority of editors (26 out of 31). Most commentators conceded that Panama had justifiable grievances; but almost all said that a UN meeting in Panama was no way to settle them. Amb. Scali's casting of the third U.S. veto in UN history, against 13 favorable votes in the Security Council (and Britain's abstention), attracted more attention in the headlines than in the editorials. Those mentioning the veto usually approved it–whether heartily (Indianapolis Star) or reluctantly (Kansas City Star, Prov. Journal).[39]

Treaty changes acceptable to the editors included dropping of the "perpetuity" provision, reduction in the area of the Canal Zone, and an increase in the annual payment to Panama; but a number seriously questioned whether the Panamanian Government could operate the Canal securely and efficiently. A minority of editors held that the Canal is "vital" to the U.S. (N.Y. News, Dallas News), but Newsday said the time was long since past when the Panama Canal could be regarded as "vital to national security and prosperity." Two journals held that the U.S. should work "toward some form of international control of the Zone and the Canal" (Des Moines Register, St. Louis Post-Dispatch). Most editors believed that the U.S. had been negotiating fairly with a military strongman who had sought to compel U.S. acquiescence to Panamanian demands by arranging the UN Security Council meeting in Panama. Afterward most editors said it was "time the two nations went ahead with the delicate and complex negotiations" for a fair and workable treaty.

Attitudes Toward Wars

Although Americans were enjoying the prospects of an era of negotiation, rather than confrontation, much interest persisted in the attitude of the public toward the use of military force in U.S. foreign relations. Polling by the Gallup Organization for the Institute for International Social Research demonstrated the capacity of the American public to exercise discrimination in judgments about America's various engagements in warfare. In 1973, 61% said that participation in World War I was a "good thing," and 78% gave that judgment on World War II (only 13% said it "would have been better if we had managed to stay out"). But a plurality (49%) felt that we should have stayed out of the Korean War, and as many as 68% felt that way about the war in Viet-Nam. When asked about a future war, "if necessary to help defend Western Europe," 41% said the U.S. should go to war; 43% said No. This result shows some decline from the preceding year in willingness to use force; then 52% favored defense of our allies "if attacked by Soviet Russia."[40]

Another Gallup Poll (commissioned by the European Community Information Service) reported that respondents who had "not heard or read anything about the European Community or the Common Market as it's called" (this group amounted to 55% of the total sample) were more inclined to give a negative reply on helping to defend Western Europe. American editors continued to support the U.S. policy of opposing unilateral withdrawal of U.S. troops from Europe.[41]

Summary

These years of 1972 and 1973 were regarded as promising by Americans who welcomed detente with Peking and Moscow, without believing that the Cold War was necessarily over. Congressional efforts to re-take from the President some of the war-making power were upheld by editors in this "Watergate" period. There was great relief over the return from Viet-Nam of POWs and U.S. fighting men; but the public still regarded some wars as worthwhile (World Wars I and II). Most editors backed Administration proposals for a new treaty with Panama; but polls were not available.

Reference Notes

1. AOR of Feb. 3, 1972.
2. AOR of Feb. 18, 1972.
3. AOR of Jan. 28, 1972.
4. AOR for Feb. and Feb. 11, 1972.
5. AOR of Mar. 10, 1972.
6. AOR for March 1972.
7. AOR for April 1972.
8. AOR for May 12 and 16, 1972.
9. Watts, Wm. and Lloyd Free, *State of the Nation* (New York, 1973), pp. 203–4.
10. Ibid., pp. 217, 281.
11. AOR for March 1972.
12. AOR for June 1972.
13. AOR for July–Aug. 1972.
14. AOR for Sept.–Oct. 1972.
15. AOR for July and Aug. 1972.
16. AOR for Oct. 18 and 27 and Nov. 1972.
17. AOR for Nov. 1972.
18. Ibid.
19. AOR for July–Aug. 1972.
20. Ibid.
21. AOR for Sept.–Oct. 1972.
22. AOR for Dec. 1972.
23. Ibid.
24. Ibid.
25. AOR for Nov. 1972.
26. AOR for Jan. and Jan. 24, 1973.
27. AOR for Feb. 1973.
28. AOR for Mar.–Apr. 1973.
29. AOR for May 1973.
30. Ibid.
31. Ibid.
32. AOR for June 1973.
33. Ibid.
34. AOR for Feb. 1973.
35. AOR for Jan. 1973.
36. AOR for May 1973.
37. AOR for June and July 1973.
38. Ibid.
39. AOR for Mar.–Apr. 1973.
40. Address by Institute President Lloyd Free before American Association for Public Opinion Research, cited in AOR for July 1973.
41. AOR for July and Aug.–Sept. 1973.

XVIII
KISSINGER BECOMES SECRETARY OF STATE (1973–1975)

Pres. Nixon's appointment as Secretary of State of his long-time White House aide, Dr. Henry A. Kissinger, in August 1973, elicited many editorials praising Kissinger as eminently qualified for his new post. The editors emphasized the Secretary-Designate's "proved brilliance as diplomat and negotiator" (N.Y. Post). Sometimes referring to the rising criticism of the Nixon Administration, editors underlined the challenge of restoring morale at Foggy Bottom and expressed the hope that Dr. Kissinger's presence would help "rejuvenate the State Department by returning it to its foreign-policy-making role" (Minneapolis Star). Some said it made "good sense" to bring the State Department and the National Security Council under one manager (Milwaukee Journal); others feared the potential conflict with Congress if Dr. Kissinger remained "protected by executive privilege." Most welcomed Dr. Kissinger's promise of "national rather than partisan policy, greater congressional partnership, and public scrutiny" (Balt. Sun). Some were concerned about Kissinger's role in the secret bombing of Cambodia and the wire-tapping of his own assistants (e.g., Denver Post, Detroit Free Press); others wondered about his administrative capacity. But the Los Angeles Times did not wish to see Kissinger "mired in the necessary but essentially secondary managerial chores of the Secretary," saying; "He is too valuable as a conceptualizer and articulator of policy for that."[1]

The next two years would see the new Secretary confronted with: a new war in the Middle East, some problems related to the continuing fighting in Viet-Nam, taking Pres. Ford to the Vladivostok summit, plus newly urgent problems related to energy, food, and human rights.

Dr. Kissinger's first address as Secretary of State was delivered before the UNGA on Sept. 24; it was applauded by editors both "conservative" and "liberal" (Hearst papers, Wash. Post). These papers supported the Secretary's attitude toward the UN; and several supported Kissinger's concrete suggestions on peace-keeping and a world food conference. News that the 1973 Nobel Peace Prize had been awarded jointly to Henry A. Kissinger and Le Duc Tho caused considerable surprise and no little difference of opinion. The New York Times said the award was "at very least, premature;" but a majority of commenting editors felt that the prize was "richly merited" by Dr. Kissinger's patient and resourceful negotiations with Le Duc Tho.[2]

At this time considerable discussion was stirred by the Jackson amendment to the administration's trade bill, which made "most-favored-nation" trade treatment for the Soviet Union contingent upon Moscow's granting freer emigration to its citizens. Half of the 30 newspapers commenting opposed the amendment, fearing that the spirit of detente, "so carefully constructed" by the President and Secretary, would be destroyed. Many editors expressed humanitarian concern for the plight of Soviet citizens, but deemed it inappropriate for the Congress to legislate on the internal affairs of another country. The Hearst papers feared that insistent interference in Soviet internal affairs could "wreck detente altogether." The Louisville Courier-Journal agreed with Kissinger who "argued eloquently that quiet diplomacy, rather than trying to force the Soviet leaders to heed an ultimatum, is the only way to get the job done." Five (out of the 30) papers specifically supported the Jackson amendment as "worth a try" in the quest for human rights (Des Moines Register, Minneapolis Star). Several papers refrained from taking a stand on the issue of the Jackson amendment.[3]

1973 War

Renewal of the warfare between Egypt-Syria and Israel took American commentators by surprise; so did the military gains of the Egyptians east of the Suez Canal. Editors promptly supported the U.S. position favoring termination of the hostilities, even though some felt that a stand-still truce should not take effect until the Israelis had a chance to recoup, or balance, their initial military losses. A prompt Gallup Poll (taken Oct. 6–8) found that, as in earlier years, there was much greater sympathy for Israel than for the Arab states. But, also as before, a large part of the public refrained from voicing sympathy for either of the contesting sides. In 1973 a total of 53% expressed no sympathy (20% saying "neither side," 23% giving no opinion, 10% hadn't "heard of the trouble" in the Mideast). Among the "sympathizing" minority, 42% sided with Israel (up from 38% in 1970), and 5% with the Arabs (up from 3%). Dr. Gallup reported that the "dominant mood of the public is clearly that the U.S. should not get involved in the struggle in terms of sending American forces."[4]

As heavy fighting continued in the Mideast it became apparent that the Soviet Union was replacing Arab losses of ammunition and military equipment by means of air convoys. Israel then requested that the U.S. make replacements available to her. The positive U.S. response was strongly backed editorially. "Every effort short of committing our own troops," said the approving Chicago Tribune (also Phila. Inquirer). Less committed to the Israeli cause, but approving the re-supply policy, the Christian Science Monitor observed: "The issue is not the survival of Israel (which is not in question) but only the spoils of the 1967 war." Although polls in earlier years had shown a margin of opposition to sending military supplies to Israel, under the actual circumstances of 1973 a plurality (46% to 34%) did say the "U.S. was right in sending planes and other military supplies to Israel." As many as 63% said, in response to another Harris question, that Sec. Kissinger was "right to send arms to Israel and then get together with the Russians to work out a cease-fire." But a larger number of respondents registered approval of the U.S. for *not* sending American troops to the Mideast "even if Israel were threatened by Russian armed force" (68% to 14%). And 67% upheld the proposition, "We should not become overcommitted to Israel, or we could find ourselves in another Viet-Nam, and that would be wrong," according to Harris.[5]

Sec. Kissinger's achievement of U.S.-Soviet agreement on a cease-fire resolution in the UN Security Council during his surprise trip to Moscow (Oct. 20) was hailed with great relief and appreciation. In fact, the largest single bloc of opinion uncovered by a dozen Harris Survey questions on the Mideast was the 79% who approved the "Russian-U.S.-sponsored cease-fire order." But almost at once there were reports that the truce was not holding, and Sec. Kissinger told a news conference that the U.S. had issued a world-wide military alert; and he now hoped the USSR would concur in backing a UN resolution calling for observation forces to ensure execution of the cease-fire terms. This was upheld in editorial comment; and most editors felt that the nation should give the Administration a "minimum of confidence" pending disclosure of the background facts concerning the Soviet "threat" respecting the Mideast. A Harris Survey reported that a plurality (49%) felt that the President had *not exaggerated* the "threat of sending troops to the Middle East . . . in order to divert public attention from his troubles at home over Watergate and the tapes" (31% said the President did "exaggerate").[6]

The threat by the oil-producing Arab states to reduce exports of petroleum to countries supporting Israel found most editors saying the U.S. should "never submit to oil blackmail" (e.g., Los Angeles Times, Wall St. Journal). Some editors did point out that American re-supply of Israel could "worsen the problems for American oil companies" (e.g., Balt. Sun). Popular antipathy of "oil blackmail" was shown by the responses to two Harris Survey propositions. Fifty percent disagreed with this proposition, "We need Arab oil for our gasoline shortage here at home, so we had better find a way to get along with the Arabs, even if that means supporting Israel less" (26% agreed with this argument). A majority (58%) agreed with this statement, "If we yield to Arab restrictions over oil now, we will soon find the Arabs dictating much of U.S. foreign policy and that is wrong" (20% disagreed). Also, nearly half (49%) rejected the Arab claim that they were "justified in fighting this war to try to get back the territory Israel has occupied since 1967" (24% did agree with this Harris proposition).[7]

Disagreements among NATO members during the Mideast and oil crisis had given the alliance a severe blow, editors agreed; and several said that the Year of Europe had become a casualty of the Mideast war. Editors were confident that NATO would recover; but a number felt that Europe's "growing dependence on Middle East oil" had become one of the big factors in the "widening gap" among NATO members. Others felt that the Mideast crisis merely furthered the strain of an alliance "already ruffled by trade differences and recurring monetary crises" (Milwaukee Journal). The editors were divided about placing the blame for the rift on either Europe or the U.S. One group stressed Europe's "dangerously unrealistic" neutral or anti-U.S. stance during the "U.S.-Soviet confrontation that Pres. Nixon described with evident accuracy as the most serious since the Cuban missile crisis" (Oakland Tribune). The Scripps-Howard papers were dismayed that our allies "were unwilling to run the risk to assist U.S. policy," and said that the State Department should tell them that a lasting alliance cannot be a one-way street, and should point out that U.S. efforts in the Mideast were in Europe's interest, too.[8]

Those who found the U.S. basically at fault stressed the U.S. failure to consult with the European allies during the conflict, particularly because the Europeans "now rival this country in political and economic strength" (Minneapolis Star). According to the Chicago News, "Europe's heavy stake in the Middle East, and particularly its oil, entitled them to full information and consultation." Journals in both groups were unhappy about the rift in the alliance. "Any split in Western solidarity," said the Salt Lake City Tribune, "is sure to be exploited by the Kremlin." The St. Louis Globe-Democrat said: "The Western powers must heal their breach for a solid front against communist attempts to negotiate an overwhelming military advantage in Central Europe."

On Pres. Nixon's foreign policy actions, a Harris Survey (released Nov. 12) showed an increase in popular approval of Mideast actions (49% approval, as against a rating in the summer of 47% negative), but some slippage respecting other areas. A majority (58%) still approved the President on "working for peace in the world," but this figure had stood at 71% at the time the POWs were returning from Viet-Nam, and at 68% in midsummer of 1973. Also, a majority continued to approve the handling of relations with Russia, but this figure had dropped from 65% to 55%. These majority approvals on foreign policy stood in contrast to the President's over-all rating of

64% negative—with particularly low ratings on "keeping down the cost of living" and "handling of Watergate." In December the Harris Survey reported that after the Mideast crisis the President's rating on "working for peace in the world" shot up again from 58% to 70% between October and November.[9]

War Powers

On Nov. 7 Congress overrode Pres. Nixon's veto of the war power act; and the Congressional position was upheld by 69% of a representative sample of newspapers (24 out of 35), and also received support from the general public in a Gallup Poll. All the editors felt that the President must have power to dispatch troops abroad in emergencies; and the great majority—including the Hearst and Scripps-Howard chains—felt that this emergency power was preserved by the current legislation which made it possible for the President to use armed forces as long as 60 days (90 days in some cases) to meet emergencies. Most editors conceded that the new law did not ensure the nation against future wars, but they were pleased that it did compel the sharing of the war power between the Executive and Legislative branches. "Reassertion of Congressional authority was long overdue," said the Hearst editorial. Some critics stressed the role of "Watergate" in Congress' decision; but most felt that Congressmen had voted on the merits of the legislation. According to the Gallup Poll, 80% of a national sample agreed that "the President should be required to get the approval of Congress before sending U.S. armed forces into action outside the U.S." (only 16% disapproved). At the same time, Gallup reported that a majority (58%) opposed the idea that, "in order to declare war, Congress be required to obtain the approval of the people by means of a national vote."[10]

In December the Harris Survey reported a striking testimonial to public trust in Sec. Kissinger. Having found that 57% approved Pres. Nixon's appointment of Gerald Ford as Vice President, the Survey offered this proposition, "Ford has had no real experience in foreign affairs, and it would be too risky to trust our foreign policy to him." The result was a stand-off: 37% agreed, 37% disagreed (26% were not sure). Harris then posed this question: "If he (Ford) kept Henry Kissinger as Secretary of State, Ford could handle foreign relations," to which 67% of the nationwide sample agreed, while 10% disagreed, and 23% were "not sure."[11]

In December Sec. Kissinger attended a Brussels NATO meeting and stopped off in London to address the Pilgrims, proposing an international attack on the energy problem. The address was prominently reported in the American press and TV; and most editors voiced positive approval of international action to meet the energy shortage, although some had doubts about obtaining quick results. Several approved the Secretary's warning that go-it-alone national efforts could result in a world depression. Amid speculation about retaliatory action against the Arab nations for their oil embargo against us, only 4 out of 29 newspapers mentioned retaliation as a possibility and none asked for it. Oil price increases in Iran, Venezuela, and Canada—together with modifications of the original Arab embargo—led to editorial emphasis on the broad issue of the energy shortage, rather than on Arab actions. Some underscored Sec. Kissinger's efforts to harmonize the need of oil-producing and oil-consuming states (e.g., C.S. Monitor, N.Y. Times).[12]

1974 Attitudes

The Harris poll on public confidence in various leadership groups indicated that Americans were starting out in 1974 with greater confidence in most institutions than was the case a year earlier. One stark exception to this trend was the Executive Branch of the Federal Government; those expressing "a great deal of confidence" in the Executive declined during this "Watergate" period from 27% to 19%. But confidence in the press had risen (from 18% to 30% expressing a great deal of confidence), also in the Senate (from 21% to 30%), and in the Military (from 35% to 40%). Confidence was high in Television News (41%); and 65% of the national sample said they "depended a great deal" on this medium "to find out what is going on in Government and Politics." Newspapers were in second place (52% "depending" on them); but among the college-educated, dependence upon newspapers (56%) was almost as great as upon television news (58%).[13]

As to the international outlook for 1974, Messrs. Gallup and Harris differed in their emphases. Dr. Gallup stressed that "the gloomy economic outlook of Americans is matched by their pessimism regarding the prospects for peace in the world." Gallup found a solid majority (65%) predicting "a troubled year with much international discord." Half of the Gallup sample (50%) said that 1974 would be a year when "American power will decline," and a majority (55%) said it would be a year when "Russia will increase her power in the world." But Mr. Harris warned political aspirants that they could be making a "blunder" if they concluded that the "country wants to return to a hard line in relations with the Soviet Union" because of the strains in relations arising over the wheat deal, Jewish immigration, and the Mideast war. Harris emphasized that 69% of Americans thought it "possible for the U.S. and Russia to reach long-term agreements to help keep the peace." Harris added that majorities ranging from 72% to 91% favored accords on specific topics (e.g., troop reductions in Europe, settlement of Mideast war). He noted also that, despite widespread "dissatisfaction" with the Russian wheat deal, 72% still wanted to see "expanded U.S.-Soviet trade."[14]

Dr. Lloyd Free, in another of his periodic assessments of American opinion on foreign policy, reported on the basis of January 1974 polling a further decline in internationalist sentiment—also some gain in isolationist feeling. The following table based upon four polls during the decade, 1964–74, shows both the erosion of internationalism and an apparent gain in "isolationism."

	1964	**1968**	**1972**	**1974**
Completely internationalist	30%	25%	18%	11%
Predominantly internationalist	35	34	38	30
Mixed	27	32	35	38
Predominantly isolationist	5	6	5	14
Completely isolationist	3	3	4	7
	100%	100%	100%	100%

Dr. Free used a battery of five questions as the basis for his analysis and characterization. To qualify as "completely isolationist" a respondent had to oppose two propositions: "The U.S. should cooperate fully with the United Nations;" "The U.S. should take into account the views of its allies in deciding on its foreign policies;" and should agree that "We should go our own way in international matters, not worrying too much about whether other countries agree with us;" and "mind our own business," and "concentrate more on our national problems." Opposite answers on the part of a respondent marked him as "completely internationalist."[15]

Since two of the five polling questions used as the basis for classifying respondents dealt with attitudes toward our allies, it may be that the uncooperativeness of our allies, as perceived in late 1973 and early 1974, contributed disproportionately to the reported rise in "isolationism." Dr. Free's 1974 figures did show a further decline since 1972 in willingness to fulfill our defense commitments. Those willing to defend Western Europe from communist attacks dropped from 52% to 48%, and those willing to defend Japan fell from 43% to 37%. Dr. Free reported that the "rise in isolationism" was evident "in all demographic groups . . . but especially pronounced in certain ones: people with only a grade-school education (from 20% to 35%), families with income below $10,000 a year (from 14% to 31%, and respondents in the 30–49 age bracket (from 8% to 24%). These groups, it may be noted, are precisely those which have been least apt to engage in vigorous discussion and advocacy of foreign policy alternatives and to exert leadership in this field," Dr. Free concluded.[16]

The signing of the Egyptian-Israeli agreement on disengagement of forces in Egypt and on the Sinai front was promptly hailed by leading newspapers all across the country. The role of Sec. Kissinger in bringing about this agreement, through his "shuttling" between Jerusalem and Aswan, was also universally extolled. The Detroit Free Press declared: "Sec. Kissinger once again emerges as the master diplomat, the most skilled crisis negotiator of his time; but it remains for the Arabs and Israelis to give meaning to those (carefully drafted) phrases." The process of disengagement did in fact proceed.[17]

A changed policy toward Cuba was urged by a majority of sampled newspapers (18 out of 24). Comment was quickened when a Cuban official indicated that Cuba would be willing to begin talks with Washington if the U.S. lifted its economic blockade of Cuba. Gallup and Harris polls had earlier reported public interest in bettering U.S. relations with Cuba. Most of the commenting editors advocated normalization of relations with Cuba, and a number specifically called for an end to the U.S. trade embargo. Several maintained that Castro's threat in Latin America had "diminished considerably;" and the Hearst papers declared: "Cuba is no longer a threat; it is a potential customer." Some editors thought it logical that the process of moving toward detente with the Soviet Union and China should include Cuba; and some feared that the increasing friendliness of Latin American nations toward Cuba could estrange the U.S. from its neighbors. The Harris Survey in March 1973 had found a majority (51%) favoring U.S. "diplomatic relations with Cuba" (33% were opposed, 16% "not sure"). In April there was an even larger wave of editorials favoring detente with Cuba.[18]

In the autumn of 1973 reports from Chile of "mass killings" and "book-burnings" under the military junta prompted considerable editorial discussion, with most newspapers (19 out of 21) urging that the U.S. refrain from extending economic aid until the new regime demonstrated that it wasn't anti-democratic. Several specifically backed the Senate resolution to this effect. Diplomatic recognition, however, was approved because it represented the "factual situation."[19]

Panama; IDA

Signature at Panama (Feb. 7) of a Statement of Principles for a new treaty with the U.S. elicited a favorable response from most commenting editors (27 out of 36 papers). This majority agreed with Sec.

Kissinger when he indicated the U.S. recognized that the time for a new approach to a canal treaty was overdue. At the same time, these editors agreed that the new treaty must preserve all rights necessary to operate and defend the canal. They tended to share the Denver Post's conviction that a new treaty could "fulfill Panama's nationalistic aspirations while at the same time safeguarding whatever security interests the U.S. still considers vital." The Wall St. Journal declared: "The current treaty has become a political anachronism." The Des Moines Register was unusual in expressing its preference that the Panama Canal be under "international control."[20]

Four papers (out of the 36) rejected the idea of yielding U.S. sovereignty over the Canal (Hearst, Indianapolis Star, Richmond Times-Dispatch, St. Louis Globe-Democrat). The Hearst editorial contended that it would be "foolhardy indeed to relinquish even part of our dominion over the Panama Canal to the present unsteady and hostile government" at a time when Russia is expanding its military influence. An additional five papers were very dubious that adequate U.S. control could be maintained in a new treaty under the new "statement of principles" (e.g., N.Y. News, Pittsburgh Post-Gazette).

The Washington Energy Conference (Feb. 11–13), despite the largely negative role of France, was adjudged by editors as offering a promising start on the international effort to deal with the world energy crisis. The Chicago Tribune called this meeting of oil-consuming nations "a diplomatic triumph for the U.S.," and the Washington Post said it might "mark the renewal of the Atlantic alliance under American leadership." Editors agreed with the New York Times that work could now "begin on international programs to conserve energy resources and restrain demand." About half of the editors, however, suspended judgment concerning conference accomplishments, waiting to see the implementation of the adopted plans.[21]

When the House of Representatives voted down the $1.5 billion authorization bill for the International Development Association (Jan. 23) editors across the country spoke out in disapproval. In fact, only 2 out of 23 commenting papers failed to express disapproval (N.Y. News, Pittsburgh Post-Gazette). Editors usually noted that the U.S. had succeeded in gaining the approval of 24 other IDA sponsors for a reduction in the U.S. contribution of funds for this "soft loan window" of the World Bank. They often added that it was the poorest countries of the world which would be hardest hit by a termination of IDA loans; they called upon Congress to reverse the action.[22]

Viet-Nam

On the anniversary of the Viet-Nam cease-fire agreement many editors reviewed that agreement and discussed future policy. Although regretting the heavy casualties in the continuing fighting, all the editors were grateful that no more G.I.s were fighting and that our POWs had returned. Some newspapers were additionally gratified that the South Vietnamese had "at least held their own." Citing the continued freedom of Indonesia, Malaysia, and Thailand, the Wall St. Journal said some future historian might record that the U.S. had "fought with a high purpose . . . to stem a massive flow of cruel and intolerant zealotry that threatened to engulf the world." But the editors were about evenly divided as to the wisdom of continuing American military aid to Saigon. Opponents cited refusal of the Thieu government to hold scheduled elections and charged it with keeping 100,000 persons as political prisoners. Supporters of the U.S. policy of aiding Thieu argued that Saigon was less to blame for current conditions than Hanoi was. The Scripps-Howard editorial said: "Thanks to U.S. money and battlefield sacrifices, which bought time, South Viet-Nam has a well-equipped, million-man army."[23]

As time went on, more newspapers came out in favor of reducing U.S. aid to Saigon than maintaining the level of aid for that area. Critical of keeping the war going on Thieu's terms, the aid "cutters" said that "American dollars are as doomed to fail at settling the fighting and assuring freedom as were our hundreds of thousands of troops" (Chi. News). (Incidentally, most of the aid "cutters"–13 out of 15–were in favor of the Administration-sponsored U.S. contribution to IDA, whereas less than half of the Saigon aid supporters backed the IDA.) As noted earlier, polls in 1973 had shown a majority opposed to both military and reconstruction aid to South Viet-Nam. The poll taken for Potomac Associates in April 1974 showed 49% against "continuing to provide military equipment and supplies to the government of South Viet-Nam to help it combat the communist forces," and only 40% in favor.[24]

Relatively few American newspapers commented on the U.S. plan to expand the U.S. communications station on the British island of Diego Garcia in the Indian Ocean; but over half of these papers counseled delaying–rather than going ahead with–the plan to deepen the harbor and extend the airplane runways (10 papers for delay, 6 for going ahead, 2 non-committal). All the commenting papers noted the increasing Soviet presence in the Indian Ocean and the likelihood that this presence would increase further after reopening of the Suez Canal. The minority desirous of going ahead wanted to protect oil shipping and to prevent the Indian Ocean from becoming a "Russian lake" (e.g., Wash. Star-News, Hearst papers). The majority, however, were concerned about a big-power arms race in the area and didn't want the U.S. to be responsible for escalating it. Hardly any papers expressed absolute opposition to expanding the Diego Garcia station; and the Scripps-Howard editorial suggested that the U.S. wait to see "if Soviet vessels really come pouring through Suez; if they do, the nations in the area . . . will welcome rather than resent a bigger U.S. naval presence."[25]

Interdependence

In the considerable editorial discussion of relations with Europe, before and after the Common Market decision to hold broad discussions with the Arab nations, some editors sympathized with Sec. Kissinger's feelings of disappointment and frustration; but most editors disapproved the sharp tone of American public remarks, including Pres. Nixon's reminder (in his Chicago speech) to our NATO colleagues that an alliance is a "two-way street." The failure of some allies to facilitate U.S. efforts in 1973 to re-supply Israel may have contributed to a decline in the proportion saying, in a January 1974 poll by Potomac Associates, "the U.S. should take into account the views of its major allies"–from 80% in 1972 to 69% in 1974. Of course, 69% was still a sizable majority of Americans who wanted the U.S. to consider allied views "in deciding on its foreign policies."[26]

All editors welcomed the moderation which presently appeared on both sides of the Atlantic–at the time of Britain's pledge of cooperation with the U.S., Bonn's agreement to offset substantially the U.S. payments deficit, and Pres. Nixon's "softened" remarks at Houston. Most editors hoped that future American language would be less "abrasive;" but a minority approved the "shock treatment" by U.S. officials seeking fuller transatlantic cooperation. The papers criticizing the Administration's performance did not insist on a new "Charter" or on "showy summits;" rather they wished for a "constructive dialogue" to reach practical decisions.[27]

Editors applauded Sec. Kissinger's April 15 address to the special session of the UNGA, in which he stressed global interdependence, and outlined a 6-point program for cooperative development of the world's natural resources. Several papers, however, warned that a willingness to cooperate among the world's nations was unlikely "to be achieved very soon" (Chi. News). Some editors stressed Kissinger's warning against cartels of producers of scarce raw materials, although the Cleveland Plain Dealer added that his "conciliatory plea for cooperation" might not win over the most militant Third World nations. The Secretary's constructive goals were seen by some as challenged by a U.S. Congress "which fails to grasp his message" (Los Angeles Times). The final UN declaration was regarded as disappointing, owing more to the "LDC steamroller" than to the Secretary's "practical response" (N.Y. Journal of Commerce).[28]

When the Administration proposed to Congress (Apr. 24) a single package of economic and military assistance, chief editorial attention was given to the newest item—inclusion of $250 million of economic aid for Egypt. This was approved by all commenting editors as "sensible U.S. aid for Mideast peace" (Newsday). The importance of development aid was mentioned by about half of the editors, and one journal wondered if the total amount requested might not be too little (Los Angeles Times). A careful and comprehensive polling survey, sponsored by the Overseas Development Council, reported that over the past decade and a half popular approval for "giving assistance to underdeveloped countries" had risen appreciably. The survey said approval had increased from 51% in 1958 to 58% in 1966, and reached a "historic high" of 68% in October 1972—16% strongly in favor, 52% somewhat in favor. Only 28% were opposed (8% strongly opposed). Respondents most often gave moral or humanitarian reasons for their approval, and gave greatest support to "direct visible programs aimed at alleviating such basic problems" as hunger, disease, and illiteracy. As to the size of the program, a plurality (49%) favored maintenance (or an increase) of economic aid; whereas a majority (52%) would reduce military aid. At the same time, the poll found that certain negative propositions about aid were supported by large numbers: 79% felt that the U.S. was "doing more than its fair share in helping underdeveloped countries;" 76% said "too much of our foreign assistance money is kept by the leaders of poor countries and does not get to the people;" and 73% thought that "too much foreign aid is wasted in our own bureaucracy and never gets abroad."[29]

Mideast; Indian Blast

At the first stop on the President's 1974 journey to the Mideast and to Moscow, Sec. Kissinger held a news conference (Salzburg, June 11) in which he asked for a review of the evidence connecting him with the wiretapping of 13 Government workers and four newsmen. Editorial comment was unified in praising the Secretary's success as a diplomat, and a number expressed consternation lest Dr. Kissinger carry out his threat to resign. But about a third of the papers were critical of the Salzburg news conference as ill-placed and ill-timed. The requested review of the wiretapping evidence by the Senate Foreign Relations Committee was approved by a majority of commenting editors; but some doubted that the Secretary's "capacity to conduct foreign relations" was or would be "compromised by the tempest in his diplomatic teapot" (Wash. Star-News). Some columnists were critical of the Secretary's support of wiretaps on newsmen (Carl Rowan, Jos. Kraft, David Broder); and some sympathized with the position taken by the Secretary (Marquis Childs, Richard Wilson, Wm. F. Buckley, Jr.).[30]

Several polling results about Sec. Kissinger were published by the Harris Survey on May 30; and Mr. Harris reported that "an overwhelming 85% of the American people rate Sec. Kissinger as doing a good-to-excellent job in office; this is the highest positive rating ever recorded in the Harris Survey for a member of the Executive Branch of the Federal Government." Only 10% gave the Secretary negative marks on his performance. Three other specific propositions elicited popular approval: Kissinger "is a highly skilled negotiator, especially in dealing with the Communists" (88% vs. 4%); "no matter who is President, Kissinger should stay as Secretary of State" (75% vs. 11%); and, "he has done a remarkable job in bringing Pres. Sadat of Egypt over to the American and away from the Russian side" (67% vs. 7%).[31]

As the presidential trip proceeded to the Mideast and revealed the disengagement between Syria and Israel, the encomiums were renewed; editors tended to agree with Pres. Nixon that prospects for a Mideast settlement were "better than they have been at any time in the past 25 years." A Hearst editorial welcomed this "dramatic affirmation of this nation's new policy of trying to be more even-handed in dealing with Israel and the Arab world." According to the Chicago Sun-Times, "Mr. Nixon's latest foreign venture yielded several important benefits and the trip was a genuine, if mixed, success." One reason for editorial reservations about the trip was misgiving about the nuclear offers to Egypt and Israel. The June 14 offer to sell Egypt a nuclear plant and nuclear fuel came as a distinct surprise to American Congressmen and editors; a number promptly expressed their doubts, and approval was given by less than half of the newspapers (17 out of 36). Only 5 of these mentioned doubts about selling nuclear goods to Israel. But in the case of Egypt editors referred to India's nuclear blast (less than a month earlier) and saw a real danger that U.S. nuclear fuels could be diverted to military or terrorist uses. Those editors who approved of the sale presumed that strong and adequate safeguards would be imposed to prevent diversion of nuclear fuels, and they felt it desirable to participate in Egypt's economic development.

The Indian nuclear explosion was really a "shocker" to American editors. Almost all comments were critical. Most were skeptical about India's avowed peaceful intentions. "For India to call its explosion 'peaceful,' and to abjure all military intent is, in a word, rubbish," declared the Washington Post. Two out of 3 commenting editors also chided India for upsetting the established balance of nuclear forces and increasing the risk of global warfare—an ironic turn of events, considering India's "waspish comments on the uses and abuses of power by other nations" (Los Angeles Times). Others charged India with an "upside down sense of priorities" and with "wasting their scanty resources on an expensive and dangerous plaything" (e.g., Hearst papers, Cinci. Enquirer). But the Christian Science Monitor and the Denver Post gave India the benefit of the doubt, the former saying: "India is the first to have nuclear energy, but to forswear nuclear weapons. (If India) means this, then it will still be possible to have 'non-proliferation' in weapons." Some others also pointed out that the established nuclear powers (including the U.S.) have not worked diligently toward disarmament, as they pledged to do in the Non-Proliferation Treaty. A third of the commenting papers called on the superpowers to work anew for disarmament and set a better example for the non-nuclear nations.[32]

Moscow Summit

Like his trip to the Mideast, Pres. Nixon's visit to the Soviet Union for his third "summit" meeting with General Secretary Brezhnev was a success, both on TV and in the judgment of a majority of commenting editors. There was disappointment that an agreement was not reached on limiting offensive nuclear weapons; but this result had been anticipated by many. The Chicago Tribune declared that "the trip achieved everything that could realistically be expected of it;" and Wm. R. Hearst, Jr. added that "there may never be an agreement (on SALT) unless the cooperative spirit of detente is maintained." The "minor" accords reached at the summit (on trade expansion, heart research, energy conservation, etc.) were welcomed by many; and the Christian Science Monitor said: "If the summit keeps up the momentum of improved relations, then it certainly was worthwhile."[33]

There was a favorable editorial response to the NATO "Declaration of Atlantic Principles" initialed in Ottawa on June 19 and later signed at Brussels by heads of NATO governments. The majority felt that the new Declaration signaled no basic change in NATO, but saw the alliance strengthened somewhat by the smoothing over of differences. However, some did see the Declaration as providing a new "base from which to move forward to a more solid and workable relationship" (e.g., Louisville Courier-Journal). A few saw no gain, the Cleveland Plain Dealer seeing only "a sheepish acceptance of disunities as they showed up in the crucible of the Middle East war and the Arab oil embargo."[34]

The Cyprus crisis which produced the ouster of Archbishop Makarios on July 15 was universally deplored and usually blamed upon the military government in Athens. The multilateral attempts to restore peace by the UN, NATO, and the Common Market were approved by most. The U.S. response to the coup was criticized by a majority of commenting editors who called "the policy of backing the Greek dictators" dangerously "wrong-headed." The Turkish invasion of Cyprus was deplored by some as "barbaric" over-reaction, whereas others felt that the Turks' resort to arms was justified. Many editors praised the success of diplomatic efforts to bring about a ceasefire on Cyprus, and gave credit to the many parties which contributed to it. Several stressed the role of NATO. The changeover in both Greek and Cypriot leadership was warmly welcomed; and the Hearst papers rejoiced that "this is one crisis in which both we and the Russians seem to be on the same side."[35]

The role of the United Nations in such crises as that of Cyprus was generally appreciated; and a Harris Survey taken in April showed popular approval of a much broader role for the UN. Harris found a full majority (63% vs. 18%) agreeing with this proposition: "Today's problems require international action that only the United Nations or other international agencies can take." Further support for this principle was supplied in response to questions about specific activities of the UN. Each of the four following UN functions was supported by 85% or more of the respondents, as they indicated their desire that the UN maintain—or increase—its activity in each of these fields:

Solving the world food supply (71% would increase UN role)
Solving the world's energy problem (68% would increase)
Setting up peacekeeping forces (68% would increase)
Helping clean up air-water pollution (67% would increase).[36]

Public knowledge about the UN was, as usual, spotty. Only 18% of the sample knew that the UN membership was in the 100–150 bracket; and less than half realized that "UN resolutions are not usually binding" on member nations (47%); but 65% knew that "the UN is helping poor countries develop their economies." A majority (54%) would increase the help the UN is giving "poor countries to develop their economies." Also interesting is the fact that only 20% saw the UN as "generally working against the interests of the U.S.;" 57% disagreed with this proposition. In a general estimate of the United Nations, a solid 76% said the United Nations was "worthwhile;" this figure was less than it had been in 1967 (81%), but higher than that for 1970 (68%). Only 7% favored U.S. withdrawal from the UN; and as many as 65% would either increase or maintain U.S. support for the UN, compared with 45% in 1971. The most supportive demographic groups were: Blacks (61%), Women (52%), and those aged 18–29 (51%).[37]

Fortune magazine for May 1974 carried the results of a foreign policy poll of 600 vice presidents of America's large companies, conducted by two Yale faculty members (Prof. Bruce Russett and Betty Hanson). They found that over the past half-dozen years or so businessmen had "become distinctly more dovish, less inclined to perceive foreign relations in cold-war terms, and more inclined to favor retrenchment in U.S. defense spending and in U.S. military commitments abroad." A majority (54%) said it was "not correct" for the U.S. to send ground combat troops to Viet-Nam; and a majority favored future military action to help countries "attacked by foreign Communist forces" in only two instances out of seven listed countries (Mexico and West Germany). When the hypothetical circumstances were altered from a "foreign" attack to one led by "an indigenous Communist movement," there was no longer a majority in favor of U.S. military help. When asked about U.S. aid programs, 54% wanted a decrease in economic aid, and 71% a decrease in military assistance.[38]

At the same time, these businessmen anticipated increased American economic involvement abroad, 83% envisaging "increased involvement in foreign markets and investments." When asked to choose from a fairly long list "the most important approach to world peace," 61.5% chose the category, "trade, technical cooperation, economic interdependence." The next highest category, "military superiority of the U.S.," was named by only 10.9%. The authors concluded that businessmen's "acceptance of an American retreat from power is certainly not a simple 'isolationist' turning away from the world."

Aid and Human Rights

Increased concern about the internal repression by Pres. Park Chung Hee's government in Seoul was expressed during the summer of 1974. A number of editors were distressed by the trial and sentencing of political rivals and student demonstrators, and they were troubled that such undemocratic measures should be taken by a government receiving economic and military aid from the U.S. A majority favored reducing either U.S. economic aid or the 38,000 troops in Korea, or both. The Philadelphia Bulletin asked: "Just how solid and reliable is an American alliance with a South Korean regime whose repression . . . creates wider disaffection among its people?"[39]

News that the Turkish Government had decided to rescind its ban on the growing of opium poppies caused universal distress among editorial writers, and prompted both houses of Congress to move toward cutting U.S. aid to Turkey, unless that country were to prevent Turkish opium from reaching the American underworld. But among American editors twice as many opposed cutting aid as favored a reduction; the majority felt that an aid cut would further embitter Turkish-American relations and NATO problems—without restoring the poppy ban which they regarded as impossible of achievement in view of the strong attitudes of Turkish political parties. From the start, some editors felt that the Turkish poppy ban was doomed as a long-range solution to the U.S. drug problem, in view of the availability of drugs from numerous other countries. Some of these commentators urged that the U.S. and Turkey seek to work out the problem cooperatively.[40]

U.S. aid to Saigon also continued under editorial debate, with a minority upholding the U.S. program, but a majority of editors advocating cuts in our military aid which they felt was prolonging the fighting. The minority held that any reduction would jeopardize the Thieu government. Strong criticism of the aid came from about a third of the commenting editors when it became known that funds from AID and Food for Peace were being used for war-related purchases and programs (e.g., St. Louis Post-Dispatch, Minneapolis Tribune).[41]

Also 1974 reports that the CIA had been active in Chile stirred much editorial comment on the CIA role in that country in the years preceding the 1973 overthrow of the Allende government. A majority of editors now expressed flat opposition to any effort by a U.S. agency to overthrow or undermine the government of another country. They held that the fact that Communists engage in such activities was "no justification" for our doing so. These newspapers had generally been supportive of America's internationalist policies. On the other hand, one fourth of the editors upheld the efforts of the CIA (e.g., Hearst papers, Wash. Star-News). Another group took an in-between position; they were dubious about what the U.S. did in Chile, but they were not ready to discard entirely the option for covert activity (e.g., Scripps-Howard papers, N.Y. Times).[42]

The annual Harris Survey of public confidence in American group leadership showed a general tendency toward diminished confidence in these institutions in 1974, as compared with 1973. Two notable exceptions, however, were the increase in the number expressing "a great deal of confidence" in the Federal Executive Branch after Mr. Nixon's resignation (from 19% to 28%) and in the Supreme Court (33% to 40%), for which the Court's decision on the White House tapes was thought to be largely responsible. But in almost every other case the 1974 figures was well below that recorded in 1966. The press was closest to that earlier registration of opinion, with 25% confident in 1974 compared with 29% in 1966; but the Military, for example, had 33% expressing a "great deal" of confidence in 1974, whereas 62% did so in 1966.[43]

Congressional efforts to cut off U.S. aid to Turkey after the Turkish invasion of Cyprus were twice vetoed by Pres. Ford, and twice Congressional efforts to override his veto failed. In the considerable discussion of this question a majority (63%) of commenting editors upheld Pres. Ford's position. Some maintained that the "final compromise" between the President and Congress was "fair" since it gave him until Dec. 10 to try to work out a Cyprus settlement before actual termination of the aid (e.g., Chi. News). The main position of those supporting Pres. Ford was that a President must be able to carry out the day-by-day conduct of U.S. foreign relations. The majority felt also that cutting off aid to Turkey would not bring peace to Cyprus, and it could impair the bargaining leverage of the U.S. in seeking such a peace. Also some were concerned lest cutting off aid to Turkey undermine NATO; and some others emphasized the role of the Greek-American lobby and charged Congressmen with "putting a narrow political interest ahead of the nation" (e.g., Seattle Times).[44]

Newspapers in the minority group (33%) warmly welcomed Congress' assertion of a strong role in foreign affairs, and stressed that the Executive was refusing to carry out the U.S. law which rendered the Turks ineligible for aid in view of their "expanded aggression" on Cyprus following their "initially-justified intervention" (Phila. Bulletin). The Louisville Courier-Journal added: "It is precisely because both the Nixon and Johnson administrations took liberties with the letter and the spirit of the law in their conduct of foreign policy that Congress has grown so mistrustful of executive power and is seeking to put it on a much tighter rein." Papers in this group also felt that cutting off aid would help Sec. Kissinger in his efforts to achieve peace on Cyprus.

A Harris Survey appearing in late October reported that positive ratings for Sec. Kissinger's handling of his job had diminished from the 85% of May, but they still stood at a highly favorable level: 73% favorable vs. 22% negative (5% "not sure"). Two polls also reported popular majorities calling it "wrong" for the U.S. to "intervene in the internal affairs of Chile and try to destabilize the government": Harris, 60% against; Time magazine's poll, Soundings, 68% against. A Gallup Poll on Cuba re-affirmed earlier findings that "re-establishment of diplomatic relations" had majority approval (63%). Editorial opinion was in harmony on both the Chilean and Cuban issues. An August Harris Survey (8/26) reported that the general public disapproved of U.S. selling of nuclear reactors to Egypt (69%) and to Israel (66%). Louis Harris commented that "most people simply don't believe the repeated assurances of Kissinger and others that safeguards can be employed to make certain that a country does not convert a peacetime nuclear capability into a war-making capacity." Approval of permitting nuclear reactors to go to eight other countries was also low–ranging from 11% to 20% (Australia). Editorial opinion, it will be recalled, was also disturbed about the possibility of making reactors available to other countries.[45]

Vladivostok

Pres. Gerald Ford and General-Secretary Leonid Brezhnev met at Vladivostok (Nov. 24, 1974) at a time when a clear majority of Americans credited their new leader with "working for peace in the world" (52% vs. 38%, according to the Harris Survey). Announcement of a "break-through" in the SALT negotiations inspired many hopeful editorials, along with some incredulous ones. There was disappointment in many quarters when Pres. Ford, at his Dec. 2 news conference, disclosed the actual arms "ceilings" agreed upon. When editors understood that the mutual limitation on delivery vehicles was to be 2400 (including ICBMs, bombers, and submarine-launched missiles), and that the sub-limits on missiles to be MIRVed was 1320, they realized that the Vladivostok meeting provided for a limitation of armaments but not a reduction within the life of the projected treaty which was due to last until 1985.[46]

Since a Potomac Associates poll had recently reported that 80% of Americans did not see much danger of nuclear war with the Soviet Union (41% "not very much danger," 39% "none at all"), much of the editorial hope for the SALT talks had centered on the possibility of budget cuts arising from actual reductions in armament, rather than mere limitations.[47]

The Scripps-Howard editorial called the Vladivostok limits "certainly higher than desirable," but the agreement seemed to be worthwhile as "the best that Russia would accept" (similarly, Los Angeles Times, Indianapolis Star). According to the Des Moines Register, even though the limits were "much too high, Congress should not just say 'too high' and repudiate the President's efforts."

The second largest group of newspapers did stress that the ceilings were "too high," and that actual arms reduction seemed foreclosed for 10 or 11 years. Papers in this group often suggested that Congress find some way to move the U.S. and the Soviet Union to lower ceilings; but none of these went so far as to say that the tentative accord should be turned down. The Miami News, however, did say that to try to sell Vladivostok as "a 'cap' on the arms race was an insult to the public's intelligence." The two most negative newspapers were the New York News and Wall St. Journal, both of which felt that SALT ONE had been too advantageous to the Soviet Union and that Vladivostok gave the Russians an advantage in "throw-weight" and hence the possibility of many more warheads on their MIRVed missiles, which could tempt the Soviets to try for a first-strike against the U.S.

Among the general public, 63% assented to this Harris proposition: "just setting a limit on missiles is a major accomplishment." Louis Harris wrote that the two chief reservations expressed were:

that the ceilings "will allow for a substantial continuation of the arms race;" and "the Russians are unlikely to keep their end of the bargain" (46% agreed to this Harris proposition). When Sec. Kissinger announced in late December that the final aide memoire on Vladivostok permitted early reductions in nuclear forces, prompt and warm approval came from a number of papers (e.g., N.Y. Times, Los Angeles Times, Balt. Sun).[48]

Energy, Food

In late 1974 Sec. Kissinger in a Chicago speech outlined an international policy of cooperation to meet the continuing energy crisis which prompted a generally favorable editorial verdict. The Chicago Tribune saw a "comprehensible 5-point package likely to inspire hope," including: 1, international agreement to reduce oil imports; 2, development of new sources of energy; 3, a new international agency to recycle petrodollars; 4, continued assistance to the developing countries; and 5, solidarity of oil-consuming countries in dealing with the producers. Many editors approved the whole package, although feeling that it would "take years" to implement the Secretary's proposals. A number stressed the importance of conserving oil and reducing consumption (e.g., St. Louis Post-Dispatch), although some doubted that reducing oil consumption would bring down the price of oil (e.g., Boston Globe, Wash. Star-News). There was broad agreement with the New York Journal of Commerce that, "if the world is going to do something meaningful about its energy problems, the U.S. must do something meaningful about its own."[49]

In an interview with Business Week, Sec. Kissinger mentioned that the U.S. had the option of military action to ensure survival in the event of a renewed embargo by the oil-producing states which could threaten the "strangulation" of nations dependent on petroleum. About half of the commenting editors approved the Secretary's mention of this military option (e.g., Wash. Post, Scripps-Howard papers), whereas one-fourth of the editors said that the military option should not be considered by the U.S. (Des Moines Register, St. Louis Post-Dispatch). Other papers were non-committal. To gauge the attitude of the general public, a poll by the Chicago Council on Foreign Relations used two approaches. When the poll inquired about U.S. military action in case "the Arabs cut off" the oil supply to Western Europe, it found 21% favorable to military action, but 56% opposed. When it offered a 3-way choice in the event of "another Arab oil embargo," a plurality chose the option, "Share our oil with Europe and Japan, even if it means less oil for Americans;" almost as many (38%) said, "Go it alone, and let Europe and Japan fend for themselves." But only 6% chose the third alternative, "Invade the oil-producing countries."[50]

The UN World Food Conference in Rome in late 1974 stirred extensive editorial comment, with many discussing the complex relationship between food, oil, fertilizer, and population, and placing strong emphasis on the interdependence of nations. Many praised Sec. Kissinger's internationalist and humanitarian approach as appropriately expressing America's concern; and there was general approval of the conference goals of increasing agricultural production and creating food reserves or stockpiles. Many papers endorsed the use of food by the U.S. for humanitarian purposes; and a number felt that the U.S. pledge of 3.3 million tons of grain for famine relief was not so great as it should have been (e.g., Chi. Sun-Times, Los Angeles Times). Some voiced strong disapproval of the U.S. for using food for economic or political gain. About a third of the commenting papers called for reassessments of traditionally wasteful American life styles, and for various American sacrifices to help provide food for the needy in other nations (e.g., Miami News). The U.S. can lead "an all-out assault on hunger," said the New York Times, "only by sacrifice at home—by limiting meat consumption, for example—and by generosity abroad."[51]

Amb. John Scali's UNGA speech in December, criticizing the "tyranny of the majority," evoked considerable editorial sympathy. Virtually all of the 30 commenting papers deplored certain actions of the UN bloc composed of Third World, Communist, and Arab countries, including the decisions to ban South Africa from the 1974 General Assembly sessions and to give observer status to the Palestine Liberation Organization. A majority of commenting editorials also shared Amb. Scali's concern that the conduct of the Third World majority threatened to undermine American popular support for the UN. No newspaper was noted as calling for U.S. withdrawal from the world organization; but the Scripps-Howard papers suggested "selective U.S. support" of UN programs, and most papers approved the U.S. decision not to contribute to the UN Special Fund to aid underdeveloped countries most affected by the energy-economic crisis.[52]

As editorial and popular opinion continued to favor resumption of relations with Cuba, the U.S. was criticized for its failure to take a position at the Quito meeting of OAS ministers which could have eased those relations. It was difficult, said the Washington Post, for Washington to complain about subversion by Cuba, after publicization of the U.S. role in Chile. Most of the critics stressed that American and OAS restrictions on trading with Cuba were "no longer tenable" in an era of U.S.-Soviet and U.S.-Chinese detente.[53]

A number of editors also sympathized with the Latin American nations which stated their solidarity with Venezuela and Ecuador in complaining that certain provisions of the U.S. Trade Act of 1974 deprived them of trade preferences because of their membership in a cartel (OPEC), even though they did not join with the Arab producers in embargoing oil to the U.S. There was also sympathy because the Latin Americans had been deprived of the long-promised tariff preference on their industrial exports. The Kansas City Star, however, declared that Venezuela and Ecuador did "joyously receive the OPEC price for petroleum," and maintained that "cartels are the very antithesis of free trade."[54]

Comprehensive Poll

In March 1975 the Chicago Council on Foreign Relations published an unusually comprehensive public opinion poll which it had commissioned Louis Harris and Associates to undertake (interviewing at the end of 1974). Many aspects of U.S. foreign policy were covered; but the most important single conclusion of the poll was that Americans were not neo-isolationist in sentiment, although there were indications that the public did favor "de-militarization" of U.S. foreign policy. As many as 86% agreed that the U.S. has "a real responsibility to take a very active role in the world;" and a majority indicated their belief that foreign policy is relevant to their direct personal concerns in this interdependent world, since U.S. foreign policy has a "major impact" on such matters as gasoline and food prices, the availability of raw materials for manufacturing, and unemployment. A large majority agreed that "international cooperation is essential if we are to cope with problems of food, energy and inflation"—that such problems cannot be solved by individual countries in isolation.[55]

But this poll also confirmed the findings of other recent polls that Americans were reluctant to sanction the use of U.S. military forces overseas. The following table gives the reactions to several hypothetical situations of both the general public and a sample of 330 "leaders"—drawn from Congress and Government Departments, from business, from the press and broadcasting, and from the university-foundation world. The greater willingness of the "leaders" to use U.S. troops in defense of Western Europe and West Berlin is evident; but it may be noted that the general public did present plurality opposition in these cases—many gave "no opinion" about how they would feel. Responses to a specific question eliciting attitudes toward "our commitment to NATO, the military organization of Western Europe and the U.S." showed a clear majority (54%) in favor of maintaining (or increasing) our commitment, 13% desirous of decreasing it, but only 7% in favor of withdrawal (26% "not sure").

Attitudes Toward Use of U.S. Troops in Certain Situations

	PUBLIC			LEADERS		
	Favor	Oppose	No Opin.	Favor	Oppose	No Opin.
If Canada were invaded	77%	12%	11%	90%	4%	6%
If West Europe invaded	39	41	20	77	14	9
If Russians took West Berlin	34	43	23	55	33	12
If Israel were being defeated by the Arabs	27	50	23	41	44	15
If No. Korea attacked South Korea	14	65	21	19	67	14
If Communist China invaded Formosa (Taiwan)	17	59	24	11	79	10
If No. Vietnam launched major attack vs. South	11	72	16	6	87	7

Willingness to send troops to Asia was notably less than to Europe; but as many as 60% were willing to send to "friendly countries" (anywhere) which have been attacked "economic and military aid": 23% would send troops (and military and economic aid), 37% military and economic aid, 22% economic aid only, 9% nothing, and 9% "not sure."

Sustained support for detente with the Soviet Union was demonstrated by this 1974 poll, as well as wide approval (75%) of Sec. Kissinger's style of diplomacy. On U.S.-USSR relations, favorable majorities of between 63% and 83% were registered in behalf of nine proposed areas for specific agreement (e.g., SALT, Mutual and Balanced Force Reductions, joint space missions). At the same time, 71% thought it would be a threat to the U.S. if Western European countries were to become Communist. A majority (60%) were willing to spend money on U.S. defenses (either the current or a larger amount); and many who originally favored spending less reversed themselves if the cuts would result in our military inferiority to the USSR. While the public also supported the objective of the Jackson-Vanik amendment calling for increased emigration from the Soviet Union, an even larger number (62%) favored according the USSR the same trade treatment as other countries.

Some perspective on popularly-held goals for U.S. policy was afforded by a question in the Chicago Council poll which asked respondents to indicate the relative importance of 18 suggested goals, and also to rate the job the U.S. is doing with respect to those goals. Below are listed the top five goals (the figures in parentheses show how many thought the U.S. was doing a good (Excellent or Pretty Good) job respecting that goal):

Keeping peace in the world (60%)
Promoting our security (71%)
Securing adequate supplies of energy (38%)
Protecting American jobs (35%)
International cooperation to solve common problems (44%)

Evidence of some tempering of the messianic streak, which occasionally manifests itself in American attitudes, was shown by the fact that the public ranked the export of democracy and the export of capitalism at the very bottom of the 18 suggested goals. "Containing communism" ranked in the middle of the public's goal priorities, with 54% terming it "very important." In principle, 2 out of 3 Americans say the U.S. should put pressure on countries that "systematically violate basic human rights." A majority called it "morally wrong" for the U.S. to support "a military dictatorship that strips its people of their basic rights," even if it allows us military bases. Specific cases, however, showed some differentiation in attitude. Re South Africa, 35% said the U.S. should adopt "a more active role" than at present in opposing apartheid. There was greater disagreement (48%) than agreement (41%) with the statement that "how the Soviet Union handles the treatment of the Jews and other minority groups is a matter of Soviet internal policy and none of our business."

This poll confirmed the lack of popular enthusiasm for large-scale aid programs, and it exposed some of the beliefs underlying the people's attitudes. A majority (63%) said that aid hurts our own economy, and only 25% said that economic aid helps our economy; similarly, a majority (73%) said that aid gets us too involved with other countries. At the same time, a majority (56%) gave the U.S. positive ratings (Excellent or Pretty Good) on "helping to improve the standard of living in less developed countries," whereas only 26% of the (better-informed) leaders gave such high ratings.

An unusual feature of this Chicago Council poll was its inquiry into the public's perception of the relative current importance of various possible participants in foreign policy decisions. A "very important" role in determining policy was seen for the Secretary of State by 73% of the respondents; "American Business" was so rated by 42%, the Congress by 39%, the State Department by 38%, "The Military" by 36%, the CIA by 28%, and "public opinion" by 19%. The leaders almost unanimously stressed the role of the Secretary of State, but assigned less importance than did the general public to the roles of American Business, the Congress, and the State Department. When asked which participants should be more important than they are, 49% of the general public said Congress should have a more important role, and as many as 58% said that public opinion should play a more important role.

Viet-Nam Concluded; Arms Traffic

As the fighting in Viet-Nam continued—despite the Paris accord of 1973—the largest group of editors continued to uphold Congress in opposing any increase in U.S. military aid to Saigon. We must avoid any "step" toward deeper re-involvement in Viet-Nam, said the Des Moines Register in a typical expression of this group's view. Firm support for additional aid did come from staunchly anti-Communist papers which had long favored ample aid for that purpose; several leading papers indicated that they might favor more aid for Thieu if he would show greater willingness to try for a political settlement in Viet-Nam. In February a Gallup Poll found 78% opposed to "sending $522,000 in additional military aid to South Viet-Nam and Cambodia."[56]

The giving of arms to other countries was frowned upon by the general public—65% according to the Chicago Council's poll. But there has been one major exception to this general attitude: military aid to Israel. In 1967 the Harris Survey found people slightly opposed (39% to 35%) to military aid to Israel; in 1973 they changed to support it (46% to 34%); and in 1974 they were decidedly favorable: 66% to 24%, according to the Chicago Council poll.

The practice of "the U.S. *selling* military equipment to other nations" was disapproved by a majority (53%), according to the 1974 (Chicago) poll; 35% were in favor, and 12% were "not sure." When the U.S. in 1975 terminated its 10-year-old embargo on the sale of arms to Pakistan and India, the commenting editors realized that the change chiefly affected Pakistan, because India had been purchasing weapons from the Soviet Union, as well as manufacturing many of its own. Under these circumstances a plurality of editors (12 to 8) approved the lifting of the U.S. embargo. Less editorial attention was accorded the issues of arms for Saudi Arabia or Ethiopia; but most commenting editors deemed it dubious for the U.S. to sell arms to Saudi Arabia.

The initial reaction to the fall of Saigon to the North Vietnamese, and to the stream of refugees desiring to enter the U.S., was publicization in the press and on TV of the objections and fears that some Americans expressed in letters to Congressmen and to state and federal officials, that the newcomers would be a burden to taxpayers and competitors for jobs. But the 1975 newspaper editorials were virtually unanimous in stating America's responsibility to accept and re-settle the refugees from South Viet-Nam and Cambodia. A number shared Pres. Ford's anger over the original manifestations of hostility to the influx of refugees; and nearly all rejected the expressed fears as exaggerated and unjustified. A majority felt that the refugees could be absorbed without serious dislocation to the economy. Over half of the editors called on Congress for swift passage of the funds needed to transport and re-settle the refugees; and some noted with approval the disappearance of anti-refugee sentiment from public notice and the upswelling of volunteers working to help the newcomers.[57]

Editors spoke also of our continuing commitments, despite the exodus from Indochina; and of their sustained interest in peace in the world. "We must remain internationalists for our own salvation," said the Houston Post; but "we must give up intervention." The New York Times maintained that "a new consciousness that power must be used wisely, without exaggerated faith in its military application alone, is a far cry from isolationism." The Christian Science Monitor urged that our pledge to Japan be promptly reaffirmed—along with that to South Korea, although the Monitor hoped Pres. Park would desist "from following in Thieu's tragic footsteps" by a further domestic crackdown.

A Gallup Poll (May 8) confirmed that Americans in 1975 were reluctant to commit military force to the defense of other countries; but the poll stressed that this sentiment was much the same after the fall of Saigon as it had been in 1971. (In the case of West Germany, however, there was a sizable decrease in interventionist sentiment during these four years.) The accompanying table gives, for both 1971 and 1975, the proportions of respondents who were "interventionists" (either willing to send troops or supplies) and "isolationists" (who didn't want the U.S. "to get involved" or gave no opinion).

Another significant development in editorial opinion was that several leading papers expressed their belief that "this is no time to signal a retreat" by slashing the defense budget. This sentiment extended to some papers which had previously advocated a "hard look" at requests for military expenditures (e.g., Balt. Sun, Detroit Free Press, N.Y. Times). However, several papers adhered to their belief that appropriations for new weapons systems (e.g., B-1 bomber, Trident submarine) be reduced in the interest of cooling the arms race.

The public was unhappy about the triumph of Hanoi in Indochina and the plight of the South Vietnamese; but there was satisfaction that the fighting was over and that the U.S. had been able to receive many refugees. Similarly, the American public was gratified by the termination of the fighting in the Middle East and the improved prospects for peace there. A majority of editors seemed to feel that the U.S. was doing what it could about the food and energy prob-

Public's Views on Commitments: 1971 and 1975

	INTERVENTIONISTS		ISOLATIONISTS		
	Send Troops	Supplies	Not get involved	No Opinion	Total
Mexico '75	42%	25%	23%	10%	100%
1971	45	26	19	10	100
England '75	37	30	24	9	100
1971	37	33	19	11	100
Germany '75	27	32	33	8	100
1971	28	41	22	9	100
Japan '75	16	35	40	9	100
1971	17	34	38	11	100
Israel '75	12	42	37	9	100
1971	11	44	33	12	100
Turkey '75	9	29	49	13	100
1971	10	36	37	17	100
Taiwan '75*	8	27	54	11	100
1971	11	30	45	14	100

*Question was phrased "Nationalist China."

lems; but there was also considerable unhappiness about U.S. aid going to repressive governments, and disappointment that Vladivostok had not produced agreement on actual reduction of nuclear armaments.

Few editors spelled out a comprehensive new foreign policy, but a number agreed with several of the policy recommendations of the Los Angeles Times: a "policy of world involvement, supported by a freeing of trade, a strong military establishment, a generosity of economic assistance, and an expansion of American crops to help buffer world food emergencies."[58]

Reference Notes

1. AOR for Aug.–Sept. 1973.
2. AOR for Oct. 1973.
3. Ibid.
4. Ibid.
5. AOR for Oct. and Nov. 1973.
6. Ibid.
7. Ibid.
8. AOR for Nov. 1973.
9. AOR for Nov. and Dec. 1973.
10. AOR for Nov. 1973.
11. AOR for Dec. 1973.
12. AOR for Dec. 1973 and Jan. 9, 1974.

13. AOR for Jan. 1974.
14. Ibid.
15. AOR for July 1974; Free in Donald Lesh, ed., *A Nation Observed* (Washington, 1974), p. 145.
16. Ibid.
17. AOR for Jan. 1974.
18. AOR for Jan. and May 1973.
19. AOR of Nov. 12, 1973.
20. AOR for Feb. and Mar. 7, 1974.
21. AOR for Feb. and Mar. 1974.
22. Ibid.
23. AOR for Feb.–Mar. 1974.
24. AOR for April 1974; Watts & Free, *State of the Nation 1974* (Washington, 1974), p. 326.
25. AOR for April 1974.
26. Ibid.; Lesh, op. cit., p. 143.
27. AOR for April 1974.
28. AOR for May 1974.
29. Ibid.; Paul Laudicina, *World Poverty and Development: A survey of American Opinion* (Overseas Development Council, Washington, 1973).
30. AOR for June 1974.
31. Ibid.
32. Ibid.
33. AOR for July 1974.
34. Ibid.
35. AOR for Aug. 1974.
36. Ibid.
37. Ibid.
38. AOR for Sept. 1974.
39. AOR for Aug. 1974.
40. Ibid.
41. AOR for Sept. 1974.
42. AOR for Oct. 1974.
43. Ibid.
44. AOR for Nov. 1974.
45. Ibid.
46. AOR for Dec. 1974.
47. Ibid.
48. AOR for Jan. 1975.
49. AOR for Dec. 1974.
50. AOR for April 1975.
51. AOR for Dec. 1974.
52. AOR for Jan. 1975.
53. Ibid.
54. AOR for April 1975.
55. AOR for Feb.–Mar. 1975.
56. AOR for Jan. and Apr. 1975.
57. AOR for May–June 1975.
58. Ibid.

XIX

MAJOR OPINION DEVELOPMENTS (1940–1975)

The replacement of isolationist policies by more activist foreign policies for the United States was a process which developed step-by-step throughout the decade following Hitler's attack on Poland in 1939. In this process of establishing war-time and post-war U.S. policies, culminating in the NATO alliance in 1949, the American public typically affirmed its support for the policies presented by the Executive Branch of the Government. Public support was particularly evident for policies designed to safeguard U.S. national security: joining international security organizations, entering defense alliances, sending military and economic aid to threatened nations, even waging two wars in Asia. After Pearl Harbor there was no public pressure against the Government for many years which could be compared to that which had pushed for the Ludlow Resolution of early World War II days, which called for a popular referendum prior to U.S. engagement in war. In fact, until the modification of policy as to the Viet-Nam War there was no major foreign policy position which can be credited to either popular or Congressional pressure upon the Executive Branch. The movement from isolationism to activism was led by the Executive and supported by the public and the Congress.

Critics of the public's role in foreign policy are wont to stress the volatility and changeability of public opinion; but anyone who has followed the development of U.S. policy in the two decades after 1949 must be struck, rather, by the public's tendency to maintain once-established opinions and policies. The extension of U.S. defense commitments to the Far East and Middle East in the 1950s, via the Congressional resolutions requested by Pres. Eisenhower, was promptly backed by the American public—as was Pres. Kennedy's firm and vigorous course in the Cuban missile crisis. Also the public and Congress supported Pres. Johnson's request for the Gulf of Tonkin resolution; but in 1968 the public did modify its support of the Viet-Nam War to the extent of favoring a limit on the escalation of dispatching U.S. ground troops there. After a quarter-century on an active internationalist course, the U.S. public (and Congress) now showed a considerably reduced willingness to use armed force to achieve national objectives. The tendency of the public to scrutinize more closely the foreign policy proposals of the Executive Branch was heightened further at the time of the Watergate debate.

Apart from the limitations placed on military activity, the desire of the majority of Americans to break away from past isolationism, and to take an active part in world affairs has persisted in recent years and widened in scope. The basic decision that the U.S. participate in an international organization to maintain the peace, the United Nations, has continued to be strongly held. On some other policies, such as aid to less developed countries, or immigration, the public has given support to the general principle advanced by the Government, but has refrained from pressing for the full implementation of policy recommended by the Administration. The liberal trade policy fell into this category, winning growing editorial and popular support until nearly the close of the 1940–1975 period when polls showed a rise in public sentiment for "protecting American jobs." The heightened public appreciation of the interdependence of nations has meant that a much wider range of topics was regarded as appropriate for international action in 1975 (pollution, famine, energy, etc.) than in 1940.

The typical pattern of the foreign policy process after 1940–Executive leadership followed by public support–included many instances involving U.S. armed forces over the next quarter-century (Berlin, Korea, Lebanon). But the impact of the Viet-Nam War ultimately prompted Congress to adopt legislation seeking to limit the powers of the President to initiate military ventures overseas–without depriving him of the power to act swiftly to meet an attack. This legislation was approved by a majority of leading American editors, and of the general American public. But foreign policy initiatives by the Executive were not invariably supported by Congress and the public in the period prior to 1965. When the Executive after World War II sought to establish an International Trade Organization (ITO), it ran into opposition in the business community and refrained from mounting a big appeal to the general public. Another major action by the Executive, Pres. Truman's relief of Gen. MacArthur during the Korean War, failed to win the approval of the general public; but it was supported by an overwhelming majority of the nation's leading editors.

State Department

The public was well aware of the great foreign policy role of the Presidency throughout this period (1940–1975); and it registered increasing awareness of the role of the State Department–making perhaps its greatest increase during the time of Sen. Joseph McCarthy (R-Wis.). During World War II the public seemed more ready to make complaints about the State Department than about some other federal Departments (e.g., War, Interior). Polls have usually shown some citizens ready to grouse about the inefficiency of government workers and Departments; but usually there have also been some citizens highly appreciative of the State Department's constant endeavors for "peace." In the polls of this period Americans appeared to be more appreciative of our ambassadors than of State Department personnel, and also to believe that the American Foreign Service was more proficient than that of most countries.

When Sen. McCarthy persisted in charging that there were Communists on the State Department payroll, many of the public credited the charges; and most people thought it a good idea to be extra vigilant about weeding out any workers of dubious loyalty and preventing such from being hired. Respecting the Secretaries of State, about 60% of polling respondents had formed a favorable impression of Sec. Marshall; and popular approval of Sec. Dulles also was usually around the 60% mark. Sec. Acheson started out with a comparable degree of appreciation, but many Americans came to think that he and Pres. Truman were not sufficiently concerned about rooting out Communists, and Acheson's vote of approval declined—even to the point that on some occasions the polls reported greater sentiment in favor of his resignation than for his continuance. This did not mean, however, any diminution in public support for such Truman-Acheson major policies as participation in the UN, the Marshall Plan, and NATO; but there was public wavering on Truman-Acheson policies for the Far East (which had not received the bipartisan support of the three major policies just mentioned).

The greatest change in public attitudes toward the Department and its leadership came when Pres. Eisenhower and Sec. Dulles succeeded Pres. Truman and Sec. Acheson. About one-fourth of the public had been voicing approval of the outgoing leaders; but on Inauguration Day in 1953 public approval zoomed to 60% or more. The same Department was now seen differently. Nevertheless, Sen. McCarthy was still able to stir doubts about "softness on Communism"—even in Eisenhower's government.

The greatest approval for a Secretary of State in this 35-year period under review has been accorded Henry Kissinger. His travels to Peking as Pres. Nixon's White House Assistant had brought him to special public notice; and his role in securing the Paris agreement on Viet-Nam had further built up public appreciation. His service as Secretary of State inevitably brought decisions and actions which produced some negative opinions; but Kissinger remained in 1975 better known, and more favorably, than any other Secretary of State of this generation.

Establishing Post-War Policies

For Congress to shift from the neutrality legislation engendered by the public's isolationist beliefs to the adoption of the lend-lease policies calculated to prevent the domination of the world by the Axis powers required a substantial change in American public opinion. The process took place over a period of more than two years, but perhaps the crucial shift in public opinion took place in the spring of 1940 when Americans witnessed the over-running of Western Europe by Hitler's forces, and realized a need for defensive measures on America's part. By the time of Pearl Harbor the American public realized that it was in its own interest to "take an active part" in world affairs; and by the time of the Dumbarton Oaks conference of 1944 the public realized that there was need for American participation in an international organization to maintain peace.

In seeking to establish two of its important post-war policies, the Government did not assume that its citizens would spontaneously respond to world events with appropriate detailed programs, but undertook to educate them by extensive information campaigns: on both the United Nations, and (later) the Marshall Plan. (Both campaigns succeeded in mobilizing public approval.) Americans in 1945 accepted the official advocacy of the United Nations, although the information campaign doubtless prompted many Americans to exaggerate the peace-keeping potentialities of the new organization. The nearly unanimous vote of the Senate in approving the UN Charter demonstrated the change in public opinion since the time when the Senate failed to approve the Charter of the League of Nations incorporated in the Treaty of Versailles.

During the war years Americans came to feel that their traditional desire to alleviate the human problems caused by disaster and famine should be directed toward the relief of those people who were suffering from deprivations caused by the war. The American public supported UNRRA until the most grievous suffering had been alleviated and until it was felt that in some countries (especially in Eastern Europe) relief was being distributed on a partisan political basis, rather than on the basis of human need.

The 1946 British Loan was enacted without receiving majority support in public opinion polls, but it enjoyed overwhelming approval by American newspaper editors and commentators. The 1947 program of aid to Greece and Turkey was undertaken without time for an extensive information campaign; but it, too, had the approval of the great majority of editors. Opinion polls showed popular support for economic aid to the two threatened nations, but reluctance to approve military aid. Later, of course, the general public came to approve military aid to our allies both in NATO and in Asia.

When Sec. Marshall first proposed his plan for European reconstruction it was supported immediately by the more-educated segment of the American public; and it came to receive majority support from all educational groups after the ripples flowing from the

Government's large-scale information campaign had reached many elements of the general public. The principle of Pres. Truman's proposal of Point Four technological assistance to less developed countries also won acceptance from the public. This was confirmed by Congressional enactment of an unbroken series of aid programs, demonstrating the sustained willingness of a majority of the public to pay taxes for this purpose.

The public's traditional aversion to alliances was overcome first with reference to the Western Hemisphere, then Western Europe, and in the following five years was extended to the Pacific basin. The public became as supportive of these forty-some alliances, as it had been opposed to such ties during most of the 19th and 20th centuries; and here again the change did not take place overnight. Americans now believed that allies were required for the nation's defense in the modern world; and this belief was reflected in the many treaties approved by the Senate pledging U.S. support to numerous nations, if and when they should be threatened by aggression.

Relations with Communist Countries

The American public welcomed Soviet participation in World War II on our side of the conflict, although not forgetting the Molotov-Ribbentrop pact of 1939–41 or the fact that it was Hitler's attack which brought the Russians into the war. Americans supported lend-lease for the Soviet Union, but there were increasing misgivings about the consequences of such aid for Russian domination of Eastern Europe. The Yalta agreements in 1945 briefly quieted such doubts for the majority, and USSR cooperation in establishing the United Nations was welcomed. The predominant view was to accept Soviet steps toward cooperation and to hope for the best; but later Soviet expansionist moves–in Iran and toward Greece and Turkey–as well as Soviet resistance to international control of atomic energy and vetoes in the UN caused cumulative doubts. Many Americans even felt that the UN would be more effective if the Soviet Union were not a member. By the time of the Communist take-over of Prague (Feb. 1948) the Cold War was on and recognized as such; and Americans became ready to help the Western European nations in setting up NATO as a defense against Communist expansionism. The war in Korea was seen as further demonstrating the need to counter a Soviet drive for domination. The willingness of the American public to uphold Pres. Eisenhower's efforts to improve relations through summit meetings was dashed by Khrushchev's torpedoing of the Paris summit, his renewal of the Berlin tussle, and his introduction of offensive missiles into Cuba. The more fruitful Soviet response to Pres. Nixon's overtures was welcomed by the American public, which particularly praised the reaching of agreement on SALT. The U.S.-Soviet wheat deal was enthusiastically received; and other agreements for US-USSR cooperation in space, medicine, and anti-pollution continued to be approved by the American public. Now 80% of the public felt that there was only a little danger of getting into an atomic war with the Soviet Union (39% said "no danger at all").

Attitudes toward the "Iron Curtain" countries and China were similar to those toward the Soviet Union, with considerable public tendency to regard Communism as "monolithic." Differentiation of attitudes toward the countries of Eastern Europe was subsequently encouraged by the revolts in East Germany and Hungary; but it took some time for the public to accept the development of even non-strategic U.S. trade with Eastern Europe.

In 1948–49 a few commentators suggested it could be realistic for the U.S. to recognize Peking, but after the Communist Chinese military action against the U.S. forces in Korea virtually no one advocated such a course. Sentiment favorable to Chiang-Kai-shek's Republic of China, and its continued seating in the United Nations, remained stable for two decades. The thaw with the People's Republic of China has developed officially only since 1971; since then visits of Chinese to America have been welcomed by the public, and there has been general satisfaction that the two countries are again in communication. While there has been desire for full diplomatic relations with the PRC, the public has wanted to keep its ties with Taipei until some final solution is reached (even though polls since 1971 have shown very little support for defending Taipei against military attack from Peking).

European and Other Allies

The American public's sympathy for Western Europe was well established prior to U.S. entry into World War II. This attitude continued to be notably stable, despite some suspicions from time to time of Britain or of de Gaulle. Basically, Americans continued to believe that it was necessary to the U.S. to have allies in order to maintain its own security in the world. Americans repeatedly expressed approval of close cooperation with Western Europe; but only a minority (around 20%) have ever declared themselves in favor of Atlantic Union. Some American Congressmen and editors sought to induce closer cooperation among the Western Europeans; they welcomed the Coal & Steel Community and the Common Market. But the majority of the American public did not follow such European developments. By 1948 Americans did favor military aid to Western Europe, and by 1949 they favored the defense commitments of the NATO pact.

From time to time a minority of Congressmen and editors bewailed Europe's degree of cooperation with us, the most common complaint being a failure of our NATO partners to carry their proper share of the defense costs. During the brief Mideast war of 1973 some editors were indignant over the failure of our NATO allies (except Portugal) to permit the U.S. to utilize their territory in connection with our re-supply of Israel. But most of the time Americans regarded our NATO allies as helpful and congenial. It may be noted that when Americans voiced support for defense agreements in the 1940s and 1950s most of the polling questions presumed that the U.S. would be acting in concert with other countries (whether Latin American, European, Asian, or United Nations). Still, disappointment with the extent of assistance from other United Nations members in Korea was not sufficient to prevent undertaking additional commitments in the 1950s. Also, while the Chinese intervention in Korea prompted a majority of Americans to tell polling interviewers that our entry into the war was a "mistake," they did not actually turn away from the policy of "containing" Communist expansionism. The public opposed a Korean settlement which would sanction substantial Communist gains through aggression, and it approved subsequent agreements to block further Communist aggression.

United Nations

Despite revised opinions about the potentialities of the United Nations for peacekeeping, and annoyance with actions of the new Third World majority, the American public has given strong and sustained support to U.S. membership in, and cooperation through, that organization. Various crises in the years after 1945 demonstrated to the American people that the new organization could not settle disputes and declare peace in every emerging crisis. Beginning with the Rio Pact and NATO, the public approved treaties of alliance with two score countries, as at least valuable supplements to operations under the UN Charter. Public support for military action to stop Communist expansion did not imply a belief in the general acceptability of military action as a technique of foreign policy in circumstances not involving "vital American interests." In the Arab-Israeli conflict of 1948 there was no majority approval for sending U.S. armed forces to stop the fighting and maintain order there. A large polling majority said the U.S. should *not* by itself send troops to Palestine; but 50% did approve U.S. participation in case the UN decided to send an "international police force" to keep order there. At the same time, most press commentators stipulated that this should be accomplished only by vote of the U.S. Congress. In the case of the 1956 war, Americans backed the efforts of their government to secure UN action ending the fighting in Egypt; only 7% said later that the U.S. should have "done more" to help Britain and France in their action there.

Such UN initiatives as the Declaration of Human Rights were approved by most commenting editors, mainly as a means of educating other UN members (including the Communists) in the importance of such rights as Americans had long honored in their Bill of Rights. But the idea of signing a treaty on human rights did arouse objections in some quarters (including Congress) lest a "UN treaty" supersede the American Bill of Rights. The Bricker amendment (intended to limit the American Executive as well as to hamper adoption of "UN treaties") was not adopted by the Senate; but neither was the Convention on Human Rights. There was little public outcry over this treaty failure (or the failure of the Bricker amendment); and it was not until much later that U.S. foreign policy—and the American public—gave a prominent place to human rights.

It may be noted, however, that during the first decade of the United Nations two movements—of contrary import—arose seeking to alter the relations of the United States to the United Nations: 1, the movement of world government sought to increase the role of the United Nations in world and U.S. affairs; 2, the Bricker amendment sought to decrease the role of the United Nations in American affairs. But American popular impressions in the 1950s of large-scale public revulsion against the UN were not founded in fact; never more than 12% or 13% of the public were recorded as favoring U.S. withdrawal. But each of the two movements just mentioned did gain some support within the public and in Congress; and the Government had to deal with both of these currents of opinion by statements to Congress and to the public. In each case the effort to push the Executive failed. Very helpful to the Executive in these conflicts was the tendency of editorials and public opinion to support the status quo—or at least not to be persuaded to take up the cudgels against it.

The swift UN action to cope with aggression in Korea raised estimates of the UN for a brief period; but after the large-scale intervention by Communist China estimates of UN capabilities tended to revert to earlier levels. The majority of the American public have backed UN efforts to deal with the African crises which started with the Belgian Congo, even though a minority have been critical of what they regard as "interference" in a country's "internal affairs." Further intrinsic difficulties of the UN were revealed by its inability to compel some members (France, USSR) to pay assessments for peacekeeping actions in Africa.

The proliferation of UN members, as the former colonial areas gained their independence, turned out to mean also the end of the almost automatic majority which the U.S. was able to count on in the first decade of UN history. Despite the initial U.S. public antipathy to the veto power under the UN Charter, the majority of editors have approved the U.S. resort to the veto (in cases involving Israel and Panama). The public did come to support a reduction in the U.S. regular contribution to the UN (to 25% of the total); but the public has also acquiesced in large U.S. contributions to voluntary funds which support UN activities in such fields as refugees, development aid, and food production. As the UN has enlarged its role in such activities, and in problems of energy and the environment, Americans have regarded these expanded activities as highly appropriate, if not essential.

The American public—as well as the UN—has been, and is, concerned about the arms race. While the general public has not favored giving away any atomic secrets, editorial opinion did back the U.S. 1946 offer to place atomic energy under international control. The public has been favorable to limiting and reducing armaments, but also insistent that any agreements be enforceable and calculated to minimize the possibilities of "cheating." The signing of multilateral treaties prohibiting the militarization of Antarctica and bacteriological warfare, and banning the military use of the sea beds and space, has received public approval and is regarded as somewhat encouraging; but it is generally felt that the real problem is the US-USSR race in nuclear weapons. Another weapons issue finds some editors opposing U.S. military aid to repressive governments.

Trade; Aid; Immigration

During most of the postwar period the views of the public tended to be supportive of government policy in the less publicized fields of trade, foreign aid, and immigration. The Administration's desires for a liberal tariff policy tended to be upheld in editorial comment and in public opinion polls. Similarly, the public accepted the foreign aid program in principle, although the general public (and many editors) have not insisted on particular dollar figures requested by current administrations. Editors and important organizations tended to back government appeals for greater immigration into the U.S., whereas the general public viewed increased immigration with considerable reluctance—although the phrasing of polling questions to admit escapees from Communism, or relatives of U.S. citizens, has sometimes sufficed to win grudging acceptance from a majority (especially when unemployment has not been prominent in the national consciousness).

Editoral support for the Reciprocal Trade Agreement program, already substantial in 1945, tended to grow steadily; support from business and labor organizations was also strong. Among the general public, sentiment favorable to lower tariffs and the principle of reciprocity usually resulted in approval of the RTA program in opinion polls. Only a few years after the end of World War II, Americans concluded that we should permit trade with West Germany and Japan on the same terms as with other friendly countries. But concern about the menace of Communism led to editorial and popular opposition to selling goods of military or strategic value to Communist countries; and some Americans opposed any trade with Communist countries as "aiding the enemy." However, a while after the Cuban missile crisis, editors and people noted that Western Europeans were engaged in lucrative trade with Communist countries and felt that American firms could do so too. After Congress eased the restrictions on trade with Yugoslavia and Poland, there was some criticism of the importation of "Polish ham" and other products; but, generally speaking sentiment to liberalize trade with Communist countries increased until, and after, the large grain deals with the Soviet Union in the 1970s. Congress at this time amended an Administration bill, providing "most-favored-nation" treatment for the Soviet Union, to make application of this principle contingent upon liberalization by the Soviet Union of its regulations on emigration.

In all three of these fields (trade, aid, immigration) support of the Executive's programs has tended to increase with the education of the respondent, which probably means that the more highly-educated Americans were more aware of, and could more readily appreciate, the factors which led the Administration of the day to advocate its programs. The ignorance of the American public concerning America's relatively small recent contributions to foreign aid is a striking feature of any over-all analysis of American public information and understanding of foreign affairs. To overcome this significant lacuna in public understanding, Government efforts have usually not been more attention-compelling than the appointment of a more or less prestigious committee to analyze the situation and make a public report.

Stability of Opinion

Public support for U.S. foreign policies, as mentioned earlier, has tended to persist during the postwar years. The size of the majority desirous of replacing isolationism with an active role in world affairs remained much the same from 1942 to 1975. In fact, the subjects which are regarded as appropriate for international action are more numerous today than they were 35 or 40 years ago. The decision to participate in the United Nations as "a step toward peace" has been firmly held; and the proportion of the public saying the UN is "important to the U.S." has continued at a high level.

The maintenance of peace has also been thought to require both a strong national defense and the assistance of allies to "contain" Soviet expansionism. At the same time, Americans have constantly favored "negotiations" over "confrontation" and have favored summit meetings between the leaders of the Communist and "free" worlds; and they have consistently desired to limit and reduce armaments. Also conceived as helping world peace have been U.S. policies of liberal international trade, foreign aid, and immigration, as well as the extension of relief at times of disaster. These policies also have usually been sustained by American opinion.

Public support of foreign policies can be affected by major changes in the outside world. The entry into the Korean War of massive numbers of Communist Chinese did lead some Americans to change their earlier verdict and conclude that our intervention in Korea was a "mistake." But this conclusion did not diminish public support for such recently adopted foreign policies as membership in the UN and NATO, and supplying our friends with economic and military aid.

The stability of opinion supporting Government foreign policies was doubtless strengthened by the absence of major differences of opinion associated with geographic region or political party affiliation. Opinion polls have shown minimal regional differences on foreign policy: the spread of percentage between East and Far West has usually been no more than 5% or 6% on major policies–rarely registering a spread of 8% or 10% (although the South did sometimes exceed other regions by a larger amount in its support of the Viet-Nam War).

Similarly, political partisanship has had little to do with attitudes toward such policies as membership in the UN or NATO, or our programs of economic or military aid. Partisanship was a factor during the McCarthy era in attitudes toward the Secretary of State (and the "kind of job" he was doing); but even then it was not an absolutely controlling factor. During that same period there was obvious partisan division on such controversial question as whether the Administration was "responsible for the loss of China." On most questions of foreign policy partisan feeling has been quite absent (the polls often giving identical figures for Republican, Democratic, and Independent support), and little difference in attitude toward seating Communist China in the UN or toward "cold war" issues. These were long-lived attitudes, although they did eventually change. Differences by sex were not usual either; but on questions of war the differences have sometimes been considerable–especially in the case of the Viet-Nam War, when women were much more opposed than men to continuing the fighting. Differences in attitude by educational background, however, have frequently been significant–particularly with reference to foreign aid programs, the United Nations, and immigration.

Opinion Changes

During the 35 years under review there have been some significant changes in public attitudes, especially in attitudes toward the use of military force and toward appropriations for foreign aid. But these have not been sudden or whimsical changes; they have taken place over long periods of time. Indeed there was little major change throughout the period, 1941–1966, denominated by Prof. Klingberg as a period of "extroversion."[1] In 1968 Dr. Free's polls began to show an appreciable diminution of the "internationalism" that had previously been the dominant sentiment among the public. But this diminution was by no means a reversal; there was a minor increase in "isolationist" sentiment, but a greater increase among those holding "mixed" opinions.[2]

The change about foreign aid requires little discussion because the decline in its ready acceptance has become familiar as it developed over a period of years, and some reluctance to tax ourselves for "give-aways" seems understandable. Opinion polls suggest there may have been a gradual increase in the number of people who approve of aid for developing countries; but in actual appropriations the U.S. has been steadily losing rank in percentage of GNP devoted to aid. This is clearly a matter of international significance, affecting America's place in the world.

The spring of 1968, after the Tet offensive in Viet-Nam, marked an important shift in public permissiveness about the use of U.S. military force (especially ground troops) to deal with problems in other countries. (It may be recalled that three years earlier the dispatch of U.S. troops to the Dominican Republic caused a substantial storm of protest against such unilateral action in advance of a decision by the Organization of American States.) In 1968 the U.S. decided not to escalate further the ground war in Viet-Nam; and the presidential candidates of both major parties (Nixon, Humphrey) pledged to end that war. In the following year (1969) Louis Harris reported significant declines in the willingness of Americans to "go to war" to defend other countries—even our allies. While Americans of the 1970s came to believe by a majority that participation in the two world wars of this century was appropriate, they felt that our two Asian wars were "mistakes"—not to be repeated. They felt that the cost of pursuing the Korean and Indochinese actions against the expansion of Communism was higher than the nation should pay in the future (and conditions in Korea and Indochina were not thought to be greatly improved as a result of U.S. military intervention).

While opinion polls on our defense commitments do not give authoritative insights into future actions, they made clear that in the early 1970s only a minority said they favored defense actions in Asia or the Mideast, and that past determinations to defend Western

Europe and Japan had been weakened below the point of majority conviction. Even the defense of West Berlin, so popularly accepted in the Kennedy days, seemed to be becoming assimilated to that of other capitals behind the Iron Curtain (e.g., Budapest, Prague) which were not regarded in the 1950s and 1960s as warranting a "war" in their defense. After our experiences in Korea, the Dominican Republic, and Viet-Nam, Americans apparently concluded that "collective security" agreements did not always mean that the U.S. could count on great military aid from others, and that in practice the U.S. would be acting chiefly on its own. This realization may help to account for the decline in the polling figures on going to the aid of allies, as compared with the 1950s.

Policy Changes

With these changes in public opinion, it is not surprising to find changes in policy executed by the Chief Executive and by the Congress. Pres. Nixon not only announced the gradual withdrawal of U.S. forces from Viet-Nam, but in the Nixon Doctrine he declared a "lower profile" for the U.S. in its exercise of military force in the world. These policy changes were warmly welcomed by American editors and the general public. The President did not agree with Congressional efforts to curb the war powers of the Presidency; but these efforts, too, were welcomed by the press and the public.

Pres. Nixon came into office with his pledge to end the war in Viet-Nam; but fighting there by U.S. soldiers did not cease until 1973, even though there were dramatic demonstrations in the streets of Washington and other American cities by thousands of Americans demanding a prompt end to the war. The majority of the American public accepted the continuation of the fighting, with regret, but for two main reasons: they still believed that prevention of Communist aggression in Viet-Nam was a desirable objective; and 2, that any peace settlement should not only include the return of our POWs but afford the people of South Viet-Nam as great an opportunity as possible to rule themselves. Opinions about subsequent military moves, such as the incursions into Laos and Cambodia and the bombing of North Viet-Nam, did fluctuate—as Americans shifted in their perceptions of the likelihood that such moves would contribute to their basic hopes. Ever since 1968 Americans had felt that the costs of war should not be escalated; but they were not ready simply to give up the effort without any gains to show for it.

In 1972 Pres. Nixon, between his China and Moscow summits, ordered the mining of all North Viet-Nam ports; this move pleased fewer editors than it alarmed, because they were fearful that the Kremlin would call off its summit session. But the general public approved Nixon's bold action, 59% vs. 24%. After the Viet-Nam peace agreement was signed in January 1973, however, Nixon's continued bombing over Cambodia was not supported by popular opinion.

War Power

With public approval, Congress undertook to limit the power of the President to initiate military actions overseas—without depriving him of the power to act swiftly to meet an attack. Whether the War Powers Act is a realistic brake on the foreign affairs powers of the President may be arguable; but it is clear that the Executive since the mid-1960s has had to pay greater attention to potential opposition to the use of military force overseas than at any other time during the preceding quarter-century. From 1945 to 1965 the American public usually gave prompt support to military actions undertaken by a President. Such was the case at the time of the Berlin air lift, at the beginning of the Korean War, in Pres. Eisenhower's dispatch of Marines to Lebanon, in Pres. Kennedy's firm stands on Berlin and during the Cuban missile crisis. The American-sponsored effort of Cuban exiles at the Bay of Pigs gave Pres. Kennedy a burst of popular approval; but Americans did not favor the use of American soldiers against Cuba.

Pres-Johnson's 1965 moves in Viet-Nam received prompt public support; but opinion was somewhat divided on dispatching U.S. troops to the Dominican Republic. After the U.S. brought the matter before the OAS and the U.S. force became part of an inter-American force maintaining order there, a majority of editors voiced their approval; but a minority still felt that the U.S. had applied force too precipitately. Public pressure against the use of force overseas can clearly have a pervasive effect on our relations with many countries.

At the same time a majority of editors continued to oppose the unilateral withdrawal of the large contingent of American ground troops stationed in Europe, despite the various and repeated efforts of Dwight Eisenhower and Mike Mansfield to reduce their numbers. In 1974 a Watts-Free poll reported that "over the next few years the total military power of the U.S." should be kept at the present level (42%) or increased (40%).[3] Also, it will be recalled that in many instances where the polls indicated less than majority support for U.S. troops to go to the aid of an attacked ally, there continued to be willingness to send military supplies, and economic aid, to the victim of attack.

Foreign Policy Goals

Significant changes in the foreign policy goals held by the American public were revealed by the Chicago Council poll taken at the end of 1974. While the top goals of keeping peace and promoting our national security were held to be dominant throughout the period of this study (1940–1975), in 1974 one goal that was prominent in the early years of this period, the containment of Communism, had dropped to a middle-ranking position (among 18 goals mentioned in the polling question), and a brand-new goal now stood in third place: securing adequate supplies of energy. Fresh emphasis was also given in 1974 to the goal of "protecting American jobs;" and organized labor reversed its support for a liberal trade policy and voiced concern over the tendency of "multinational corporations" to "export U.S. jobs."

While there was support for a "lower U.S. profile" in the world, it is clear that during the 1970s the U.S. also continued to be much more "active" in world affairs than was the case before 1940. During the period of "introversion" that recurred after 1966 (or so), the deep concern with human rights at home seemed to overflow our national boundaries; and there was also increasing American interest in the global problems of hunger and population, along with the concern about "repressive" regimes.

Toward *non-Communist* countries, which were thought to be repressive, editors tended to advocate reduction of U.S. military and economic aid. This was clearly the case with South Korea; and a similar attitude was shown in editorials on aid to the Thieu government even during the Viet-Nam War. In the case of Chile the primary public concern was over the activities of the CIA, but considerable sentiment was expressed against aid for the "repressive" military junta.

Toward *Communist* countries, where the issues were likely to arise over trade and cultural exchanges rather than U.S. aid, the internal repression of the governments tended to figure little in most editorial discussions. This is clearly true with reference to China and Eastern European countries, and most newspapers favored trade with these countries. But the minority of insistently anti-Communist papers often cited the repressive character of Communist governments they didn't want the U.S. to have closer relations with. In the case of the Soviet Union, the editors condemned the Kremlin's treatment of dissidents; but most of them tended to disapprove the technique of the Jackson amendment to the Trade Act. Evidently editors tended to feel that the U.S. was more responsible for the existence and perpetuation of repressive acts by non-Communist governments which were actually receiving U.S. aid, than it was responsible for acts by Communist regimes with which we maintained trade and cultural relations without sending aid.

Adequacy of Public Information

Throughout this period under study there have been significant complaints from editors and the general public about the inadequacy of the information on foreign affairs available to the public. After the revelations about the hitherto secret CIA activities, there were criticisms of U.S. actions against governments in Iran, Guatemala, and Chile; and during the Viet-Nam War there were charges of "government lies" about the prosecution of that war. Complaints against the Government were less prominent at the times of the State Department's (and White House's) information campaigns on the United Nations Charter and the Marshall Plan; but even then public understanding was by no means complete, although the campaigns did succeed in mobilizing public support. Also, people did not wholly approve the presence of a great-power veto in the UN Charter (although years later most editors came to feel that it was useful for the U.S. to possess it).

Only about one quarter of the people appreciated one of the fundamental principles of the Marshall Plan—that the European nations get together and develop a cooperative program for their joint economic recovery; but the majority of Americans did approve the aid program and, on the momentum of the campaign for the Marshall Plan, went on to support economic aid to many less developed countries. But the American public has continued to be seriously mistaken about at least two important aspects of the aid program: the continuing need for such programs; and the comparative U.S. effort in this field.

There is an inevitable gap between the understanding held by government leaders and bureaucrats on the one hand and the general public on the other hand—between editors and other media specialists on foreign affairs and the man-in-the-street. Nevertheless, public discussions have tackled aspects of the energy problem, the tariff, and the environment; and the job of building understanding is obviously immense. In fact, the United States is pioneering in the practice of democratic control of foreign policy; no great nation with world-wide responsibilities has demonstrated how the mass of its voters can be given an ample understanding of world affairs. The United States, confronted with this tremendous challenge, can take some encouragement from the advances which have been registered during the past generation. Citizen attitudes will affect our foreign policy, whether they are based upon sound information and interpretation or not. Fortunately, the American citizens who actively participate in the public discussion of foreign affairs—writing letters to the editor and to their Congressmen, and leading community or group discussions on foreign policy—have tended to come from the better-informed and more-educated strata of the public.

The record of the 1940–1975 period indicates considerable hope for success in building a better-informed public if this is made a deliberate objective. The isolationism of the 1930s is gone; and there is the record of Government leadership which has overcome initial popular resistance or reluctance in case after case: joining the international organization for peace, rehabilitation of ex-enemy countries (Germany and Japan), establishment of cooperative relations with leading industrial nations, building a basis for a liberal international trade policy, assistance to emerging nations in the Third World, and amelioration of relations in the Middle East. The public's approval of an active world role for the U.S. has remained vigorous and forward-looking; and the constantly rising level of education within the public should be advantageous in gaining public understanding of the new issues in our foreign relations.

Reference Notes

1. Op. cit. in note 3, Chapter I.
2. Op. cit. in note 9, Chapter XVII.
3. Op. cit. in note 24, Chapter XVIII.

BIBLIOGRAPHICAL NOTE

The present study is based mainly upon opinion analyses prepared in the State Department for current use, which are now available at the National Archives in Washington, D.C. These records of the Office of Public Opinion Studies from 1943 to 1975 are located in the Diplomatic Branch (Record Group 59) and are completely open.

It may be helpful to cite here pertinent public opinion surveys (which have provided a wealth of data for the 1940–1975 period) and some studies which illuminate the relation between the American public and U.S. foreign policy. *The Gallup Poll* (New York 1972) gives polling questions and results from 1935 to 1971; and subsequent volumes of the same title cover polls from 1972 through 1979 (Wilmington, Del.). Elmo Roper's polls, also going back to the 1930s, are now preserved at the Roper Center, Inc. with access from Williams College, Yale University and the University of Connecticut (postal address: Office of Archival Development and User Services, Box U-164R, Univ. of Conn. at Storrs, 06268). Also available at the Roper Center are polls by the National Opinion Research Center which asked many questions about foreign policy in the 1940s and 1950s. Louis Harris has given his own analysis of his most significant polls on foreign and domestic affairs from 1963 to 1973 in his *Anguish of Change* (New York 1973), and additional data are given in the *Harris Survey Yearbook of Public Opinion* (1970–1973).

Political Beliefs of Americans (New Brunswick, N.J. 1967) by Hadley Cantril and Lloyd Free is based upon polls by the Institute for International Social Research; and Dr. Free has published subsequently significant data on American foreign policy attitudes in collaboration with Wm. E. Watts: *State of the Nation* (New York 1973) and *State of the Nation 1974* (Washington 1974); and with Donald Lesh in *America Observed* (Washington 1974). See also *Hopes and Fears of the American People* by Albert H. Cantril and Charles W. Roll, Jr. (New York 1971).

A relatively brief overview of *The Public and American Foreign Policy, 1918–1978* (New York, Morrow, 1978) was written by Ralph B. Levering and published by the Foreign Policy Association. Prof. Frank L. Klingberg's article, "The Historical Alternation of Moods in American Foreign Policy" appeared in *World Politics* for Jan. 1952. Robert E. Osgood's *Ideals and Self-Interest in America's Foreign Relations* (Chicago 1953) provides a helpful analysis of public thinking about foreign policy from the end of the 19th century to Pearl Harbor. In 1950 Gabriel Almond published his comprehensive and influential study, *The American People and Foreign Policy* (2nd Ed., New York 1960).

Henry M. Wriston's *Diplomacy in a Democracy* (New York 1956) offers practical insight into the role of the public. Both foreign and domestic issues are analyzed by V. O. Key in his *Public Opinion and American Democracy* (New York 1961). In the early 1940s Jerome Bruner interpreted a number of foreign affairs polls in *Mandate from the People* (New York 1944). Dorothy Robins described the activities of American organizations in connection with the establishment of the United Nations in her *Experiment in Democracy* (New York 1971). In 1958 popular opinion about the United Nations was comprehensively analyzed by Wm. A. Scott and Stephen B. Withey in their *United States and the United Nations* (New York). A volume entitled *Mobilizing Consent: Public Opinion and American Foreign Policy, 1937–47* was published in 1976 by Michael Leigh (Westport, Conn.). On U.S. trade policy, a comprehensive study was published in 1963 by Raymond A. Bauer, Ithiel deSola Pool, and Lewis A. Dexter, *American Business and Public Policy, the Politics of Foreign Trade* (New York).

Alfred O. Hero has been a prolific author of intensive studies of various aspects of the relation between American public opinion and U.S. foreign policy: *Mass Media and World Affairs* (Boston 1959); *The Southerner and World Affairs* (Baton Rouge 1965); and analyses of the views of labor (1970) and religous groups (1973). Prof. James Rosenau has published a study entitled, *Public Opinion and Foreign Policy: an operational formulation* (New York 1961), also *National Leadership and Foreign Policy: A case study in the mobilization of public support* (Princeton 1963) which focused on the foreign aid program. Rosenau has also edited *Domestic Sources of Foreign Policy* (New York 1967). An intensive study of opinion on foreign aid in the 1970s was undertaken by the Overseas Development Council and analyzed by Paul Laudicina in *World Poverty and Development: A survey of American Opinion* (Washington 1973).

The Public's Impact on Foreign Policy (Boston 1972) by Prof. Bernard C. Cohen described the impact of the public on State Department personnel and Foreign Service Officers; Cohen has also published a thoughtful study on *The Press and Foreign Policy* (Princeton 1963). Prof. Ernest A. May has written an interesting chapter on "An American Tradition in Foreign Policy: The Role of Public Opinion," in Wm. H. Nelson, ed., *Theory and Practice in American Politics* (Chicago 1964).

The annual volumes, *The U.S. in World Affairs*, published by the Council on Foreign Relations in New York for the years 1945 through 1970, are very helpful in providing coverage of pertinent Congressional discussions and many of the high spots of public opinion.

INDEX

ABOUT THE AUTHOR

H. Schuyler Foster brought to his assignment as public opinion analyst in the U.S. State Department pertinent experience in Political Science as student (B.S. Dartmouth 1925, A.M. Harvard 1928, Ph.D. Univ. of Chicago 1932) and teacher (Ohio State Univ. 1929–35, 1936–37, 1938–43; Harvard Univ. 1935–36). His articles on public opinion and foreign policy have appeared in *Foreign Affairs, Public Opinion Quarterly*, *Department of State Bulletin*, and other journals. At the State Department he was concerned with analyzing American opinion on every foreign policy issue receiving sizable public discussion from World War II to 1975.

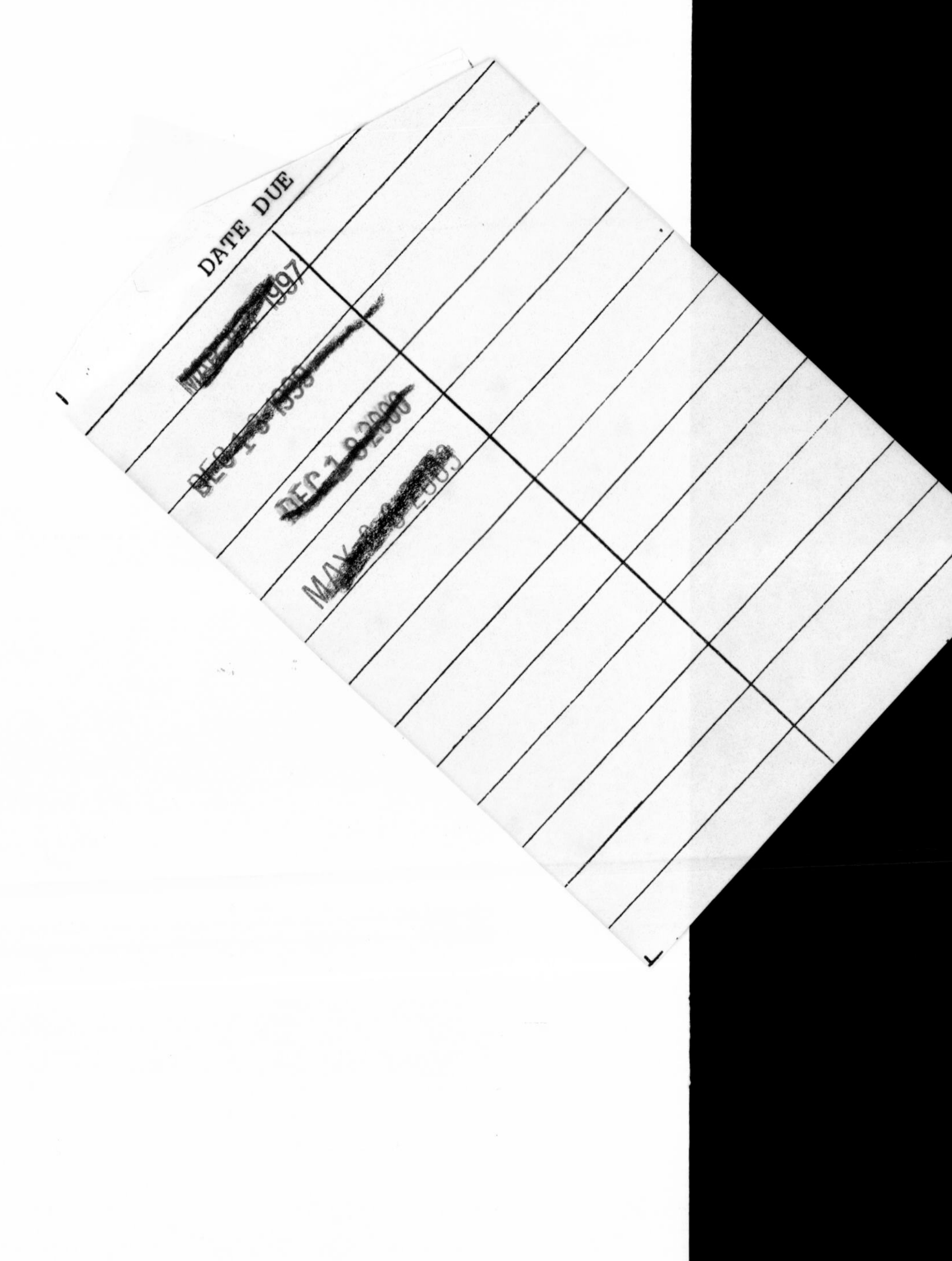